Benefits Management

Wiley Series in Information Systems

Editors

Richard Boland

Department of Management Information and Decision Systems, Weatherhead School of Management, Case Western Reserve University, 10900 Euclid Avenue, Cleveland, Ohio 44106-7235, USA

Rudy Hirschheim

Department of Information Systems and Decision Sciences, Ourso College of Business Administration, Louisiana State University, Baton Rouge, LA 70803, USA

Advisory Board

CURRENT VOLUMES IN THE SERIES

Benefits Management

Delivering Value from IS & IT Investments

John Ward
Elizabeth Daniel

John Wiley & Sons, Ltd

Other Wiley Editorial Offices

John Wiley & Sons Inc., 111 River Street, Hoboken, NJ 07030, USA

Jossey-Bass, 989 Market Street, San Francisco, CA 94103-1741, USA

Wiley-VCH Verlag GmbH, Boschstr. 12, D-69469 Weinheim, Germany

John Wiley & Sons Australia Ltd, 42 McDougall Street, Milton, Queensland 4064, Australia

John Wiley & Sons (Asia) Pte Ltd, 2 Clementi Loop #02-01, Jin Xing Distripark, Singapore 129809

John Wiley & Sons Canada Ltd, 22 Worcester Road, Etobicoke, Ontario, Canada M9W 1L1

Wiley also publishes its books in a variety of electronic formats. Some content that appears in
print may not be available in electronic books

Library of Congress Cataloging in Publication Data

Ward, John, 1947–
    Benefits management : delivering value from IS & IT investments / John Ward,
    Elizabeth Daniel.
        p.   cm. — (John Wiley series in information systems)
    Includes bibliographical references and index.
    ISBN 0-470-09463-X (cloth : alk. paper)
    1. Information technology—Management.   2. Information storage and retrieval
    systems—Business.   I. Daniel, Elizabeth, 1962–   II. Title.   III. Series.
    HD30.2.W368 2006
    658.4′038′011—dc22   2005017407

British Library Cataloguing in Publication Data

A catalogue record for this book is available from the British Library

ISBN-13 978-0-470-09463-1
ISBN-10 0-470-09463-X

Typeset in 11/12.5pt Palatino by Integra Software Services Pvt. Ltd, Pondicherry, India
Printed and bound in Great Britain by T.J. International, Padstow, Cornwall
This book is printed on acid-free paper responsibly manufactured from sustainable forestry
in which at least two trees are planted for each one used for paper production.

Contents

About the Authors

John Ward is Professor of Strategic Information Systems and Director of the Information Systems Research Centre at Cranfield School of Management. Prior to joining Cranfield, he worked in industry for 15 years and he currently acts as a consultant to a number of major organizations. As well as publishing many papers and articles, he is co-author of the book *Strategic Planning for Information Systems*, now in its 3rd edition. He has served two terms as President of the UK Academy for Information Systems and has been a member of its board since 1994.

Elizabeth Daniel is Professor of Information Management at the Open University Business School. Prior to joining OUBS in 2005, Elizabeth worked in the IS Research Centre at Cranfield School of Management where she researched and taught in the fields of e-business and IS strategies and benefits management. She has a particular interest in IOS and IS in marketing and supply chains. She has published many papers in leading academic journals and a number of management reports. Elizabeth has a first degree and PhD in Physics and an MBA from London Business School. She has spent over 10 years in industry, starting her career as a medical engineer and subsequently working as a strategy management consultant.

Series Preface

The information systems community has grown considerably in the twenty years that we have been publishing the Wiley Series in Information Systems. We are pleased to be a part of the growth of the field, and believe that this series has played, and continues to play, an important role in the intellectual development of the discipline. The primary objective of the series is to publish intellectually insightful works that reflect the best of the research in the information systems community. These works should help guide the IS practitioner community regarding what strategies it ought to adopt to be successful in the future. Books in the Series should also help advanced students – particularly those at the graduate level – understand myriad issues surrounding the broad area of management of IS.

To this end, the current volume – *Benefits Management: Delivering Value from IS and IT Investments* – by John Ward and Elizabeth Daniel is an especially welcomed addition. This book explores the numerous issues surrounding the difficulty organizations have in achieving the expected benefits from their IT expenditures. The issue of obtaining the hoped for economic benefits from IT has been a particularly thorny problem for the field; one that has caused many, if not all, managers considerable headaches. That is why this book is so valuable. Professors Ward and Daniel set out a process that they refer to as 'benefits management', which organizations can follow to achieve the payback they anticipate from their IT investments. Their refreshing perspective on the problem of IT value is both insightful and cogent. This volume should be on the bookshelf of every IS academic and practitioner. We are delighted to have it as part of our Wiley Series in Information Systems.

Rudy Hirschheim

Preface

Supermarket admits IT systems are flawed and goes back to manual systems – company writes off millions of pounds.

Computing, 19 October 2004

£456m child support IT fiasco – system was badly designed, badly tested and badly implemented.

silicon.com, 18 November 2004

Reports in the press continue to recount the stories of failed IS and IT investments. Indeed, despite over almost four decades' experience of using and investing in information systems, it might appear that organizations have made little progress, with project failure rates doggedly sticking to around 70%.

While the statistics suggest that organizations have not learned how to implement new IS and IT successfully, they conceal more than they reveal. Early failures were often about system capability and reliability. Improvements in the underlying technology and systems development and design methods have reduced the number of failures due to technical or 'supply-side' issues. Significant delays and cost overruns were other reasons why IS and IT investments were often judged to be unsuccessful. However, once again, the falling cost of technology and the increasing adoption of standardized packages have done much to ensure more projects are delivered on time and on budget. But even when projects hit budget and time, many still fail to deliver the business benefits that were expected.

So why does this continue to occur? It is partly because the uses of IS and IT are becoming increasingly more complex, often impacting large areas of the organization and affecting many different people both inside the organization and, increasingly, external parties, such as customers and suppliers. Also the pace of change, including the personal use of IT and the Internet, combined with the uncertainties of the business environment, and continuing developments in IT, make decisions about investments in new systems and technology increasingly difficult. Failure is more likely to occur if uninformed or hasty decisions are made.

It is also partly due to the way that organizations manage the investments. Until recently the improvements in management techniques were mainly supply side driven, to improve the certainty of delivering a working technical solution. Little attention was paid to managing the 'demand side' more effectively – the activities required to identify and manage the benefits intended from the investment. This requires a greater understanding of the nature of the benefits that can be achieved, what needs to be done to cause them to occur and the role of business managers in the realization of the benefits. As argued in this book, existing methods and processes do not directly or adequately deal with the issues at the core of benefits delivery. Therefore, what is required is a new way of working that enables experienced individuals to combine their business and technology knowledge, to increase the benefits achieved from IS/IT investments.

This book describes a process and practical tools and frameworks that organizations can employ to enable them to improve the realization of value from their investments. The single most important tenet of the approach presented is the dependency of business benefits, not only on the implementation of IS and IT, but also on changing organizational processes and relationships and the roles and working practices of individuals and teams inside and, in some cases, outside the organization. Indeed we have found that within many organizations, the benefits they are seeking do not always require investment in additional IS and IT, but can be realized with existing systems and technology, if only they could achieve the appropriate changes in the ways their staff work. This inherent interdependency of *benefits* realization and change *management* is the reason why we refer to the process presented in this book as '*benefits management*'.

The process and the underlying tools and frameworks presented in this book were derived from extensive research undertaken by the Information Systems Research Centre (ISRC) at Cranfield School of

Management in the mid-1990s. The original research programme, which was carried out in collaboration with a range of organizations, from both the private and public sectors, lasted three years. Since then, the tools and frameworks have been further developed and refined, in conjunction with other major organizations. Over the last 10 years, key elements of the benefits management approach have been adopted by over 100 organizations based in the UK, Europe, USA and even in locations as remote as China. Its use by so many and such varied organizations has shown how effectively it can be applied in practice. The widespread application has also provided us with significant real-world insights into the use of the approach, much of which is captured in this book.

John Ward is also one of the authors of another book in this series, *Strategic Planning for Information Systems*, which provides a comprehensive discussion of how organizations can develop a coherent and appropriate IS/IT strategy. For those who are not familiar with the strategic planning book, Chapter 2 of this book discusses the development of an IS/IT strategy and presents an overview of the key tools and frameworks that can assist in the formulation of such a strategy.

We would argue that, even when an organization has a well-defined strategy, another set of challenges remain, which affect the organization's ability to successfully implement the investments that are essential to realizing the value intended from the strategy. The benefits management approach provides the means by which organizations can address many of those increasingly critical implementation challenges.

Structure of the Book

In order to help the reader, the structure of the book is illustrated in Figure 0.1. The book considers activities needed to effectively realize benefits at two levels: the organizational level and the level of the individual project or investment.

Chapter 1 traces the use of IS and IT within organizations, including the high expectations caused by the arrival of e-commerce and e-business, and introduces the different types of benefit that can be realized. The chapter also considers the issues and challenges organizations have to understand, and address effectively, if they are to select the most appropriate investments to make and then manage

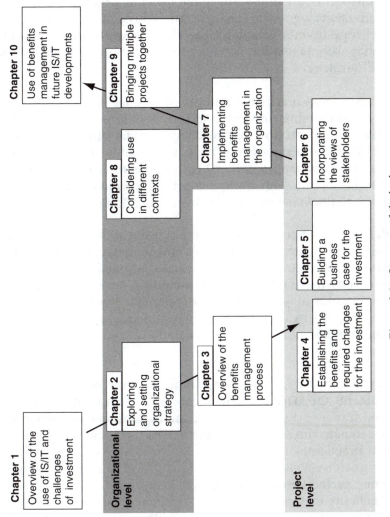

Chapter 1
Overview of the use of IS/IT and challenges of investment

Organizational level

Chapter 2
Exploring and setting organizational strategy

Chapter 3
Overview of the benefits management process

Chapter 8
Considering use in different contexts

Chapter 9
Bringing multiple projects together

Chapter 10
Use of benefits management in future IS/IT developments

Chapter 7
Implementing benefits management in the organization

Project level

Chapter 4
Establishing the benefits and required changes for the investment

Chapter 5
Building a business case for the investment

Chapter 6
Incorporating the views of stakeholders

Figure 0.1 Structure of the book

them successfully. The problems with current investment management approaches, most of which are dominated by financial appraisal
and justification, are discussed. While such activities are important,
we argue that not only are these often poorly done, they are not
sufficient to ensure that the benefits of investments are adequately
understood or actually realized.

To be able to identify and manage the benefits, organizations need a
clear understanding of the strategic rationale or business reasons for
IS and IT investments. Chapter 2, therefore, presents tools and frameworks that allow an exploration and determination of organizational,
IS and IT strategy.

Chapter 3 discusses why a new approach is needed to address the
limitations of existing methods and describes how benefits management both differs from, but also complements, other proven ways
of improving the results from IS/IT investments. The chapter then
presents an overview of the entire benefits management process,
from the initiation of an investment, through planning and implementation to final review.

Chapters 4, 5 and 6 consider use of the process at the level of individual projects or investments. The tools and frameworks that underpin
the approach are presented and their use discussed. Examples of the
application of the tools are given, including an extended example
of their use in a major enterprise-wide IS/IT investment in a food
processing company. This example is begun in Chapter 4 and is built
on in the subsequent two chapters, such that a complete benefits plan
is presented.

Chapter 7 considers how organizations can introduce the benefits
management approach, the practicalities of adopting the process,
tools and frameworks and how they can be used in conjunction with
other established investment and project management methodologies
and best practices.

A premise of the benefits management approach is that the nature
of the benefits that can be realized depends on the specific context
of the organization. Chapter 8 considers the use of the approach in
a variety of contexts, including distinct types of organisation and
different application types that are commonly being deployed.

As organizations are undertaking more complex and far reaching
change initiatives, they increasingly have to manage both major

change programmes that are, at least in part, enabled by IT and also a range of individual IS/IT projects. Chapter 9 discusses the application of the benefits management approach in change programmes and how it can be used to improve the governance of the organization's portfolio of IS/IT investments.

Finally, Chapter 10 considers expected future developments in IS and IT and, in particular, how the benefits management approach can help with the new challenges they may present. The chapter also discusses and exemplifies how the approach can be used to help in the formulation and implementation of business strategies, thereby providing closer links between what an organization intends to achieve and how its investments in IS/IT and change programmes will produce the benefits inherent in those intentions.

Acknowledgements

We are grateful for all the help and support we have been given in writing this book, including the many hundreds of both business and IS/IT managers, whose application of the tools and ideas presented in the book have enabled us to refine the process to that presented here. Their use has not only ensured that the process has been robustly tested in a wide variety of settings, but has demonstrated its relevance and value. The examples used in the text have all been drawn from use by real organizations and we would particularly like to thank them for their contribution.

We would also like to thank current and former colleagues at Cranfield School of Management, who played a significant part in developing and refining the concepts, ideas and techniques: Phil Taylor, Roger Elvin and, especially, Peter Murray.

Finally, we are both particularly appreciative of the help provided by Carole Hutchings in preparing the manuscript and by Carol Ward, for her careful reading of the manuscript and insightful comments in improving its quality.

1
The Challenge of IS/IT Investments

Managers considering the current role and value of IT within their organizations can be forgiven for feeling they are at a crossroads and being given very little help with which direction they should go, either from their colleagues or from outside commentators and experts.

The demand from colleagues within the organization for new systems, improvements to existing systems and increased support seems to grow continuously. Such demands will be supported by descriptions of the expected improvements, either claiming cost savings from improved efficiencies or increased revenue generation from the creation of new services or capabilities. Many of these arguments will be well founded. However, these demands must be set against the reality that IT budgets are finite and in many cases these budgets are being reduced. Although for many organizations budgets are linked to the prevailing trading climate, this also suggests that senior managers are not as convinced of the positive outcomes from IT spending as those further down the organization. This may also be a reaction to the overblown expectations that accompanied the dot.com boom of the late 1990s, when many claims were made for how internet-based initiatives would change organizations and even create a 'new economy'.

Equally, commentators appear to have conflicting advice on the subject. Articles in the press and respected management journals constantly describe how organizations have improved their operations, generated new business opportunities and outperformed their competitors by means of well-selected and deployed IT. In their discussion of IT investment approaches, Ross and Beath (2002) describe how United Parcel Service (UPS) invested $11 billion over a 10-year period to create a centralized data repository, built a global network, implemented enterprise-wide applications and shared databases and implemented disaster recovery operations. This has resulted in UPS being able to exchange 88% of all transactions and package information electronically, significantly improving the efficiency and hence the cost base of its operations, while also being able to pursue new business opportunities. This, they state, has allowed UPS to reassert its leadership in its industry, with *Fortune* magazine naming it the most admired mail, package and freight company in 2000.

In contrast, the provocatively titled article, 'IT doesn't matter' (Carr, 2003), suggested that the considerable investments organizations continue to make in IT are wrong headed. The author argued that the decreasing costs of IT, be that processing power, data storage or data transport, coupled with the significant sums that organizations have spent on these capabilities, have resulted in ubiquitous powerful IT – something that every organization can own. He therefore reasoned that, since all organizations can tap into this capability, it cannot provide competitive advantage to any one firm. Carr developed his argument by likening IT to earlier broadly adopted technologies that have shaped modern-day industry, from steam engines and railways to the electricity grid and telephone networks. These technologies he referred to as 'infrastructural' and observed that, unlike the results of most company proprietary R&D work, these developments are more valuable when shared with other companies rather than kept private.

He continued that such infrastructural developments initially result in standard technology becoming available to all firms, but after time, even the way that technology is used becomes standardized, with best practices being well understood and even built into the technology. This reduces the possibility for competitive advantage for any one firm even further. In the case of software, because many business processes and activities have become embedded in software, those processes are replicated as standard across organizations. As any IT manager is well aware, customization of packages is expensive and often results in reduced interoperability, but without which there is little distinction between organizations. The ability to deliver software over the Internet, as standardized web services, Carr argued, will exacerbate the standardization and commoditization even further. The growing use of the term 'utility computing', where the leading vendors will rent their applications rather than sell them, further underlies this move to commoditization.

A study by a group of US academics (Mata et al., 1995) explored the issue of sustained competitive advantage from IT. They concluded that many issues related to IT, such as technology, access to capital and technical IT skills could not provide sustained competitive advantage. The only factor that could provide this was IT management skills, described as *'the ability to conceive of, develop and exploit IT applications to support or enhance other business functions'*. Skills required to achieve this include the ability of IT managers to understand the business needs of other functional managers and to work with these managers to develop and exploit appropriate systems. The authors concluded that these IT management skills were often tacit, composed of many hundreds of small decisions and had a strong social element to them. They were therefore difficult for competitors to imitate and hence could, if developed, provide a source of sustained competitive advantage.

The Development of IS/IT within Organizations

As the competitive pressures on organizations have changed over the last four decades, so the expectations from IT in helping to meet those challenges have changed. As shown in Table 1.1 (Farbey et al., 1993; Renkema, 2000), the early days of IT adoption within organizations were characterized by the automation of routine activities to improve efficiency. As IT adoption became more widespread, the emphasis began to shift from using IT solely to reduce costs to also using it to improve the quality of firms' operations and products.

Table 1.1   *The development of IT support for business (after Farbey et al., 1993; Renkema, 2000)*

Decade	Market demands	Ideal firm	IT performance criteria	Technology base	IT applications
1960s	Price	The efficient firm	Efficiency	Mainframe – batch processing	Data processing/ automation of routine tasks
1970s	Price, quality	The quality firm	Efficiency + quality	Mainframe – batch processing	Functional efficiency
1980s	Price, quality, choice/delivery time	The flexible firm	Efficiency + quality + flexibility	Personal computing	Personal productivity
1990s and beyond	Price, quality, choice/delivery time, uniqueness	The innovating firm	Efficiency + quality + flexibility + innovative ability	Networks	Organizational transformation

In many industries, the 1980s saw a movement away from production being determined by raw materials and production capacity, to production being set by customer demand. Fluctuations in this demand caused firms to focus on the flexibility of their operations. The advent of the PC in this era, allowed a more distributed application of IT, for example at individual workstations within factories, within warehouses and in smaller regional offices. This application closer to the point of need, both enabled and further encouraged the increasing demand for flexibility.

The New Economy

The 1990s, and the dawn of the new century, has seen the dramatic growth in the networking of PCs, supporting increased communication between individuals, thus spawning the whole domain of IT-enabled knowledge management. In addition to human-to-human interaction, increased networking, through the increased adoption of standards, has improved the integration between applications addressing the issue of localized adoption of IT that often resulted in unconnected 'islands of automation'.

The 1990s saw the commercial adoption of the most notable of these networks, often described as a 'network of networks', the Internet. This spawned the whole domain of e-business and its associated emphasis on innovation, both in the products and services supplied to business customers and consumers, and also in the business processes supporting this product and service delivery.

Despite the downturn in sentiment towards the dot.com companies in April 2000, e-business continues to be a strategic imperative for many businesses. Firms recognize that e-business can assist with numerous objectives, such as enriching the dialogue with customers, streamlining internal business processes and developing deeper relationships with key suppliers. However, this domain also poses many challenges such as the entrance of new competitors, the blurring of market boundaries and the emergence of new business models.

A number of researchers have suggested that in such environments competitive advantage is transient, rather than sustainable and hence the emphasis for today's firms is on innovation. Managers must therefore concentrate on renewing rather than protecting their sources of competitive advantage. No longer can they rely on the assets, staff, products, IT and other resources that they have assembled to provide their present competitive position. The dynamic nature of the current business environment requires them to be able to combine these resources in new ways and to develop new resources, and to do this repeatedly, if they are to compete successfully.

Productivity Gains from IS/IT

Farrell (2003) explored the link between productivity, at both industry and organizational level, and the expenditure on IT. Her study focused particularly on the 1990s and sought to see if the considerable expenditures on IT that were witnessed during that decade resulted in corresponding increases in productivity. She found that the latter half of the 1990s saw an increase in labour productivity, particularly in the USA, which coincided with a dramatic increase in the spending on IT. However, she also found that those gains in productivity were not evenly spread across industries, despite all industries increasing their IT spending. Indeed in the US, just six sectors accounted for 76% of the country's net productivity gain. From this she concluded that *'IT is of great, but not primary, importance to the fate of industries and individual companies'*.

From her study, Farrell concluded that the prime cause of the increased productivity witnessed is intensifying competition within an industry and hence on the individual firms. This increase in competition, she stated, causes managers to increase innovation, which in turn increases productivity. IS/IT is just one way, although if used well, a very powerful way, in which such managers can innovate in order to either meet or exceed the increased competition. In considering where and how IS/IT has been used most effectively to improve productivity, she observed certain patterns. These include the application of IS/IT to those areas or levers in the business that matter most (see Box 1.1). These will vary from industry to industry, for example in consumer retailing, systems that improve distribution and logistics, merchandising and store management will have the greatest effect, whereas in banking it is systems that can automate lending and process large-scale back office transactions. This suggests that it is more specialized applications, tailored to particular sectors that will have the greatest impact on productivity. Indeed, she found that general-purpose applications, such as CRM systems, have to date tended to yield poor results. Interestingly, and consistent with the approach suggested in this book, she also found that IS/IT adoption had most impact on productivity within organizations when it was accompanied by managerial and organizational changes.

Box 1.1 IT and organizational value

Does IT provide value to organizations and, if so, how is that value generated are perennial questions, both for the managers within organizations who must invest ever greater sums in IT and seek to harness value from such investments, and for academics wanting to shed light on these challenging activities. Melville et al. (2004) propose a single, overarching model that brings together or integrates previous studies looking at this topic.

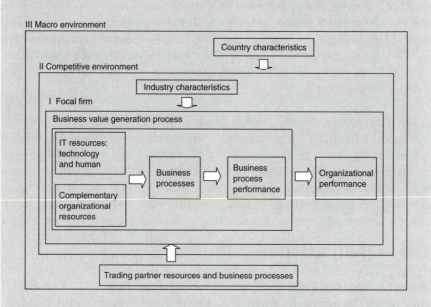

Figure 1.1 *The business value model (after Melville et al., 2004, p. 293) Copyright © 2004 by the Regents of the University of Minnesota. Used with permission*

Their derivation of the proposed model is based on the resource-based view (RBV) of the firm. This strand of strategic thinking proposes that rather than a focus on the external market in which an organization operates, strategy should be based on a consideration of the resources they have at their disposal or can easily acquire. Such resources include not only physical and financial assets, but also the skills and experience of the staff within the organization. The RBV suggests that if a resource is rare, then it can provide a source of temporary advantage or value to an organization that possesses it. However, in order to provide sustained value, a resource should be both rare and difficult to imitate or substitute.

The model of how IT acts to provide business value within an organization is shown in Figure 1.1. IT resources, which are recognized to consist of both technology and human resources, together with other complementary resources, such as appropriate working practices or culture, are combined and applied to the processes that make up the activities of the organization. Improvement of these processes may be expected to lead to improved organizational performance, although it is noted by the authors that this is not always the case.

The model also shows that the derivation of value by an individual organization will be affected by its trading partners, the industry in which the organization operates and the macro-environment. In particular, the authors observe that partners with whom the firm is trading electronically may try to appropriate some of the value generated by any inter-organizational systems. Additionally, in highly competitive markets the value generated by the use of IT may be appropriated by customers.

The Generic Benefits of IT

In their book exploring evaluation methods for IT, Farbey et al. (1993) present a generic list of benefits that may be expected from IT investments. Their book, which is based on an empirical study of project evaluation in 16 organizations spanning a range of industry sectors, presents a list of benefits drawn from those projects and is augmented by benefits identified in the then existing literature. While the authors stress that the nature and scope of benefits is obviously dependent on what the project is trying to achieve and will vary by particular organizational or market context, they note that such a generic list of benefits would be welcomed.

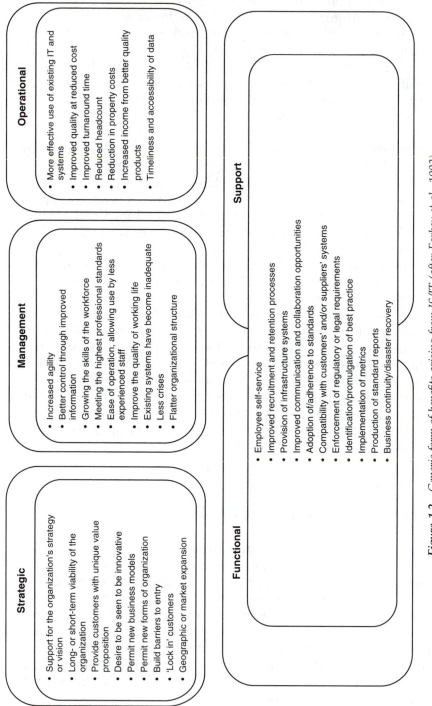

Strategic

- Support for the organization's strategy or vision
- Long- or short-term viability of the organization
- Provide customers with unique value proposition
- Desire to be seen to be innovative
- Permit new business models
- Permit new forms of organization
- Build barriers to entry
- 'Lock in' customers
- Geographic or market expansion

Management

- Increased agility
- Better control through improved information
- Growing the skills of the workforce
- Meeting the highest professional standards
- Ease of operation, allowing use by less experienced staff
- Improve the quality of working life
- Existing systems have become inadequate
- Less crises
- Flatter organizational structure

Operational

- More effective use of existing IT and systems
- Improved quality at reduced cost
- Improved turnaround time
- Reduced headcount
- Reduction in property costs
- Increased income from better quality products
- Timeliness and accessibility of data

Support

Functional

- Employee self-service
- Improved recruitment and retention processes
- Provision of infrastructure systems
- Improved communication and collaboration opportunities
- Adoption of/adherence to standards
- Compatibility with customers' and/or suppliers' systems
- Enforcement of regulatory or legal requirements
- Identification/promulgation of best practice
- Implementation of metrics
- Production of standard reports
- Business continuity/disaster recovery

Figure 1.2 Generic form of benefits arising from IS/IT (after Farbey et al., 1993)

The resulting list of benefits is categorized according to Mintzberg's view of the structure of an organization described in *Structure in Fives* (1983). In this view of an organization, Mintzberg's intention was to differentiate the elements of a firm according to the *people* contained in each and the activities they undertook. This people-centric view of the organization is a valuable starting point for considering the benefits that arise from the use of IS/IT, since an assumption that underlies the whole benefit-centred approach described in this book is that IS/IT delivers benefits when it allows individuals or groups to improve the performance of their roles or tasks within the organization. Use of the Mintzberg framework underlines that the benefits arising from the adoption of IS/IT cannot be considered in isolation from those individuals who are making use of the new systems.

A version of the Farbey et al. framework, updated to reflect current developments in IS/IT is shown in Figure 1.2.

The meaning of each of the five elements of the organizational structure is shown in Table 1.2. The first three organizational elements shown in this table are relatively easy to understand, even if there may be a discussion about where the boundary should be drawn between them, and remain current today. However, it would seem to be difficult to distinguish between the last two categories. Mintzberg, from whom the underlying model is taken, described the functional component of the organization as containing staff whose role is to influence the *way* in which people work. Such individuals would originally include operations researchers and work-study teams and more recently systems and business process analysts, change managers and, in some firms, internal audit staff. As shown in Table 1.2,

Table 1.2 *The five elements of an organization (after Farbey et al., 1993)*

Organizational structure element	Description
Strategic	Includes people charged with overall responsibility for the organization's direction
Management	Includes middle managers who operate in order to transform the strategic vision into operational reality
Operational	Refers to people who perform work related directly to the production of products and services
Functional	Includes people who serve the organization by affecting others' work
Support	Includes people who provide support for the organization outside the basic production of goods or services. These are often specialists in certain disciplines

he describes the support element of the organization as those staff whose work lies outside the direct production of the products or services of the firm. While a distinction can be drawn between IS/IT support for this activity and that for the functional area of a firm, in practice the distinction is slight. Increasingly the provision of new and improved infrastructure within an organization is intended to improve the *way* in which staff work. For example, the provision of email within an organization is to allow richer, faster and lower cost communication among staff, which will impact how they work with their colleagues. For this reason the benefits arising from application of IS/IT in the functional and support activities will be discussed together.

While a detailed examination of any of the individual benefits would require a consideration of the context of the project, the organization and even the industry in which it operates, Figure 1.2 illustrates a number of generic benefits that can be realized from IS and IT. The figure, and the structure chosen by the authors, clearly shows that IS/IT can generate benefits in all areas of the organization. Many of the benefits continue to be operational gains, such as the reduction in the time taken or costs incurred to complete a task or process or an improvement in the accuracy of an activity. These benefits are consistent with the early uses of IT within firms in the 1960s and 70s, and are often where firms commencing their use of IS/IT focus their efforts. However, Figure 1.2 shows there are also a significant number of benefits that can be linked to the management and strategic development of an organization.

Strategic Benefits

The opportunity for organizations to realize strategic benefit from IS and IT has been possible ever since its early use for business applications, back in the 1960s. However, the advent of e-business in the 1990s caused a particular focus on the use of IS and IT to define or redefine strategy. Many organizations developed new business models, often where IS or IT was not simply a support to the existing organization, but *was* the organization (Amit and Zott, 2001). Well-known examples where IS effectively defines the strategy of the organization include organizations born during the dot.com era, such as Amazon and Lastminute.com. However, a number of firms that preexisted that era have made such significant use of IT to run their internal operations and to work with suppliers and customers, that IT is now key to their existence (see Box 1.2).

Box 1.2 Using IS/IT to define organizational strategy

An example of an organization that makes such extensive use of IS and IT in its operations that it now defines the organization is Dell Computers. The use of information systems starts with customers being encouraged to use the organization's website (www.dell.com) to place their orders. The easy-to-use site guides users through the configuration of a PC that meets their needs, screening out combinations of components that are not optimal. Once the order has been confirmed, purchase orders for the necessary components are automatically generated by Dell and sent to their suppliers. This rapid transmission of orders back to suppliers allows Dell to hold little stock and results in a stockturn of around 60 times per year, a figure that is six times higher than their competitors.

The close communication with suppliers and low stock holding, enabled by IT, allow Dell to define itself as 'building PCs to order'. The benefits of such an approach are significant. Customers get exactly what they want, rather than what a manufacturer has chosen to make many months before, as occurs in the automotive industry. Dell also removes the risk of being left with slow to move finished goods, a particular risk in the high-tech sector, where falling cost and increasing performance of many components mean that such stock can depreciate in value very quickly. Indeed, the electronic customer ordering and payment operated by Dell is so efficient that the company has a positive working capital for such orders.

In other organizations, where IS/IT has not been adopted to such a significant level, it can still offer significant strategic benefits. For example, it may allow the organization to provide a unique service to its customers, differentiating them from the competition and, ideally, 'locking their customers in'. Many e-business developments sought to generate such unique customer value propositions, often by opening internal systems up to customers to provide them with an improved service.

The efficiency savings offered by IS/IT may be so significant that they allow an organization that otherwise would be in severe difficulties to remain viable and even be able to compete effectively with others in their industry. Small and medium sized businesses in particular are often encourage to explore the use of IS/IT to allow them to *'level the playing field'* with their larger competitors, who benefit from economies of scale. One of the benefits predicted for the electronic procurement marketplaces that flourished during the late 1990s, was that they would reduce the buying costs smaller businesses often face. By combining orders with other small businesses and also reducing the transaction costs associated with purchasing, it was expected that such marketplaces would allow smaller businesses to achieve a cost of goods similar to that of larger organizations. To date, there is no evidence that smaller businesses have brought their purchasing together in order to negotiate bulk discounts. However, such marketplaces have clearly demonstrated the ability to reduce the administrative costs associated with purchasing.

Another strategic reason for adopting IS/IT is a desire to be seen to be innovative. A study undertaken by Daniel and Storey (1997) into the rationale for the then new online banking services being offered by the retail banks found that this was one of the benefits being sought from such systems. A number of other potential strategic benefits were also identified by banks, such as the ability to provide a better service to existing customers and an ability to attract new customers and to target new customer segments. However, interestingly, the ability of the service to protect or enhance their existing reputation for innovation was cited by the banks interviewed as one of the key benefits sought from such systems. This may have been because, at the time, it was clear that uptake would be very slow and, although in the future such systems may allow reduction in the costly branch networks operated by these banks, in the short to medium term, internet banking would only add to the cost and complexity of the organization's operations. Justifying the development on cost savings would not therefore be possible. Developing a reputation for successful innovation is key to many consumer markets, since growing revenues increasingly depend on such innovations. Maintaining such a reputation is important, since studies have shown that consumers are more ready to accept new services from proven innovators.

Management Benefits

Farbey et al. (1993) use the term management in Figure 1.2 to describe the activities of middle managers within the organization. These individuals operate at a business unit level and are often tasked with the collection and sharing of information, together with decision making based on that information, often about the most appropriate use of resources and are also responsible for the development of their staff.

Agility has become an increasingly popular term in all areas of business. As many markets are seen to be becoming more dynamic, and are changing in unexpected ways, organizations must learn how to change frequently and rapidly. The ability of an organization to change in order to accommodate market dynamism is being termed organizational agility. In theory, agility is not dependent on IS/IT, but in reality this is the only practical means of creating the speed and accuracy required (see Box 1.3). While agility can be developed at the organizational level, and be considered as an organizational benefit, it is often more feasible to address agility at the business unit level and hence here it is considered as a management benefit.

Box 1.3 Agility in action: the case of Barclays and the Woolwich

In a further exploration of workforce agility, Breu and Hemingway (2001) undertook a number of case studies. In one of these they report how the development of a B2E portal by Barclays Bank played a key part in making their merger with the Woolwich, which took place in July 2000, effective more quickly.

The portal allowed information presented to staff within the organization to be personalized according to an individual's role, physical location, personal preferences or the subsidiary in which they worked. The Woolwich remained as a distinct brand with its own branches, but the staff in those branches were rapidly assimilated within the Barclays Group by presenting them with both the group-wide and Woolwich-specific information they needed to function in the newly merged organization.

Now, whenever a new member of staff joins the organization or someone within it changes their roles or locations, they can simply reconfigure the selection of information they will see.

The B2E portal is also being used to disseminate management information (MIS) to senior managers within the group. When combined with mobile technologies such as phone, laptops and PDAs, access to the MIS via the enterprise portal ensures that all managers have access to the most up-to-date and consistent view of the state of the organization, which they can use to make effective business decisions.

A study by Breu et al. (2002) considered the concept of agility in the particular case of a knowledge-based workforce. Their study, which is based on a large-scale postal survey, found that highly agile organizations demonstrated 10 aspects of competence, which can be grouped into five areas, as shown in Table 1.3.

Interestingly, their study found that workforce agility was not strongly correlated with the adoption and use of new technology *per se*. Rather, it was the new working models that such technologies allowed that showed the greatest relationship with agility. The ability to develop virtual teams within the organization and with other organizations and the development of communities of practice were all related to increased agility. As noted by the authors, hot-desking, mobile working and home working, which are all aimed at improving the working of individuals, were not as strongly related to agility as those models that involved the collaborative working between groups and teams. In addition to collaborative working models, the study found that access to consistent and accurate organizational and customer information is a key prerequisite for organizational agility.

Other benefits from the use of IS/IT that may be expected to accrue to the middle management layer of the organization include better decision making and control at the business unit level, largely through the access to improved information. While the obvious limitations of the information that organizations currently hold include

Table 1.3   *Capabilities required for workforce agility (after Breu et al., 2002)*

Capabilities for workforce agility	
Intelligence	Responsiveness to changing customer needs
	Responsiveness to changing market conditions
Competences	Speed of developing new skills and competencies
	Speed of acquiring the skills necessary for business process change
	Speed of acquiring new IT and software skills
	Speed of developing innovative management skills
Collaboration	Effectiveness of cooperating across functional boundaries
	Ease of moving between projects
Culture	Employee empowerment for independent decision making
IS	Support of the IT infrastructure for the rapid introduction of new IS

it being out of date, inaccurate or incomplete, a less obvious, but commonly encountered problem is that of duplicated information. Many organizations report spending considerable time debating which of a number of information sources should be used as a basis of decision making or trying to reconcile differing information. The considerable expenditures witnessed by organizations on data warehouses is frequently driven by the wish to resolve this limitation and provide *'a single version of the truth'* to everyone in the organization.

Benefits also sought by this level of the organization are often related to the skills of the workforce. This may include the development of systems that allow employees to develop their skills or knowledge, for example the use of computer-based training (CBT) systems. A report on the use of IT in the workplace by the iSociety (2003) describes the use of such a system by a leading firm of accountants to train their staff on the important regulatory issue of money laundering. As the report describes *'training consists of watching a video, reading the policy statement and completing the full computer based training'*.

Information systems may also be deployed with the intention of allowing staff with limited experience or skills to carry out a given activity to a required standard. Many telephone call centres suffer from high levels of staff turnover, with levels of 100% per annum not being unknown. In such cases, the provision of information systems that provide script information to a screen in front of the call handler, including prompts to ask the customer questions and answers for frequently asked questions (FAQs), allows such organizations to provide a consistent level of service regardless of such high turnover in staff.

Despite the economic slowdown of the early 2000s, and the redundancies announced by many businesses, the importance of retaining and attracting the best staff is a key concern. IS and IT are often viewed as opportunities to improve the *'work–life balance'* that can be offered to staff. For example, many firms are exploring the opportunities for mobile working so that staff can work at locations that suit them and even at times to suit themselves. This may include the opportunity to work from home or, for organizations located on multiple sites, may allow a reduction in travel between those sites, with colleagues collaborating via IT-based systems. As well as improving the working life of staff, such systems and technology can reduce the travel costs incurred by organizations and may even allow them to reduce their property costs. Interestingly, while the opportunities for such flexible working sound attractive, research is beginning to suggest that it is not always appreciated by staff, and can have associated disadvantages or 'disbenefits'. These disbenefits are discussed in the following section.

Operational Benefits

Benefits are classified as operational in the model of Farbey et al. (1993) when they are associated with the production of the goods and services the firm provides. This production is frequently comprised of a number of interrelated processes. Each of these processes can be considered as a number of inputs to the process, actions or activities that comprise the process and a range of outputs that either become inputs to the next process, or are the finished goods or services produced by the organization and are passed to customers or users.

When taking such a generic, process view of an organization's core activities, it can be seen that IS or IT can only act in a limited and structured number of ways. First, it can act on the inputs to the process, the process itself or its outputs, and for each of these, it can act in three basic ways: to increase efficiency, that is to improve the use of resources, usually cost; to improve the quality, which is often associated with accuracy; or to reduce the time taken for the process, that is, increase its speed. Any system may impact all three stages of the process and in all three ways, or more usually, a number of stages and in just one or two of the three basic ways described.

The use of such logic to identify the possible benefits arising from an information system that will allow patients, whose doctor has referred them to their local hospital for an X-ray examination, to choose a date and time for that appointment that is convenient to them is shown in Figure 1.3. This project, called 'Choose and Book', forms part of the Connecting for Health programme (formerly the National Programme for IT) being pursued in the UK National Health Service. Currently when a patient requires an X-ray, their GP sends a letter of request to the local hospital, which will send the patient an appointment. Many hospitals are left with wasted appointment slots,

Business process / Areas of possible benefit / Basic attributes of IT	'Choose and Book' Allowing patients to book X-ray appointments at a hospital		
	Inbound – booking appointment	Business process – performing X-ray	Outbound – reporting X-ray results
Efficiency (lower cost)	Cost associated with paper requests for X-rays and paper records (e.g. storage) removed both at GP's surgery and hospital	Reduced cost per X-ray due to reduction in unused slots DNAs – did not attend	Reports of X-ray can be sent electronically to requesting GP removing costs associated with paper reports
Accuracy (quality)	Complete and accurate record of patient received by X-ray department e.g. name, address, date of birth, hospital number	Complete electronic record of X-rays undertaken on each patient ensures radiological guidelines on exposure are not exceeded	Missing or delayed reports can cause electronic alert on GPs' systems, ensuring all requested X-rays are carried out and all results are received and acted on
Speed	Electronic or telephone request for X-ray received from patient or GP removes delays associated with traditional postal requests	Reduced need to complete or correct inaccurate patient information prior to examination reduces time taken for each appointment – allowing more appointment slots per day	Electronic reports of X-ray remove delays associated with traditional postal reporting – and allow treatment or follow-on tests to be commenced sooner

Figure 1.3 IT's improvement of operational business procedures

since when patients find their date or time inconvenient they fail either to attend or to inform the hospital in time for the appointment to be given to another patient. With the system that is being developed, either the doctor will book an appointment during the patient consultation or the patient will book the appointment themselves by telephone or online. It is expected that by allowing the patient to select the date and time of the appointment the number of wasted slots, called 'DNAs' (did not attends), will be significantly reduced. The system will also offer other benefits, such as the reduction in costs and delays associated with traditional postal booking arrangements. The reduction in these delays will allow the results of the X-ray to be known by the requesting doctor sooner and hence allow treatment or follow-up tests to be instigated as soon as possible. Also, by recording all of the X-rays given to a certain patient to be built up, the system will ensure that radiological guidelines on exposure are not exceeded, improving the quality of the service offered by the X-ray department.

Such consideration often shows that the efficiency gains associated with IS/IT can result in staff productivity improvements. If this is the case, then firms must consider how they wish to realize that productivity improvement. This could involve reducing the head-count within the business or redeploying staff on other, higher value adding tasks. IS/IT may alternatively, or additionally, offer other forms of efficiency gains, such as improvement in the use of plant, land or other assets including intellectual property. Once again, firms must consider how they wish to realize this gain. Can they sell the asset or lease it to another organization or, if not, can they put it to another value-adding use?

Functional and Support Benefits

In his model of the internal value chain (see Chapter 2), Porter (1985) identifies certain activities that are intended to support the core activities associated with the production of the goods and services made by the firm. These support activities include human resources, legal, finance and IT. Both Figure 1.2 and the case described in Box 1.4 show how the introduction of IS/IT within these specialist support areas can provide benefits, both within the specialism and for the wider business.

Many organizations are developing a self-service approach to support functions. This involves providing staff with online access to information and tools that allow them to carry out tasks such as selecting and tracking employee benefits, claiming expenses and arranging travel themselves. Such services can take away repetitive enquiries from specialist staff within support functions such as HR and allow them to apply themselves to more value-adding work. It can also improve the service offered to the staff within the organization, allowing them to get rapid responses to their enquiries and complete reservations on the spot. Research in a wide range of organizations (Breu and Hemingway, 2001) has shown that there is a strong correlation between the use of self-service for support activities and highly performing companies. It would seem there is a two-way mechanism in operation. By allowing both operational and functional support staff to become more productive, self-service can lead to an improvement in the performance of an organization. Equally, high performing organizations have a proven track record in being able to spot and develop effective systems and have identified employee self-service to be such systems.

Box 1.4 Winning the 'war for talent'

One of the world's major software vendors uses IS to improve both the quality and the efficiency of its recruitment process. The organization receives many hundreds of applications from potential recruits every day, most of these by email, but a few via traditional post. The paper applications are scanned to produce an electronic version then all applications are parsed to produce information that can be fed into a database of applicants. All applications receive an acknowledgement within 48 hours of being received.

The information in the applicant database is then matched against open job positions. The database is also scanned by HR staff to ensure that good candidates are not missed. Once candidates who the organization might like to interest have been identified, HR staff liaise with the relevant managers to arrange a suitable time for the interview to take place. All the information known about the candidate is sent electronically to the manager before the interview to ensure that he or she is fully briefed and so the interview can be most effective for both parties. Following the interview, feedback on the candidate is sent back to HR and entered into the applicant database. If additional interviews are deemed appropriate, follow-up questions suggested by the first interviewer can be stored and will be passed to subsequent interviewers. This ensures that the interviews

Box 1.4 (Continued)

build on each other and particular areas of the candidate's skills or experience can be fully explored.

The whole process not only ensures that the organization finds the people who best match their needs, but also gives the candidates a good impression of the organization. Even when unemployment rates are high, recruitment has been described as a *'war for talent'*, and such systems can improve the ability to match individuals to open positions and present the organization in a better light than other employers.

The provision of improved IT infrastructure within the organization, and some of the consequent benefits that this can give rise to are shown within the functional/support components of the Farbey et al. model shown in Figure 1.2. Such IT infrastructures would include voice and data networks, both wired and wireless, servers and PCs and mass data storage facilities. The benefits are shown in the functional/support area due to the fact that the implementation and operation of those infrastructures are undertaken by the IT function, which in most organizations is viewed as a support activity to the core business. However, while some benefits of such infrastructure deployments accrue directly to the IT function, such as lower maintenance costs or reduced data storage costs, the majority of benefits are realized by wider areas, if not the entire business. This is similar for other support functions, for example, the deployment of an improved recruitment system, as described in Box 1.4, benefits the HR department, in that it makes them more efficient, but it also improves the suitability of the candidates recruited to all areas of the business.

Tangible and Intangible Benefits

Benefits arising from IS/IT are often described as either tangible or intangible. *Tangible* benefits are those that can be measured by an objective, quantitative and often financial measure. Examples of such benefits would be the revenue generated by the launch of a new e-commerce website or the cost savings caused by discontinuing the licences to certain software packages. These benefits can easily be measured and in both of these cases the unit of measurement could be financial. Such benefits are often termed 'hard', as opposed to the 'soft' benefits discussed later and many organizations concentrate their consideration of new IS/IT investments solely on such hard benefits.

In some cases it may be that a benefit has a quantitative measure, but it is not financial. For example, provision of training courses to staff within an organization can be accomplished by providing those courses through online resources. The benefit of this system could be expressed as the number of courses that are offered online, to show the breadth or diversity of the service. However, it is usually difficult to associate the access to these online courses directly to any financial benefit.

Intangible benefits are those that can only be judged subjectively and tend to employ qualitative measures. Examples of intangible benefits include improvements in satisfaction, either of customers or of employees, or an improved ability to make decisions. Some organizations that recognize the importance of such qualitative issues to their organization, work hard to develop suitable measures. The importance of customer satisfaction to the major supermarkets, in the UK and elsewhere in the world, has led them to develop very sophisticated customer satisfaction indices. Past data and modelling shows them how changes to the index directly impact the amounts spent by shoppers. Any initiative is therefore carefully considered in terms of how it will impact this customer satisfaction index. Other organizations recognize the importance of such intangible benefits, but understand that they cannot derive a financial value for them. However, they are recorded in the business case for new investments, where they are viewed as important as more tangible benefits.

Different types of benefits and how they may be measured are discussed in more detail in Chapter 5.

Emergent Benefits

In their study, Farbey et al. (1993) identified that many of the IS/IT projects studied, in addition to the anticipated benefits, gave rise to unplanned or emergent benefits. Many of these unplanned benefits appear to be 'second order' benefits, that is they arose from achieving an initial or planned benefit. For example, they describe how a firm offering professional services had deployed a network within their offices and between their regional offices, to improve the communication between staff. It was only once this network was in use, it was realized that it could be used to switch work between offices, to the point where they could take advantage of cheaper labour and property costs outside London.

Interestingly they found that unplanned benefits tended to be more intangible than the planned benefits. This is likely to be largely a function of the emphasis many firms place on a financially justified business case or ROI, as discussed later. However, such qualitative or intangible benefits are often associated with how individuals perceive the system and how satisfied they are with it. Such benefits are therefore important in contributing to considerations such as employee satisfaction.

The Disbenefits of IS/IT

While the adoption of IS/IT by an organization is driven by the desire to realize benefits, such adoption may also be accompanied by some form of disadvantage or downside, either to the organization as a whole, or to groups or individuals within it. These adverse effects we term *'disbenefits'*.

The dominant focus for much adoption of IS/IT tends to be the realization of benefits by the organization. Such a focus tends to either ignore the benefits at the level of individuals or groups within the organization or only explore these benefits if they are consistent with the organizational benefits sought. In the worst cases organizational benefits are often achieved at the expense of an individual's ability to improve their working conditions or way of working. Box 1.5 describes how the use of knowledge management systems, particularly when used in conjunction with dispersed teams, can provide considerable organizational benefit, but significant disbenefit to the individuals on whom the success of the systems relies.

Box 1.5 IT as a jealous mistress

Many organizations are interested in knowledge management and collaboration and have developed or are in the process of developing systems to support these activities. A study by

Griffith et al. (2003) investigates how such systems, particularly when used by remote or dispersed staff, may provide benefits to the organization but at the expense of the individuals on whom they rely to be successful.

Any discussion of knowledge management should commence with a discussion of the important concepts of explicit and tacit knowledge. Explicit knowledge is that knowledge that can be expressed and hence codified. This is often called objective or fact-based knowledge. In contrast, tacit knowledge is the knowledge that cannot be easily expressed. It is the knowledge held in the 'heads' of individuals that has been acquired over time, usually from many interactions with others, and which is often also termed experience or skills.

The intention of most knowledge management initiatives within organizations is to ensure that as much explicit knowledge as possible, or at least that most valuable to the organization, is expressly captured. Such initiatives also aim to ensure such knowledge is fully and correctly identified and stored such that it can be retrieved and reused by others. These initiatives also aim to find ways and means to transform tacit knowledge into explicit knowledge, so that this might be stored and shared with others. Indeed, while explicit knowledge may easily leak away or be copied by others, firms recognize that their key asset is often the tacit knowledge of their employees and are keen to try and capture as much of this as possible just in case it walks out of the door!

The paper by Griffith et al. asserts that IT can play the role of a jealous mistress between an organization and its employees. They suggest that IT used to support collaboration in virtual or dispersed teams increases the transformation of tacit knowledge to explicit knowledge, since individuals are encouraged to express their knowledge in order to collaborate with other team members. However this dispersed way of working reduces the ability to produce new, individually held tacit knowledge, due to the removal of the rich interactions from co-located peers that the generation and acquisition of such knowledge is reliant on.

They suggest that such IT support for virtual collaboration therefore benefits the organization but not the individual. The

Box 1.5 (Continued)

organization may therefore gain from this in the first instance, but this will be short lived as without certain safeguards to mitigate the effects described, individuals will not be keen to work in such environments. In order to address this, the authors state that organizations must allow individuals the opportunity to replace their personal tacit knowledge. This, they suggest, can be achieved by the use of systems that support rich interactions such as the personal experimentation and learning-by-doing that are necessary to transfer tacit knowledge among individuals.

The most extreme disbenefit that may arise for individuals from the adoption of IS/IT is the loss of their job. As shown in Figure 1.2, many of the benefits sought are associated with the improvements in operational efficiency, which are linked to increased productivity and frequently to a consequential reduction in headcount. Many organizations seek to redeploy such individuals in other areas of their business, often in more value creating, and hence more satisfying roles. However, other organizations are keen to realize a reduction in their cost base or may find that the staff released are not suitable for other roles in the organization.

Other disbenefits that may be associated with the adoption of new IS are standardization of tasks and the associated deskilling of roles and loss of autonomy. Many organizations keen to reap the rewards of the control and standardization of processes have adopted workflow systems to control and monitor the stages in their key processes. Computer systems control the flow of activity between individuals, who are given a certain time to complete their allocated tasks. The completion of tasks is monitored by the system and failure to complete such tasks on time is flagged to a manager. While such systems offer many benefits to organizations, often including improved cycle times and consistency of approach, they tend to reduce the creativity and autonomy of the individuals involved. While the reduction in these aspects may be appropriate in areas such as the approval of bank loans or the processing of an insurance claim, workflow systems are increasingly being applied to areas that are considered highly creative or non-routine, such as developing marketing campaigns, new product development and the handling of legal cases.

The use of expert systems that codify the expert or professional knowledge in a certain subject area is also being adopted by more organizations. These include businesses and public sector organizations, such as healthcare providers. Again, while these systems provide the organization with a means of ensuring a consistent approach, they often reduce the autonomy of individuals.

New information technologies may also represent a mixed blessing to those who must use them. An example is that of remote or mobile working. Many organizations are interested in exploring the use of new technologies to achieve this way of working for their staff. The organizational benefits that may be sought from this approach include less 'dead' time when staff are unable to work because they are travelling, resulting in increased productivity and the ability to reduce property costs, by encouraging activities such as hot-desking. While the ability to work anywhere, anytime, often appeals to staff at first, including the ability to work from home, before long they find that they are expected to work all the time and everywhere. Working hours, it is found are not reduced due to improved productivity, rather they are increased with staff being expected to be contactable at all times. Studies have also shown that many staff do not like hot-desking, since the lack of a fixed location to return to reduces their ability to have regular contact with colleagues. Perversely, the provision of improved communication networks, allowing mobile and home working, results in many staff feeling increasingly 'disconnected' from the organization.

Net Benefits: The Measure of IS Success

In 1992 DeLone and McLean proposed perhaps the most widely used framework for measuring the success of information systems (DeLone and McLean, 1992). Since its publication almost 300 studies of IS success have made use of or cited this framework. Ten years later, these authors considered both the studies that had been based on their original framework and the developments that had occurred in this time in IS/IT use in organizations. This led to their proposing a refined version of this framework, which is shown in Figure 1.4 (DeLone and McLean, 2003).

In their initial model, DeLone and McLean identified six factors which contribute to the success of an information system: systems

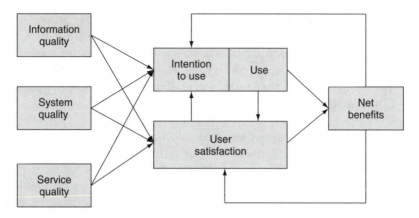

Figure 1.4   *DeLone and McLean IS success model (after DeLone and McLean, 2003)*

quality, information quality, systems use, user satisfaction, individual impact and organizational impact. In their revised model, they suggest, in addition to the measures of information and system quality, the inclusion of service quality. This reflects that many IS organizations within firms undertake the dual role of information provider and service provider (supporting end users). Most interestingly for this consideration of benefits, the authors also reframed their description of the outcomes of the use of the system. Rather than consider only the impact on the individual and the organization, they note that the effects of many current information systems now extend beyond the organization, with impacts on customers, suppliers, the industry and even on society. Instead of including measures at all of these levels, the authors group all of the impact measures into a single category called 'net benefits'. This term, they state, is in their opinion the most accurate descriptor of information system success.

The use of 'net benefits', the authors concede, raises the issues that will be dealt with in detail throughout this book, that is: what qualifies as a benefit?, for whom?, and at what level should this be considered (individual, manager, senior management)? They suggest that the answers to these questions will depend on the particular system, its context and whose perspective of success is being considered. Finally, inclusion of the word 'net' is stressed as important, since in agreement with our earlier discussion of disbenefits, few system developments are wholly positive, without some negative consequences for some individuals or groups.

Current Investment Appraisal Approaches

The most frequently observed approach to the appraisal of IS/IT investments is the preparation and assessment of a financial business case (Ross and Beath, 2002). Such a case is frequently built around a calculation of the return on investment (ROI) expected from the project. Indeed, the ROI approach is so popular, particularly in the USA, that the term is often used synonymously with the term business case.

A fuller discussion of investment appraisal methods will be given in Chapter 5. However, an outline of the key approaches is given here, since an understanding of the underlying concepts and assumptions that comprise these approaches sheds light on their limitations, which affect not only investment appraisal, but also project implementation. Understanding these limitations highlights the need for a new approach and also begins to suggest the issues that it should address.

Return on investment calculations require the financial outcomes expected from the project, in the form of additional revenues or reductions in costs, to be forecast and compared with the costs that will be incurred in undertaking the project. The time over which it is acceptable to count those additional revenues or cost savings will often be specified in an organization's policies or derived from the useful life of the system under consideration. More sophisticated financial approaches to project appraisal recognize the *'time value of money'*. That is, money has an opportunity cost and money earned or saved today has a greater value than money earned or saved in the future. Discounted cash flow (DCF) and net present value (NPV) methods require projects to be described as streams of cash flows, which are then reduced by a discount rate the further in the future they occur.

Such quantitative financial approaches have the benefit that the results are easily compared to those from other projects, either within the IT function, or with capital expenditure projects in other areas of the business. Senior managers are happy with financial descriptions of projects; it is how they are used to expressing activities within the organization. This perceived comfort and the comparability of projects expressed as an ROI or DCF-based case allows managers to use these cases to prioritise projects within the organization, either to allocate scarce resources or to decide in which order projects should be carried out. However, such approaches either require a financial value to be placed on the more qualitative benefits arising from the investment or, as commonly occurs, such benefits are given no value and are omitted. Furthermore, as will be discussed in later chapters, these traditional approaches to IT investment are likely to encourage the funding of piecemeal applications, rather than true enterprise-wide capabilities firms need to compete in today's increasingly dynamic environment. Such approaches also encourage the funding of safer, incremental projects, rather than more strategic investments.

While determining the additional revenues or savings associated with a project is often far from simple, it has also to be recognized that the cost side to these calculations is difficult, as demonstrated by the massive overspending reported on many projects. While this may often be due to projects that run late, a significant proportion of such cost variances are due to a lack of understanding of the different sources of cost that a project will incur. As we will discuss throughout this book, many IS/IT investments require a significant degree of associated working practice and process change in order to deliver benefits. This change management is often omitted or severely underestimated when determining the costs of an investment.

Although Ross and Beath (2002) note the continued dominance of financial methods on the appraisal of IT projects, their study of the methods major companies had used to undertake this activity found that there were some alternative approaches. Of the companies interviewed, they found that the majority had funded at least one e-business initiative, which was the focus of the study, simply on the basis that it was perceived to be 'strategic'. No formal business case was required for such projects. Allied to this, a significant number of companies interviewed reported setting aside a separate budget for e-business 'experiments'.

Such approaches undoubtedly have a number of advantages compared to the solely financially based approaches, not least in that they allow the inclusion of less tangible benefits, but they also have limitations. In particular, they do not facilitate prioritization between projects, which is often the biggest challenge facing organizations. Also these less rational, more instinctive approaches are more susceptible to being dominated by persuasive or charismatic project champions. While these approaches seem visionary to those at the top of the organization, to those lower down, they often suggest that the usual financial justification procedures do not apply to the 'pet projects' of senior managers.

Limitations of Current Appraisal Methods

A survey of over 100 companies by Cranfield School of Management (Lambert and Edwards, 2003) explored the implications of current approaches to IS/IT investment appraisal. The key findings from their survey are shown Table 1.4.

Ineffective Appraisal Processes

The survey found that while IT investment appraisal was seen as important, the majority of organizations felt that their investment appraisal processes were ineffective.

Many companies are now finding the traditional financially based approaches limiting. The strategic importance of IT has caused them to consider balancing the return on individual projects, as expressed in ROI calculations, with the need to create organisation-wide capabilities. They must also be able to leverage or improve existing systems while at the same time being able to experiment with new ways of doing business, the returns of which may be very uncertain.

While there is a recognition that information system investments are made to yield benefits to the organization, traditionally business cases have not been explicitly stated in these terms. In many organizations the business case that is required from project teams is a highly financial document. This emphasis is likely to make projects where the benefits are difficult, if not impossible to financially quantify, hard to justify. However, it is such projects that may be contributing to those

Table 1.4 *Survey of IS investment appraisal*

	Yes	No
Is IT investment appraisal seen as important by business managers?	55%	45%
Do you have an effective investment appraisal process?	22%	78%
Are business managers adequately involved in IT investment appraisal?	30%	70%
Does the appraisal process consider the implications of business changes?	10%	90%
Do people making decisions understand the business cases?	25%	75%
What % of projects deliver the benefits that justified the investment?	27%	73%

areas of the business that are most important to the organization, for example customer care or employee satisfaction. The dominance of a financial mindset within the investment appraisal process will tend to favour cost cutting or efficiency projects, which although worthwhile, should not be allowed to exclude projects that will improve effectiveness or innovation within the organization.

The money available for new projects is finite within any organization and, in difficult trading conditions, that funding can become very limited. This results in severe competition among projects, which leads to the inevitable consequence that project teams will endeavour to present their business case in the best possible light, often overstating the financial benefits or return from the project in order to secure funding. Research has shown that many organizations fail to conduct post-implementation reviews. Lack of resources and other commitments mean that the time is not found to carry these out and those that are undertaken often focus solely on the technology implementation, rather than determine if the organization achieved what it intended from the project. Without such reviews being performed, the tendency to overstate the return or benefits expected from a project will continue, since those involved will not be called to account later.

It should be noted, that while finite financial resources may be a severe limitation to the undertaking of information systems projects, the lack of other types of resource can be equally limiting, if not, in some cases, even more so. A frequent limitation is that of skilled or experienced staff. Lack of access to IT staff with specialized skills, or experienced IS project managers or of business managers with sufficient time to devote to the project are common examples. While, it may be argued that additional financial resources could address such constraints, this is not always true. In the case of IT or business managers, as discussed before, Mata et al. (1995) note that the effective management of IT is a capability that is not easily transferred between organizations, since it relies on a good understanding of the particular context of the organization and good relationships between staff in different areas, all of which will take some time to establish.

The observation that managerial resources may be more of a scarce resource than capital was made by Strassmann (1999) in his discussion of IT productivity. He notes that capital has become a commodity, which is readily available for a price that is commensurate with the risk involved. The importance of skilled management, rather than the availability of capital was clearly demonstrated in the dot.com boom of the late 1990s. At that time many venture capital organizations were happy to pour significant sums of money into start-up organizations with highly inexperienced managers. The money invested could not make up for the lack of experience of the managers and many of the organizations failed. While it may be argued that this was due in large part to the lack of uptake of services by customers, managers with greater experience or ability should have been able to address their slower than expected growth in revenues and develop their strategy accordingly. Those dot.com firms that did survive this era, such as Amazon and Lastminute.com, did not have greater funding than many of those that did not survive, demonstrating the enduring need for effective management.

Lack of Involvement of Business Staff

That business managers believe IT is essential to improving the performance of their organizations is underlined by the finding that a majority of managers view IT investments as important. However, the rapid advances in technology make it difficult for business managers to keep abreast of developments and the technical-language of many IT staff further excludes them.

A study by the iSociety (2003), exploring the role and use of IT in workplaces in the UK, identified a separation between the IT staff within an organization and the rest of the business. They found that there were three types of separation: spatial, cultural and structural, one or more of which may be present in an organization. Spatial separation arose from IT staff often being in locations distinct from users, either in the bowels of the building or on another site. This spatial separation tends to result in each group being 'out of sight and out of mind' of the other, resulting in a lack of knowledge or appreciation of the work and working practices of each other.

However, even without physical separation, the report describes a cultural divide between IT staff and others within the organization, summed up by the common feeling of 'them and us'. They quote a survey (Harding, 2003) that found half the office staff surveyed believed that IT staff 'spoke another language'. While it may be tempting to address the divide between IS and the business by means of the formal structures within the organization, a study by Chan (2002) found that a critical success factor for the effective use of IS was the existence of strong informal relationships. Multidisciplinary teams, flexible divisions of work and the exchange of knowledge between different types of staff were found to be critical to developing an innovative and effective IS capability.

Finally, the lack of understanding at senior levels within the organization can result in the institutionalization of structural barriers between IT and the rest of the business, at its most extreme when such senior managers choose to outsource IT activities to another organization. A tale, perhaps more apocryphal than strictly accurate about the lack of senior participation in the adoption of IT, is given in Box 1.6.

Box 1.6 The president's emails

The archives of the Bill Clinton presidential library contain 40 million emails – mostly memos and notes exchanged between aides and cabinet members.

Careful examination of these emails showed that just two were sent by Bill Clinton himself – and one of them may not even count as it was sent as a test to see if the commander-in-chief understood how to send emails.

And what of the other email? Allegedly, it was an email to astronaut and senator John Glenn on his return to outer space after a 40-year hiatus. According to Reuters, the former president sent the email to the space shuttle while in orbit around the earth (that's the shuttle, not Bill) with the help of Clinton staffers!

While this does not prove the president was a techno-phobe, for a government that was promoting the benefits of e-government, this cannot be considered as leading by example.

Source: *The Weekly Round Up*, Silicon.com, 30 January 2004

Need for Business Change

Table 1.4 also shows that the survey respondents did not believe their appraisal of new IT projects considered the implications of business change. Listening to the promises made by the vendors of information technology, it could be believed that all an organization needs to do to improve its performance is to implement a given application or set of hardware, often termed the 'silver bullet' approach to IT deployment (Markus and Benjamin, 1997). However, considerable research has shown that such implementations should not simply be exercises in technological deployment, but to be successful, should also be accompanied by complementary changes in processes, the working practices of individuals and groups, the roles of individuals and even the culture of the organization. The report by the iSociety (2003), states this need accordingly: *'New technology is not transformational on its own . . . appropriate use requires considerable complementary investment in people, processes, culture and support . . . some or all of these things are usually missing'.*

The traditional business case fails to identify the changes in these social aspects of information technology adoption, either due to an ignorance of their importance from those preparing the business case or the realization that their inclusion will increase not only the cost of the project, but also the time required and risk involved.

A helpful theoretical model that explains the steps involved in creating value from IS/IT, and highlights the importance of business change in this process, has been proposed by Soh and Markus (1995). As shown in Figure 1.5, this model identifies three distinct processes that must be successfully undertaken. The first is the conversion of purchased IS/IT into assets that can be used by the firm. The second is the effective use of those assets by the firm, which captures the need to undertake business change in order to achieve effective use. Finally, this effective use must be transformed into meaningful improvements in organizational performance. These three stages relate to the ends, ways, means view of strategy development, which

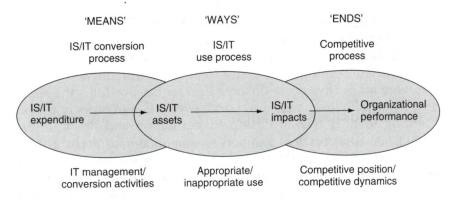

Figure 1.5   *How IT creates business value (after Soh and Markus, 1995)*

will be discussed more fully in Chapter 2. However, it should be observed here that, to date, most emphasis on strategy development has focused on the two end processes identified in this model, that is the means and the ends, with little attention to the vital process that connects these two, that is the new ways of doing things that will allow the new IS/IT assets to deliver improved impacts to the organization.

The recognition that IS projects have a strong social, as well as technical aspect, highlights the need to consider the project from the perspective of those groups or individuals that will be impacted. These groups or individuals, often termed stakeholders, can be expected to react differently to the system depending on what they perceive is *'in it for them'*. If stakeholders are required to make use of the system, or are needed to change their working practices in some way, then their view must be considered if the system is to be effectively implemented.

Need for Prioritization

The limited availability of financial and other resources results in the need for organizations to be able to prioritize the many projects and activities they are undertaking in the information systems and technology domain. When working with organizations, prioritization is often cited as one of the areas they view as most critical, but which they feel least able to do. It is recognized that if an organization can identify what is really important to its future prosperity, it can stop those activities that are not. By doing less, it will be able to deploy additional resources on the important activities and hence be able to do them faster and, more often than not, better.

The current approach to the majority of businesses cases means the only way to prioritize projects is by identifying those with the greatest, or fastest, financial return. However, as also discussed earlier, this is likely to result in a tendency to favour cost reduction projects over more innovative ones. Chapter 2 presents a portfolio, the applications portfolio that can be used to classify different types of project according to their overall business contribution and the ability to produce an appropriately justified business case for each of these types. By recognizing that different types of project will give rise to different types of organizational benefit, and hence business case, this portfolio can be used to prioritize projects more effectively within an organization.

Lack of Guidance for Implementation

The emphasis of the early stages of information systems project planning on the need to produce a business case that will secure funding for the project often results in little thought regarding implementation of the project, if the case for funding is successful. Any consideration of implementation will usually be driven by those responsible for the deployment of the underlying information technology, with detailed project planning carried out around the selection, development, deployment and testing of this aspect of the project. As discussed earlier, most business cases fail to include consideration of the business changes associated with successful implementation of the project. Without this complete picture of what implementation of the project entails, it is no wonder that sufficient thought cannot be given to how the full set of changes will be managed.

Failure to Deliver Benefits

The statistic that over 70% of IT projects are seen to fail to deliver the intended benefits is well known, both among members of the business community and the IT community itself. The promulgation of this statistic results in increased scepticism from the business users and defensive behaviour from the IT staff, resulting in a greater divide between the two sides and a further reduction in constructive communication, the very activity that is needed to address this poor track record. Interestingly, this high failure rate does not only apply to IS/IT projects, but applies to a wide variety of project types, suggesting that it is not something inherent in IT but reflects how complex projects of all types are managed within organizations.

Historically many IT projects did fail. Both the press and academic sources are littered with examples of IT projects that overran their estimated timescales by years and spent their allocated budgets many times over and such stories can still be found. Today, the improved reliability of both software and hardware, the use of standard packages and the increased experience among both internal IT staff and supporting external staff mean there are fewer overruns in cost and timescales. However, this improvement in deployment has not stopped the perception of the majority of IS projects as failures, despite the IT being implemented on time and on budget, because of the failure to deliver benefits to the organization. This may be due to a number of reasons. Perhaps the project was never capable of delivering the intended benefits, in which case, this should have been identified early in the project planning phase and the project cancelled. However, in most cases the project does have the potential to deliver worthwhile benefits to the organization, but the organizational and social aspects of change associated with delivering the benefits are not identified or addressed and hence those benefits are not realized.

The Need for a Fresh Approach: Benefits Management

The foregoing discussion of current investment appraisal approaches and their limitations suggests the need for a better way to approach the management of information systems projects. As with any project, it is important to get things right from the outset or considerable time and cost can be wasted in reworking activities already undertaken. A new approach should therefore commence with improved project identification and planning. It should also address the other limitations already described, such as the overreliance on financial business cases, a lack of inclusion of the social aspects of information system projects and the lack of review mechanisms at the end of projects.

In the mid-1990s an extended research programme was undertaken by the Information Systems Research Centre (ISRC) at Cranfield School of Management to address the limitations of existing approaches. The research programme, which originally lasted three years but has since been the focus of further research and development activity, was undertaken in conjunction with a number of major private and public sector organizations. The process and tools resulting from this work have been extended and refined from experience gained from the many organizations that have adopted the approach in the last seven to 10 years. Key elements of the approach are now in regular use by over 100 organizations based in the UK, Europe, USA and even in locations as remote as China.

The overall approach developed, termed *benefits management*, can be described as shown in the definition box.

> **Definition: Benefits management**
>
> The process of organizing and managing such that the potential benefits arising from the use of IS/IT are actually realized.

As emphasized in this definition, the approach developed was based on a process that is a set of steps to guide the planning and implementation of IS projects, such that the potential benefits from that project are realized. The key steps of the process are formulated as interrelated tools or frameworks that can be used to guide and structure the planning and actions needed to implement a project successfully.

The subsequent chapters in this book explain and illustrate, with practical examples, the benefits management process and its underlying tools and frameworks. Before addressing the detailed stages of the process, it is worthwhile considering how the benefits management approach compares with traditional approaches to IS projects and the improvements that it has been shown to yield. This comparison and the improvements resulting from the benefits management approach are shown in Figure 1.6. While we would not claim the activities on the left-hand side of this diagram are wrong or unnecessary, experience from the use of the benefits management approach shows that these activities on their own are insufficient to deliver benefits to the organization. Use of the benefits management approach can enable organizations currently on the left-hand side to move to the right-hand side of this figure.

From ⟶	*To*
• Technology delivery	• Benefits delivery
• Value for MONEY – low level task monitoring	• VALUE for money – benefits tracking
• Expenditure proposal – loose linkage to business needs	• Business case – integration with business drivers
• IT implementation plan	• Change management plan
• Business manager as onlooker/victim	• Business manager involved and in control
• Large set of unfocused functionality	• IT investment that is sufficient to do the job
• Stakeholders 'subjected to'	• Stakeholders 'involved in'
• Trained in technology	• Educated in exploitation of technology – talent harnessed
• Carry out technology and project audits	• Obtain business benefits then review with learning – leverage more benefits

Figure 1.6 Comparison of benefits management with traditional IS project approaches

Benefits Delivery

Central to the benefits management approach is the identification of and focus on the potential benefits that can arise from the investment. This focus is continuous throughout the project, from the initial planning stage, through appraisal and implementation, to the final review of the project. Technology delivery remains a key part of the project and, as described later, robust project and systems methodologies should be adopted to ensure that this part of the project is successful. However, too often technology delivery becomes the *raison d'être* of the project at the expense of the benefits the system will deliver to the users and the organization. Many of the implementations of customer relationship management (CRM), enterprise resource planning (ERP) and e-business systems have been driven as much by the promise of vendors and a fear of being left behind by competitors, as by a clear statement of the benefits they will yield the organization. Too often project managers find themselves in the situation that their organization *'has bought Siebel'* or *'is going wall-to-wall SAP'* and they are then left to implement the chosen application without a clear understanding of the expected benefits and the organizational changes that will be required.

A Focus on Value

Money is the language of business and translating all projects, not just IT projects, to a financial case allows senior business managers to believe that they understand the value of the project. While it is not necessary for senior managers to have a detailed understanding of IT or the workings of IS, the continued reduction of business cases to financial numbers and ratios reduces those managers understanding of the role IS or IT can play in their organization. Given also that the financial approach is unlikely to give a full picture, since more qualitative or intangible benefits are likely to be excluded from the case, this lack of understanding is likely to be exacerbated.

It has also been mentioned that it is often easier to identify the costs associated with a project than the benefits or value that it will yield. This leads to the statements commonly used to describe projects that focus on their cost, rather than their value to the organization:

'we are investing £2m in an e-procurement system'

'our £36m global ERP rollout'

'the development budget for 2005 is £4m'.

The emphasis on financial measures to justify projects also results in their use to monitor the progress of projects. This has obvious appeal since it is relatively easy to monitor the expenditure incurred on a project as it progresses, but it gives no information on the progress towards achieving the benefits required from the project, the real reason for the investment.

This use of financial measures to track progress also extends to measuring the success of projects, which are often judged as successful if they were delivered on time or on budget, regardless of the impact of the system on the operation of the organization. While overruns in either of these would not be encouraged, a project that takes longer or costs more, but delivers the intended improvements to the organization should not necessarily be judged as a failure.

A Business Case Linked to Organizational Strategy or Objectives

This focus on the financial case for IS investments, and the relative ease of assessing the cost of a project compared to the value of the benefits it will generate, results in the investment cases often being effectively an expenditure proposal, rather than a true business case. To be comprehensive, the business case should state clearly how the intended project will contribute to the strategy and performance of the organization. In the benefits management approach, described in this book, the planning for a project and the subsequent development of the business case commences with an understanding of the current and expected *drivers* acting on the organization. As introduced in Chapter 3 and discussed more fully in Chapter 4, drivers are the strategic forces acting on an organization that require the organization to make changes to what it does or how it conducts its business activities. In generating this list of drivers, the perspective of the senior management of the organization is taken, to ensure that the identified drivers are actually strategic to the future of the whole enterprise, rather than merely affecting the interests of certain departments or functions. All projects should be considered in the light of how they can contribute to the drivers and hence what is most important to the organization. The result is a project and business case that is tightly coupled to what the organization wishes to achieve.

The Importance of Change Management

The lack of recognition of the importance of the social element to IS and IT deployment often results in the need for the degree of change to working practices to be overlooked. In particular, the tendency for such projects to be led by IS staff, rather than business staff, exacerbates this lack of recognition of the impact that the system will have on individuals and groups. This may well not be intentional, but is often driven by inadequate understanding of how the business operates by those in the IT department. Many organizations are trying to address this issue by having individuals from within the business participate in IS/IT projects and even lead them. However, they may fail to release those individuals from their day-to-day responsibilities and hence involvement in the project becomes an additional burden for which they have little time. Such instances can result in participation in the early stages of a project, and then leaving it with the IT team until it is ready for delivery. If the project is more than six months in duration, it can be expected that many factors, both within the project and in the wider business context, will change. These are often related to the changes required to how staff within the organization work or their attitudes to the project, rather than to the technology itself. Continued involvement of the business managers is required to identify and address these issues as they emerge.

Commitment from Business Managers

The rapid pace of change of IT, coupled with the technical language of IT staff, frequently causes business managers to feel that they do not understand IT in the same way that they believe they understand marketing or other areas of the business. They therefore feel vulnerable when involved in appraising IS/IT projects, contributing to their preference to have such projects expressed in hard financial terms. This feeling of vulnerability was expressed by business staff in those organizations which took part in the original research project as a feeling of being *'an onlooker or victim where IT is concerned'*. The benefits management process seeks to address this issue by proposing tools and frameworks that both the business staff and IT staff use together, in order to ensure both communities contribute their knowledge and that the combined knowledge produces something neither group could have developed alone. The tools and frameworks are all intended to be used in workshop settings, to encourage participation from multiple individuals from both the business and IT groups. It has been found through the extensive experience of using the process that this approach encourages collaboration, more than the sequential passing of documents between individuals and that those involved often actively enjoy the experience, something many of them say has not happened in previous IS/IT projects.

IS/IT Sufficient to do the Job

IS and IT vendors are keen to promote the many features of their products and, all too often, organizations believe that the list of features equates to a list of benefits that the systems will provide to their organizations. However, it is seldom the case but can result in organizations buying and installing systems that either do not meet their needs or are overcomplex. As a result those systems tend to be under-utilized and hence fail to deliver the expected benefits. The benefits management approach looks at this issue from the other direction. Rather than start with the features and functions of the technology or system, benefits management elicits what is causing the organization to consider the investment and what the project is expected to deliver. It is only when this and the required change management actions have been identified that the IS and IT required should be assessed, leading to a technology specification that is *'sufficient to do the job'*.

A focus on the IT that is sufficient to do the job does not imply that organizations should purchase under-specified hardware or software that would soon be insufficient to meet their needs, rather it is to counter the emphasis of many vendors on the long list of features and functionality that they can provide. It is often the case that vendors sell their products in packages or suites. It may therefore be the case that it will cost little more to buy some additional functionality than the cost of the minimum requirements. The additional functionality should be evaluated to see if it contributes benefits that would address the strategy or objectives of the organization. However, if it does not, it should not be purchased or, if bundled in, should not be implemented. Implementing features that are not required is likely to slow the project down, cause additional need for changes to working practices and may result in an overcomplex system that is under-utilized. Theory on the adoption of new information systems states that there are two main factors that determine if a new system will be used (Venkatesh et al., 2003). These are how much the system helps the user in their job and how easy it is to use. If this latter factor is reduced due to unnecessary functionality, it will result in a reduction in use of the system.

Involvement of Stakeholders

Just as business managers may feel they are a 'victim' in IS/IT projects, others who will be impacted by the system often believe that they are *'subjected to IS/IT'*, rather than feeling that they are contributing to and shaping the project. This can at best result in a system that meets their needs but has induced a feeling of resentment that must be overcome if the system is to be used to full effect and, at worst, result in a system that does not meet their needs and therefore is not used.

The lack of involvement of stakeholders may be due in part to their fear or lack of understanding and interest in IS/IT. However, it is also often due to the attitude and activities of the IT staff within the organization. The report by the iSociety (2003) quotes Rose's (2002) work on this subject. He describes IT staff as less concerned with maintaining the quality of contact with others and gaining an understanding of how the organization works than other groups of staff. He also found that they spent less of their time advising, persuading or counselling others; rather they spent their time analysing and dealing with problems that were technical or system related. As he said in summary: *'The work of [IT professionals] as a whole is systems orientated not people orientated'*.

An important part of the benefits management approach presented in this book is the consideration of the project from the perspective of a wide set of stakeholders. Ideally, as many of those stakeholders, or their representatives if they are large groups, will be involved in planning the project, they will maintain a continuing interest and participation in the tracking and realization of benefits. In addition to encouraging participation in planning and implementation activities from a wide range of stakeholder groups, the benefits management approach includes a particular set of tools that specifically uncovers the views of each stakeholder group and identifies actions that may be needed to encourage their cooperation.

Educated in the Use of Technology

Surveys continue to show that firms invest little time and money in training their staff to use IT and IS. This problem tends to be particularly severe in the UK, with such surveys showing that compared to other European countries, organizations spend less per head of workforce on IT training, leading to reduced effectiveness in these activities. Many projects are started with a defined training budget. However, this is often not sufficient to provide enough training for individuals to become familiar, let alone confident with the new system (see Box 1.7). Even when a project does start with an appropriate training budget, if the system runs late or over-budget, it is often the training budget that is reduced to make up the shortfall elsewhere.

Box 1.7 The (in)adequacy of training budgets

The limited expenditure on staff training is highlighted by the activities of a major, worldwide professional services firm. The firm has recently been implementing a global financial system at a cost of tens of millions of pounds to improve the accounting, time recording and billing activities of the organization. All 15,000 staff in the organization are required to use the system to record their activities, if the expected benefits are to be realized. A significant budget has been set aside for training staff to use the system. However, when the large number of staff and the average charge-out rate to clients of many of those staff are considered, the training budget equated to just 20 minutes per member of staff!

Rather than provide formal training for staff, the iSociety report (2003) found that much training was left to informal, on-the-job training, undertaken by colleagues. Even with formal training in place, such informal training is beneficial since use of a system will depend on the details of a particular context. However, the existence of such informal mechanisms should not be taken as an opportunity for managers to abrogate their responsibility to provided basic systems, technology and even business skills training.

While training staff in how to use technology and systems is important, this is not sufficient in itself. To ensure projects deliver the full set of potential benefits it is usually necessary, not only to teach individuals which screens to access and which keys to press, but to demonstrate to them how the system can improve the role that they carry out for the organization. This training in the impact or exploitation of the technology should include an appreciation of how use of the system will impact others and other processes in the organization. Even if a user has been trained in how to use a piece of technology or a system, if they do not understand why they are using it, or how it can help them perform their role or improve the performance of the organization, their use of the system will be less than optimal. Equally, undertaking this education in exploitation will allow individuals to consider new ways of using the system or technology in their particular role, harnessing their experience and creativity.

Many systems today may not offer a net benefit to the individual. Rather the major benefits accrue to the entire organization. This may include knowledge management and CRM systems, where individuals are expected to share their expertise or customer contacts. Without a clear understanding of how their use will benefit the organization, individuals will be reluctant to use them. A lack of appreciation of the wider picture leads to individuals by-passing the new systems and continuing to store information on their local databases and personal devices. This tendency does not only apply to operational staff, but even to senior managers, who should be supporting company-wide initiatives. A survey from BT (2004) among senior managers found that 29% of those interviewed kept essential customer information on their own handheld devices and a further 12% held that information on paper records.

Undertake a Post-Implementation Benefits Review – Capture Learning

While many organizations have been keen to describe themselves as learning organizations, as discussed previously, very few carry out post-implementation reviews, seriously limiting their ability to learn collectively from the experience gained from projects. All too often, competing pressures mean that the project team is disbanded as soon as the project is finished and sometimes even before it is completely finished.

The benefits management process includes a post-implementation benefits review as an important component of the project. This review should not concentrate on the use of technology or on the project management, rather technology and project audits should be carried out separately. Instead, the benefits review should explore which of the planned benefits have been realized, whether there were any unexpected benefits arising and which planned benefits are still expected but may need additional attention to ensure they are realized. Actions should then be put in place to ensure that these benefits are realized. The benefits review should also consider if, given what the project team have learnt and how the organization has changed, there is an opportunity for further benefits to be realized. It is often not possible at the outset of a large project to foresee all the benefits that can be realized when the system is in operation. Many of the current large-scale enterprise system deployments, such as

ERP systems and enterprise portals, are initially intended to remove problems resulting from the existing systems. Once the organization becomes used to operating without these problems, which are often acting to reduce efficiency, they can then consider how the system can be used to improve overall performance and also how it can now be used to do new things and develop innovative ways of working.

The Rewards for Managing Benefits

In a detailed study of 11 strategic IS/IT investments (McGolpin and Ward, 1997), varying in cost between £5m and £100m and carried out across a range of industries, a number of factors differentiating the two projects that were judged highly successful (the benefits exceeded expectations) and the two that were successful (the expected benefits were achieved) from the seven less successful investments were identified (see Figure 1.7). The commitment and involvement of senior management has been identified in many studies as a success factor, but although all the projects were commissioned by senior management, only in the four successful ones was that involvement maintained throughout the projects. In particular, senior management ensured that responsibility for benefit delivery was clearly allocated to individuals and that the investment was seen as an integral component of a strategic change programme. However,

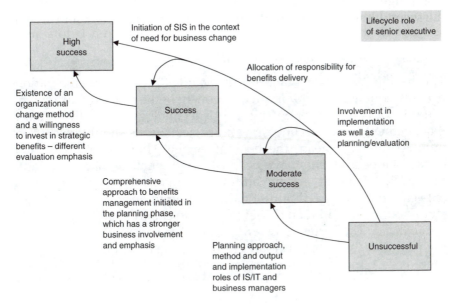

Figure 1.7   Factors affecting the success of strategic IS investments

the study also found that the successful projects were characterized by a comprehensive approach to planning and managing the benefits intended from the project. In addition, in the highly successful projects, existing change management processes were used to ensure that the business maximized the value of the IT investment through associated changes to business practices.

In the moderately successful and unsuccessful projects the emphasis was on delivering a working technical solution. The effective deployment of proven systems development and project management methodologies delivered some of the expected benefits in the moderately successful investments, but in the four 'failures' even these best practices were not adequately followed.

The Problems of Not Managing Benefits

The problems associated with following traditional approaches to project planning and evaluation, and the improvements that can arise from adopting a benefits led approach are illustrated in the case described in Figure 1.8. This 'before and after' case concerns the implementation of an ERP system in a Scandinavian optical equipment manufacturer. The case allows a direct comparison within the same firm, since this organization implemented such a system twice. The first implementation, which did not follow a benefits approach, was judged such a failure that the system was re-implemented. In the second implementation, the system went in on budget and ahead

FIRST ATTEMPT – FAILURE	SECOND ATTEMPT – SUCCESS
IS led, with insufficient knowledge of the business function concerned	Business function led, by a newly recruited manager, experienced in the function, supported by IS
Belief that the requirements were simple and already known – just use the package to automate current process	Site visits and reviews of other companies' procedures to establish best practice and system requirements
Belief that this was a low risk and straightforward implementation	Knowledge that this would require some major changes
Lack of business buy-in led to both the new and old (mainly manual) system remaining in place and little move by the business to adopt the new system	New procedures completely replaced the previous system and all staff were required to use them; facilities for the old system withdrawn
Little business change	Organizational and business process changes
Bespoke amendment of package. Longer and more complex system build and difficulty applying upgrades	Minimal changes to the package and innovative use of built-in facilities. Shorter delivery timescale and easy future upgrade paths
Costs, no benefits	Benefits have exceeded expectations

Figure 1.8 *Before and after the use of a benefits management approach (after IMPACT, 1998)*

of schedule, but, most importantly, all the expected benefits were realized.

Figure 1.8 illustrates the key differences in approach for the two implementations. In the first attempt, the project was very much a case of technology push, with IT believing the business would benefit from the deployment of a new information system. However, this technology view, with little understanding of how the business actually worked, resulted in a system that did not meet with the approval of users. These users were then reluctant to give up the existing ways of working, including their paper-based and local systems. Finally, to try and encourage uptake, the project team agreed to undertake a number of significant changes to the software package so that it could conform to the way that many of the users currently did their jobs. The result was a large number of bespoke amendments to the package, which caused serious cost and time overruns and resulted in an ongoing issue about support for the system. Despite the changes made to the package, the users were not satisfied since they felt they had been put through significant upheaval, in order to simply end up with a system that did just what they were already doing.

The second attempt at implementation of the ERP system was approached quite differently. Rather than being viewed as a straightforward implementation of a piece of software, it was recognized to be significant change project, which happened to be enabled by an information system. Viewing the system as a change management issue caused the organization to appoint a business manager to lead the project who could work closely with the IT department. A business manager who had experience of implementing such a system elsewhere was recruited for this lead role. An important part of the project was the identification and implementation of new procedures and best practices to accompany the implementation of the new system. To ensure compliance with the new procedures, the existing ways of doing things were decommissioned. While the introduction of any new procedures is never easy, it was particularly difficult in this case given the scepticism among the staff about this type of system following the first unsuccessful implementation. However, with clear communication of the benefits that were expected from the system and the associated changes, together with actions to aid the changes identified, staff were willing to comply. The result was an achievement of benefits that exceeded expectations, which would have a positive effect on the development and deployment of systems in the future.

The Importance of a Common Language: Information Systems and Information Technology

Before undertaking an exploration of how the benefits from information systems might better be realized, it is worthwhile considering the terms that are used in this field. Some terms are often taken as synonymous, or at least used interchangeably, by business managers, IT specialists and others commentating on these subjects. This lack of clarity in usage can lead to misunderstandings and even barriers, particularly between staff within the business and IT department. The following section discusses major terms in common use and defines how they will be used throughout this book.

Information systems (IS) and *information technology* (IT) are terms that are often used interchangeably. This is discussed by Ward and Peppard (2002) and the definitions and usage adopted in this book are consistent with the approach of these authors. They note that information systems (IS) existed in organizations before the advent of information technology more than 40 years ago. Even today, they stress that many information systems continue to function within organizations with technology nowhere in sight.

Information technology (IT), they state, refers to the technology on which modern information systems operate or run. That is, it refers specifically to the hardware, software and telecommunications networks that underpin modern information systems. Some commentators and organizations, particularly in the government and public sectors use the term *information and communication technologies* (ICT), rather than simply IT, in order to stress the convergence of traditional hardware and software with the networks that characterize communications technologies.

Our definition of information systems is adopted from the UK Academy for Information Systems (UKAIS), a body of both practitioners and academics interested in the study and improvement of information systems usage. They describe information systems as '*the means by which people and organisations, utilising technology, gather, process, store, use and disseminate information*'. Thus, although, as stated earlier, information systems can exist without the use of information technology, our interest in this book will be those information systems that are supported by information technology. This definition of information systems is in agreement with the discussion of this subject by Checkland and Holwell (1998). They stress that information systems exist to serve, help or support people undertaking their daily tasks and in order to create a useful system, it is first necessary to determine what *is* to be supported, that is the information system, and subsequently to consider *how* this may be achieved, that is the information technology that is required. Too often, rapid advances in the performance or capability of technology and the promises of technology vendors have caused organizations to start their considerations with the capabilities of the technology rather than by clearly identifying what the technology is to serve or support.

The UKAIS also notes that the use and study of these systems includes both the underlying technological and social aspects. Within the business sphere, this social dimension is concerned with how individuals, teams and even whole organizations adopt and use information systems and how this use, in turn, shapes those information systems. Adopting the definitions just given clearly demonstrates that a consideration of information systems must take into account not only the technologies that enable them but also the inherent social implications. It can therefore be seen how the interchangeable use of these terms can lead to misunderstandings between the users of information technology and those providing it. Overreliance on the term information technology at the expense of information systems devalues the importance of the social dimension, which, as has already been stressed, is critical to the realization of benefits.

Another term that is often used when discussing information systems is *applications*. Applications are information systems that are used to accomplish a specific business activity or automate a particular process. Examples of simple applications are the word processing and spreadsheets found on virtually every PC. More sophisticated applications are used to accomplish activities such as general accounting, production scheduling or warehouse management. Such applications are often now sold as *suites*, comprising a number of separate applications. For example, the ubiquitous personal computing suite from Microsoft, Office, contains the word processing and spreadsheet applications just mentioned as well as others such as a graphics application, a database application and software for operating personal diaries and accessing email. Recently there has been a trend to develop very large suites of applications that, when implemented, impact the activities of many processes or functions within an organization. These are being termed *enterprise systems*, examples including ERP and CRM systems and enterprise portals.

Organizations still face the difficult decision of whether to develop information systems or applications in-house to meet their specific needs, often termed *bespoke* or *customized* applications, or to buy a standard package from a software vendor. Prior to the 1990s, there was a tendency to develop bespoke applications, with the logic that little or no competitive advantage could be gained if a number of organizations in an industry had the same software package. More recently, the pendulum of opinion has swung in the direction of advising organizations to buy standardized packages, in which the vendors could embed best practice gained from their exposure to multiple organizations. As argued by both Carr (2003) and Mata et al. (1995), and discussed earlier in this chapter, it is not the software itself that will confer competitive advantage to any organization, but the skill that the management of the organization has in putting that software to work to address the objectives of their business and create changes to improve performance. The large enterprise suites offer a partial compromise to this dilemma as they allow organizations to configure the standard applications to best suit their circumstances and needs.

A Further Complication: E-Commerce and E-Business

Two other terms now in common usage, which like information systems and information technology are often used synonymously, are the terms electronic commerce (e-commerce) and electronic business (e-business). Kalakota and Whinston (1997) define *e-commerce* as '*the buying and selling of information, products and services via computer networks*', the computer networks primarily being the Internet. Hence e-commerce describes trading activities focused outside the organization itself, for example with customers and suppliers. *E-business*, in contrast, describes the automation of an organization's business processes, both within the organization and with outside trading partners. E-commerce, which was the first of the two terms to be coined with the opening of the Internet to commercial use in the mid-1990s, can therefore be considered as a subset or special case of the broader term, e-business, which grew in popularity when it was realized that the protocols that underpinned the public Internet could be deployed successfully within organizations to improve internal communication and working.

During the late 1990s, almost every business was considering how they might make use of the Internet. Sadly, this interest was more often than not fuelled by the observation that competitors were adopting this way of working or addressing customers, and a belief that it would cause their stock to be more attractive to investors, than a clear understanding of the real value it could add to an organization. This ill-thought-out rush to develop internet sites, often likened to the landgrabs undertaken in settling the west of the USA, contributed to the dot.com bust witnessed by the fall of the NASDAQ in March 2000. Despite the downturn in sentiment to the dot.com companies, many organizations have continued to develop e-commerce and e-business-based activities. However, their investments are now more measured and rather than being seen as something quite distinct, as they often were before 2000, such developments are now viewed as further information systems and technology-enabled changes. Rather than being justified by faith, or by a fear of being left behind, such developments are now required to demonstrate benefits to the organization and hence, like traditional information systems projects, can benefit from the methodology set out in this book to improve the identification and realization of those benefits.

Summary

Given the continued perception of the majority of IS/IT investments as being unsuccessful, there is a need for a fresh approach to how projects are undertaken. We suggest this should be a process approach that encompasses the entire lifecycle of the investment, commencing with the early exploration of the idea and planning the project and continuing throughout implementation and including a review, when it has been completed. The focus throughout the project should be on the realization of benefits, since that, after all, is the reason the organization is undertaking the investment. A major feature of the benefits management process we describe in the following chapters is the recognition of the importance of the need for organizational and business changes to accompany the deployment of technology and how the realization of benefits is dependent on the successful achievement of these changes. Since a wide variety of stakeholders are therefore likely to be affected by these changes, this suggests the need for a range of individuals to be involved in the benefits realization process, something that does not always happen with more traditional project management approaches.

As will be described, the starting point for the development of a benefits plan for a project is an understanding of the strategic drivers acting on the organization and its planned responses to these. An understanding of these drivers can show whether the investment being considered addresses areas that are important to the organization. It can also help in prioritization. As financial and management resources are finite in all organizations, deciding which projects *not* to do is often critical to being able to resource the ones that really matter. A number of tools and frameworks have been developed in the strategic and general management domain to help with the process of identifying and analysing possible strategies and making appropriate choices. The importance of a well-thought-out and clearly stated strategy as the starting point for the realization of benefits from individual projects is underlined by the presentation and discussion of a key set of these tools and frameworks in Chapter 2.

Once the business strategy for the organization has been determined, it is necessary to develop an IS and IT strategy. Ward and Peppard (2002) describe how this essentially has two parts to it: the IS demand, which describes the organisation's demand for information and systems to support the overall strategy of the business; and the IT supply, which describes the provision of IT capabilities and resources required to achieve this. The IS demand element will include an identification and prioritization of the projects that will best meet the stated objectives of the organization and should thus show how individual investments contribute, both on their own and in combination with others, to support the identified business strategy. While the IS strategy should support the business strategy, there is also a recognition that IS can shape the business strategy. This dynamic interrelationship between these two activities is termed *strategic alignment*. The nature and role of IS and IT strategies is discussed further in Chapter 2.

2
Understanding the Strategic Context

Before an organization can consider or pursue the development of a particular information system, it is first necessary to understand the relevance of the investment to the three interrelated strategies that should have been defined by the organization. These are the business, the IS and the IT strategies. Only when these strategies have been agreed can it be determined how individual investments contribute to what the organization is trying to achieve. While projects that do not directly contribute to the identified strategy of the organization may well generate useful outcomes, the greatest benefits are likely to arise from projects that enable the organization to achieve its chosen strategy.

The chapter first discusses two different perspectives of business strategy formulation that consider the external or internal environment of the organization and how these different perspectives can be brought together. A number of tools or frameworks that can be used to determine and develop business strategies are then presented. Having described the formulation of a business strategy, consideration is then given to IS and IT strategies. A discussion of the distinctions between business, IS and IT strategies and how these are interrelated is presented. The issue of how organizations can better categorize and understand the mix of IS investments they are currently undertaking and have planned is then discussed by means of a framework termed the applications portfolio. The IS strategy is then examined in more detail, by considering the competences required for effective IS development and use by an organization.

The range of tools and frameworks discussed here, and the depth of discussion of each, is appropriate for their use in the context of the benefits realization process. However, there are many other strategy tools and frameworks, both business and IS oriented, that can be used in addition; for those, and also a fuller discussion of the ones presented here, the interested reader is referred to one of the many comprehensive texts on the subjects of business strategy (see, for example, Hill and Jones, 1998; Johnson and Scholes, 1999) or IS strategy formulation (see, for example, Galliers and Leidner, 2003; Ward and Peppard, 2002).

It should be noted that an industry or market is not static and will change over time. Companies must therefore constantly keep their chosen strategies under review. Some changes may be outside the control of the firms competing in these markets, such as economic and legal changes. Other changes will be caused by the strategies being pursued by other players in an industry or market, such as the development of new products, new distribution channels or changes in pricing. Analysis of an industry or market and the development of a business strategy are therefore both dynamic and interrelated. Rather than be viewed as a one-off event, undertaken for example during the annual planning cycle, they should be kept under regular review.

The need to develop business, IS and IT strategies is not the sole preserve of private sector organizations. Public sector and not-for-profit organizations must also constantly scan the external environment and also take account of their internal resources and capabilities, in order to develop strategies that match the two in ways that best meet the needs of their various constituents or stakeholders. Indeed, such organizations often have a large number of stakeholders, whose needs may at times be conflicting. The development of strategies often therefore has the additional challenge of balancing the needs of these different stakeholders in an acceptable and achievable way. The tools or frameworks presented in this chapter, and indeed throughout this book, are suitable for use by both private and public sector organizations. However, it may be appropriate in some cases to change the terms used in the latter case. For example, rather than use the term 'customer', substitution in the framework of the term 'citizen' or 'client' may be more appropriate.

The Competitive Forces and Resource-Based Views of Strategy

All organizations are interested in finding ways in which they can ensure their long-term viability, whether they are private firms looking to maximize their shareholder value, or public sector and not-for-profit organizations seeking to maximize their effectiveness. A significant part of this quest for long-term viability will be an identification of what the organization is trying to achieve and why. A business strategy can be described as *'an integrated set of actions aimed at increasing the long-term well being and strength of an enterprise relative to competitors'* (Porter, 1980).

Interest in the formal development of corporate strategies began to grow markedly after World War II and a number of tools and techniques to guide and structure this activity were developed during the 1960s and 1970s. Some of these, such as the Boston Consulting Group's grid or matrix, are still proving useful today. These approaches encouraged a focus on analysis and, where possible, measurement of factors in the external marketplace in which the company operated or was considering entering. This focus on the external environment as a basis for strategy development was continued by the individual who has perhaps had the greatest influence on modern strategic thinking, Michael Porter (1980, 1985). Porter suggested that there were structural factors within industries and markets that resulted in some offering a greater potential for profitability or increased viability (see the later discussion of five forces and external value chain analysis). Organizations should therefore identify these more attractive industries and markets and operate within them. This approach to strategy development is referred to as the 'competitive forces' view of strategy.

In the 1990s, some strategic thinkers (Barney, 1991; Grant, 1996; Wernerfelt, 1984) began to suggest an alternative view of strategy development. This was in part driven by the observation, in contrast to Porter's suggestions, that the greatest variation in profitability between firms was not between firms in different industries, but between firms in the same industry. This suggests that it is not so much differences in the structural factors within industry that determines the profitability of firms, but what is inside an organization and the idiosyncratic ways this allows them to compete. Rather than consider the external environment, it was suggested that an organization should consider the assets or resources it has at its disposal and what it is able to do and particularly do well, that is, its competences and capabilities. If these resources, competences and capabilities are valuable, rare, inimitable (difficult to imitate) and non-substitutable – the so-called VRIN attributes – they can be used to implement value-creating strategies that will provide sustainable competitive advantage. This consideration of the internal context of the organization in strategy formulation is called the 'resource-based view' (see Box 2.1).

Box 2.1 Resources, competences and capabilities

In considering the resource-based view of strategy, the terms resources, competences and capabilities are often used inter-changeably. A discussion of the terms, and how they are related, is given here and shown in Figure 2.1.

Resources are the assets, both tangible and intangible, that an organization owns or can access in order to pursue its chosen strategy. These resources may be *physical*, such as buildings and plant, *human resources*, *financial resources* or *intangible resources*, such as know-how, brands and patents. Resources may be categorized into two types: those that are similar to those available to competitors or easy to imitate and those that are unique to the organization.

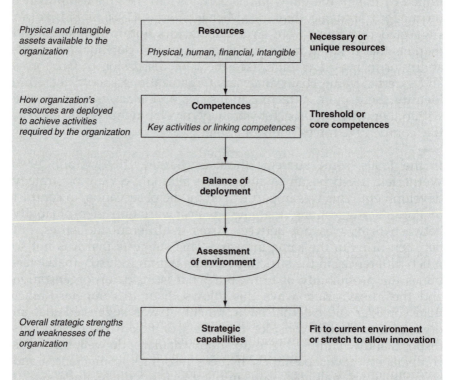

Figure 2.1   Resources, competence and capabilities (after Johnson and Scholes, 1999)

Competences describe how resources are deployed through processes in order to achieve the activities of the organization, such as product design, marketing, production, distribution and customer liaison and support. Competences are also required in order to achieve effective linkages between these activities. Organizational competences, rather than the underlying resources themselves, are often the key to organizational performance. As with resources, competences can be categorized into two types, those that are similar to others in the industry and those that allow the organization to outperform the competitors in that area. The latter are often called *core competences*.

The competences required within an organization can be explored by means of the internal value chain analysis discussed later in this chapter. The competences required by a supply chain or network can be explored by means of the external value chain analysis, which is also discussed.

The strategic capabilities of the organization describe the ability of the organization to meet the opportunities and threats of the external environment, that is, they describe the strategic strengths and weaknesses of the organization. The challenges posed by the external environment may be assessed by means of frameworks such as a PEST analysis and Porter's five forces analysis, discussed later in this chapter.

Strategic capabilities are determined by the resources and competences available to the organization and how these are balanced, combined and deployed. Meeting the demands of the external environment suggests a need for the strategic capabilities to *fit* the current environment, but there may also be a requirement to *stretch* the capabilities in order to participate in, or even create, new opportunities.

More recently, strategic thinking has sought to balance the competitive forces and resource-based views of strategy. Long-term success, it is suggested, will result for organizations that can align their resources and capabilities in ways that match the demands of the environment. An approach that considers the balance of the external and internal attributes of the organization is the dimensions of competence framework presented later in this chapter.

One particular strand of thinking, which recognizes that many markets are becoming increasingly turbulent and volatile, has suggested that in such environments competitive advantage is transient, rather than sustainable (Eisenhardt and Martin, 2000; Teece et al. 1997). Managers must therefore concentrate on *renewing* rather than *protecting* their sources of competitive advantage. No longer can they rely on the assets, staff, products, brands and other resources that they have assembled to provide their present competitive position. Rather they must be able to combine these resources in new ways and to gain additional resources, and to do this repeatedly, if they are to compete successfully, so-called 'dynamic capabilities'. Such capabilities are viewed as critical to the future success of firms, so much so that it is said that the threat to survival will not come from competitors, but from within the firm, somewhat akin to the processes of adaptation and selection witnessed in the natural world.

Ends, Ways, Means

Our discussion of the competitive forces and resource-based views of strategy can be summarized by considering three major elements of strategy formulation and implementation available to organizations: the *ends* they wish to achieve, the *ways* in which they can operate and the *means* they can draw on. Different strategic philosophies advocate starting the process of strategy development at different points, as shown in Figure 2.2.

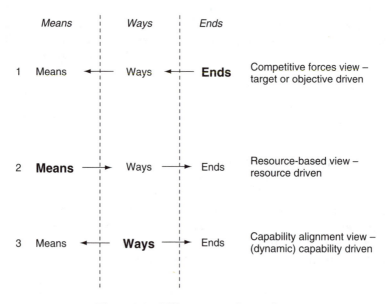

Figure 2.2   Different strategic paradigms

The competitive forces approach to strategy development stresses the objective assessment of the external environment and encourages an organization to determine which industry it wishes to participate in and, within that industry, what market segments should be addressed. Thus this approach focuses on the ends that the organization wishes to achieve, which in turn results in a concentration on targets and objectives. Having determined the required ends, it is assumed that the organization can find the required ways and means of realizing these. Difficulties will often arise when it is found that no satisfactory ways and means are available.

The focus on the ends to be achieved from strategy is typical of many US and UK organizations, due in large part to the origins of the competitive forces paradigm. A reliance on target setting in order to guide the actions of organizations was one that was adopted on a large scale by UK central government in the management of public services in the 1990s. By early 2004, the adoption of this approach in isolation was seen largely to have failed and many of the imposed targets had been dropped.

The resource-based view adopts the opposite starting point to that of the competitive forces view. Rather than commence with a top-down view of the desired objectives or ends for the organization, this approach first considers the range of means that are available to the organization. These means include the financial, people, plant and knowledge resources the organization has or can draw on. Such approaches tend to be reactive and while these can often work well in the short term, particularly in being able to respond quickly and effectively to market changes or competitors' actions, they may well founder over time due to the lack of a coherent long-term vision and limited creative capabilities. Once again, while not universally adopted, this approach is typical of many Japanese firms, particularly in the 1970s and 80s.

The third approach is to concentrate on the ways available to an organization, that is how it can operate in order to create a strategy that generates customer or user value. As we have seen already, as most markets are becoming increasingly dynamic, organizations cannot rely on an analytical approach to understanding their industry or market, since that market is changing in rapid and unexpected ways. Equally, they cannot rely on the collection of resources that have provided them with competitive advantage in the past. Rather, they must learn to develop capabilities that allow them to '*integrate, reconfigure, gain and release resources – to match and even create market change*'

(Eisenhardt and Martin, 2000). Studies have shown that these capabilities are often tacit, take considerable time to develop, are composed of many hundreds of lower level skills and have a strong social element to them. This means they are difficult for competitors to imitate and hence can, if developed, provide a sustained competitive advantage. This 'third way' of considering strategy can be found in the approaches adopted by a number of firms within continental Europe.

Rather than be considered as an end in itself, IT should be considered a means or resource that is available to the firm. As observed by a number of commentators, the most recent being Carr (2003), most IT is now available to all organizations, and therefore cannot provide an advantage to one single firm for long. Instead the generation of sustained advantage is likely to come from the ways in which it is deployed or implemented and used by the enterprise. As described already, the complex and often tacit nature of the capabilities required for effective implementation and use by an enterprise means that they cannot be quickly or easily acquired, but require long-term development within the organization. The particular competences required for effective IS deployment and use are discussed in the last section of this chapter.

PEST Analysis

All businesses operate within the broad economic and social environment. The particular attributes and workings of that environment are in a large part determined by the country or countries in which the organization is based or in which it sells its products and services. However, as events such as the Asian financial crisis and 9/11 have shown, the societies and economies around the world are becoming increasingly interconnected and events in one country can have serious ramifications on the operation of industries and markets in others.

As a precursor to more detailed strategy development, organizations are encouraged to explore the broader external environment in which their organization will operate by means of a political, economic, social and technical (PEST) analysis. In this analysis the current and future impact of each of the factors on the operation of the organisation is considered, as outlined in Table 2.1. The analysis should focus on a given product or service in a particular geographic market or region, since the impact of the four factors will vary for different products and different countries. If necessary, the

Table 2.1 PEST analysis

PEST analysis factor	Issues to consider in analysis	Typical questions
Political (should also include legal)	The impact of political, legal and regulatory environment on the organization, its suppliers and customers	• Is the political regime conducive to the type of business I wish to undertake – and how stable is this regime? • Are the legal and regulatory frameworks sufficient to allow a well-functioning organization to flourish?
Economic	The impact of the local macro- and micro-economy on the operation of the organization and its suppliers and its customers. Also to consider, how the economy is related to other economies	• What is the impact of local interest, tax, exchange and inflation rate on the operation of my organization and those of my suppliers and customers? • Are these stable enough to allow a reasonable planning horizon? • Is there a pool of suitable staff to draw from? Are local wage rates and the skills of available staff acceptable?
Social	The impact of social changes on the operation of the organization, its suppliers and particularly the needs and wants of its customers	• What social changes are occurring that may affect the demand for our products or services e.g. in many western economies people are getting married later, having fewer children, resulting in declining birthrates. This is coupled with an increased greying of the population due to people living longer
Technical	The impact of new technological developments on products and services offered by the organization and on how the organization operates. While IS/IT will have a major impact on many businesses, other fields of development such as science and engineering should also be considered	• Are new technologies being developed that will allow us to improve the products and services we offer to our customers or the way in which these are produced? • Will new technologies make our current offerings obsolete? • Can we adopt these new technologies? What are the benefits and risks?

analysis should then be repeated for other products or services and across other geographic territories. The analysis can help identify new opportunities for the organization, for example, changes in the social behaviour of consumers may suggest the development of a new product or service. Equally, the analysis can highlight challenges to the organization, such as the introduction of new legislation that requires changes to products or production methods.

Industry Attractiveness and Competitive Forces Analysis

An industry is deemed attractive when it offers the opportunity for those competing in it to generate an above average return for their owners or investors. However, not all industries offer high returns, since they may have structural factors that limit the opportunities. Although different firms competing in the same industry will generate different levels of profitability, since they all compete in different ways, the competitive forces view considers the structure and attractiveness of an industry as an essential ingredient in the profitability of a firm. Industry attractiveness is most often assessed using a framework called Porter's five forces.

Michael Porter (1985) proposed one of the best known analytical frameworks for strategy development with his *Five Forces Model*. This model states that in any industry, whether it is domestic or international and whether it produces a product or provides a service, the nature of competition is embodied in five forces:

- **threat of new entrants**: the threat of entry into the market by new competitors
- **power of suppliers**: the bargaining power of suppliers to the industry
- **power of buyers**: the bargaining power of customers in the market
- **industry rivalry**: the intensity of the rivalry among the existing competitors
- **threat of substitutes**: the threat of substitute products and services replacing the demand for existing products and services.

These five forces in combination determine industry profitability, since they influence the prices firms can charge for their goods, the prices they have to pay for the raw materials and the investment they need to make in R&D, plant, marketing and sales. Generally, as any one or a combination of the forces increases, the profitability that may be expected from that industry is reduced. The forces, together with factors that tend to reduce the profitability of an industry, are shown in Figure 2.3.

Ideally, companies should look for industries where as few as possible of the five forces are strong. However, finding such perfect markets is difficult, since if they did exist many competitors would also be drawn to them. Companies should therefore consider developing strategies that shift the market forces in their favour.

New Entrants

New entrants in a market may result in an oversupply of the product or service, which can force price reductions throughout that market. They may also cause the resources necessary to make the product, such as raw materials or skilled staff to be in high demand and therefore scarce and more expensive. Interestingly, new entrants are most likely to be attracted to a market in which they think the current players are earning high returns. Hence it is in the interest of the current players in a market not to appear to earn excessive profits since it will tend to encourage new entrants.

New entrants are dissuaded from entering a market by barriers to entry. These are factors that make it difficult for a new player to compete with the incumbent players. Barriers can include factors such as capital requirements, access to the necessary input goods and services, routes to market and the requirement for specialist knowledge. Restricted access to the factors necessary for production or advantages gained from experience, such as learning curve effects and proprietary knowledge, particularly when this is protected by intellectual property rights, can increase the barriers to entry and reduce the threat of new entrants to an industry.

Power of Suppliers

Suppliers control the inputs to the product or service being considered. In some sectors, such as manufacturing industries, this may mean the access to key raw materials but in other sectors this may include elements such as skilled staff, specialist knowledge or the supply of capital. Suppliers will have increased power over a buyer, if the cost of switching to another source of supply is high. This may be because the supplier is the sole supplier of the items in question, they are the only ones in a given geographic area or they have specialist knowledge.

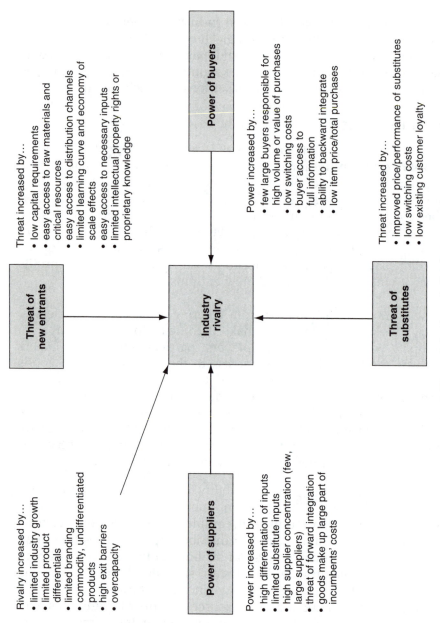

Threat increased by...
- low capital requirements
- easy access to raw materials and critical resources
- easy access to distribution channels
- limited learning curve and economy of scale effects
- easy access to necessary inputs
- limited intellectual property rights or proprietary knowledge

Threat of new entrants

Power increased by...
- few large buyers responsible for high volume or value of purchases
- low switching costs
- buyer access to full information
- ability to backward integrate
- low item price/total purchases

Power of buyers

Rivalry increased by...
- limited industry growth
- limited product differentials
- limited branding
- commodity, undifferentiated products
- high exit barriers
- overcapacity

Industry rivalry

Threat increased by...
- improved price/performance of substitutes
- low switching costs
- low existing customer loyalty

Threat of substitutes

Power increased by...
- high differentiation of inputs
- limited substitute inputs
- high supplier concentration (few, large suppliers)
- threat of forward integration
- goods make up large part of incumbents' costs

Power of suppliers

Figure 2.3   Porter's five forces

The size of a supplier relative to the company will influence its power, with larger suppliers tending to have greater power. The value of the goods or services supplied may also influence the power balance in a market. If the items purchased from a supplier represent a high proportion of the value of the finished goods or services, then that supplier will tend to have increased power. Conversely, the power of suppliers is likely to be reduced if the items purchased only represent a small proportion of the value of the finished goods. Suppliers may have additional power if they have alternative markets in which they can sell their goods and services, for example in manufacturing, machined parts may be suitable for both car and aircraft assembly, reducing a supplier's reliance on the assemblers in either industry.

Power of Buyers

Satisfying customer needs and wants can be considered the core endeavour of most enterprises. Successful organizations are ones that can do this while also capturing a share of the value they create in order to be profitable. Factors that increase the power of buyers in an industry, and hence are likely to reduce the value that can be retained, include the size of the buyer, relative to the producing firm. The larger the buyer, and the more it accounts for the output of the firm being considered, the more power it will have in negotiations about price and other terms. Buyers will also have increased power if they have low switching cost, that is they can easily and at low cost, buy the goods or services in question from another source.

Industry Rivalry

The nature and intensity of the rivalry among existing players in a market can be determined by a number of factors as shown in Figure 2.3. These include stagnating markets, in which there is limited opportunity for growth and hence the existing incumbents must battle for market share. A limited ability to differentiate products and services also increases competition among existing players. Branding, the provision of additional complementary services, such as after-sales service, and additional distribution channels can all help to increase perceived product and service differentiation and hence reduce this force within an industry.

One factor that can be important in some industries is the barriers that prevent companies from leaving a market. These may include the cost of decommissioning a plant or the cost of redundancy payments to staff. If companies are reluctant to leave an industry, even if their profits are below the level desired, it is likely to lead to overcapacity in the market, which results in downward price pressure and hence further reductions in profits.

Threat of Substitutes

The threat of substitutes describes the likelihood of customers seeking alternative products and services. These may allow the customer to carry out the same activity as current products, either at lower cost or in a better way or may completely obviate the need for the current products or services. For example, the rise in the use of word processing applications and email is reducing the reliance on the fax machine to transmit documents, and the development of the pocket calculator has obviated the need for slide rules and books of logarithmic tables to undertake calculations.

Traditional forms of IS/IT have had a significant impact on the structure and attractiveness of many industries and the rise of e-commerce in the late 1990s has increased that impact, particularly in consumer-based markets. The impact e-commerce has had on the structure and attractiveness of industries is described in Box 2.2 in order to help exemplify the application of Porter's Five Forces Model.

Box 2.2 Impact of e-commerce on industry forces

New Entrants

E-commerce can act to lower the barriers to entry in many markets and therefore can encourage new companies to enter these markets. The entry of Amazon (www.amazon.com) to the book retailing market back in 1995 provides such an example. Before that time anyone wishing to sell books throughout the USA or Europe would have needed to open a store in every neighbourhood or distributed a paper catalogue to a large number of homes. The required investment would have been enough to stop most entering the market and competing with the well-known and established incumbent players such as Barnes & Noble and WH Smith. Interestingly however, e-commerce did not only allow Amazon to enter this market it also allowed it to exceed the service offered by traditional bookstores in a number of ways, for example, access to a vast array of titles, recommendations based on what you have already bought and, in many cases, lower prices when compared to traditional stores.

Power of Buyers

E-commerce is increasing the power of buyers in many markets, be they consumers or other businesses, by improving the availability, and hence the ease of finding product information. The time and cost customers incur in looking for information about products or services is termed search costs and these can be considerable in the physical or traditional marketplace. This cost causes buyers to reduce their search to a limited number of suppliers. They are therefore reliant on incomplete information and cannot be sure of getting the item that best meets their needs or the best price. E-commerce reduces search costs since it allows customers to easily compare products from different suppliers. Certain websites, such as Kelkoo.com, even undertake the information collection and comparison on behalf of the customer.

Buyers can be supplied with a significant amount of detail about the product, including a picture or a 3D image or, in the case of products that can be digitized, a sample of the product. Having obtained this information, customers can often then buy the chosen item online with a few clicks of their mouse.

Power of Suppliers

E-commerce offers suppliers an opportunity to reduce their search costs for customers. Companies can publish details about their products and services on the web and advertise these on related or frequently used sites and so allow buyers from around the world to find them. If a company succeeds in significantly increasing demand for its products by finding many new customers, then it is in a more powerful position with regard to its existing customers and can either increase prices or change other terms of their trading relationship.

Although e-commerce can help suppliers find new customers, it is likely that the ease with which those customers can shop around will still put downward pressure on prices. Suppliers of specialist or unique products will be less vulnerable to downward price pressure but in many sectors the benefits of finding new customers will be matched or even outweighed by decreasing prices.

Box 2.2 (Continued)

Industry Rivalry

E-commerce has increased the rivalry among existing players in some industries. Many e-commerce developments are reactions to services being developed by competitors, for example, in the retail banking market. Most of the major banks wish to offer their customers a number of different ways or channels in which they can access their account. Once certain banks started offering internet banking, then the other banks were forced to offer this service also, or risk losing customers to their competitors. In the USA, Wells Fargo, and in the UK, the Royal Bank of Scotland and the Nationwide, were some of the early organizations offering online banking but within one or two years all of the major banks followed their lead and are now offering this service. Today internet banking is not seen as a differentiator in the retail banking sector, rather it is now simply 'the cost of doing business'.

In addition to offering the ability to improve customer service, internet-based services offer the potential to lower the costs to serve those customers. This also drives a competitive reaction between the incumbents in a market. If some organizations can reduce their operating costs through e-commerce services, then the other firms in that market will be left uncompetitive, unless they also launch e-commerce services or find other ways of reducing costs to similar levels.

This reaction to competitors' services is not unique to e-commerce. However, e-commerce is leading to the extreme example of firms not only competing with other firms but actively competing with themselves. This behaviour, termed *cannibalization*, occurs when a company launches a service or product that they know will compete with its existing services or products. An example of such cannibalization is shown by the US stock broking firm Charles Schwab. Schwab established an online unit, called eSchwab that offered low priced online share trading. After some time of running both the full-price offline brokerage and the discount online brokerage, Schwab closed the full-priced service down and effectively transferred all its business to the online operation – cutting an estimated $125 million off its revenues in the process. Since then the number of online accounts has grown considerably, vindicating the chosen approach.

Threat of Substitutes

For some products and services, e-commerce can offer customers different ways to satisfy their needs and therefore poses the threat of substitution in these markets. Examples of this include the online discount brokerages just discussed that have largely replaced the full-service brokerages, at least for the small private investors. Other industries that have been significantly impacted by e-commerce include the sale of books and travel and the distribution of news, personal advertisements and popular music.

External Value Chain Analysis

Having identified an industry that appears to be attractive or having understood the forces within their current industry, a firm should next consider in more detail which other firms they must work with in order to produce, market and distribute the goods and services required by their customers. In most industries it is very rare that a single organization undertakes all of the value-adding activities from raw material production to the delivery of the final product or service to the customer. The firm is usually one in a number of firms linked in a chain or system, with each firm specializing in one or more of the value adding activities involved. The analysis of such systems of interconnected firms was, like the five forces analysis, proposed by Porter (1985), and is referred to as external or industry value chain analysis. He also proposed how the internal activities within a firm should be considered when carrying out value chain analysis. This is called internal or organizational value chain analysis and is discussed later in this chapter.

The intention of external value chain analysis is to represent the way in which the various organizations within an industry contribute to the value that is eventually delivered to the customer or consumer. A generic value chain is shown in Figure 2.4. The diagrams should be annotated with the value-adding activities undertaken at

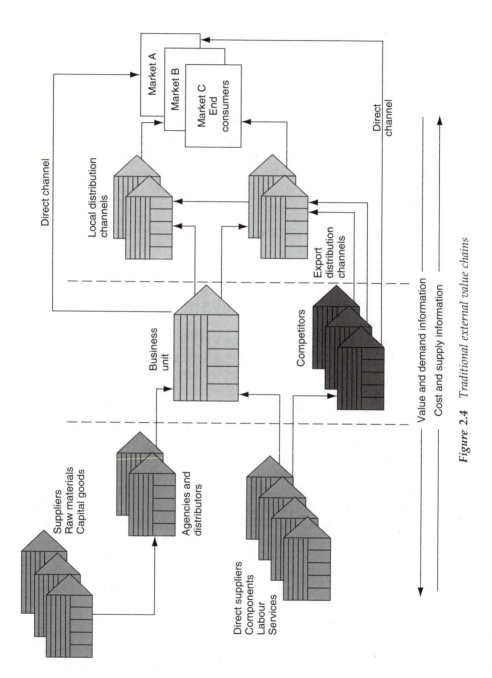

Figure 2.4 Traditional external value chains

each stage in the chain. For example, in the case of the automotive value chain, the distributors operate showrooms, hold stock, arrange test drives and provide financing, usually via a third-party finance house. The value chain should also be annotated with the flow of physical goods, both parts and finished goods, and the flow of information between the parties involved. The annotated chain can then be examined to see how the performance of the value chain can be improved.

One activity that can often be improved in a value chain is the flow of information between individual organizations. As shown in Figure 2.4, information on the demand for goods should flow from right to left, from the end consumers to the firms upstream in the supply chain. Equally, information from the suppliers on the availability of materials and parts can be shared with those downstream in the value chain. How well demand and supply information can be matched at all points in the chain will make a major contribution to the efficiency of the industry, that is the removal of the need for excess capacity and stock holding, but also the effectiveness of the chain, for example, how quickly it can respond to changing customer or market demands. Such improvements in the performance of the value chain are in turn likely to result in increased performance of the individual firms within the chain. Opportunities to improve the flow of information to all parties in the chain, either in the quantity of information, its accuracy or its timeliness should be actively examined. This will increasingly rely on an improvement in the level of integration achievable between the information systems of the participating organizations.

It is recognized that many firms do not interact in a linear way and the terms value network and constellations, among others, have been coined to describe the non-linear relationships between some firms. While the case of a linear value chain has been considered here, the basic principles discussed can be applied to other forms of networks between firms.

Traditional IS/IT, and particularly e-commerce, has had a significant impact on the external value chain in a number of industries. In many industries e-commerce is being used to enable companies to 'go direct', that is, deal directly with the end customer or parties further down the value chain, cutting out existing intermediaries. This is termed *disintermediation* and can be seen in, for example, the travel market, where airlines, car rental companies, holiday companies and train operators are allowing consumers to buy directly from their websites, removing the need for traditional travel agents.

While in certain cases intermediaries have been removed from the value chain, in others new intermediaries have been introduced. Provision of any online service requires a firm and its customers to make use of the telecommunications network, an internet service provider and software, such as an internet browser. E-commerce also provides the opportunity for new online intermediaries based on information processing, termed *infomediaries*. Examples of such firms include the internet search engines, including the highly successful Google and the consumer-to-consumer marketplace, Ebay.

E-commerce can also be used to improve the existing linkages between organizations in a value chain or system. This is most commonly achieved by building electronic links between firms and exchanging data between them. An example of such improved linkages between individual organizations in the supply chain is shown in Box 2.3.

Box 2.3 Improving information exchange: Tesco information exchange

Tesco, the leading supermarket in the UK, has developed an extranet-based system to allow it to share point-of-sale (POS) data with its suppliers, the Tesco Information Exchange (TIE). The system is aimed primarily at the management of promotions. With around 10% of goods in a typical store being on promotion at any one time, the effective management of promotions is an important area for the supermarket chain, however, the sales of such items can be very hard to predict in advance, with previous non-promotion sales figures being of little help.

TIE allows Tesco to share near real-time sales data directly from its stores with its suppliers. By sharing this information so promptly, suppliers can see if sales are higher or lower than expected and can amend their production and dispatch accordingly. This ensures on-shelf availability is maximized while waste due to out-of-date stock is reduced to a minimum. The system is based on a secure extranet, over which suppliers can see the sales of their own products but not those of competitors. Tesco, like all the other big food retailers in the USA and UK operate extensive EDI systems for stock replenishment. The TIE system is seen as an addition to these existing systems rather than a replacement.

Internal Value Chain Analysis

Internal value chain analysis considers a firm as a set of separate but linked activities, by which the organization transforms inputs into outputs that customers value. Each step should add value to the process, or if not it should not be undertaken.

Figure 2.5 shows a simplified internal value chain for a car manufacturer. It can be seen that the activities of the company are divided into primary and support activities. Primary activities are directly concerned with the production of the organization's goods or services. These are typically divided into the five categories:

- **Inbound logistics**: activities concerned with the replenishment, receiving, storing and distributing the materials needed to produce the finished goods or services. In the case of the car manufacturer, this activity includes the ordering of parts required by the ongoing production plans and the receiving and routing of these parts to the correct part of the production process at the correct time. Given the drive within the automotive industry to minimize the stock of parts by adopting just-in-time manufacture coupled with the move to mixed production lines, the activities involved in inbound logistics in this industry are highly complex.
- **Production**: activities involved in producing the final goods and services from the inputs. In the case of the automotive manufacturer, this obviously consists of all of the activities required to produce the final car, including testing and quality control procedures.
- **Outbound logistics**: activities required to store and distribute the final products and services to customers. In the case of services, this may require the organization to provide facilities where the customer can come and receive the service, rather than have it taken to them. For the example, in the case of a hospital or a restaurant, the user or customer is required to come to the premises of the provider. In the case of the car manufacturer, outbound logistics would entail the transportation of cars to their dealers, either to meet particular customer orders or to hold for display purposes.

Many parts of the automotive industry are facing considerable oversupply and effective management of the considerable stock of finished cars is an important activity.

- **Marketing and sales**: provide the ability to take and process orders for the items produced as well as seeking to understand the needs of customers and to make them aware of the products and services of the organization. In the case of the car manufacturer these activities would include national advertising to generate awareness and demand and support for more local advertising and promotion by dealers.
- **Service**: includes operations such as installation, repair and training. Increasingly, environmental legislation requires that such operations must also take responsibility for decommissioning or retiring of the original product. For example, in Europe the End-of-Life Vehicle (ELV) Directive requires automotive manufacturers to take responsibility for the recycling of old cars at no additional cost to the final owner.

Primary activities correspond to the operational and management elements of an organisation identified by Mintzberg (1983) and shown in Figure 1.2 to structure the possible benefits arising from the use of IS/IT.

The support activities shown in the internal chain are those that allow the primary activities to be undertaken as efficiently and effectively as possible. They are typically divided into the following:

- **Procurement**: activities related to identifying the optimum suppliers for the inputs required for production and also those required for the firm to operate, such as capital equipment and maintaining relationships with these suppliers. With the growing recognition of the value of strong supplier relationships, this activity is receiving increased attention.
- **R&D/innovation**: activities associated with developing new products and services. R&D and innovation activity can also be focused on improving production processes and other processes within the organization. In the case of the automotive industry, much effort is being made by all of the major manufacturers to design a standard or 'global' car that can be produced at any of their plants around the world and sold to customers in different countries with only minor modifications.
- **Human resources**: recruitment, development, reward and retention of staff in all areas of the organization. In the case of the large car manufacturers, this activity will span operations around the globe and will require attention to many cultural differences.

- **Firm infrastructure**: this includes strategic planning, finance, accountancy and other tasks needed to support the primary activities. Typically, IS/IT are included in this part of the analysis. The infrastructure also includes the context in which the organization operates, that is the organizational structure, its control systems and culture. Since top management exert considerable influence on shaping these parts of the organization, they should also be viewed as part of the firm infrastructure.

The support activities correspond to the functional, support and strategic elements of an organization identified by Mintzberg and shown in Figure 1.2. In particular many of the activities included in the term firm infrastructure relate to the strategic element.

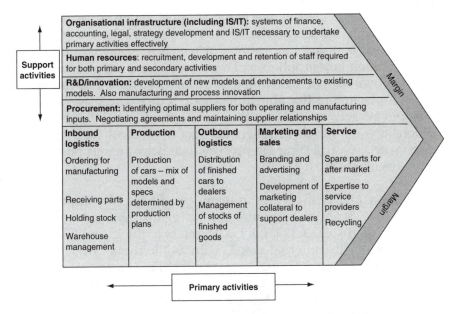

Figure 2.5   Internal value chain

Organizations undertaking internal value chain analysis should consider how each primary and support activity adds value to the final customer offering and how it helps the company to sustain its chosen strategy. As stated earlier, if an activity is not adding value or sustaining the strategy it should be improved or discontinued.

While the value-adding activities that make up a firm's value chain may provide competitive advantage, it is likely that over time these will be copied by competitors. The performance of a firm is likely to be more robust and difficult to imitate if value is added in the linkages between the activities (Johnson and Scholes, 1999). IS/IT can enable a company to improve the linkages between its separate activities and hence help sustain its competitive advantage. The improved linkages may be between the primary activities of the firm. For example, the sales department could share up-to-date sales data with others in the firm via a company intranet or portal. This access to timely information could allow the marketing department to tailor promotional activity to where it would be most effective and also allow production to tune their output to the actual demands of customers. Linkages can also be effected between primary and support activities. Information collected by the field service operation could be shared with R&D to allow issues with existing products to be quickly addressed or for new products to be developed. Linkages can also be developed between the support activities of the firm. The automotive industry, which was discussed earlier, is currently pursuing 'supplier-led innovation', in which the car manufacturers work with their key suppliers and encourage these suppliers to work with their own suppliers, in order to identify potential innovations to the major assemblies that constitute modern cars. The success of this development activity rests on the organization sustaining effective relationships with their suppliers and hence requires R&D to work closely with their colleagues in procurement, who are responsible for supplier relationships.

The ultimate aim of IS/IT use in many companies is to allow information to flow seamlessly throughout the organization to wherever it is needed. Microsoft's CEO, Bill Gates, refers to the IS and IT linking the activities of the internal value chain as the digital nervous system of the firm (Gates, 1999). He asserts that how companies gather, manage and share information within their organizations, that is how they link the activities depicted in the internal value chain, will increasingly determine which firms succeed or fail.

Alternative Internal Value Configurations

Porter's linear value chain is well suited to describing and understanding the value-adding activities of traditional manufacturing and retailing companies. However, it is less suitable for the analysis of service and network businesses. It is not only difficult to assign activities in such firms to the five generic primary activities, but the resulting chain often obscures rather than clarifies the value creation mechanisms in the firm. Stabell and Fjeldstad (1998) consider an insurance firm and ask: what is received, what is produced and what is shipped? They observe that few insurance executives would consider uninsured people as the raw material from which they produce insured people. Neither would they consider themselves as a paper transforming company, transforming blank sheets of paper into insurance policies. Clearly such a firm's value-adding activities include the assessment of risk via actuarial calculations, reinsurance of that risk, claims handling and customer relationship management. However these activities are difficult to depict as a linear value chain. These authors therefore pose two alternative configurations of internal activities that can be used to analyse the value-adding steps within an organization.

The Value Shop. Value shops are organizations that solve specialist problems for customers or clients. Firms that can be modelled as value chains undertake a set of activities in a fixed sequence that allows it to produce a standard product in large numbers. In contrast, firms that can be considered as value shops vary their activities and their sequence of application dependent on the nature of the customer or client problem. Examples of value shops are professional service firms such as those in the fields of law, architecture and consultancy. Certain functions or parts of firms that are themselves value chains can operate as value shops, for example, the research and development activity within a manufacturing firm is problem solving in nature, and hence best characterized as a value shop.

Value shops are typically populated by experts in the particular domain in which the organization specializes. The activities of particular firms are likely to be couched in terms of the language of these experts and specialists in that firm, however a generic set of primary activities can be drawn from the field of problem solving and decision making and are shown in Figure 2.6.

Many organizations in the public and not-for-profit sectors are examples of value shops, that is, the activities they undertake and their sequence will depend on the particular client, citizen, pupil or patient problem in question. Some public sector organizations, such as the healthcare, social care and educational organizations and the police force, are increasingly trying to establish standard operating procedures in order to ensure best practice is both shared and adhered to. For example in the UK National Health Service, 'clinical pathways' that indicate the ways in which patients with certain conditions should be treated have been developed. Similarly, in the UK police force, a best practice approach to the investigation of crime has been developed. However it is recognized that such procedures are only guidelines and significant professional judgement will continue to be required to take account of the unique circumstances or context of each individual or incident.

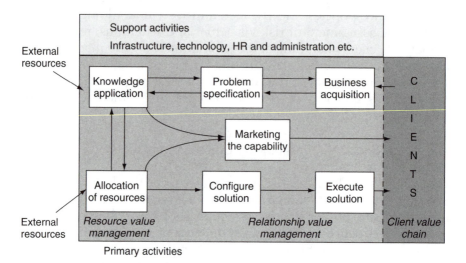

Figure 2.6   *The value shop (after Stabell and Fjeldstad, 1998)*

The Value Network. Firms that can be modelled as value networks are those that provide a networking or mediating service that allows customers to be linked to other customers. Examples of such firms are telephone companies, banks, insurance companies, postal services and online auctions and exchanges. The networking between customers can be direct, as in the case of telephone companies that provide communications infrastructure or indirect, as in the case of banks that pool the money from depositors and in turn lend this to borrowers, without putting the two groups directly in contact.

The term network is used to stress that the value such companies deliver to any particular customer is the set or network of other customers with whom they can interact or communicate. The value of the service provided by the firm increases with the number of other customers who use or can be accessed through the network, termed the 'network externality' effect.

The primary activities for value networks include the operation of the network infrastructure, the provision of services to users and the management of contracts, either with those users or for others providing support or services to the network. Support activities are similar to those found in other value configurations and include human resources, R&D, procurement and IS/IT.

A summary and comparison of the three alternative internal value configurations discussed is shown in Table 2.2.

As observed in the earlier discussion of the external value chain, most firms tend to operate in conjunction with other firms. These will most often be of the same type. In the case of value chains, this will result in connected chains, where the output of one firm forms the input of the next firm in the chain. In the case of value shops, one professional organization may refer a client to another organization for the solution to a particular part of their problem. As an example, a GP may refer a patient to a consultant for particular specialist medical tests that she cannot carry out herself. Finally, firms that are based on networks increase their coverage by interconnecting with other networks. An example is the use by banks of correspondent banks in overseas countries in order to increase their geographic coverage and hence offer more value to their customers.

Table 2.2 *Comparison of alternative value configurations*

	Value chain	Value shop	Value network
Value creation logic	Transformation of inputs to products	Resolving customer problems	Linking customers together
Primary activity categories	• Inbound logistics • Manufacturing • Outbound logistics • Marketing and sales • Service	• Problem finding and acquisition • Problem solving • Choice • Execution • Control/ evaluation	• Network promotion and contract management • Service provisioning • Infrastructure operation
Sequence of activities	Sequential	Cyclic	Simultaneous, parallel
Key cost drivers	• Scale • Capacity utilization	• Cost of experts	• Scale • Capacity utilization
Key value drivers	• Product cost • Product specification	• Expertise • Reputation	• Scale • Capacity utilization
Industry structure	Interlinked chains	Referred shops	Layered and interconnected networks

Balancing the External and Internal Contexts: The Dimensions of Competence

The two distinct views of organizational strategy commonly encountered, that is the external, competitive forces view and the internal, resource-based view, were discussed earlier. A framework for strategy development that seeks to bring these two views together was proposed by Treacy and Wiersma (1993). This model suggests that any organization, whether it is a for-profit or a not-for-profit organization, can find a route to market leadership by excelling at one or more of three generic activities. These activities, termed the dimensions of competence and shown in Figure 2.7, are:

- **operational excellence**: a focus on business processes to outperform others by delivering consistent quality to customers at acceptable costs
- **customer intimacy**: tailoring products and services to the needs of particular customer groups, exceeding expectations and building loyalty
- **product leadership**: continuing product innovation that meets customers' needs. This implies not only creativity in developing new products and enhancing existing ones, but also astute market knowledge to ensure they meet, or even anticipate customer needs.

Organizations can use this framework by considering how well they perform on each of these dimensions compared to their competitors or a similar organization to their own if they are in a non-competitive market. If no actual benchmark measures of performance are available, then the comparison can be purely qualitative, that is by discussing the question: 'How do we think we compare with other organizations in our market or industry?' Those involved in these discussions should then mark their position on each of the three axes accordingly. If their performance is similar to that of other organizations they should mark themselves on the dark 'ring of parity' shown on Figure 2.7. If they are performing better than others on any or all of the three dimensions, they should mark themselves outside this ring on the relevant axis or axes. This is termed the *zone of prosperity*. If they are performing less well than competitors on any dimension, they should mark themselves inside the ring. Finally, if their performance in any one, or more than one, dimension falls a long way short of their competitors, they should mark themselves inside the central circle on the relevant axes.

The contention is that excellence in at least one of these dimensions of competence, matched by satisfactory performance in the others, that is they are judged to be on or just inside the ring of parity, can lead to a strong competitive position. If an organization believes that its performance in two or more of the dimensions falls within the central circle, then it is likely to be struggling for survival.

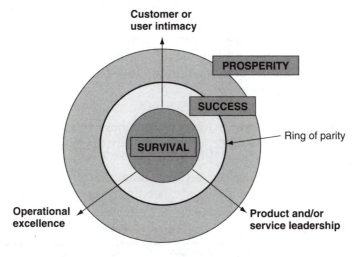

Figure 2.7 The dimensions of competence

It is most important for those involved in this analysis to consider and record what is causing the organization's performance to be as it is. This will often be due to factors within the firm, such as the availability of resources and organizational competences. The consideration of the organization's performance relative to other firms in the market, together with discussion of the causes of this level of performance, allow the dimensions of competence framework to bring together the external, competitive forces view of strategy formulation and the internal, resource-based view. An example of the use of the dimensions of competence model is given in Chapter 4.

Linking Business, IS and IT Strategies

The relationship between business and IS strategies was discussed at the end of Chapter 1 in terms of the need to find *strategic alignment* between them (Venkatraman et al., 1993). Figure 2.8 depicts the relationship between the business, IS and IT strategies proposed by Ward and Peppard (2002), which draws on earlier work by Earl (1992). It is suggested that organizations carry out an assessment of both their external marketplace and their internal resources and competences, using the tools described in the preceding sections and any additional tools and frameworks from elsewhere that are found to be useful. This assessment is used to develop an explicit strategy for the organization that answers the basic questions: *where* is the business going and *why* has this direction been chosen? The answers to these questions should be stated as clear objectives for the organization. Including objectives for both the short and medium term will ensure that they generate a sense of direction for the organization. They should also clearly encapsulate the nature and degree of change that will be required for the organization to move from where it currently is to where it wants to be.

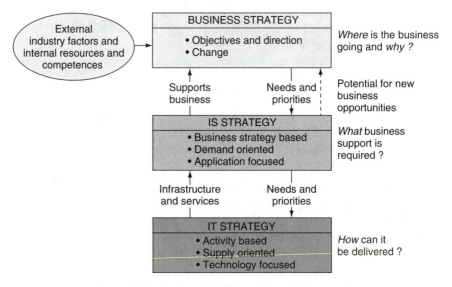

Figure 2.8   *Linking the business, IS and IT strategies*

IS should be considered as just one ingredient that supports or enables the delivery of the identified business objectives, other ingredients being business activities such as marketing, HR, or research and development. The IS strategy should take the business strategy as its starting point and consider *what* information systems or applications are required to enable the identified objectives, that is it should be oriented to the demands of the business and focused on applications that can meet these demands. The business strategy therefore suggests the needs and priorities that must be met by the IS strategy and a framework that can aid in the prioritization of applications, called the applications portfolio, is discussed later in this chapter.

While the business strategy will in most cases set the direction and objectives that should be met by the IS strategy, there will be some cases where IS can lead to the generation of new strategic opportunities. For example, with the advent of e-commerce, many new businesses were launched either by startups or by existing organizations. These were based on the ability to offer goods and services directly to consumers over the web. Hence the opportunities offered by e-commerce shaped the strategies pursued by these organizations. Organizations should always be open to such opportunities and hence the loop between the business and IS strategy should not be viewed solely as unidirectional but as iterative.

It is important to stress that the IT strategy should be distinct from the IS strategy, otherwise the latter tends to become dominated by technology issues, rather than showing how applications can meet the stated business needs. The IT strategy should address the technology, infrastructure, resources and specialist skills needed; that is it should describe *how* the IS strategy will be delivered.

One challenge that faces the development of an IS strategy and the supporting IT strategy is the fact that both IS and its basic constituent, information, permeate every function or area of the business. Any strategy must therefore be consistent with the individual strategies developed in each of these functional areas, while also being coherent enough to be able to efficiently and effectively meet the overall direction and objectives of the organization.

Balancing the Portfolio of Investments: The Applications Portfolio

The applications portfolio (Ward and Peppard, 2002) provides managers with a framework which they can use to balance the IS requirements suggested by the business strategy, by enabling the contribution of current, planned and potential systems or applications to the realization of that strategy to be better understood. It also highlights the different types of benefits that the investments will deliver and the complexity of the changes needed to fully realize them. In turn this leads to the need for quite different approaches to resourcing, developing, implementing and operating the four different types of applications indicated by the framework. The portfolio is illustrated in Figure 2.9.

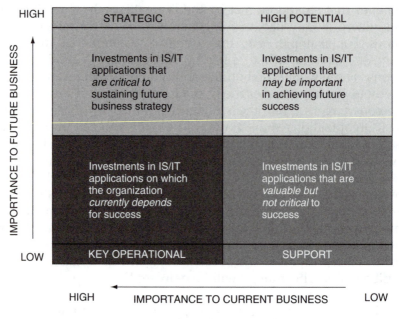

Figure 2.9   *The applications portfolio*

As discussed later in this chapter, many IS managers face significant challenges in prioritizing the many activities they and their staff are asked to undertake. This often results in them spreading their finite resources too thinly to be truly effective. The applications portfolio can help organizations find an appropriate mix of IS activities or projects and allow the resource to be concentrated on those areas that are most important to the organization. These projects are then finished more quickly and, perhaps more importantly, to higher standards. This then allows the project teams to move on to further projects that will be beneficial to the organization.

The applications portfolio classifies applications into four types, dependent on their current or expected contribution to future business success.

High Potential Applications

High potential IS applications play a similar role to the R&D activities undertaken by an organization. These applications allow an organization to experiment with new systems or technologies to understand the business opportunities and benefits they offer, together with the costs that are likely to be associated with such developments. Once these are better understood, managers are able to make informed decisions as to whether further investment is worthwhile now, or may be worthwhile in the future, or, indeed, if the idea should be abandoned.

High potential applications have certain characteristics: they are by their very nature high risk and may fail to show a return on the investment made if it is decided that the idea has insufficient promise and is abandoned. They will often be championed by an individual who is highly committed to the idea and they lend themselves well to the development of prototypes, in order to demonstrate the value of the application to others. Despite the inherent risks, high potential applications are important to the future success of an organization, since it is through the experimentation with new ideas, that firms can develop systems that can provide them with future competitive advantages.

Strategic Applications

While high potential applications are uncertain, and may or may not provide tomorrow's competitive advantage, strategic applications are those that already provide advantage or will do in the near future. Strategic applications will play a key role in enabling the business strategy, particularly those parts of the strategy that differentiate the organization from its competitors. These applications are often in response to market requirements, particularly customer requirements. They may well have been high potential applications, which the organization has 'learnt' more about and now understands how they can contribute to improved performance and how they can be deployed effectively.

Since they provide differentiation, it is hard to argue that applications that a large number of the incumbents in an industry already have, or have planned, are strategic. Differentiation can only be derived from applications that are distinct or are being used in different and innovative ways. This does not suggest that strategic applications must use 'bleeding edge' technology. Indeed, given that the future success of the organization is going to be dependent on such applications, it is better that they do not use leading edge technologies, but ones that are tested and proven, at least in other contexts.

Key Operational Applications

Key operational systems are those that are critical to sustaining the current performance of the organization. Such systems include the basic transaction processing and recording systems for most types of business, such as the point-of-sale systems in supermarkets and the transaction processing and reconcilement systems in banks.

While the effective operation of such systems is key to the performance of the organization, they do not usually differentiate the organization from its competitors. Rather, they are likely to be fairly consistent across an industry and can therefore give very little competitive advantage. Indeed, the effective operation of these systems is likely to be considered as 'mandatory' for survival in an industry. Their effective operation therefore acts more to avoid disadvantage than to provide advantage.

Key operational applications may have formerly been strategic applications that have become well established throughout an industry. An example would be the provision of ATMs (automatic teller machines) by the retail banks. When these were first introduced in the 1960s and 1970s, a network of such machines provided a point of differentiation for a bank and could be considered as a strategic application. Now they provide no differentiation and would be considered as key operational systems.

Support Applications

These applications tend to be aimed at improving business efficiency and individual productivity. They are valuable to the business but do not sustain the operation of the business or provide differentiation from competitors. Examples of such systems are the provision of personal applications such as word processing and spreadsheets on the PCs of individual staff. These applications increase the efficiency of individual staff, but for most businesses do not contribute directly to the goods and services produced by the organization.

Due to their widespread use throughout the organization, maintaining support applications can often consume a large part of an organization's IS and IT resources. However, with no advantage being derived from such systems, organizations should resist this tendency to consume resources at the expense of other types of applications. By indicating the resources, either staff time or financial investment required for the development, operation and maintenance by the applications in each of the four categories, the applications portfolio can help recognize and adjust inappropriate spending patterns.

While organizations would expect to have a range of applications that are spread across the four different types shown in the portfolio, there is no ideal distribution. An appropriate spread of applications for a given organization would depend on the context of the organization, in particular its current performance relative to competitors in its industry. Considering the dimensions of competence model shown in Figure 2.7, if an organization considers itself outside the ring of parity on the three axes, then it can invest resources into strategic and high potential applications which will build on this success. If the organization considers it is less successful than competitors on one or more of the axes, particularly if it is much less successful on any of them, then it should concentrate resources on key operational systems that will enable it to regain parity with its competitors in the area of weakness.

We will return to the use of the applications portfolio in later chapters. The issue of the forces or drivers on the organization, causing the development of new IS, is discussed in Chapter 4. It is shown how particular types of drivers tend to be associated with applications in each quadrant of the portfolio. The different types of benefit that may be expected from the four different types of applications distinguished by the portfolio are discussed in Chapter 5.

An example of the use of the applications portfolio for a supermarket chain is shown in Box 2.4.

Box 2.4 Applying the applications portfolio: a supermarket chain

An example of an applications portfolio for a supermarket chain is shown in Figure 2.10.

Like a number of the leading supermarket chains, this organization is exploring the use of radio-frequency (rf) identification of goods. As well as improving the tracking of goods during distribution and in warehouses, this technology allows the items in shopping baskets and trolleys to be recorded without needing

Box 2.4 (Continued)

to pass each item over a scanner. Shoppers could simply pass their entire basket or trolley through the reader thus reducing queuing time at the till, thereby increasing customer satisfaction. However, the reliability of such systems, and the cost of the rf tags is still questionable, resulting in this application being considered as high potential.

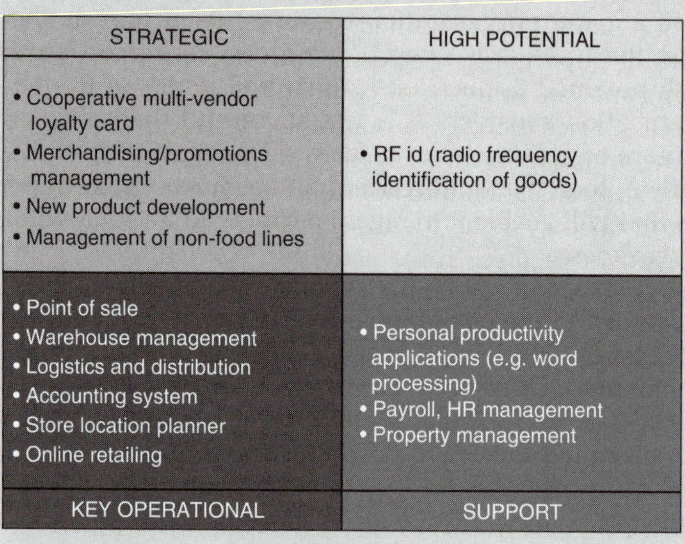

STRATEGIC	HIGH POTENTIAL
• Cooperative multi-vendor loyalty card • Merchandising/promotions management • New product development • Management of non-food lines	• RF id (radio frequency identification of goods)
• Point of sale • Warehouse management • Logistics and distribution • Accounting system • Store location planner • Online retailing	• Personal productivity applications (e.g. word processing) • Payroll, HR management • Property management
KEY OPERATIONAL	SUPPORT

Figure 2.10   Applications portfolio for a supermarket chain

The organization has a number of systems that it considers to be strategic, that is these systems provide significant advantage relative to their competitors. The organization has recently joined forces with a number of other leading retailers to offer a loyalty card that offers shoppers the opportunity to collect rewards on purchases from any of those participating. The ability to collect rewards from a wide range of retailers makes the scheme more attractive to customers, resulting in greater participation. Equally, the wider range of information that can be collected on the purchases made by customers provides a more complete picture to the participating retailers, allowing better understanding and hence an improved targeting of offers. Cooperating with other retailers also allows joint promotions to be developed. Being an early participant in such a scheme provides advantage, since it allows greatest choice over the other retailers involved. Particularly, it allows the other supermarkets to be excluded and limits their ability to develop a similar network.

Other systems that are considered strategic are a system to improve the effectiveness of the merchandising of goods, particularly those on promotion, a system to improve new product development and a system to manage the stocking and sale of non-food items. Due to limited growth there is intense competition in the supermarket sector in both Europe and the USA, so winning market share from competitors is therefore the route to success. Price cutting, through the effective operation of promotions, innovation through the introduction of new products and the diversification into non-food items are the current major weapons. The systems identified as strategic allow improved management of these three activities, particularly by improving the communication and information sharing with suppliers. A similar promotions management system is described in Box 2.3.

The supermarket operates a number of key operational systems, which include their point-of-sale systems, that record the sale of goods, and the warehouse and distribution systems that control the flow of goods from suppliers to the stores. While customers will not be attracted to the supermarket by the use of such systems, indeed, they will largely be hidden from view, ineffective use will result in goods being out of stock, one of the major contributors to customer dissatisfaction.

During the 1990s, in many developed countries the performance of supermarket chains was largely driven by their programme of store openings. As it has become harder to acquire new sites the basis of competition has moved away from expansion to fighting for market share, as already discussed. Systems to identify the optimum new sites that would have in the past been considered strategic are now less important and hence considered key operational. Similarly, online shopping, which was once considered highly strategic back in the 1990s, now offers little differential advantage since it is offered by all the major players.

Box 2.4 (Continued)

The supermarket operates a number of support applications, including those to manage their HR function and payroll and those to manage their property portfolio, such as the payment of rates and utility bills. Such systems would be common to all types of business and while the effective operation of such systems is important, the key focus should be on efficiency.

With systems in all four quadrants, the portfolio shown in Figure 2.10 appears well balanced and reflects a healthy performance. As discussed earlier, if the chain were experiencing difficulties relative to their competitors, then more focus should be placed on the key operational systems necessary to bring their performance in line with those competitors before they should invest heavily in the development of more strategic systems.

Working with the Applications Portfolio: The Why, What and How of Investments

In order to place new or existing applications in the appropriate quadrant of the applications portfolio, it is often helpful to pose three simple questions.

Definition: Why, what and how of a potential investment

Why is the investment being made – why does the organization need to change and how critical to its future is the successful management of the changes?

What types of benefit is the organization expecting to achieve by making the changes – to reduce costs, improve operational performance, gain new customers, create a new capability etc.?

How can a combination of IT and business changes deliver those benefits at an acceptable level of risk?

The answers to these questions, including instances where the answers to these questions are not known, will suggest where the application in question should be placed on the portfolio. Applications where the answer to the first question is primarily about reducing costs and improving efficiency are likely to be support systems. Such applications tend to show the greatest degree of certainty, since they often address activities the organization is currently doing and it is likely that an answer, at least in outline, will be known to both the subsequent two questions, that is what the organization hopes to achieve and largely how it could go about this.

For cases where the answer to the first question is mainly concerned with improving the performance of current activities or processes, then the application is likely to be key operational. For such applications, there may be less certainty than for support applications. An answer may be possible for the 'what the organization hopes to achieve' question, that is what processes will be impacted and by how much they should improve, but it may be less clear how this can be achieved.

If the answer to the first question is about gaining significant advantage compared to competitors, then the application is likely to be strategic. Since the application, as already discussed, must be relatively new or used in a new way, then it is likely that the organization may not have well-defined answers to the last two questions. Finally, the greatest area of uncertainty will be with high potential applications. These may be recognized when the organization is unable to answer any of the three questions in more than the broadest terms. This occurs because such projects are often undertaken in order to understand the benefits a new technology or business model might offer the organization, that is, it is about evaluating a new opportunity, rather than finding a solution to an identified problem.

The relevance of these three questions to the benefits management process is introduced in Chapter 3 and explored in detail in Chapter 4.

Organizational Information Competences

In an extended study undertaken with several major organizations to examine the specific competences organizations need to effectively develop and exploit new information systems, Ward and Peppard (2002) developed the model shown in Figure 2.11. This model links business strategy with IS demand and exploitation by the business and IT supply and can therefore be considered an extension of the model shown in Figure 2.8.

The six major competence areas identified in the model are defined as follows:

- **Business strategy**: the ability to identify and communicate an effective strategy for the organization, including an evaluation of the implications of IT-based opportunities as an integral part of this strategy.
- **Define the IS contribution**: the ability to translate the business strategy into processes, information and systems investments and change plans that match the business priorities identified. This should be the basis of the IS strategy.
- **Define the IT capability**: the ability to translate the business strategy into long-term information architectures, technology infrastructures and resourcing plans that enable the implementation of that strategy. This should be captured in the IT strategy.
- **Supply**: the ability to create and maintain an appropriate and adaptable information, technology and application supply chain and resource capacity.
- **Deliver solutions**: the ability to deploy resources to develop, implement and operate IS/IT business solutions that exploit the capabilities of the technology.
- **Exploitation**: the ability to maximize the benefits realized from the implementation of IS/IT investments through effective use of information, applications and IT services.

As indicated by the shaded area in Figure 2.11, the three competence areas, business strategy, defining the IS contribution and exploitation, are all related to the IS requirements or demands within the business. The other competence areas are related to the supply of applications, technology and skills to fulfil those requirements. As with other supply and demand models, not only should the organization seek to develop competences in all six areas identified, an appropriate balance between IS demand from the business and IT supply should be sought.

The six areas of competence identified can be further decomposed to a greater level of detail as described in Ward and Peppard (2002).

While certain of the competences identified are required from the IS function, such as IT supply, others extend well beyond the traditional boundaries of this function and include organization-wide competences. Indeed, competences such as exploitation, that is the realization of benefits from the effective implementation of IS/IT, should exist in the business areas where those systems and technologies are going to be deployed. The recognition that IS competences are required throughout the organization, and not solely in the IS function, can help to diagnose the causes of poor performance in IS development and use. In organizations that are experiencing difficulties with deriving benefits from IS/IT, the limitation may not be within the IS function, which may be very skilled at designing technical architectures and developing systems. The limitation may well be that they are not supplying the systems the business really needs, due to this not being communicated to them accurately or, as is often the case, the inability of the business to be able to effectively deploy and exploit the systems that are supplied.

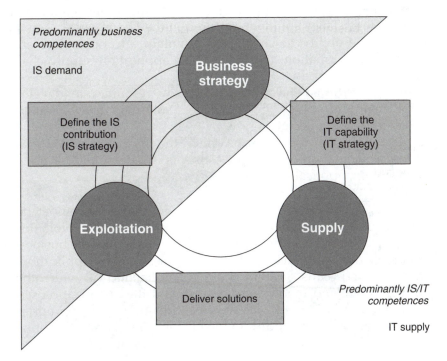

Figure 2.11   *IS competences (after Ward and Peppard, 2002)*

The IS/IT model proposed, particularly at the level of the detailed competences, can be used by organizations in a diagnostic mode. Managers, usually working together in a workshop setting, can consider their current performance in each of the competence areas relative to their required performance. Due to the organization-wide nature of the IS competences, as already discussed, the managers participating in such an assessment should be drawn from various business functions, in addition to managers from the IS function. The identified gaps in performance are where the development or improvement of competences should be concentrated.

The Challenge of Implementation

Workshops undertaken with mixed groups of managers from a wide range of organizations have shown that there are some of the detailed competences that a large number of organizations find challenging. These are shown in rank order in Figure 2.12. The two areas that organizations tend to find the most difficult are the development of an effective business strategy and the delivery of benefits from IS investments.

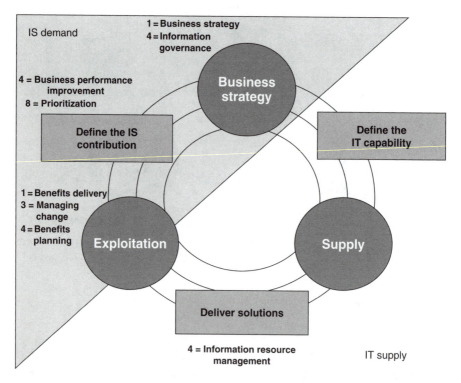

Figure 2.12 *IS competences' common areas of weakness (after Ward and Peppard, 2002)*

Managing the organizational changes associated with the exploitation of new IS was identified as the area where organizations felt they had the next greatest problem. As discussed in Chapter 1, IS/IT adoption is rarely the 'silver bullet' espoused by software vendors. To realize benefits, such purchases must, almost always, be accompanied by changes to how the organization's processes work and, within those, how individuals are expected to work. As explored throughout this book, these changes may well be more difficult and time consuming than the purchase and deployment of the underlying technology.

Four detailed competences were judged equally to be the next most challenging to the organizations studied. These were: benefits planning, information governance, information resource management and business performance improvement. Benefits planning is defined as the ability to explicitly identify and plan how to realize the benefits from IS investments. Information governance is concerned with the development of information management policies and the roles and responsibilities of individuals within those policies, whereas information resource management deals with the development and operation of processes that ensure that data, information and knowledge management activities meet organizational needs and satisfy corporate policies. These processes operate within the frameworks and policies developed within the information governance activities and the issues experienced in these two areas are interrelated. Business performance improvement relates to the ability to identify the knowledge and information needed to deliver the business objectives through improved management processes.

Prioritization of the applications and technologies identified as beneficial to the organization was identified as the next competence area in which organizations believe they are underperforming. The applications portfolio, discussed earlier in this chapter, can help organizations understand the mix of application types that they currently have and have planned. A mix that is appropriate for their current level of performance, as assessed by the dimensions of competence framework shown in Figure 2.7, can then be sought.

Overall, Figure 2.12 shows that the majority of the detailed competences that are problematic in many organizations are those related to IS demand, as opposed to IT supply-side issues. The increased adoption of packaged software and the improved reliability of hardware, taken with the increasing skill levels of many IS professionals, mean that many IS functions can develop and implement technology and systems to a high standard. Identification by the business about which systems are required, via the formulation of a clear and effective business strategy, and how IS contributes to that strategy are still problems.

Summary

The competences that appear most challenging to organizations are those relating to the exploitation of IS. Identifying and planning the benefits that can be realized from particular applications prior to development and implementation, together with managing the organizational change that is an inherent part of realizing those benefits, are both identified as areas where organizations believe they have significant weaknesses. Organizations also believe they have problems monitoring and evaluating the benefits that have been or are being derived from existing applications. Without this ability to learn from existing systems, it is difficult to improve the deployment and use of new systems and so this weakness in the area of exploitation perpetuates.

The next few chapters of the book describe a process, termed benefits management, that organizations can adopt to develop and improve the three specific competences discussed earlier: benefits planning, the associated management of organizational change and benefits delivery – the monitoring and evaluation of the identified benefits. Chapter 3 presents an overview of the process and its relationship to well-known project management and system development methodologies. Chapters 4 to 6 then cover, in detail, a set of tools and techniques that enables organizations to develop sound business cases, and comprehensive benefits plans for their investments, thereby increasing the benefits actually realized.

3
The Foundations of Benefits Management

In the previous chapter the 'macro' IS competence revealed in surveys of chief information officers (CIOs) and IT directors as the least well developed in their organisations was 'exploitation'. All three component competences – benefits planning, change management and benefits realization – were, on average, deemed to be weak, resulting in an inability to gain the full benefits from IS/IT implementations. These are intrinsically business-based competences, although how an organization decides to implement and supply IS/IT solutions will have a significant influence on the development of those competences. Therefore improving them will mean changing the ways that IT specialists work with business managers and users.

This situation is not new, but effective management of IT implementation and adept use of its capabilities are becoming increasingly integral to improving business performance and achieving intended business strategies. It is therefore essential that business managers are not only responsible for deciding on IS/IT investments and priorities, but also for the delivery of the benefits that justified the investments, given the costs and risks associated with IT implementation and business changes.

Figure 3.1 suggests that an inability to realize the benefits of particular IT investments has significant implications beyond each of the investments. The lack of ability to deliver benefits reduces the organizational understanding of the business value that IT can provide, which leads to an inability to make consistent or appropriate investment choices or set priorities. This in turn limits an organization's ability to identify how IT can be best used to improve performance or support new strategic developments. As a result, business strategy formulation often does not adequately include the consideration of opportunities available from new IT-based options or threats arising from the deployment of IT by others in the industry. It could be argued that the money many organizations wasted in the period 2000–2001 on ill-thought-out 'ventures' in e-business was, at least in part, due to business managers' lack of knowledge about the benefits that IT might deliver and the changes in business practices that were needed to cause the benefits to flow.

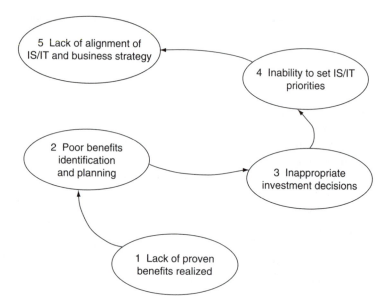

Figure 3.1　The implications of poor benefits management

This chapter first considers the reasons for the continuing poor record of organizations in realizing the intended benefits from IS/IT investments due to the incompleteness of existing methods and processes. It then describes how that gap can be filled by an approach that specifically addresses benefit identification and realization, but also enables closer integration of other methods to increase investment success. The stages in a proven 'benefits management' process are then outlined and the key differences from other existing approaches and practices are discussed.

Subsequent chapters explain in depth how tools and techniques used within the process framework can enable organizations to identify and deliver the benefits available from different types of IS/IT investment.

The Need for Another Process for Managing IS/IT Investments?

Over the last 30 years a range of processes and methodologies have been developed to improve the success rate of IS/IT developments and implementations. However, as discussed in Chapter 1, overall success in terms of investments that deliver the expected benefits seems stuck at around 30%. This is not to imply that nothing has been learned or that the processes and methodologies do not work. The investments being made today are more varied, more complex and more pervasive than in the past and often have a more significant impact on the business and organizational performance. But the conclusion can be drawn from the lack of improvement that existing methodologies and processes are insufficient and new thinking and approaches are needed if the success rate is to improve.

Existing methodologies have tended to be developed to address the 'supply-side' issues that affect organizations' abilities to specify or deliver an appropriate IT solution, to manage the project that is being conducted or to assess whether or not to make the investment. Given general agreement that the weakest area of competence is *exploitation*, none of these, other than some change management methodologies, deals explicitly with the set of issues that affects benefits realization. The change management methodologies were not normally devised for IT enabled change and need to be adapted to fit with the IT supply-side methods, which still tend to dominate the 'way things are done'.

It is not the purpose of this book to critique existing methodologies either collectively or individually, but their purpose and scope need to be understood to differentiate the benefits management approach described in detail here and also to show, later in the book, how this approach is complementary to and can be integrated with the 'best practices' from other processes and methods. Each of the types of methodologies is briefly outlined below and references are included to further sources of information about them.

IS/IT Strategic Planning

Modern approaches to strategic IS/IT planning tend to be frameworks within which tools, techniques and design processes are used to achieve the objectives of: identifying IS/IT-enabled business opportunities; aligning IS/IT investments with business strategies and priorities; sourcing and implementing IT architectures, infrastructure, applications and services; and developing organizational resources, competences and capabilities to deploy and utilize the technology effectively (see Ward and Peppard, 2002). Most approaches recognize that the *formulation* of comprehensive long-term strategies is not feasible in the context of increasingly rapid business and technology change and strategies have to be adapted frequently to deal with emergent issues and opportunities. However, the elements of the IS/IT investment plan should either be derived from conscious strategic analysis or be validated against the organization's business imperatives and objectives.

Systems Development

Methodologies such as SSADM (Structured Systems Analysis and Design Methodology) and DSDM (Dynamic Systems Development Methodology) are processes and methods designed to ensure that the right system is developed in the most appropriate way to meet agreed functionality, quality and performance requirements. Other methodologies such as SSM (Soft Systems Methodology) (Checkland and Scholes, 1999) address the organizational and people issues to ensure the right problem is being solved in a feasible and effective way. Others such as ETHICS (Effective Technical and Human Implementation of Computer-based Systems) (Mumford, 2003) and MULTIVIEW (Bell and Wood-Harper, 1998) balance the technological and organizational viewpoints. Avison and Fitzgerald (2002) provide comprehensive descriptions and a comparison of different methodologies.

Project Management

Methodologies such as PRINCE2 (Project Management in a Controlled Environment) are essential for managing activities and resources associated with a project to deliver the system and complete the tasks to agreed times and costs. Most organizations now recognise that this is a shared responsibility between business and IT management. Ultimately, it is the organization that suffers the real consequences of poor project management and business project managers are often appointed for major IS/IT investments, although their roles and responsibilities are not always clear. McManus and Wood-Harper (2002) discuss different project management methodologies.

Investment Appraisal and Evaluation

These terms are often used interchangeably, but to provide some clarity, investment appraisal is used in this book to mean pre-investment assessment, whereas evaluation implies assessment during and after implementation. There are many methods, ranging from standard financial techniques for calculating the expected return from IS/IT investments from an economic perspective, to more organizational assessments that allow for less 'tangible' benefits (i.e. those that cannot legitimately be converted to financial values) to be included (see Farbey et al., 1993; Renkema, 2000). Most project management methodologies include a post-implementation evaluation stage and processes have also been developed to enable more 'active' evaluation over the whole investment lifecycle, rather than at just the 'go/no go' decision (Remenyi et al., 1997).

Change Management

The term methodologies is perhaps less appropriate in the area of change management than 'frameworks' or 'approaches', except in the sense of proprietary methods from consultancies. All approaches recognize that the nature of the changes (for example, process or organizational), the extent of change (how much of the business or organization is affected) and the degree of innovation (or how radical the changes are) should determine the way the changes are managed and by whom, both in terms of the activities involved and the style of management needed. Several frameworks have been developed to assess the overall type of change being undertaken, its characteristics and consequently the steps required both to accomplish it and for managing the project, programme or initiative that is established to deliver the change. Of particular relevance to 'IT-enabled' changes are the frameworks described by Benjamin and Levinson (1993), Kumar et al. (1998) and Simon (1995) – these are considered in more detail in Chapter 6. Discussions of different approaches to managing 'strategic' change can be found in Balogun and Hope Hailey (2004) and Pettigrew and Whipp (1991).

Risk Assessment Techniques and Risk Management Processes

These are usually components of comprehensive systems development or project management methodologies or are included in investment appraisal methods, depending on the nature of the technical and financial risks involved. However, few of these techniques assess the risks from the perspective of how they affect the delivery of the available benefits, by considering the organization's ability to cope with the range of business changes needed. This aspect of risk assessment and management is considered in Chapter 5.

As already stated few organizations have a process focusing specifically on the output or demand-side issues of identifying and managing the business benefits required. All of the above methods do include some components of relevance to managing the benefits, but as ancillary rather than primary activities. Even in many investment appraisal approaches, identifying benefits is largely done to enable a business case to be developed, to justify the IT costs and to obtain funding. Investment appraisal can be considered as an event, or 'one day' in the life of the investment (albeit an important one!), within an overall process of *benefits management*, as defined in Chapter 1.

Since the purpose of any IS/IT investment is to deliver improvements to organizational performance, it would seem logical that the key process around which others should fit is benefits management rather than the project management, investment appraisal or systems development approaches. These should be adapted to match the types of change involved in the investment and the nature and range of benefits expected to be achieved. How the benefits management process relates to the other processes and approaches is therefore as depicted in Figure 3.2. These relationships and their implications are considered in more detail in Chapter 7.

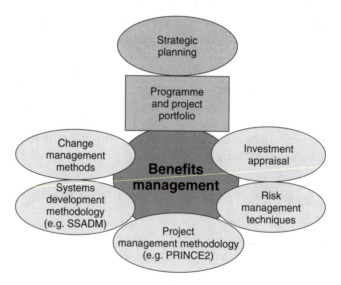

Figure 3.2   The context of benefits management

The Origins of the Benefits Management Approach and Process

The process described here was developed by studying what actually happened in a number of major information systems projects in large organizations across all sectors of industry, commerce and public bodies. Some were actively trying to manage the benefits, others were not. By studying the projects and particularly by conducting in-depth post-implementation reviews, it was possible to understand why some projects were more successful than others in delivering benefits. A new approach, which consisted of the process described here and a set of new and adapted tools and techniques, was developed. By applying the approach to subsequent, new projects it was possible to both avoid the 'loss' of benefits that were clearly achievable and in most cases to identify and realize more extensive benefits than from previous, similar investments.

Another outcome of applying the approach was that IT costs were actually reduced for some investments. In extreme cases projects were cancelled because no benefits could be delivered, but more commonly the essential IT functionality required could be identified more explicitly in relation to the benefits an organization wanted, thus eliminating IT costs that delivered nothing of value. It was also possible to reduce the amount of IT functionality deployed, by making more changes in business practices to utilize package software 'off the shelf' or to reduce procedural complexity rather than automate it.

Since the completion of the original research and development programme, the approach, process and the tools and techniques have been refined, extended and improved as a result of the feedback from the organizations that have used them. Experience from many of those organizations is reflected in this book – some as explicit examples and some more generically. Many organizations have realized that this approach is not only applicable to IS/IT projects and can be used to improve the success of other change programmes, business developments and strategic initiatives. Of course, in more and more of these, IT is one of the enablers of change and many organizations have taken the stance that, apart from infrastructure projects, there are now really no IS/IT projects *per se* – there are only change projects that have significant IS/IT components.

This chapter describes the 'basic' process that was developed for major IS/IT application investments and projects, for both custom-built and packaged software applications. How the process and tools and techniques can be adapted for IT infrastructure and other types of change programmes is discussed in Chapters 8 and 9.

Although the benefits management process is applicable across the whole investment portfolio, its value increases as the issues associated with delivery of benefits become more complex. The inputs to the process provide a first understanding of the range and complexity of the tasks involved. This can be done by asking the three 'why, what and how' questions as in the application portfolio analysis discussed in Chapter 2.

An assessment of the answers to these questions provides the background to setting objectives for the project and identifying the key stakeholders, both external and internal, and their potential role in the project. The benefits management techniques then focus on the relationship between the enabling technology and changes to processes, structures and working practices to identify the best way of realizing the maximum set of benefits from the investment.

An Overview of the Benefits Management Process

In considering the activities required to manage the delivery of benefits, it is assumed that the IT-based system is delivered to specification, i.e. the technical implementation is achieved successfully. However, as the process proceeds and the changes needed to gain the benefits become clearer, the technical specification will undoubtedly have to be revised. It is assumed that the change control processes in the development methodology can deal with this. The other related activities are the organizational and business changes of many types that have to be made to deliver the benefits. The benefits management process should be the driving mechanism for managing these change activities.

The benefits management process draws on the model for managing strategic change developed by Pettigrew and Whipp (1991), by recognizing that the process by which a major change is managed needs to be relevant to the content of the change involved – in this case primarily IT enabled change – and must be appropriate to the prevailing organizational context – both internal and external. The process also recognizes and includes some of the best practices developed in Total Quality Management (TQM) and business improvement and process excellence approaches and methods (such as Six Sigma). As well as creating a number of new techniques specific to benefit identification, definition and realization, it incorporates a number of tools and techniques from different sources to address particular aspects. It also enables organizations to utilize their existing methodologies in conjunction with the benefits management process and toolkit.

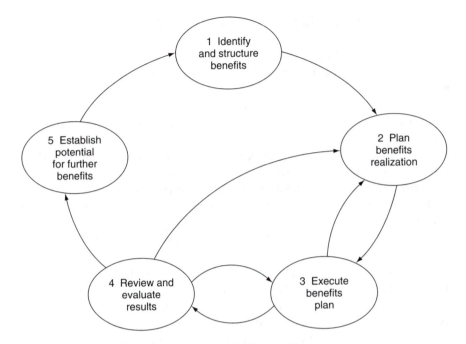

Figure 3.3 *A process model for benefits management*

The five stages in the iterative process and the links between the stages are shown in Figure 3.3 and are described in outline in the following sections.

Identifying and Structuring the Benefits

Based on the outcome of the IS/IT strategic analysis and planning activities and discussions, the overall business rationale for a new or improved use of IS/IT will have been identified and the overall nature of the business contribution expected from the investment can be determined i.e. whether it is strategic, key operational or support, as described in Chapter 2. If the nature of the contribution is uncertain, then the investment should first be put through an R&D stage (as per the high potential segment of the portfolio), to understand what the possible benefits are and if they are relevant and achievable. While the entirety of the benefits management process does not really apply to the R&D investments, a simplified version and some of the techniques can be used to enable the benefits to be identified and assessed.

The purposes of the first stage of the process are to:

- establish agreed objectives for the investment that ensure it relates to one or more of the drivers for change in the organization
- identify all the potential benefits that could be obtained by achievement of the investment objectives
- understand how a combination of IS/IT functionality and business changes can cause the benefits to be realized
- establish ownership of the benefits and determine whether they can be measured to prove that they have occurred
- identify any organizational issues or implications for particular stakeholder groups that could hinder or even cause the project to fail
- produce an outline business case to decide whether to proceed further or stop the investment now.

These points introduce a few terms that need to be defined clearly and explicitly, so that there is consistency in the language used by everyone involved and misunderstandings are avoided. The definitions and their implications are explained in more depth during the discussion of the use of the tools and techniques in the next three chapters. However, it is helpful to introduce the definitions of the most important concepts here.

Definition: Business and organizational drivers

Views held by senior managers as to what is important to the business – in a given timescale – such that they feel changes must occur. Drivers for change can be both external and internal but are specific to the context in which the organization operates.

Definition: Investment objectives

Organizational targets for achievement agreed for the investment in relation to the drivers. As a set they are essentially a description of what the situation should be on completion of the investment.

Definition: Business benefit

An advantage on behalf of a particular stakeholder or group of stakeholders.

This implies that the benefits are 'owned' by the individuals or groups who want to obtain value from the investment.

Definition: Stakeholder(s)

An individual or group of people who will benefit from the investment or are either directly involved in making or are affected by the changes needed to realize the benefits.

Identifying the potential and achievable benefits involves an iterative process of establishing the investment objectives and the business performance improvements that the technology and associated changes could deliver. The achievement of each objective could well deliver a variety of different benefits across the organization and also to trading partners and customers. The process is inevitably iterative since objectives may be modified and new benefits identified as ideas and options are considered.

For each potential benefit it is important to be as precise as possible about *where* in the business, or in trading partners, it will occur, in order to determine how it can be measured and who in the organization should be responsible for its delivery. As will later be explained in more detail, if the benefit cannot be measured or no one owns it, it does not really exist.

All business performance improvements are measurable in some way and so are all of the benefits delivered by information systems. Some can be measured directly, for example, staff reductions due to automation or a decrease in product rejects due to quality control data. Many of these can also be converted into financial values. Where this can be done, it should be, to enable an economic appraisal to be made. In other cases the benefit and its measurement may be less direct. Better timing and control of deliveries could lead to more satisfied customers, an improvement that may lead to increased sales or at least fewer lost sales due to delivery problems. The level of customer satisfaction will need to be measured and some estimate made of the sales implications of improved delivery. In essence, every benefit should be expressed in ways that can, in due course, be measured, even if the measure will be subjective, for example, customer or staff opinion. If there is no possible way of measuring the benefit it should be discarded.

Next, the feasibility of achieving each of the benefits needs to be considered. The first step as already mentioned is to determine ownership of the benefit and hence responsibility for its delivery. This is easy to identify if the system is mainly within one function or area of the business, but it is more difficult when the system crosses functions, especially when reorganization and rationalization of tasks across functions are integral to the delivery of benefits. Responsibility may have to be shared, but then this must be made explicit. Again, given that a manager is made accountable for the delivery of each of the intended benefits, any benefits lacking such ownership should be removed from the list.

The Interdependence of Benefits and Change

Having identified and allocated responsibility for benefits to stakeholders, the next step is to determine the changes required for the delivery of each benefit and how the IS/IT development will enable these to occur.

A key output from this activity is described as a *benefits dependency network*, which relates the IS/IT functionality via the business and organizational changes to the benefits identified. Developing such networks is also an iterative process, since as required changes are identified, a network of interrelating changes and benefits will evolve, and the feasibility of achieving some of the benefits will be questioned.

Equally, further benefits may well be identified. Creating the network requires knowledge to be shared among business managers and key stakeholders, including the IT specialists so that they all understand what the benefits are and how realizing each of the benefits depends on specific changes that need to be made.

There are essentially two types of change, in addition to introducing new technology.

Definition: Business changes

The new ways of working that are required to ensure that the desired benefits are realized.

Business changes cannot normally be made until the new system is available for use and the necessary enabling changes have been made.

Definition: Enabling changes

Changes that are prerequisites for achieving the business changes or that are essential to bring the system into effective operation within the organization.

Enabling changes are often 'one-off' changes, such as defining and agreeing new working practices, redesigning processes, changes to job roles and responsibilities, new incentive or performance management schemes, and training in new business skills (as well as the more obvious training and education in the new system). They can often be made, and sometimes have to be made, before the new system can be introduced.

As with the benefits, ownership and responsibility for each change has to be identified and agreement reached on the evidence needed to determine whether or not the change has been successfully achieved.

Before embarking on the significant amount of work involved in the development of a comprehensive benefits plan, a 'first-cut' business case should be prepared to assess whether there are sufficient potential benefits to justify the approximate expected cost and to define the further work needed to produce the full investment justification. If the achievable benefits are clearly insufficient, the project should be stopped.

It is also advisable to carry out an initial stakeholder analysis to identify all the relevant parties involved and assess whether, based on the balance of benefits and changes that affect each stakeholder group, the necessary commitment of resources and knowledge will be made to the project. In this step, potential negative impacts on particular stakeholders need to be identified, so that actions can be considered to mitigate these 'disbenefits'. Stakeholder analysis is considered in more detail in the next stage of the process, but for some projects much of the assessment can be made in the first stage.

Planning Benefits Realization

The main purposes of this stage are to develop a comprehensive benefits plan and a business case for the investment, which will be submitted to management for approval. In order to do this the following also have to be achieved:

- a full description of each of the benefits and changes, with responsibility for delivery clearly defined and agreed
- measures for all the benefits and, where appropriate, estimates of the expected 'values' of each benefit at the end of the investment. This assumes that many of the improvements can be quantified in advance and, for some, financial values calculated. The basis and rationale for such estimates must also be made clear
- measurements to establish the current 'baseline' at the start of the investment, which may require new measurements to be introduced to ensure the benefits resulting from the project are accurately attributed to it
- agreed ownership of all the changes and actions in place to address all the stakeholder issues that may affect the achievement of the changes
- the evidence or criteria to be used to assess whether each change has been successfully carried out
- a complete and fully documented benefits dependency network to show all the benefit and change relationships.

A full description of the contents of a benefits plan and business case (including risk assessment) and how to carry out the activities involved is provided in Chapter 5, because the contents are products of the tools and techniques that are described in the next two chapters. Like any plan it includes activities, responsibilities, timescales, resources and deliverables, but perhaps most importantly a clear description of the relationships and dependencies that are critical to achieving the investment objectives.

Benefits Realization: the Stakeholder Perspective

Before the dependency network and resulting benefits plan can be finalized and a sound business case proposed, a thorough stakeholder analysis should be completed. The purpose of stakeholder analysis is to understand organizational and people factors that will affect the organization's ability to implement the required changes and achieve the expected benefits. This is effectively an aspect of risk analysis, which considers the implications for the project in terms of how different stakeholder perceptions can impact particular components of the benefits plan. Some stakeholders will be mainly beneficiaries of the investment, others will largely be involved in the changes and some will be both beneficiaries and responsible for significant changes.

Anyone affected by the system or the process of development should be considered as a stakeholder since the view they have of the investment may influence the outcome. It may have been possible to identify all the relevant stakeholders at the start of the project and involve them in creating the network and benefits plan, but this is not always feasible and an analysis of stakeholders and their real or perceived issues is needed, so that actions can be established to manage them. These actions should become additional enabling changes on the benefits network. Alternatively, some stakeholder groups may have genuine concerns that cannot be addressed during the project and the investment scope or implementation plans may have to be modified to avoid serious conflict and possible investment failure. Some of the 'disbenefits' that have been identified may be deemed unacceptable and, again, the objectives or scope of the system may need to be revised.

The main objective is to address the 'what's in it for me?' problem of IS/IT investments. Projects often fail due to the lack of cooperation of parties who are not considered central to its success, but whose ability or willingness to accept change is essential to delivering the business improvements required. The purpose of assessment is to obtain ownership and buy-in of relevant individuals and groups, and to identify organizational factors that will enable or frustrate the achievement of the benefits.

Another reason for the analysis of stakeholder interests is to consider aspects of business change outside the particular project and the possible implications on achieving the benefits. For instance, other business initiatives, reorganization and possible changes in key stakeholders may have a significant impact on the project. A number of techniques for carrying out a stakeholder analysis are discussed in Chapter 6. Only when this assessment has been completed and the feasibility of achieving the target benefits thoroughly tested, should a business case requesting funding for the IS/IT investment be developed.

The steps involved in stages 1 and 2 of the process can be summarized as a set of questions that have to be answered to produce a benefits plan. These are shown in Figure 3.4.

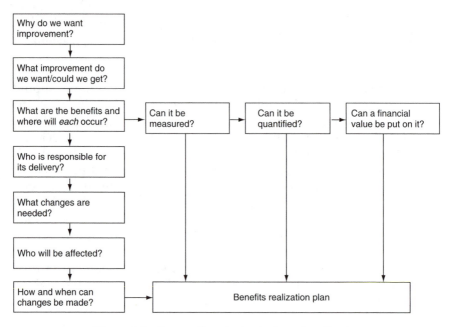

Figure 3.4 *Key questions in developing a benefits plan*

Executing the Benefits Plan

As with any plan, the next stage is to carry it out and adjust it as necessary, as issues and events affecting its viability occur. Monitoring progress against the activities and deliverables of the benefits plan is just as important as for the IS/IT development plan and the two plans are components of the overall project plan. It may be necessary to establish interim targets and measures to evaluate progress towards key milestones or the final implementation.

Normally a business project manager is appointed to ensure that the project is delivered to meet the business needs without undue disruption or risk. The role that a business project manager can and should fulfil is considered in detail later in the book, but one aspect of that role is to be the 'custodian' of the benefits plan on behalf of other business stakeholders and to ensure that each of the stakeholders carries out his or her responsibilities as defined in the plan.

As the project evolves, inevitably the plans will have to change, due to changes in resources and personnel plus unexpected events or problems that have to be assessed and dealt with. It is the business project manager's responsibility to decide, in consultation with the other relevant business managers, what action to take in terms of reviewing the scope and specification of the system or the business and enabling changes. In some instances the investment justification may need complete reappraisal to decide whether the project should continue. The starting point for any interim review should be 'what is the effect on the benefits and our ability to achieve them?' to both ensure that actions are appropriate to the overall project objectives, rather than just the immediate problem and that all the relevant stakeholders are involved in decisions to change the plan.

During implementation, further benefits may also be identified and, again, the business project manager should obtain agreement on appropriate action to revise the plan to accommodate the benefit or defer any action until stage 5.

Equally it may become apparent that intended benefits are no longer feasible or relevant and the benefits plan should be modified accordingly, along with any consequent reduction in the IS/IT functionality or business changes. Factors outside the benefits plan itself, such as changes in the organization or problems in meeting the requirements at the intended cost will, of course, initiate reviews of the project deliverables and plan and, in turn, cause a reassessment of the benefits plan and even the business case.

Reviewing and Evaluating the Results

One of the factors that differentiates successful from less successful companies in their deployment of IS/IT is the management resolve to evaluate IS/IT investments *after* completion. A survey of approaches to managing IS/IT benefits in 60 major organizations (Ward et al.,

1996) revealed that only 26% of the companies always reviewed projects after completion to determine whether benefits were delivered – a finding in line with other research. Most respondents also believed that their organization's investment appraisal processes were not appropriate for the types of investment now being undertaken and 45% admitted overstating the benefits to gain approval, in the full and certain knowledge that no evaluation would be made after implementation!

As discussed in Chapter 1, the purposes of a benefit review involve both assessment of the investment itself and organizational learning:

- to determine and confirm which planned benefits have been achieved
- to identify which expected benefits have not been achieved and to decide if remedial action can be taken to still obtain them or if they have to be foregone
- to identify any unexpected benefits that have been achieved and any unexpected 'disbenefits' that have resulted
- to understand the reasons why certain types of benefits were or were not achieved and provide lessons for future projects
- to understand how to improve the organization's benefits management process for all projects.

Once the new technology, system and business changes have been implemented, there should be a formal review of what has and has not been achieved. This is a business review aimed at maximizing the benefits gained from the particular investment *and* increasing the benefits from future investments. All comprehensive project management, systems development and change management methodologies include a review process following implementation and they should be carried out prior to the benefit review. The results of those assessments may provide explanations for the non-delivery of intended benefits, as well as knowledge to improve the management of future projects or systems design and implementation.

The evaluation should involve all key stakeholders and focus on what has been achieved, what has not (or not yet) been achieved and why, and identify further action needed to deliver outstanding benefits, if possible. The reasons for lack of benefit delivery may be due to misjudgements or lack of knowledge in preparing the benefits plan or problems during its execution. Another aspect of this review is to identify any unexpected benefits that have arisen and understand how they came about. This again may prove valuable input to improve the first stage of future projects. Equally any 'disbenefits' that resulted should be understood in order to try and avoid them recurring in future projects.

It is worth stating that any post-implementation review should not become a 'witchhunt'; it must be an objective process with future improvements in mind, not a way of allocating blame for past failures. If it is seen as a negative process, honest appraisal and a constructive critique of what has happened become impossible and the whole process falls into disrepute or is not carried out.

Establishing the Potential for Further Benefits

Research referred to earlier (Ward et al., 1996), found that it is difficult to predict all of the benefits of a system in advance. While 90% of survey respondents supported this view, in only 15% of their organizations was there any specific activity or process to search for further benefits at the end of projects. Some benefits only become apparent when the system has been implemented (or been running for some time) and all the associated business changes have been made.

Therefore, having reviewed what has happened, it is equally important to consider what further improvement is now possible following the implementation of the system and associated changes and in the light of the new levels of business performance that have been achieved. This should be a creative process similar to stage 1, involving the main stakeholders and any others who may be able to contribute, using the increased knowledge now available to identify new opportunities and the benefits they offer. These benefits may be achievable through further business changes alone or may require more IS/IT investment. In the latter case these potential benefits should be the starting point for investment consideration via the steps in stage 1 of the process.

If this is not done, many available benefits may be overlooked. If maximum value is to be gained from the overall investment in IT, benefit identification should be a continuing process from which IS/IT and business change projects are defined. This 'benefit-driven' approach to determining the investment portfolio, as well as maximizing the return from each investment, is considered in Chapter 9.

Table 3.1 summarizes the main activities involved in each of the process stages.

Table 3.1   *Stages and main activities of the benefits management process*

Stage	Activities
1 Identifying and structuring the benefits	• Analyse the drivers to determine the investment objectives • Identify the benefits that will result by achieving the objectives and how they will be measured • Establish ownership of the benefits • Identify the changes required and stakeholder implications • Produce first-cut business case
2 Planning benefits realization	• Finalize measurements of benefits and changes • Obtain agreement of all stakeholders to responsibilities and accountabilities • Produce benefits plan and investment case
3 Executing the benefits plan	• Manage the change programmes • Review progress against the benefits plan
4 Reviewing and evaluating the results	• Formally assess the benefits achieved or otherwise • Initiate action to gain outstanding benefits where feasible • Identify lessons for other projects
5 Establishing potential for further benefits	• Identify additional improvements through business changes and initiate action • Identify additional benefits from further IT investment

What is Different about this Approach?

The purpose of the benefits management process is to improve the identification of achievable benefits and to ensure that decisions and actions taken over the life of the investment lead to realizing all the feasible benefits. This approach recognizes the criticality of business manager involvement in achieving organizational value from IS/IT and is complementary to the current range of methodologies and processes, not a replacement for any of them. Improving existing methodologies, which largely deal with the complexity of the 'supply side' of investments, will not address the gap on the 'demand side'. The benefits management process was developed to fill this gap. Each element of the process can be aligned with steps or deliverables in other methodologies and, as depicted in Figure 3.2, the benefits management process can be the means of integrating the other approaches, since it maintains the focus on the purposes of the investment, rather than the means of delivery.

The majority of value from IT comes from the business changes that it enables the organization to make. The investment is in 'IT-enabled change', not just technology, to achieve improvements in business and organizational performance through better processes, relationships and ways of working. The achievement of benefits obviously depends on effective implementation of the technology, but evidence from project success and failure suggests that it is organizations' inability to accommodate and exploit the capabilities of the technology that causes the poor return from many IT investments. This has been recognized and addressed in the socio-technical approaches to systems development, but these methods do not specifically consider the links between the technology and business changes and the way they are brought together to deliver particular benefits. The 'benefits plan', which is the main deliverable of the first two stages of the process, and the benefits dependency network which underpins the plan, are means of ensuring these links are made. The benefits plan is also the basis for the business case, not only for obtaining funding, but also for managing the project, since it includes not only *what* benefits are intended but also *how* each one can be achieved.

In essence, the most obvious difference in this approach is the benefits plan and its role in 'governing' the investment process. But, perhaps more importantly, the approach and the associated tools and techniques change the nature of the involvement of business managers and other stakeholders in the management of the investment throughout its lifecycle. In particular, the first stage of the process is designed to encourage the stakeholders to share their collective knowledge to reach agreement on the overall outcome they expect and to determine whether they are able and willing to undertake the changes needed to reach the objectives. That will to a large extent depend on the benefits each stakeholder perceives and hence the emphasis on the ownership of benefits.

Gaining business ownership of the benefits and the change programme requires more than a new process, better tools and another plan. The mode of engagement between the IS/IT specialists and business stakeholders also has to change. The process and tools are designed to enable business managers to become more effectively involved in IT developments and in control of the parts of the project only they can make successful, while respecting the fact that they are inevitably busy people with many competing priorities for their time. Research has shown, to quote Walsham (1993), 'the participation of users and other stakeholder groups in the design and development process can be considered essential'. However this is difficult to achieve by asking the stakeholders to fit in with the methodologies of the IS/IT specialists, which are not an intuitive or convenient way of working for most business managers.

Inevitably this approach is more demanding of management time, especially at the start of projects, but experience has shown that clarity and agreement about what the project should deliver, as early as possible, prevents significant and expensive corrective action later – assuming that corrective action is actually possible. It does, however, make more effective use of the time managers can devote to the project, by improving the communication about those aspects of the investment that are most critical to its success. As was stated earlier, this type of approach, which enables the collective knowledge of the key stakeholders to determine what the benefits are and how they will be realized, is also effective in stopping investments that had no real chance of success, before major expenditure is incurred. Cancelling projects should always be a business decision, based on a benefit/cost assessment, that is, what is it worth spending to get the benefits, rather than, as is often the case, a cost/benefit assessment, which asks whether enough benefits can be found to justify the expected cost.

The other key difference in this approach is the emphasis on post-implementation evaluation of the extent to which benefits have been achieved, and the assessment of the further benefits that are now available having completed the investment and achieved some or all of the objectives. Exploiting the learning that has been gained from previous IT investments is essential to increasing the value from future investments. That will not happen without formalizing the reviews as integral parts of the process and ensuring that they are carried out.

Some of the key differences of this approach are shown in Figure 3.5.

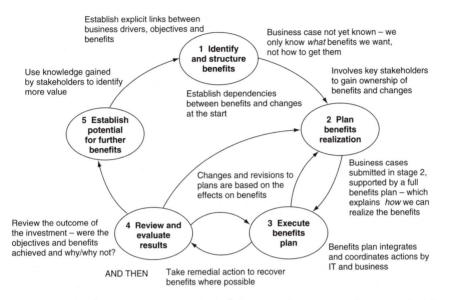

Figure 3.5 *Key areas of difference in the benefits management approach compared with others*

Summary

In Chapter 1 the challenges faced by organizations to increase the value from their IS/IT investments were discussed and, in Chapter 2, the low level of organizational competences in exploiting IS/IT was revealed as an underlying cause of the difficulty in dealing with these challenges. These inabilities to plan for and manage the benefits and associated changes successfully can lead to an 'ineffective use process' in the three-stage model of Soh and Markus (1995) and also to inappropriate investments in IT assets, which add cost but do not improve the performance of the business. The benefits management process discussed in this chapter does not, of itself, overcome these problems. But it has been successfully used in many organizations, with the tools and techniques described later in the book, to change the way IS/IT investments (and other change programmes) are managed, resulting in improved benefit delivery.

It is an additional process, but one that specifically addresses the core issues in realizing the available benefits. This is not only because it recognizes the inextricable link between change and benefit, but also provides a way of maintaining that link by more appropriate involvement of business stakeholders at the inception and throughout the lifecycle of the investment. In turn, this changes the working relationships between business managers and IT specialists, based on a clearer understanding of how investment success depends on the collective knowledge and abilities of everyone involved in the project.

Using the *ends–ways–means* logic of strategic management, the *ends* in this case are the realization of more value from IS/IT investments. The *means* normally implies the functionality or capability of the technology, available technical resources and the abilities of those designing and implementing the new system. This view often neglects the knowledge and skills of business managers and other stakeholders, which are essential to understanding how, in the particular organizational context, the new IT capabilities can actually be used to improve performance. This, in turn, causes the business resources, especially people's time, to be used ineffectively in relation to the activities required to realize the benefits. Existing methodologies tend to treat that knowledge mainly as an input to a process to design and deliver a technical 'solution' that meets expressed requirements. It seems to be assumed too often that, if the requirements are met, the benefits will somehow arrive. All the available evidence suggests this is rarely the case.

Realizing value from IS/IT investments depends on the *ways* in which an organization uses its collective technical, business and managerial knowledge and skills to identify what it can achieve through a combination of technology and other changes, and the *ways* it uses its resources to achieve the investment objectives. The benefits management process provides the foundations of a new way of managing IS/IT investments that makes more effective use of the means that most organizations already have at their disposal, but which all too often are not being combined to create the organizational competences necessary to obtain all the benefits available from their IS/IT investments. The tools and techniques and how they can be used to bring about new ways of managing are discussed in the next three chapters.

4
Establishing the Why, What and How

This chapter introduces and describes the use of some of the tools and frameworks that enable the key questions posed in Chapters 2 and 3 to be answered for a particular investment. Those questions are: why is the investment being made; what types of benefit is the organization expecting to achieve; and how can a combination of business changes and IT deliver those benefits?

The frameworks and tools presented in this, and the following two chapters, are described in terms of their use in completing the first two stages of the process shown in Figure 3.3, that is, in identifying and structuring the benefits of a particular investment and the preparation of a benefits plan and business case. However, in the execution or implementation phase of the project (stage three in Figure 3.3), the knowledge provided from the use of the tools and frameworks should be used to guide the project management, systems development and change management activities, as described in Chapter 3. The progress of the project should be reviewed against the results of this initial analysis to determine the steps to be taken to address any discrepancies. This may either require additional effort applied to the business changes that were identified, or require the analysis to be revisited in light of any unexpected or emergent constraints. In a similar way, the information produced and documented using these techniques will provide the baseline against which to undertake a formal review at the end of the project, that is, stage four in the benefits management process shown in Figure 3.3, and also a means of identifying further benefits that may be realizable.

The chapter ends with an extended example of the use of the tools by a food processing company seeking to improve control over their administrative and control processes. This example is further developed in Chapters 5 and 6, in order to generate a complete benefits plan.

Why: Identifying Business and Organizational Drivers

In undertaking the business, IS and IT strategic analyses and planning activities discussed in Chapter 2, new ideas and opportunities for the use of IS and IT will have been identified. Use of the applications portfolio, shown in Figure 2.9, will define the expected contributions to the business, for example, whether an investment opportunity is strategic or key operational. The benefits management process is then used to explore and analyse the potential benefits of each investment, identify the change activities required to realize the benefits – the benefits plan – and develop the business case.

While ideally, organizations should undertake a strategic analysis of their business and the contribution IS and IT can make before undertaking a benefits analysis, in some cases this does not occur. Quite frequently such strategic planning is undertaken at senior levels but not communicated or shared with others in the business. Staff lower down in the organization are therefore often unclear about the strategic direction and thus how individual applications or investments can contribute to this.

In order to address this lack of shared understanding it is suggested that all benefits management work commences with a discussion to clarify and confirm what the strategic influences or forces on the organization are. Even if there is a well-communicated business strategy, it is important to ensure there is a common and consistent understanding of the rationale for the strategy and the implications of the organization's objectives. This activity, which is called *driver analysis*, seeks to establish and understand the forces or drivers acting on the organization, which require the organization to make changes either to what it does or to how it conducts its business activities. In generating this list of drivers, senior managements' perspective of the organization is taken, to ensure that the identified drivers are actually strategic to the future of the whole enterprise, rather than merely affecting the interests of certain departments or functions. Often localized priorities are found to conflict with the best interests of the future of the whole organization. Also, as is described in Chapter 5, when developing a business case, it will strengthen that case if it can be clearly linked to what is important to the senior management of the organisation.

The timescale over which these drivers should be considered will depend on the industry sector in which the organization operates. For example, the utilities and transport sectors, which require significant investments in fixed infrastructures, may need to take a five- to 10-year horizon for their strategic analysis and planning. For organizations in sectors such as the nuclear industry, mining or waste disposal an appropriate horizon may be up to 20 years. In contrast, for those operating in very fast moving or turbulent environments, such as fashion goods or information technology, a one- to two-year horizon would be more appropriate.

As introduced in Chapter 3, drivers can therefore be described as views held by senior managers as to what is important to the business – in a given timescale – such that they feel changes must occur. Drivers for change can be both external and internal but are specific to the context in which the organization operates. They should be described in enough detail to ensure that they are explicit to its particular situation over the specified timescale and ensure there is an understanding of why change is needed and the implications of not taking action to respond to the drivers. For example, rather than simply record 'increase market share', an organization should be clear as to why they wish to increase market share. Is it because they have been losing market share to a particular competitor or is it that they wish to increase it for a specific reason, for example, it would allow them to have greater influence over setting prices in their industry or be automatically included in invitations to tender for government contracts?

Sources of Drivers

In terms of their origins, strategic drivers that affect IS/IT investments can essentially be of three types, as shown in Table 4.1.

Most projects originate from one of these but eventually will have to take account of the other two. Context originated projects will have more uncertainties about scope and the intended outcome and will demand more input from senior business managers in the formative stages. Outcome driven projects will have to consider the different options that might exist to achieve the outcome and even whether it can be fully achieved. The danger with content driven projects is that the focus on the IT issues and often an assumption that 'it just has to

Table 4.1 Origin of strategic drivers

Origin of driver	
Content	Issues are IT related, for example, providing infrastructure to enable mobile working, consolidation and rationalization of intranet sites or moving away from an unsupported platform or application
Context	Issue lies in internal or external context of business area under consideration. For example, a merger, a reorganization, regulatory compliance or a significant directive from HQ
Outcome	Issue is focused on a specific outcome, such as retention of market share, cost reduction or integration of online customer channels to provide new customer services

be done' means that other potential benefits that could be achieved from the project are overlooked. Project teams should beware of a tendency to turn all projects into 'content-driven' projects because the IT development process, with its inherently strict logic, is easier to manage than the more ambiguous or 'softer issues' associated with the other types of project.

Many drivers will be external to an organization, due to the industry or marketplace in which it operates, or the general business or economic environment. For example, changing customer behaviours, increasing costs of key resources or the actions of competitors may well result in drivers on the organization that require it to change its current products or modes of operation. External changes may also result from legislation or regulation, either of the particular industry in which the organization operates, or of all businesses in that geographic market, for example, the Working Time Directive for all organizations in the European Union.

Drivers will also arise from within the organization. For example, many organizations are concerned about their ability to share and reuse the knowledge that they have generated. They describe themselves as 'reinventing the wheel' every time they undertake a new project and therefore feel a strategic imperative to improve knowledge sharing or management within the organization. Other organizations are concerned with their ability to attract and retain the best talent in their industry or sector. This may be because there is a shortage of individuals with particular skills or the organization does not provide appropriate career development paths or even that the working environment is considered too stressful. Finding an acceptable or, better still, attractive balance for staff between their work and home life may also be important in attracting and keeping staff and therefore a strategic driver. How IT is deployed can have a significant effect on this balance, often to the benefit of individuals but in some cases can be a cause of staff alienation, as reported by the Work Foundation study 'Getting by, not getting on' (iSociety, 2003).

Strategic Drivers, Dimensions of Competence and the Nature of Change

One effective method of establishing the drivers acting on a business, and the degree of change required to address these, is to use the dimensions of competence framework, based on the work of Treacy and Wiersma (1993), discussed in Chapter 2. This framework seeks to bring together a consideration of the external or competitive environment in which an organization operates with a similar consideration of its internal resources or capabilities. The framework asks managers to assess where they are in relation to their competition according to three dimensions of competence: product or service leadership, customer intimacy and operational excellence.

Identification of performance 'behind' that of competitors on one or more dimensions will suggest the need for incremental changes to address and overcome the perceived or known disadvantages. If the organization is assessed to be a long way behind its competitors or, in non-competitive markets, performing well below what is expected by stakeholders, it is probable that there is the need for more radical change in order to 'catch up' or stop further deterioration in performance. Such situations may also require the identification and elimination of activities that are seriously hampering the performance of the organization, which may only be possible by organizational restructuring, the replacement of many ineffective legacy systems or outsourcing a number of business processes.

Performance below that of competitors or what is expected by stakeholders on just one of the three dimensions will suggest drivers relating to improving performance in this area, requiring targeted change to address specific problems or weaknesses. Performance that is comparable to that of competitors in any or all of the three dimensions will suggest drivers that are related to maintaining this status quo. The changes suggested by such drivers are likely to be incremental in nature and intended to maintain 'business as usual'.

While it may be thought that any organization that is performing better than their competitors or exceeding stakeholder expectations has no need for change, it should be stressed that their external environment will continue to change, often driven by the activity of competitors or the rising expectations of a range of stakeholders. Such organizations must continually refresh or even reinvent themselves if they are to continue to be leaders in their field. Being in a leading position implies that the organization should search for opportunities for innovations or performance improvements that will increase the gap between them and their main competitors. Innovations may require some radical changes, although this may not appear as critical or difficult as the radical change required by laggards in an industry. As the fate of many of the organizations described in Peters and Waterman's seminal work *In Search of Excellence* (1980) demonstrated, maintaining a leading position cannot be taken for granted and requires considerable creative skill and the ability to change before being caught or overtaken by the competition.

The need for radical change is usually associated with organizations that are performing well below competitors or expectations, but it will also be required by organizations that are currently performing at an acceptable level on all the dimensions, but have identified the need for change due to drivers affecting a combination of the dimensions. For example, Reuters, the information agency, had to change radically, by creating new products and services as well as reducing its costs, to maintain its leading position, as the sources of similar information expanded dramatically following the commercialization of the Internet.

The linkages between performance levels identified by the dimensions of competence framework and the associated nature of change are summarized in Table 4.2.

Strategic Drivers and Application Types

Figure 4.1 shows how generic or typical drivers tend to relate to the different types of IS/IT investment as described in the applications portfolio discussed in Chapter 2. It can be seen that high potential applications, that is, those that require further investigation and therefore should be considered and managed as R&D activities, often result from a radical new business idea or new technology, or some other need or opportunity to create change within the organization or in the market in which it operates.

Table 4.2 *Nature of change suggested by the competence analysis*

Performance from dimensions of competence	Associated nature of change	
Performance well below that of competitors on one or more of the three dimensions of competence	Elimination of problems and constraints and potentially radical change	Improvements by removal of problems, constraints or inefficiencies
For organizations with, at least, parity on all axes and an advantage in one dimension – opportunities exist to move considerably ahead – outside the ring of parity – in one or more dimension	Innovation and potentially radical change	Performance improvements from doing something new or in a completely new way
Performance below that of competitors on one of the three dimensions	Targeted improvement	Level of change required to meet specific business objectives and/or achieve more effective use of resources
Performance equal or better than competitors on all axes	Business as usual or incremental improvement	Managing a stable situation to avoid disadvantage

STRATEGIC	HIGH POTENTIAL
Perceived market requirements Competitive pressures Achieve business changes	Innovative business idea New technology opportunity Create change
Improved performance of existing activities (effectiveness) Integration/rationalization to speed up business processes Industry legislation	Cost reduction and efficiency improvements through automation General legislation
KEY OPERATIONAL	SUPPORT

Figure 4.1 *Typical drivers for different application types*

Strategic applications are often developed as a response to competitive pressures within the industry or to achieve a competitive advantage by satisfying a market need ahead of the competition. Applications or investments that can be considered as key operational often result from a need to improve the effectiveness of current operations in order to overcome known causes of current competitive disadvantages or to avoid becoming disadvantaged in the future. This may result from unfavourable comparisons with other firms in the industry or from a level of performance that is no longer acceptable to the organization. Such improvements in effectiveness are often accompanied by cost savings, but this is not normally the main objective for the investment. Finally, investments in support applications are driven by the need or desire to increase the efficiency and reduce the costs of specific organizational activities. This is often achieved by removing time-consuming and error-prone steps in current processes or by the automation of information tasks and clerical activities.

Establishing Investment Objectives

The business and organizational drivers exist independently of any decision to invest in a particular opportunity or project within the organization. Indeed, those drivers originating outside the organization will persist, even if the organization chooses to 'hide its head in the sand' and do nothing about addressing them. However, assuming the organization wishes to make changes that address some or all of the drivers, it is necessary to assess whether and how individual opportunities or investments, identified in the strategic analysis and planning stage described in Chapter 2, will achieve the necessary changes. The first requirement is to establish an agreed set of objectives for the investment or project.

Investment objectives should be a set of statements that define the 'finish line' for the project, or paint a picture of the way things will be if the project is successful. Success criteria are therefore often included in the statement of the objective. However, these tend to be high level statements, rather than detailed operational measures. As discussed later, such detailed measures should be applied to the individual benefits that will be realized from the project, if the investment objectives are met. The identification and use of appropriate measures is an important part of the benefits management process and is discussed further in Chapter 5.

While it is impossible to be prescriptive, projects should have a few clearly stated and compelling investment objectives, rather than a long list of incremental and overlapping ones. The longer the list the harder it is to remember what the objectives are and the task of achieving them all becomes more complex and difficult and the greater the probability of conflict, misunderstanding or confusion over the relative priorities among the objectives. Experience of applying the benefits management process in a large number of organizations and with very different types of project has shown that the majority of projects can be described perfectly well in between three and six carefully worded objectives. There is often a tendency to think that a project's significance is dependent on the number of objectives rather than the importance of each of them.

The linkage between investment objectives and drivers is discussed further later, but it is important to note that each of the investment objectives should explicitly address one or more of the drivers, to ensure that the project will clearly contribute to achieving changes that are important to the organization's future. A formal definition for investment objectives is introduced in Chapter 3 and included in the glossary.

SMART Objectives

An increasingly popular means of creating compelling and manageable objectives for projects is to test each objective against the 'SMART' checklist shown in Table 4.3.

As is discussed further in Chapter 5, although it is important to define how the eventual achievement of the objectives and also the benefits will be determined, this does not mean that all objectives must be associated with a quantitative measure. Subjective

Table 4.3 SMART objectives (after Doran, 1981; OGC, 2004)

Objectives should be...	
Specific	Precisely describe a well-defined accomplishment in a way that all stakeholders to the project can understand
Measurable	Be capable of being measured or it being known that the objective has been achieved
Achievable	Realistic given the context in which the organization is operating and the constraints that it has
Relevant	Address issues that are important to the organization.
Time bounded	Be associated with a particular timeframe in which the objective should be met

measures, such as those related to the customer perceptions of service improvement or product quality, or staff views of the working environment are acceptable.

Linking the Investment Objectives to Drivers

Having identified the drivers, both external and internal, acting on the organization and determined the objectives for the particular initiative or project, it is necessary to bring these together by considering each objective in turn and deciding which of the drivers it addresses, as shown in Figure 4.2.

As indicated in this figure, not all drivers will be addressed by a particular initiative or project. Any organization will have a wide range of drivers acting on it and a project that claims to be able to address all of these is likely to be too large and complex ever to be successful, since the drivers will affect many parts of the organization and their impact will be over different timescales.

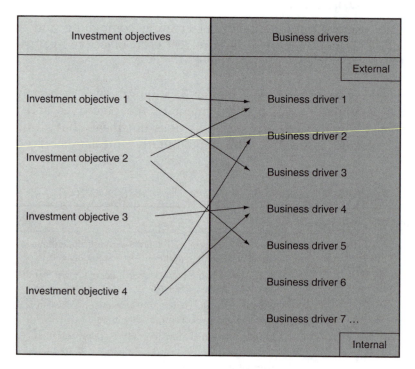

Figure 4.2   Bringing investment objectives and drivers together

Clearly, any projects that do not address at least one of the business drivers should not be considered any further, since it will not be possible to develop a credible business case for the project. The fact that a project only addresses one, or a very few drivers, does not mean it should have a low priority. By definition, each driver is important to the future of the organization and it may be that the project is the only way that the organization can effect the changes needed to address this issue.

The project team should be ever alert to preventing the project objectives evolving over time, to become more related to the functionality that can be delivered by the chosen software, rather than to the business contribution that is required. As research into the implementation of enterprise systems has shown, many strategic investments to create new organizational capabilities can become essentially software replacement projects (Ward et al., 2005). Ensuring that the investment objectives are and continue to be linked explicitly to the drivers should prevent this happening.

Concerns may also arise over its relationships with other initiatives or change programmes that may overlap with the project or on which there are critical dependencies. Alternatively, the discussion may identify opportunities to increase the chances of success by building on changes created by other initiatives. In order to capture these issues and concerns and also to allow the agreed objectives and how

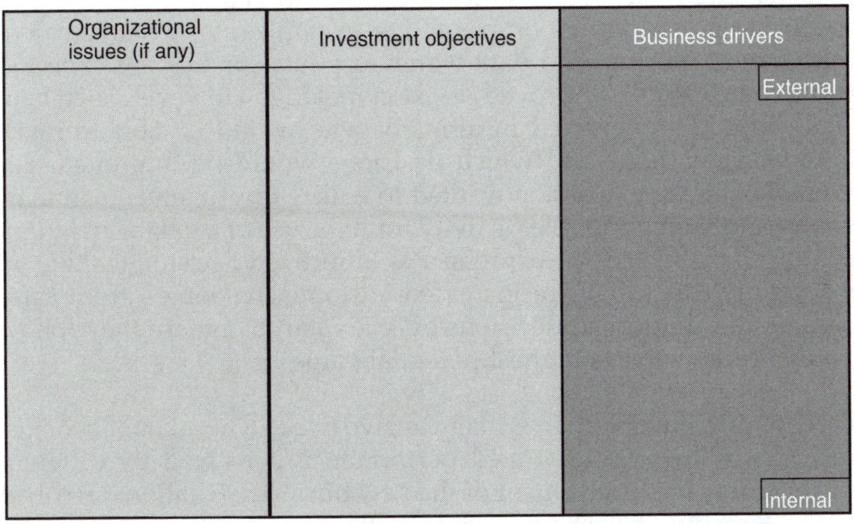

Organizational issues (if any)	Investment objectives	Business drivers
		External
		Internal

Figure 4.3 Framework for drivers and objectives analysis

they address the strategic business drivers to be clearly communicated, it is suggested that a framework similar to that shown in Figure 4.3 is adopted. As with a number of the benefits management frameworks, as will be explained later in this chapter, it should be completed from right to left. External and internal refer to the nature and origins of the drivers identified. For example, changes in the marketplace are likely to give rise to external drivers, whereas the need to address unacceptable cost structures within the organization would be an example of an internal driver.

An example of the use of the framework shown in Figure 4.3 to link investment objectives to drivers is given in the extended example at the end of this chapter.

What: The Business Benefits

Having agreed the investment objectives, it is then possible to consider the business benefits that will be realized. Since the objectives are phrased in terms of targets for achievement wanted from the investment, the benefits can be identified by considering the performance improvements that will be realized if each of these objectives or targets is achieved.

As discussed in Chapter 3, a business benefit can be defined as an advantage on behalf of a particular stakeholder or group of stakeholders. An important attribute of the benefits is that they should be specific to an individual or group. For example, many management information systems and data warehouse investments are expected to yield the benefit 'improved decision making'. However, such benefits should be expressed in terms of who would be able to make improved decisions and which decisions would be improved. For example, if an organization wanted to realize improvements in marketing campaigns and sales activity from the use of a data warehouse, then the benefits may be expressed as 'improved decision making by marketing staff to ensure increased customer responses from campaigns' and 'improved decisions by sales staff to ensure they follow up the leads with the highest potential value'.

Each investment objective is likely to give rise to a number of benefits, each describing the improved performance perceived by different stakeholders by achievement of the new business situation described in the objective. For example, one of the objectives may have been agreed as 'to increase the loyalty of customers'. Such an objective is likely to follow from identification of drivers on the organization resulting from an increasing defection rate among customers. If the organization could increase customer loyalty from the investment being considered, then a range of different benefits could be expected to arise in relation to the roles and interests of different stakeholders. For example, increased customer loyalty might be expected to yield a number of benefits: 'improved satisfaction for customers', 'reduced spending of the promotions budget on customer (re)acquisition (by marketing)' or 'reduced administration costs in customer accounts'. If, as in many industries, loyal customers are found to spend more than new customers due to trading up to higher value products and services, 'increased sales of high margin products (leading to increased bonuses for the sales staff)'.

How: The Benefits Dependency Network

The earlier chapters of this book have stressed that the realization of benefits from IS/IT investments will in the majority of cases be dependent on changes to business processes and relationships and the ways individuals or groups work within the organization. Such changes are often overlooked or, if not overlooked, they may be underestimated and under-resourced. As expressed by Melville et al. (2004) in their exploration of how IT can generate value within an organisation, discussed in Chapter 1: *'Improvements in processes and organisational performance [from IT] are conditional upon appropriate complementary investments in workplace practices and structures'.*

The central framework in the benefits management process is designed to enable the investment objectives and their resulting benefits to be linked in a structured way to the business, organizational and IS/IT changes required to realize those benefits. The framework, called a *benefits dependency network,* is shown in Figure 4.4.

The network should be created from the right of the page to the left. Construction of the network commences with understanding the drivers acting on the organization; agreement on the investment objectives for the particular initiative or project; and identification of the business benefits that will result if the investment objectives are achieved.

Having identified the drivers, investment objectives and business benefits, it is then necessary to identify the changes to the ways individuals and groups work that are a necessary part of realizing the potential benefits identified.

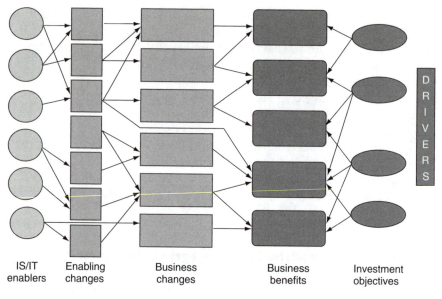

IS/IT   Enabling   Business   Business   Investment
enablers   changes   changes   benefits   objectives

Figure 4.4 *The benefits dependency network*

Each benefit should be considered in turn and the changes that would be necessary to realize that benefit should then be identified and described on the dependency network. Two distinct types of change need to be recognized. *Business changes* are those new ways of working that will be required permanently in the future if the benefit is to be achieved and sustained. In contrast, some changes are only required to be undertaken once and these are termed *enabling changes*. These one-off changes may be necessary to allow the enduring business changes to be brought about or may be related to bringing in the new system and ensuring it is used effectively. Definitions of business and enabling changes are given in Chapter 3 and also included in the glossary.

Business Changes

Business changes have, so far, been described as new ways of working that will be required by the organization in the future. They may include a wide range of different types of change, particularly for large enterprise-wide system deployments. The types of change frequently identified include:

- adoption of new or redefined processes
- new roles and responsibilities
- operation of new teams, groups, divisions

- new governance arrangements
- use of new measures and metrics
- use of new appraisal and reward schemes
- new practices for managing and sharing information.

Changes may well be required in many different parts of the organization. In some cases, many individuals or groups will have to make similar sets of changes and in others each group will have to undertake changes specific to their roles and activities.

While business changes may be considered as the way the organization wishes to work 'for ever more', it is recognized that the organization will be undertaking other investments and changes. These may require the business changes resulting from one project to be reviewed and changed again after a relatively short period. Such constant change now appears to be a standard part of the operation of many organizations.

Enabling Changes

In a similar way to a variety of types of business change being needed, there is also a wide range of enabling changes that may be required in order to ensure the identified benefits are realized. These may also involve many different groups or functions in the organization.

Enabling changes required may well include some of the following:

- training in how to use the new system or technology
- education in how the new systems can improve the performance of individuals, groups or the whole organization
- definition of new measures and the information needed to use them
- collection of current performance data to provide a baseline for future comparison
- mapping of current processes and the design of new processes
- definition of new roles, job descriptions, responsibilities and organizational structures
- establishment of rules and practices for the migration of data from legacy systems or collecting the new information required
- business rules and standard practices managing the information lifecycle (acquisition, renewal, retirement)
- decommissioning of legacy systems

- definition of new application and information governance structures
- reallocation of resources/budgets.

Again, as for the business changes, these enabling changes should be described in terms of the specific implications and requirements of the particular investment.

Enabling changes tend to be required either before the system goes live or shortly thereafter. For example, training in the use of a new system is often undertaken just before the system goes live so that staff, and perhaps customers and suppliers, are ready to use the system as soon as it is available. The decommissioning of legacy systems should ideally occur shortly after the new system goes live. A short overlap ensures that a smooth changeover can occur both for business operations and technical support and allows the organization to have the 'backup' of the existing systems in case of teething problems. However, if the old systems remain operational for too long, it may be found that users do not switch to the new system and hence do not adopt the ways of working, leading to limited benefits being realized.

Enabling IS/IT

Once the major business and enabling changes have been identified, the information technology or systems required need to be considered. This may result in the need for additional changes, particularly enabling changes. If this is the case, these should be added to the relevant part of the network.

The IS/IT enablers can be described as shown in the definition box.

Definition: IS/IT enablers

The information systems and technology required to support the realization of identified benefits and to allow the necessary changes to be undertaken.

IS/IT investments may require the purchase or development of new systems or technology or changes to existing IS/IT applications and infrastructure. The approach of deferring consideration of the technology is intended to ensure that the focus of the investment is on what the organization wishes to achieve and the related change management, rather than the technology options and solutions that are available. As discussed in Chapter 1, IS and IT vendors are keen to promote the many features of their products. All too often, organizations simply believe that this list of features equates to a list of benefits that the systems will provide. This can result in organizations buying and installing systems that either do not meet their needs or are overcomplex. Having explored all other areas of the investment it is then possible to consider what IS/IT is *'sufficient to do the job'*.

Such an approach is not meant to encourage organizations to purchase IT that has limited capabilities or capacity, but to enable them to clearly understand what is required and what is not, in terms of providing relevant, realizable benefits. The explicit linkages shown on the benefits dependency network should more easily allow potential capacity and capability constraints as well as the new functionality implications to be identified and hence more appropriate technology and system purchase decisions to be made. For example, if benefits have been identified from having all of an organization's customers in one system, such as a data warehouse or a single billing system, then it should help ensure that the assessment of alternative suppliers' products will be based on the costs of holding and accessing all customer information in a single system and whether it can accommodate expected growth in customer numbers.

Having undertaken the identification of the benefits and the required business and enabling changes, it may become apparent that the organization does not need to invest in new IS/IT. Indeed, it is often found that if the changes identified could be undertaken, many of the benefits could be realized with current systems, indicating that the problem is the way individuals are working or using existing systems or the inability of the organization to implement 'best practice'.

A concentration on the business benefits and the change management implication at the start of the process will also encourage business managers to become involved. As also discussed in Chapter 1, the effective engagement of business managers is often lacking and it is recognized as a factor that repeatedly causes organizations to fail to realize benefits from IS/IT. Discussions that are essentially about the functionality of IS/IT, or are dominated by this, are usually of little interest to business managers who can even feel threatened due to their lack of technology understanding and are therefore unable or unwilling to contribute to the project. As has been stated before, one key aspect of the benefits management approach described in this book is to create an environment in which both business and IS/IT staff participate fully and willingly in the discussions, to contribute and share their knowledge and learn from their colleagues.

An example of a completed benefits dependency network is given in the extended example at the end of this chapter.

Origins of the Benefits Dependency Network: Right-to-Left Working

The format of the benefits dependency network is derived from a well-known technique in project management called Precedence Diagramming Method (PDM) (Dobson, 2003). In PDM the activities within a project are shown in nodes connected by arrows that denote dependencies between tasks. The approach, which is often incorrectly called PERT charting after the Program Evaluation and Review Technique for project management, can also be termed activity on node charting. This is in contrast to the other popular charting method of ADM (Arrow Diagramming Method) or activity on arrow, which shows nodes connected by arrows on which the activities are indicated.

PDM commences with a starting node on the left-hand side of the page and connects all the activities in the project in the sequence in which they must be undertaken and completed across the page to a finish node on the right-hand side. Each activity or node in the network, apart from the start node, therefore has one or more predecessors – that is an arrow or arrows coming into it from activities that must be finished before it can be started. Similarly, each node except for the finish node has at least one successor – an arrow from it to the subsequent task or tasks. A number of methods for describing the links between changes and benefits, for example, 'results chains' (Thorp, 2003) are based on the PDM technique.

The benefits dependency network, as shown in Figure 4.4, has a similar form to a completed PDM network. The desired finish is the achievement of the investment objectives and delivery of the associated benefits, which are therefore shown on the right-hand side of the diagram. The necessary steps required to achieve these, that is, the business and enabling changes, are shown on the left-hand side of the network. However, a significant difference between benefits dependency and PDM networks is the order in which the elements are identified. In the latter, having identified the desired outcome and key activities for a project, a network is usually built up from the start to the finish, that is from left to right. In the benefits network, as just described, the network is built up from right to left. The investment objectives are agreed and these are used to identify the specific benefits that might be expected. Consideration of each of the benefits or benefit streams is then undertaken in order to identify the necessary business and enabling changes and the required IS/IT. Joining up the network will be discussed further later, but having derived the network from right to left, implementation will tend to occur from left to right, although some activities may be started before earlier ones are complete. The project activity will commence with the purchase or development of the necessary IS/IT and by undertaking the enabling changes that are the prerequisites to making the enduring business changes happen.

Joining Up the Network: Highlighting Dependencies

The dependency network diagram in Figure 4.4 shows each investment objective giving rise to one or more benefits. Hence arrows are drawn from the objectives to the benefits. As discussed earlier, implementation will tend to occur from left to right, with the IS/IT, enabling and business changes required before benefits can be realized. These are therefore connected with arrows from left to right.

The network can be joined up as it is being produced. That is, each objective could be considered in turn and the benefits that would arise from its achievement, the required business and enabling changes and the necessary IS/IT could be identified, before moving on to consideration of the next objective and its associated benefits and changes. Alternatively the benefits arising from all the investment objectives are identified before moving on to consider how individuals and groups within the organization would have to change their working practices, in relation to the set of benefits and the enablers for the range of changes. Having identified these major building blocks of benefits and changes, they can be connected up as shown in Figure 4.4. In this approach, the connecting-up process can be used as a sense or completeness check of the changes and benefits identified.

Box 4.1 describes the derivation of a benefits dependency network for an investment that will improve the booking of patient appointments in the healthcare sector.

Box 4.1 'Choose and Book' in public healthcare

At over £6billion, the National Health Service (NHS) in the UK is currently undertaking what has been estimated to be the largest civilian investments in IT (NHS, 2005). 'Connecting for Health', as it is being called, has a number of strands of activity: a centrally managed email and directory service for all organizations in the NHS; the provision of an electronic health record for all citizens; the use of IT to improve prescribing; systems to capture and distribute medical images; and the ability of patients to choose a date and time for appointments.

This last strand of the programme, which has been termed 'Choose and Book', was discussed in Chapter 1. The intention is that patients whose doctor has referred them to their local hospital for a consultation, a therapy or a diagnostic test, such as an X-ray examination, should be able to choose a date and time for that appointment that is convenient to them (www.chooseandbook.nhs.uk). Currently, when a patient requires an X-ray or similar procedure, their GP sends a letter of request to the local hospital, which will send the patient an appointment. Consequently, many hospitals are left with wasted appointment slots, since when patients find their date or time inconvenient they fail to attend or to inform the hospital in time for the appointment to be given to another patient. With the system that is being developed, either the doctor will book an appointment during the patient consultation or the patient will book the appointment themselves, either by telephone or online. It is expected that by allowing the patient to select the date and time of the appointment, the number of wasted slots, called 'DNAs' (did not attends) will be significantly reduced.

A simplified benefits dependency network for the project is shown in Figure 4.5. A number of benefits are indicated, including improved patient experience, a reduced unit cost per X-ray due to the reduction of DNAs and cost savings for both GPs and hospitals since there would no longer be a requirement for referral and appointment letters. If the system can also be used to transmit the results of tests back to GPs and to update the patient record, then additional benefits can be expected. For example, the requesting doctor can know the results of the X-ray sooner, and hence cause treatment or follow-up tests to be instigated more quickly. Also, by recording all of the X-rays given to a certain patient, the system will ensure that radiological guidelines on exposure are not exceeded, improving the quality of the service offered by the X-ray department.

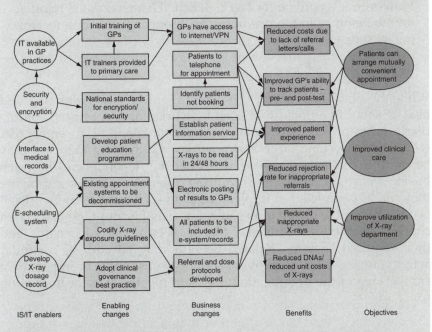

Figure 4.5 *Benefits dependency for 'Choose and Book' project*

The network shows a simplified set of the necessary changes and the supporting IS/IT. These changes involve not only staff within the radiology department, or even within the hospital, but are reliant on external parties, such as GPs and patients. Without these being prepared or being encouraged to undertake the necessary changes, then it can be seen that the majority of the benefits expected will not be realized.

It also shows that certain benefits rely on resources or capabilities outside the project. For example, with many tests such as X-rays, it is not only having the test procedure completed that is important, but it is having those results interpreted by a relevant expert to generate a report. While electronic transmission back to the referring physician may reduce the delays associated with the handling of paper-based reports, these delays may be trivial compared to those introduced in the process if there is a

Box 4.1 (Continued)

shortage of experts to generate reports. Our example therefore
shows the need to reduce the time for reporting to 24 or 48 hours.
However, it would be for any individual hospital developing its
own benefits plan to consider what reporting period is feasible
for its staff.

While the simplified network shown in Figure 4.5 looks compact and
neat, it should be noted that such networks for real projects, particularly large projects that span multiple functions of an enterprise,
will tend to become large and complex. Connecting them up may
be quite a challenge as there will often be dependencies between
business changes, with some requiring other changes to occur before
they can be completed or implemented. In such complex networks, it
is often helpful to group or organize the benefits and their associated
changes into 'benefit streams', that is, sets of related benefits and
their required changes. Related benefits may all address a similar
activity, for example, improving service to customers or impact on a
similar area of the organization, for example, the sales or marketing
function.

Definition: Benefit streams

A set of related benefits and their associated business and
enabling changes and enabling IS/IT.

The most important rationale for joining up the network is to understand the dependencies between the identified changes and the realization of benefits. The linkages show that a given benefit will only be
realized if the connected changes are successfully achieved. Considering each benefit, it is worth asking 'is this benefit significant enough
for us to make the associated changes?'. Measuring and quantifying
benefits and assessing their importance are discussed in Chapter 5,
where the issue of building a business case is addressed. However,
even at this early stage of exploring a project, it is often known
which benefits are essential to realising the maximum value from
the investment.

Conversely, consideration may begin with the nature of the changes identified on the network. If a change is seen to be particularly challenging, for example, something the organization has tried many times in the past but has not achieved, then how can it expect to be successful this time? If any change on which a benefit is dependent is seen to be unachievable or highly problematic, then that benefit should be removed from the network. The issue of investment risk for projects is considered more fully in Chapter 5, however, it can be seen that the explicit recognition of the dependency between organizational changes and the realization of business benefits is an aspect of risk analysis for the project.

Measurement and Ownership

Having developed a first version of the benefits dependency network, including considering the achievability of the required changes, it is necessary to add further information, to each of the benefits and changes, to complete it. These additions are intended to examine further how feasible the project is and ensure that the benefits can be realized from the investment.

Each benefit should be considered in turn and two important aspects identified. First, it should be considered whether the benefit could be measured. Before undertaking the often significant work involved in producing a robust and well-founded business case, it is worthwhile at this stage specifying how individual benefits might be measured. This will also often improve the clarity or precision about what was meant by a particular benefit. For example, a benefit may have been expressed simply as 'increased sales'. However, in considering how this might be measured, it may become apparent that sales are likely to increase for a number of reasons. It would then be realized that the measure should not be 'increase in all sales', but only the sales increase that can be attributed directly to the investment in question, for example, sales of a new service or to a new customer group or in a new geographic market. Consideration of measurement of the benefit would therefore lead to a more precise wording of the benefit as appropriate, for example; 'increased sales of new service line' or 'increased sales to younger age group'.

Second, each benefit should have an owner assigned to it. A benefit owner should ideally be an individual who gains the advantage inherent in the stated benefit and therefore is willing to work with the project team, either personally or through the resources and influence that he or she has, to ensure that the benefit is realized.

> ### Definition: Benefit owner
>
> An individual or group who will gain advantage from a business benefit and who will work with the project team to ensure that benefit is realized.

As will be discussed later, the benefit owner cannot necessarily be described as 'making the benefit happen' or 'being responsible for realizing the benefit', since the changes necessary to deliver the benefit may need to be undertaken by others outside his or her sphere of control or influence. These are termed change owners and are also discussed later.

While it is preferable to have an individual owner for a benefit, it may be appropriate to have more than one. For example, if an expected benefit from a particular investment has been identified as 'increased sales of a new product' and the organization is divided into three regional sales operations, then the three regional sales managers or directors should be named as the benefit owners. Although organizational structures might make it necessary to identify more than one benefit owner, large groups should not be named as benefit owners. For example, if the deployment of a new system containing complete product information were being considered in a call centre, it would no doubt provide benefits to the call centre staff, since they would have better information with which to answer customer enquiries. However, rather than cite the many call centre staff, the benefit owner should be specified as the call centre manager or other individual who was directly responsible for the operation of the centre.

Citing large groups of individuals as benefit owners has the risk that, if they have to make decisions to enable the benefit's delivery, they are unlikely to have much influence on others in the organization. Obtaining agreement from everyone in the group, especially if they have varied opinions, will also be difficult. While such large groups of staff should not be named as benefit owners, their views of the project, particularly 'what is in it for them' and how will they be affected by the required changes, is critical to realizing the benefits and should be expressly addressed. How the views of such stakeholder groups can be explored and addressed is discussed in Chapter 6.

In addition to identifying measures for the benefits, measures or 'evidence of achievement' that can demonstrate that the required business and enabling changes have been successfully made should be established. Once again, considering how the achievement of each change could be assessed is likely to cause more careful consideration of what is meant by the change and particularly how critical its successful completion is to realizing the levels of improvement associated with the dependent benefits. For example, one enabling change identified in many networks is that of 'training users on the new system'. In considering how the achievement of this should be measured, there is a range of alternatives, both to measures, but also to how the training is provided. Is it sufficient to offer training courses, so that people who believe they require it can attend? Or is it important that everyone is trained how to use the system and attending the course is mandatory? It would then be important to measure the number of staff involved who did not attend the training. It would be better still to measure how effective the training was in terms of the ability of individuals to use the full functionality of the new system thereafter. In which case some evaluation of how well individuals have acquired the necessary skills and knowledge at the end of the training, and perhaps how well this has been retained after a few months, should be set up.

It is also necessary to identify change owners, named individuals or groups who will be responsible for making each of the identified changes happen successfully.

> **Definition: Change owner**
>
> An individual or group who will ensure that a business or enabling change identified is successfully achieved.

The change owner should be the named individual, or people in a specific role, in whose area of responsibility the identified change resides. The change owners may not be personally responsible for making the changes, but are accountable for the changes being effected successfully. They therefore must be committed to the project to dedicate sufficient personal time and knowledge to planning and managing the changes and influential enough to ensure the necessary resources are made available to carry out the changes. As with the benefit owners, it is preferable to have a single individual named as the change owner, otherwise, if problems arise in achieving a given change, the responsibility for resolving them may become unclear.

The addition of benefit owners and measures, and the responsibilities for changes and the evidence of their achievement to a benefits dependency network is shown in Figure 4.6.

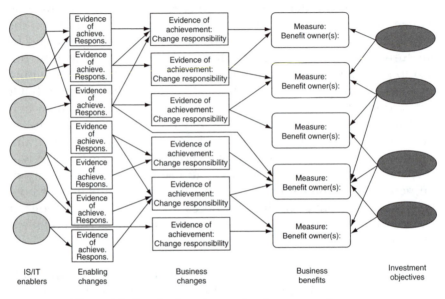

Figure 4.6   *Benefits dependency network: owners and managers*

The Nature of Benefit and Change Ownership

In the case of change owners, those named should be senior or influential enough to ensure the change identified will be achieved successfully and when needed in the project plan. If it is necessary to name a very senior person, it can be reasonably assumed that they will not have day-to-day involvement in making the change happen and this will be delegated to others. However, if difficulties are encountered in successfully achieving the change, then the change owner will use their resources or influence to ensure they are addressed and, if possible, overcome.

While the benefit owners are not necessarily required to be responsible for the changes, their involvement in the project should be active rather than passive. They should work closely with those who are managing the changes, to address any issues that might cause uncertainty about achieving the benefits and they should use their knowledge and, where necessary, resources, to help resolve the problems. The benefit owner should therefore also be senior or influential enough to ensure that others understand and carry out their responsibilities in the project.

Although benefit and change owners should be senior enough to address any difficulties arising in the project, this does not mean that ownership should always be escalated to very senior levels. Usually, smaller investments that are confined to one or two areas of the organization can have middle managers as both benefit and change owners. However, in large projects, almost inevitably, changes have to be coordinated across a number of business functions or processes and the involvement of more senior managers is often required.

One test that should be applied to all benefit and change owners is their interest and perceived commitment to the project. As is discussed further later, the tools and frameworks discussed in this chapter should not be used by an individual or the project team working in isolation. They should be used to facilitate knowledge sharing and agreement between the project team and project stakeholders, including those who are likely to be responsible for the changes and benefits expected. The role of benefit and change owner should not then be a responsibility that is 'awarded' to someone who has not been involved but should be a role that the appropriate individuals nominate themselves for. A lack of willingness to take on the responsibilities probably suggests a lack of interest or commitment to the project. Lack of interest by a number of the identified change or benefit owners, especially of the more critical changes or most significant benefits, should make an organization question whether the investment is actually still worth pursuing.

Project Team and Operational Staff as Owners

By definition the benefits identified in a network are those that are expected in the future operations of the organization and should therefore be owned by business managers and staff rather than dedicated project staff. Similarly, the business changes are those that are required to the processes and practices of the organization and therefore responsibility for achieving those changes must also rest with operational managers.

Organizations can adopt essentially two different approaches to organizing and resourcing projects. Some assemble project teams by assigning or seconding staff on a full-time basis for the duration of the project. This approach is often adopted for large or business critical projects or where specialist knowledge or skills are required. It enables projects to be undertaken quickly, but it can cause the project to become isolated from the realities of practical issues affecting how the organization works and can leave operational staff feeling that the new system and changes have been 'done to them'. Projects involving a significant number of external consultants or contractors are particularly prone to developing a life of their own, leading to a lack of buy-in by line managers and staff.

The alternative approach is to ask operational staff to undertake the project alongside, and in addition to, their existing responsibilities. Such teams are often supported by a number of dedicated staff, such as IT specialists and a programme manager. This has the advantage that the project should remain closely aligned with the operations of the organization, but it has the downside that it is likely to take longer and coordination of activities is more complex, as staff have to balance the project priorities with the need to 'keep the shop open'.

These two different approaches will result in different patterns of ownership of benefits and changes on the dependency network. In the former case where there is a dedicated project team, the individuals in that team should only feature on the network as being responsible for some of the enabling changes. In the latter case, members of the project team who also have ongoing operational responsibilities can take responsibility for both enabling and business changes and business benefits. However, any dedicated staff in such teams can still only take responsibility for enabling changes.

Recognizing where ownership by different individuals on the network is appropriate and, in particular, understanding the limited responsibilities of dedicated project staff is important. Many organizations wish to ensure good performance from project teams, recognizing that the projects are often critical to the future of the organization. They therefore try to incentivize the team by making them responsible for the delivery of benefits from the project. However, benefits from IT are only likely to be realized from the changes to everyday operations and activities and project staff can rarely be responsible for achieving such changes.

An appreciation of appropriate ownership of benefits and changes is also important for the structuring of agreements with software suppliers or consultancy firms, especially with the risk-sharing agreements that are often being adopted in the public sector. In large or complex projects, organizations may wish to incentivize or share risks with external suppliers or partners. They are therefore increasingly seeking to make these external organizations responsible for the benefits, invoking financial or other penalties if the required benefits are not delivered. However, as in the case of in-house projects, the realization of benefits from IT is dependent on the achievement of changes within the organization, which, again, can rarely be the responsibility of external parties. They can, of course, be held responsible for the on-time and on-budget delivery of the technology and other enabling activities, such as training or the redesign of business processes. However, they cannot, for example, ensure the effective ongoing operation of those new processes, which is the responsibility of the operational staff within the organization. The use of the benefits management tools in different contexts, including that of risk-sharing projects such as the private finance initiatives (PFI) in public sector projects is discussed in Chapter 8.

A Balance of Benefit and Change Owners

Having identified owners for each benefit and change in the network, as shown in Figure 4.6, it is then important to understand the balance and relationships between the those responsible for or affected by the changes and those receiving benefits. If different names appear on the left-hand side of the network from those on the right, it should be considered whether those individuals will be prepared to lead the changes required, if they are going to receive little or no benefit. This can be a significant issue in some projects and it needs to be addressed as early as possible, otherwise it can lead to difficulties later. How this is best done will depend on how well the drivers and investment objectives are understood and accepted by all the stakeholders. If those responsible for actually undertaking the changes support what the organization is trying to achieve and have been consulted regarding how this can best be done, they are more likely to agree to make the necessary changes. Their cooperation may also be dependent on their involvement in other ongoing or planned projects. If they appreciate that others will receive major benefits from this project, but other projects are being undertaken that, in turn, will provide them with benefits, they can be expected to be more cooperative. The impact of the balance of changes required to benefits realized, forms an important part of stakeholder analysis and is discussed in Chapter 6.

An alternative approach to dealing with an imbalance between the benefit and change owners is to consider if the project can be restructured or rescoped, in order to provide those who have to change for the benefit of others with some benefits from the project. It may be necessary to forego some of the benefits, if it is considered that those individuals or groups identified on the left-hand side of the network will not be willing or able to make the necessary changes. Obviously this trade-off will depend on the significance of a particular benefit to the organization.

Benefit and Change Templates

While the benefits dependency network is the recommended means of exploring the linkages between the realization of benefits and the need for change, the resulting networks can become very large and difficult to read. It is therefore suggested that, after a network has been agreed, the information and logic it contains is transferred to a more straightforward layout, where more detail can be added to begin to develop the benefits plan. It is suggested that the formats shown in Table 4.4 are adopted. One should be used for benefits, referred to as the *benefit template*, and the other for changes, termed the *change template*.

In the case of the benefit template, each benefit identified on the benefits dependency network should be entered in a new row in the first column. The intention is then to set out for each of the benefits, its owner and the changes on which it is dependent. Similarly, a change template identifies the required change, whether it is an enabling or business change, who is responsible for ensuring the change occurs and any other changes on which it is dependent. It is advisable to develop a coding system to number the benefits and changes in order to retain the links defined on the network.

Additional information, to complete the templates, which will result from considering issues such as type of benefit, expected value, resourcing the changes and the timing of the realization of benefits, is discussed in Chapters 5 and 6. Examples of use of the benefit and change templates are given in the worked example at the end of this chapter.

Table 4.4   *Benefit and change templates*

Benefit number and type and related objectives	Benefit description	Benefit owner(s)	Dependent changes and responsibilities	Measures	Expected value (if applicable)	Due date

Change or enabler number and dependent benefits	Description	Responsibility *(and involvement)*	Prerequisite or consequent changes	Evidence of completion	Due date	Resources required

Worked Example: Improved Control within a Food-Processing Organization

Background

FoodCo is a medium sized business based in the UK that prepares fresh vegetables for sale in supermarkets and use in the catering and food service industry. In addition to its state-of-the-art food preparation facilities, it owns farms where it grows much of the raw materials that are included in its products. The firm is therefore a vertically integrated producer with control from the field to the consumer's plate, which is important to an industry where safety and traceability are essential. FoodCo provides its customers with the ability to quickly trace ingredients through the process. In addition to its own farms, vegetables are bought from other growers in the UK and Europe. Only accredited suppliers are used and regular audits are undertaken to ensure that they are fully compliant with all legislation and industry codes of practice.

The firm sells its products to the leading supermarkets in the UK, particularly in the area of 'own-label' salads. It also sells via wholesalers to independent retailers, and raw ingredients to sandwich and ready meal manufacturers and to caterers. Sales are also increasingly being made in Europe. Innovation is a critical area for the food industry and FoodCo undertakes regular marketing and consumer research as part of its ongoing new product development activity.

The Challenge: Rapid Sales Growth

In the late 1990s and early 2000, the firm was undergoing unprecedented growth in sales revenues. An interest in healthy eating and eating out was being witnessed in the UK and across Europe and the high quality and fresh products of FoodCo were ideally suited to take advantage of these trends. However, despite this growth in sales, the profitability of the organization was falling. The problem was seen to be lack of control of both direct and indirect costs.

The fresh food sector has a number of challenges. While cool-storage facilities can prolong the life of many products, they cannot be stored indefinitely. There is therefore a degree of waste that must be minimized. Pricing for goods bought and products sold is also complex. Prices agreed with customers for produce are influenced by the availability of supply, which is affected by factors such as the weather and alternative demands for the underlying raw materials. Coupled to this, all food products and ingredients must be traceable throughout processing from the consumer's plate back to the original growers.

These challenges were putting pressure on the operating and administrative processes of the firm, some of which were known to be inefficient and complex. Problems were exacerbated by delays in information availability and the difficulties in reconciling information from the piecemeal systems the organization was relying on. When production volumes were more modest and less of the raw materials came from independent growers, problems due to the use of distinct, non-integrated, systems could be tolerated. However, as the scale of the operation grew more rapidly, the effects of those inefficiencies and delays had grown disproportionately, reducing the profitability of the organization. The need to overcome these problems and improve both the control and integration of the core processes and the accuracy of information within the organization was recognized. A major project was initiated to review the operational and administrative processes and systems.

Driver Analysis

The project commenced by directors and managers from key areas of the business, together with relevant IT staff and other specialists, attending a workshop to identify and agree the objectives for the investment. They also sought to derive an initial benefits dependency network for the benefits they expected to obtain and the changes to working practices required to achieve them. As a first step, the 'dimensions of competence' model was used to assess and agree the drivers acting on the organization. The diagram shown in Figure 4.7 was generated.

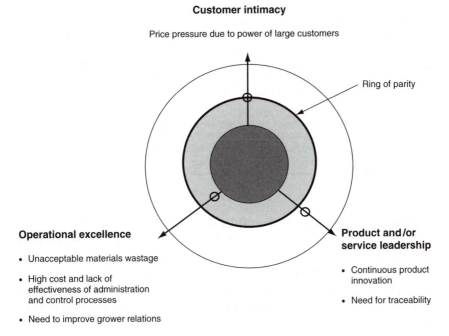

Customer intimacy

Price pressure due to power of large customers

Ring of parity

Operational excellence

- Unacceptable materials wastage
- High cost and lack of effectiveness of administration and control processes
- Need to improve grower relations

Product and/or service leadership

- Continuous product innovation
- Need for traceability

Figure 4.7   Dimensions of competence for FoodCo

A fuller description of each of the identified drivers is given in Table 4.5.

It can be seen that there were drivers acting on the organization both from the external environment and from within the organization itself. The demand by consumers for a continuous stream of new and exciting products, the pressures from regulators and public agencies for improved food handling and particularly the traceability of all ingredients and the power of the large supermarket chains all represented external drivers on the organization that needed to

Table 4.5 Drivers acting on FoodCo

Drivers	
Customer intimacy	
Power of large customers – significant price pressure	Supermarket sector is highly consolidated resulting in considerable power of key customers. Significant pressure on prices
Product and service excellence	
Continuous product innovation	Continuous demand from customers (and end consumers) for new product introductions including new packaging formats
Need for traceability	Regulation requires ability to trace product back from consumer's plate though processing to farmer's field
Operational excellence	
Unacceptable materials wastage	Perishable nature of products requires accurate matching of orders to sourcing of raw materials
High cost and lack of effectiveness of administration and control processes	Administration and control systems seen to be inefficient with many disparate systems causing delays, errors and reconciliation failures to occur in key processes
Improving grower relations	Keen to maintain good relationships with best growers. Access to high quality raw materials is a key contributor to quality of final product. Good relations with suppliers are key to maintaining supply in times of shortage

be understood, interpreted and addressed. However, the key area of weakness that required improvement immediately was agreed to be the lack of effectiveness of their internal operations. In particular, it was recognized that there was an unacceptably high degree of wastage of materials and that the administration and control processes within the organization were both inefficient and fragmented, leading to delays and errors.

Although the firm grew many of its raw materials, an increasing its proportion was being sourced from other growers and this trend would continue. The payment structure to these growers was very complicated, having a fixed price element but also a variable element that was calculated on the yield achieved from the materials and the price obtained from the final customer. The complexity of these payments was adding to the administrative burden on the organization. Payments to growers were often late, and sometimes incorrect, causing a souring of relations with some growers. These problems were all contributing to increasing costs within the business, to the extent that despite the unprecedented growth in sales volume and value, the organization was experiencing falling profitability.

The Investment: Regaining Control of the Business

The recognition that the administrative and control processes within the organization were no longer sufficient caused the team to consider the deployment of an integrated enterprise resource planning (ERP) system. Such systems can provide administrative efficiencies and improve control by providing an integrated set of applications for the core processes of an organization. Modules for activities such as order entry, production scheduling, inventory control, shipping and transport and providing after-sales service can be implemented, together with applications that carry out and manage activities such as the general ledger, supplier and customer accounts and payroll. In addition, real-time management information can be extracted from the systems to improve decision making at all levels.

While it was expected that part of the solution to their problems would be found in a new information system, it was recognized that this would not be sufficient in itself and that considerable change to how individuals and groups within the organization were currently operating would be required if the desired improvements were to be realized. It should also be stressed that buying and implementing a complete ERP suite was not a foregone conclusion. Such suites contain many applications or modules, some of which may be of little relevance or benefit to a particular organization or require too much or risky organizational change to deliver the benefits. To quote Davenport (2000): *'Successful implementation of ERP involves probably the greatest technological change most organisations have ever undergone . . . even more difficult, and important, however, are the major changes in business that come with an ERP project'*.

The approach discussed earlier in this chapter, of working back from the desired objectives and benefits, through the business changes, to the specific applications or modules required was adopted to ensure the 'minimum IS/IT to do the job' was identified.

Identifying Investment Objectives

Based on the drivers acting on the organization, it was important to focus on a comprehensive but achievable set of improvements that would directly address the issues identified. After much discussion, three investment objectives for the ERP project were agreed:

- to simplify and automate all business transactions
- to integrate key processes and systems
- to improve the financial control of business assets and resources.

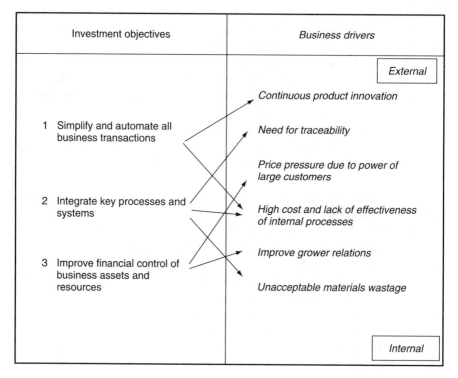

Figure 4.8   *Linking investment objectives and drivers at FoodCo*

The linkages between the agreed investment objectives and the drivers are shown in Figure 4.8. Simplifying and automating business processes would improve the effectiveness and reduce the costs per transaction of those processes. It would also provide more accurate information about activity costs and improve decision making for new product developments. Integration of separate processes and systems would improve performance by creating streamlined, simpler processes and also reduce data collection and information reconciliation costs. Integration would also help provide the required traceability for all products and reduce the levels of wastage being experienced. Finally, improved financial control would allow the organization to negotiate more effectively with its large customers to achieve an acceptable margin on its products. It would also impact positively on the payments made to growers. Being able to make these payments on time, with guaranteed accuracy, would improve relations with the independent growers.

Developing a Benefits Dependency Network

Having agreed the investment objectives, managers of the various business processes and functions set about identifying the particular benefits they should realize if the agreed objectives were met and, equally importantly, the changes to working practices that would be needed. The benefits dependency network developed is shown Figure 4.9.

It can be seen that the first objective, to simplify and automate key processes gave rise to a number of benefits. However, achieving the second objective, when processes were integrated across production, stock control and order fulfilment, would deliver the most significant benefits. Improved financial control would also give rise to a number of distinct benefits both to FoodCo and its key suppliers, the independent growers.

Similarly to the pattern of benefits, the changes needed to improve individual or discrete processes were fairly well contained and simple. For example, the physical scanning of goods currently utilized during manufacturing should be extended to dispatch in order to reduce dispatch and invoice errors. However, integration of the processes spanning the organization, from the sourcing of raw materials, through production to sales, required a more extensive and interrelated set of changes. At the centre of these changes was the need to develop and implement a new planning process, that could draw real-time information from all points in the organization to provide improved production scheduling, both in terms of resource use and changes in customer orders. An enabling change that was seen as essential to make this possible was to reduce the degree of local discretion in production planning, thus ensuring decisions could be coordinated across all stages of production.

Another key area of change concerned the key performance indicators (KPIs) used to manage the business. The automation of the new processes would produce accurate and timely information that could be used to monitor the most critical and sensitive aspects of business

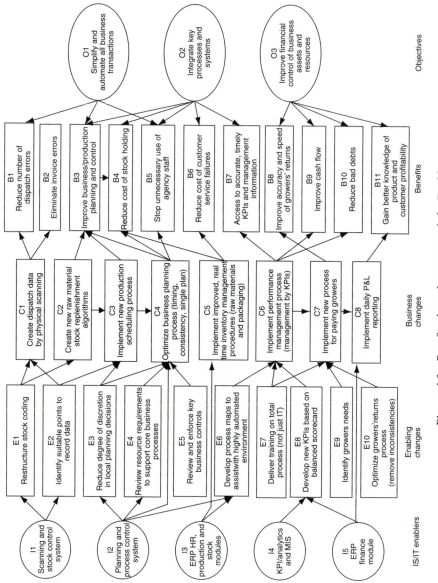

Figure 4.9 Benefits dependency network for FoodCo

performance, that is those that had the most immediate or significant effects on sales or costs. However, simply being able to produce the figures quickly and frequently would not ensure that they were effectively used – to ensure the benefits of having the information would be realized, a number of business and enabling changes had to be made. First, those indicators that most accurately reflected the level of performance and overall financial health of the organization, and which required management actions to control, had to be identified. Having done this it was necessary to define and implement new processes to ensure the identified KPI information was disseminated to the relevant managers and also that they were able to understand the implications and take prompt action to address any unacceptable variances in performance.

Having identified the expected benefits and the necessary changes, the underlying IS and IT functionality was identified. This was specified as key modules or components, thus allowing flexibility in the choice of solutions, that is, purchase of a complete ERP suite or the selection of independent systems in a 'best-of-breed' approach.

Adding Benefit and Change Owners

Having developed the network, ownership of the benefits and changes was agreed as shown in Figure 4.10. As discussed earlier in this chapter, rather than assign or delegate these to individuals who were not present at the workshop, the roles shown were those of the people who had participated in developing the network. This involvement not only helped to demonstrate their commitment to the project, but also ensured that the desired benefits and necessary changes were derived from a thorough and relevant understanding of actual business operations.

Figure 4.10 shows a good balance of responsibilities across the benefit and change parts of the network. Those who were responsible for making significant changes, in most cases, also received benefits. Although this suggests that the people involved should be willing to actively engage in the project, it was necessary to carry out a full stakeholder analysis to ensure the views of the production and other operational and administrative staff, as well as external parties, such as the growers, could be understood to prevent unexpected problems arising during implementation. This is discussed in Chapter 6.

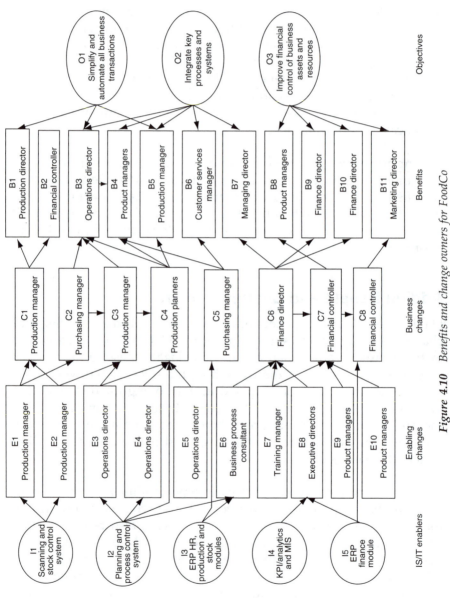

Figure 4.10 *Benefits and change owners for FoodCo*

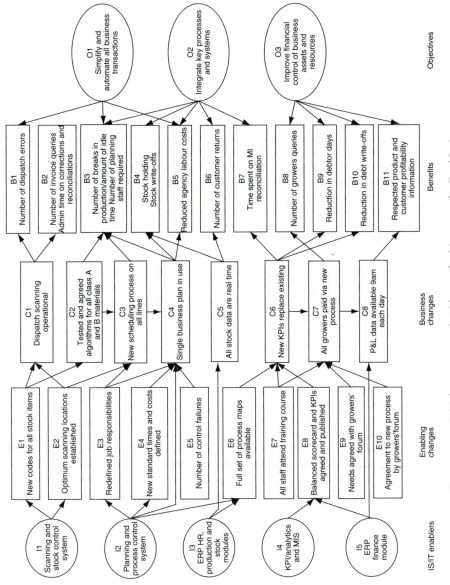

Figure 4.11 *Initial measures and evidence of achievement for FoodCo investment*

IS/IT enablers	Enabling changes	Business changes	Benefits	Objectives

IS/IT enablers

I1 Scanning and stock control system

I2 Planning and process control system

I3 ERP HR, production and stock modules

I4 KPI/analytics and MIS

I5 ERP finance module

Enabling changes

E1 New codes for all stock items

E2 Optimum scanning locations established

E3 Redefined job responsibilities

E4 New standard times and costs defined

E5 Number of control failures

E6 Full set of process maps available

E7 All staff attend training course

E8 Balanced scorecard and KPIs agreed and published

E9 Needs agreed with growers' forum

E10 Agreement to new process by growers'forum

Business changes

C1 Dispatch scanning operational

C2 Tested and agreed algorithms for all class A and B materials

C3 New scheduling process on all lines

C4 Single business plan in use

C5 All stock data are real time

C6 New KPIs replace existing

C7 All growers paid via new process

C8 P&L data available 9am each day

Benefits

B1 Number of dispatch errors

B2 Number of invoice queries Admin time on corrections and reconciliations

B3 Number of breaks in production/amount of idle time Number of planning staff required

B4 Stock holding Stock write-offs

B5 Reduced agency labour costs

B6 Number of customer returns

B7 Time spent on MI reconciliation

B8 Number of growers queries

B9 Reduction in debtor days

B10 Reduction in debt write-offs

B11 Respected product and customer profitability information

Objectives

O1 Simplify and automate all business transactions

O2 Integrate key processes and systems

O3 Improve financial control of business assets and resources

Table 4.6 Partially completed benefit template

Benefit number and type and related objectives	Benefit description	Benefit owner(s)	Dependent changes and responsibilities	Measures	Expected value (if applicable)	Due date
B2: Financial: O1	Eliminate invoice errors	Financial Controller	C1 – Production Manager	1 Customer invoice queries 2 Admin time on corrections and reconciliations		
B4: Financial: O2	Reduced costs of stock holding – including inventory reductions	Product Managers	C4 – Production Planners C5 – Purchasing Manager E3, E4 and E5 – Operations Director	1 Stock holding by product type for: (a) (RM) raw materials (b) packaging 2 Number of stock write-offs		

Table 4.7 Partially completed change template

Change or enabler number and dependent benefits	Description	Responsibility (and *involvement*)	Prerequisite (P) or consequent (C) changes	Evidence of completion	Due date	Resources required
E8 B7, B9 and B10	Develop new KPIs based on Balanced Score Card	Executive Directors	P: None C: C6 Implement performance management process	Balanced Score Card & KPIs agreed by board and published		
C2 B3, B4	Implement new raw material stock replenishment algorithms	Purchasing Manager and *Product Managers*	P: E1 Restructure stock coding C: None	Tested and agreed algorithms for all A and B class materials		

Adding Measures and Evidence of Achievement to the Network

While adding owners of benefits and changes to the network, it is important to determine a measure for each of the benefits and define how the achievement of each change will be assessed. The initial measures identified by FoodCo are shown on the benefits dependency network in Figure 4.11. As can be seen in some cases, to help demonstrate that improvements in performance are due to the new investment and have not occurred for other reasons, it is often helpful to define two or more measures for benefits or changes. The importance and implications of selecting appropriate measures are discussed in detail in Chapter 5.

Benefit and Change Templates

Partially completed benefit and change templates for the FoodCo example are shown in Tables 4.6 and 4.7 respectively. The tables can be completed after the business case described in Chapter 5 has been produced and the stakeholder analysis described in Chapter 6 has been undertaken. Each table shows just two benefits or changes, but similar details should be provided for all the identified benefits and changes.

Summary

This chapter has presented some of the key tools and frameworks used in the benefits management process. Additional tools will be presented in later chapters in the book. As stated earlier, the primary use of these tools is to identify and explore the expected benefits from a particular investment and the feasibility of achieving them, by understanding the changes to organizational structures, processes and working practices that will be required to realize those benefits. If the investment looks viable after a first pass at linking it to the drivers acting on the organization, and having generated an initial benefits dependency network, then more work can be carried out to develop a more complete and accurate network. Such work should include a more detailed statement of each of the benefits and necessary changes, including estimates of timescales required for the latter, identification of the owners for all benefits and changes and a clear statement of how the achievement of each of these can be measured or assessed. If the investment is significant and involves a large number of changes to different areas of the business, then the development of a complete network may take some time and resources to complete. However, getting it right at this early stage can avoid misunderstandings later in the project about what has to be done, by whom, to succeed with the investment. It is therefore important to ensure that all the key stakeholders are involved in creating the network.

This additional work is also essential to the development of a business case and benefits plan for the investment, which is described in Chapter 5. At the same time, for most projects, it is valuable to carry out a comprehensive stakeholder analysis, which considers the investment and change programme from the perspectives of the different stakeholders. This analysis, which is discussed in Chapter 6, will shed further light on how achievable each of the changes involved in the project is, and may lead to further actions to overcome any particular stakeholder issues that could prevent the benefits from being realized.

While developing the benefits dependency network is the starting point for examining the attractiveness and viability of investments, it is also essential to the last three stages of the benefits management process: execution of the benefits plan, review and the identification of further benefits. The changes identified on the network will form the main work packages that are to be undertaken as part of the execution or implementation phase of the project. These work packages can be specified in as much additional detail as is required to ensure their achievement and then incorporated in standard project management methodologies, such as PRINCE2. The timing of each work package will depend on any dependencies identified on the network or any resource or other constraints identified by the project management methodology. Identified owners, particularly change owners, should be involved in the planning of the work packages relevant to their change activities.

The network should be updated during the execution phase of the project. If it emerges that some of the necessary changes have become difficult or impossible to achieve, the potential impact on the realization of the dependent benefits should be assessed. Equally, if some of the benefits become irrelevant or unavailable, due to changing business circumstances, it may make some of the changes unnecessary.

When problems or other factors affecting the benefits plan arise, both those responsible for the changes and the owners of the relevant benefits should decide together what action can and should be taken.

The updated network will eventually form the baseline for the benefits review of the investment. Benefits realized can be compared to those that were expected. Where benefits have not been realized, then the associated changes can be considered and action taken to address these where they have not been achieved, if that is still possible. Finally, the network can also be used to identify the potential for further benefits. It may be that having resolved some business problems or removed constraints, further benefits are now visible. These can be the starting point for a further iteration of the process by identifying the types of change and, if necessary, the additional IS/IT functionality needed to achieve them. Alternatively, it is possible at this stage to start at different places in the network and 'build outwards from here'. For example, having successfully realized benefits from the implementation of a number of the ERP application modules, our example firm, FoodCo, might consider the additional modules that are available and evaluate whether the potential benefits they offer are now relevant and significant enough to justify further changes to working practices. The effective management of benefit reviews and the identification of further benefits are discussed more fully in Chapter 7.

5
Building the Business Case

Traditionally, the main purpose in developing a business case for an IS/IT project has been to obtain funding for a significant financial investment. However, in the context of this book and the realization of business benefits from the implementation of new systems and technology, the term 'business case' has a wider meaning. One aspect of the business case is to provide information to decide whether or not to make the financial investment, but it should also enable the organization to plan and manage the project to a successful conclusion, such that the benefits which underpin the rationale for both the IS/IT investment and the business changes are achieved.

The term 'business case' also implies that it is more than a financial justification for investment. The latter relies on identifying explicit, relatively short-term, performance improvements that will be achieved and excludes consideration of benefits that cannot be interpreted financially. While this may have been appropriate when the vast majority of benefits were accrued from efficiencies resulting from automation of clerical tasks, the integral and often critical role IS/IT plays in organizations today means that such a limited view will preclude the realization of many available benefits. These additional benefits are often associated with the term 'capability'. That is, the technology enables the organization to be able to change and evolve over the longer term to achieve its strategic aims and create new opportunities. The business case therefore has to include, where appropriate, arguments that define how it contributes to enhancing existing capabilities or creating new ones (Ross and Beath, 2002).

As described in earlier chapters, it is the complementary investments an organization makes in changes to the way business is performed and resources are deployed that deliver the majority of benefits from IS/IT. It has been shown that the level of complementary investment required to fully exploit IS/IT assets is often five times the cost of the technology itself (Brynjolfsson and Hitt, 2000). Apart from IT infrastructure investments, which only create IT assets, the business case is therefore really concerned with justifying an IT-enabled business change project. In the case of infrastructure, studies have shown that organizations that adopt a longer term strategic view of the capabilities that it creates can not only ensure that lack of investment does not inhibit business development but they also have to invest less overall, relative to those who adopt a more piecemeal, reactive investment approach (Broadbent et al., 1999). Making the business case for infrastructure investments has long been problematic and this chapter concentrates on application investments, i.e. those that deliver explicit business benefits through a combination of IS/IT and business activity changes. How the overall benefits management approach, including the business case, can be adapted for infrastructure investments is discussed in Chapter 8.

The business case is also an essential 'document' in ensuring effective coordination and management of the complex set of activities and resources involved. Representing that complexity as a simple set of financial figures obscures the real nature of the investment, by losing the understanding of what has to change in order to achieve each of the business improvements. That is not to say that a financial appraisal of the case for investment should not be made in order to decide whether it should be funded and therefore the business case must be developed in a way that enables a financial appraisal to be made as and when necessary. However, this should not be an independent decision, since at any time there will be a choice of possible investments and the decision will always be made in relation to the overall funds available and alternative ways of investing them. The investment has therefore to be understood from the viewpoints of both *what* benefits can be expected and *how* feasible it is to achieve those benefits, in comparison with alternative uses of funds and resources. This implies that all IS/IT investment business cases are developed and expressed in a consistent way so that management can compare 'apples with apples' when making decisions on funding priorities. It would be ideal if all business investments were expressed similarly and not just the IS/IT options and, for this reason, a number of organizations have adopted the approach described in this book for a wide range of investments involving business changes, such as office relocation and organizational restructuring.

As discussed in Chapter 1, most IS/IT investments deliver a range of benefits. It is necessary to understand the mix involved, how they interrelate with each other and their interdependence with the required set of changes. Hence the business case should accurately reflect those relationships, as defined by the benefits dependency network. However, in order to develop the business case it may require further activities to be added to the network, for example the need to establish more appropriate measurements to quantify the improvements.

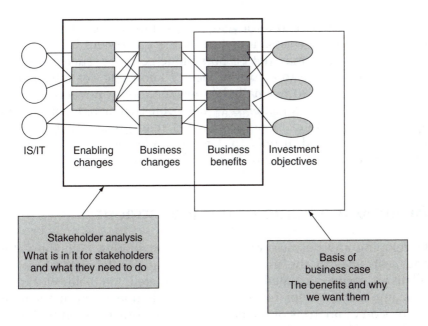

Figure 5.1 *Basis of the business case and stakeholder analysis*

Once the case can be converted to one that is suitable for the investment decision, by the addition of costs and the attribution of financial values to some of the benefits, assessments of technology and financial risks should be undertaken. How these will be interpreted will be influenced by the overall expected contribution of the investment to the business strategy, as expressed in the applications portfolio discussed in Chapter 2. However, an aspect that is often overlooked, especially for strategic investments, is the organization's capability to make the required changes and drive through all the benefits. These aspects of risk assessment are considered at the end of this chapter.

Organizational risks can be assessed and understood at an overall level, but there are also more specific issues that can influence the success of the investment. These result from particular stakeholders' expectations, interests and priorities, which inevitably will affect their commitment of time and resources to making the required changes. How these stakeholder issues can be identified, understood and managed is discussed in detail in the next chapter. In some cases this will result in changes to the business case, if there are serious issues which may prevent the achievement of some benefits (see Figure 5.1). As discussed in Chapter 7, it is sometimes appropriate to carry out a detailed stakeholder analysis prior to completion of the business case.

The approach described to developing the business case is intended to provide a comprehensive picture of the investment being undertaken. However, it may not be possible to complete such a case for all investments, due to a current lack of knowledge or information available. This would normally be the situation for novel or innovative systems – those considered as 'high potential' investments in the applications portfolio. A decision whether to proceed with further work is still needed, if only to determine whether scarce resources should be allocated to the project or used elsewhere.

Arguing the Value of the Investment

Developing any business case involves considering both the value and cost sides of the investment equation. While costs are often relatively easily calculated, or at least estimated, the major weakness in many proposals for investing in IS/IT is due to the inadequate expression or analysis of the benefits that the organization will gain. In this section we concentrate on developing a realistic assessment of the benefits.

As described in the discussion of the benefits management process in Chapter 3, developing the 'value' side of the case often requires two stages. An initial assessment based on the identification of the potential benefits, as per the dependency network, is needed to determine whether the project has any prospect of being funded and, if it has, to specify the further work needed to develop the full case to be submitted for management approval. This will involve activities to prove how the benefits can be measured and to determine which of the benefits can be quantified and expressed in financial terms.

The main differences between the benefits management approach to developing the value side of the equation, compared with more traditional approaches, are the continued emphasis on the relationship between change and benefit, the importance of benefit ownership and the need to be explicit about benefit measurement. These aspects were all introduced in the previous chapter in the context of the benefits dependency network. From the network it should be explicitly understood how each benefit relates to one or more of the investment objectives, who owns it and will drive through the realization and whether, and perhaps how, it can be measured. This information and an understanding of the types of change required to achieve the benefit are the starting points for building and refining the business case. This chapter will discuss the additional requirement of applying appropriate rigour to the evidence needed for formal justification.

Maintaining the Dependency: Benefits are the Result of Changes

The first statements in the business case should ensure there is an explicit link between the investment objectives and the context for the investment, in terms of the business objectives or drivers that gave rise for the need for change. They should be clear statements about the business drivers that mean change is essential and how the achievement of the objectives of the investment will address those drivers.

Then the benefits expected to arise from achievement of each of the objectives should be classified in terms of the main type of change that will be needed to realize it, as shown in the columns in Figure 5.2. It may seem simplistic to relate each benefit to one of only three causes, but the vast majority of benefits arise because:

1 the organization, its staff or trading partners can do new things, or do things in new ways, that prior to this investment were not possible
2 the organization can improve the performance of things it must continue to do, i.e. do them better
3 the organization can stop doing things that are no longer needed.

It is reasonable to expect senior management to be more excited by the benefits, and therefore commit more time and effort to changes, which allow new activities or innovations or those that stop wastage on unnecessary activities. It suggests that more significant action is involved than that required to improve the performance of existing activities and also that the changes will have a more dramatic and longer lasting effect on the business.

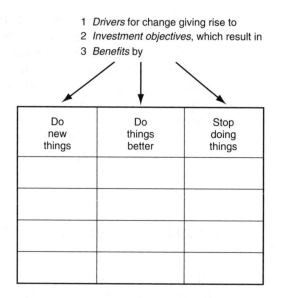

1 *Drivers* for change giving rise to
2 *Investment objectives*, which result in
3 *Benefits* by

Do new things	Do things better	Stop doing things

Figure 5.2   *The essence of the value argument: relating the benefits to change*

In some cases the definition or description of a benefit may have to be reconsidered in order to make it clear in which column it belongs and occasionally restated as two or more benefits since, for example, by stopping one thing resources can be reused to do something new. This is only a first step in arguing the case for investment, but an important one, since it retains the understanding of the link between the drivers for change and benefit delivery and it also helps determine the nature of the measures that can legitimately be used to calculate the value of the benefit and prove its realization. Clearly, it should be quite feasible to quantify and value the reduction in resources required if an activity will cease, but far more difficult to estimate the financial value that will accrue from a new activity. Equally the change management associated with creating a new activity or way of working will have different challenges from eliminating an old working practice. That is not to suggest that one is easier than the other. Often benefits fail to be delivered because old practices are still in place despite the implementation of new systems and technology.

A Structure for Analysing and Describing the Benefits

A business case is essentially a reasoned argument for investment. It should be based on the ability to measure each benefit and on specific evidence that enables the level or size of each expected improvement to be estimated. The matrix shown in Figure 5.3 defines four levels of 'explicitness' that are based on the ability to assign a value to the benefit and the degree of current knowledge about the future expected improvement. Each benefit should be initially allocated to either the *observable* or *measurable* row, assuming that it at least meets the criteria, and then an assessment made of how much is already known or could be determined, such that it might be moved upwards in the table. Each type of benefit will be discussed in turn.

Degree of explicitness	Do new things	Do things better	Stop doing things
Financial	By applying a cost/price or other valid financial formula to a quantifiable benefit a financial value can be calculated		
Quantifiable	Sufficient evidence exists to forecast how much improvement/ benefit should result from the changes		
Measurable	This aspect of performance is currently being measured or an appropriate measure could be implemented. But it is not possible to estimate by how much performance will improve when the changes are complete		
Observable	By use of agreed criteria, specific individuals/groups will decide, based on their experience or judgement, to what extent the benefit has been realized		

Figure 5.3   Classifying the benefits by the explicitness of the contribution

Observable Benefits

Definition: Observable benefit

By use of agreed criteria, specific individuals/groups will decide, based on their experience or judgement, to what extent the benefit has been realized.

Observable benefits require a clear statement of the criteria to be used to assess their achievement and also the identification of who is qualified or appropriate to make the most objective judgement. This is often the only way of determining whether many of the 'softer' benefits, such as improved staff morale or customer satisfaction, have been realized, although if these have been tracked for a period of time through surveys and the issues that the investment addresses can be isolated, it may be possible to actually measure, rather than merely observe the benefit. While such benefits, even in total, are unlikely to be sufficient to argue the investment case, they should not be ignored or trivialized. They may accrue to large numbers of stakeholders, whose change in behaviour is essential to using the new application or process, leading to the realization of the more substantial organizational benefits. Such benefits should be retained in the business case and benefits plan, even if there are ample other financial and quantified benefits to obtain investment funding.

For example, in the introduction of new EPOS systems in a super-market chain, although the main financial benefits were due to the speed at which transactions could be processed through the tills, the checkout staff would be less stressed at peak times, due to reduced queue lengths and fewer errors. This benefit made the thousands of staff involved positive about the introduction of the new system, despite the disruption to work patterns that would occur during the changeover.

In a healthcare organization, a knowledge management initiative was failing to achieve its objectives of knowledge sharing among prod-uct development and marketing professionals, in spite of financial incentives to 'provide content', until the authorship of the content was made explicit to users and the number of times the content was accessed was fed back to the author. Recognition of an individual's contribution by his or her peers was considered to be more significant than reward by the organization for undertaking an additional task.

Measurable Benefits

Definition: Measurable benefit

This aspect of performance is currently being measured or an appropriate measure could be implemented. But it is currently not possible to estimate by how much performance will improve when the changes are completed.

A measurable benefit is one where either measures exist or can be put in place that will enable the improvement in performance to be determined after the event. This obviously implies that the level of performance prior to the implementation can also be measured and that the improvement can be specifically attributed to the investment, rather than other changes. When looking at process improvements, measures may be of organizational inputs, activity levels, outputs or results. It may be necessary to have more than one measure to determine whether the benefit has been fully realized, for example, if the number of customer complaints has reduced, has that led to a reduction in the staff time spent dealing with complaints or even the number of staff involved? If the new process has meant that each complaint can be dealt with more quickly and require less investigative effort, again has this resulted in less time spent by staff per complaint? These examples are intended to show that the measure should not only be relevant to the benefit itself but also to the changes that are needed to realize it, so that the improvement can be directly attributable.

Wherever possible existing measures should be used and particularly when they are part of the organizational performance measurement system, via a Balanced Score Card or KPIs (Key Performance Indicators), since this ensures that achieving the benefit is seen as integral to overall performance improvement. It will also mean that the current 'baseline' is already known. If however, no relevant current measurement exists, which is often the case when the benefit results from doing something new, a decision has to be made as to not only what measure is appropriate, but also whether the effort required to establish the measure is worthwhile in relation to the significance of the benefit. If it is deemed too difficult or expensive to set up a measure then the benefit should be 'relegated' to observable and suitable criteria for evaluation identified.

Another important aspect to consider is whether the way the improvement is measured will encourage the types of organizational and personal behaviours required to deliver the benefit. For example, staff in a call centre were expected to spend, on average, less time per service call once a new system was installed. However, only average call times were used to measure staff productivity, and this did not reflect the range of types of call or the communication abilities of different customers. As a result some staff cut off callers who were taking more than the average time, resulting in either another call or a dissatisfied customer.

A last consideration with both observable and measurable benefits is the time period required after implementation before a meaningful measurement can be made to determine whether and to what degree improvement has occurred. Few benefits are instantaneous and most require a few weeks or even months to accrue. An estimate should be made as to when sufficient effects of the changes should be visible as measurable improvements, but before the specific benefits may become obscured by the consequences of other changes or events.

Setting Measures

Measuring business and organisational performance and setting targets for improvement is an increasingly important aspect of management. It is a complex topic, which has been the subject of considerable research and development over the last decade (the Centre for Business Performance, at Cranfield School of Management, has published a number of books and papers on best practices in performance measurement, see for example Neely (2003) and Neely et al. (2002)). As mentioned earlier the choice of performance measures influences behaviours and equally when there is a need to change behaviours the development of new measures has to pay careful attention to how they will be interpreted by the staff involved. There are a number of 'checklists' that can be used to assess whether performance measures are appropriate. Tables 5.1 and 5.2 are examples of such checklists.

Quantifying the Benefits: The Major Challenge

Definition: Quantifiable benefit

Sufficient evidence exists to forecast how much improvement/benefit should result from the changes.

Table 5.1 Criteria for effective performance measures (after the Royal Statistical Society, 2004 and HM Treasury, 2001)

Relevant	to the organization's strategy and able to demonstrate progress towards achievement
Well defined	clear and unambiguous, easy to understand both in terms of the definition of the measure and how it is calculated
Attributable	those whose performance is being measured can influence the result by their own actions and are not dependent on the performance of others
Comparable	performance can be compared over time and across different groups carrying out the same tasks
Contextual	they cannot be misinterpreted – the assumptions and limitations of the measures are understood

Table 5.2 The characteristics of a good performance measurement system (after HM Treasury, 2001)

Focused	no more measures than are necessary, clearly linked to and prioritised in relation to the organization's strategy
Appropriate	to the people who will use the information to improve performance – presentation tailored to different users
Balanced	to cover all areas of business and organizational activity – different types of measures to reflect stakeholder interests
Robust	not dependent on ways of working and organizational structures – not sensitive to organizational changes
Integrated	part of the business planning process and linked to individual and organizational success criteria
Cost effective	in terms of the cost of data collection and timeliness for use in decision making

As defined in Figure 5.3 the essential difference between measurable and quantifiable benefits is that, although measurable benefits can be shown to have been realized after implementation, no pre-implementation estimate can be made of the degree of improvement to be expected. In order to quantify benefits, evidence is needed before the project is funded to 'calculate' the amount of improvement that the changes will produce. This is relatively easy in the 'stop column' on the matrix, but more difficult in the others. Having determined the most appropriate measures for a benefit, it is essential that the current baseline can be established from which the estimate of performance improvement can be developed, by considering in more detail how the changes that deliver that benefit will affect the performance level.

One of the weaknesses of many investment cases is the lack of evidence provided to substantiate the financial benefits or the assumptions made in quantifying the benefits. Without 'legitimate' quantification, it will be difficult, if not impossible to agree a realistic financial value. Hence the step between measurable and quantifiable is the most critical in converting a qualitative argument to a sound economic case for investment. Of course, as already considered, there is always the issue of 'materiality', i.e. is the effort involved worth it? This, in turn, depends on the likely increment in performance that could be achieved, but often the task is not undertaken because there are already 'sufficient benefits to justify the investment' or 'nobody will believe the figures anyway' or some similar rationale. This is understandable, but leads to misunderstandings of what the investment is actually intended to deliver and reduces the attention paid to ensuring all the available benefits are achieved.

Ways of Overcoming the Quantification Problem

As illustrated in Figure 5.4 there are a number of ways that, assuming the potential benefit is material, the measurable to quantifiable 'barrier' can be overcome.

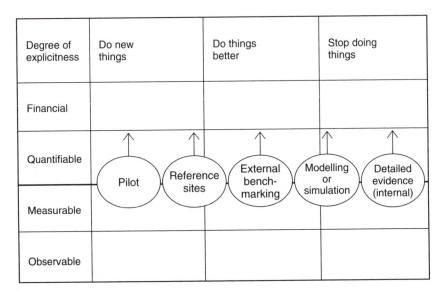

Figure 5.4 *Converting measurable to quantifiable benefits*

As stated earlier, quantification is more difficult in the new and better columns, relative to the stop column. Therefore there is generally an increasing need to obtain external data or evidence to help develop the business case, when there is limited internal experience of a specific type of innovation. Organizations that have comprehensive activity and process performance measurement and variance analysis systems, especially those that include activity-based cost analysis, may well be able to calculate and quantify the majority of improvements from internal data. But even those organizations will find difficulty in estimating the degree of improvement that can be achieved by certain IT-based innovations.

The five approaches shown in the circles in Figure 5.4 are not exclusively aligned to the columns as shown, and the more sophisticated, such as pilots and reference sites could be used for all types of benefit if the organization has no experience of implementing such changes. Equally using these approaches may help identify further benefits that could result from the planned changes. This is especially true when implementing large enterprise-wide packages, where the integration benefits are difficult to understand and describe – especially from an existing situation of fragmented and incompatible systems.

Detailed Evidence and Modelling or Simulation

Relevant detailed evidence to help quantify a benefit may take some 'digging out' from the existing systems, which tend to record performance in relation to the organization structure rather than business activities or processes. It is also often important to establish evidence over a relevant time period, such as a year or through a peak in the trading cycle. It may only be necessary to sample the data to find sufficient representative evidence from which the overall value can be extrapolated.

Some software packages, mainly in transactional or operational areas, such as ERP, Fleet Management and Workflow Systems, have simulation or modelling software that can show the level of performance that can be achieved by adopting practices and processes embedded in the application suite. These can provide a target level against which to estimate what can be achieved in the particular organizational situation. Also many companies use modelling tools in areas such as marketing planning, inventory management and sales forecasting that can also be used to explore the potential implications of changes to processes and ways of working.

Benchmarking and Reference Sites

Benchmarking aspects of organizational process performance and resource utilization is commonly used in a number of industries as the starting point for improvement programmes. This can be a valuable approach to quantifying benefits, by evaluating the changes in relation to 'best practices' in the industry, or in comparable processes in other industries (Alshawi et al., 2003; Johnson and Misic, 1999). For example, supermarkets study each other's EPOS systems performance in relation to store 'traffic', in terms of processing speed for transactions and queue lengths. The time and cost taken to process loan and mortgage applications or insurance claims are considered as 'competitive' KPIs in the financial services industry, whereas in other industries, such as electronics and pharmaceuticals, time to market for new products is a critical benchmark.

Although benchmarking is helpful for identifying potential improvements to established processes and practices by comparing the performance of similar activities in other organizations, for obvious reasons it is less useful when trying to quantify the benefits from innovations. There are two further options which can be used in the 'new column'. Unless the innovation is the first of its kind in the industry, there should be reference sites where similar changes have been made or examples where the technology is being used in other industries. The latter are usually available from the technology suppliers, which are keen to prove the benefits of their products to new customers via existing ones. Obviously care is needed to select relevant implementations and to be able to compare not only how the technology has been deployed, but also to understand the changes that were made to deliver the performance improvement. It is also important to understand where the reference organization started from, in performance terms, to be able to assess how much of the improvement they have achieved is relevant and feasible. Where organizations believe they are achieving an advantage from an innovation, it is unlikely that they will be willing to share all the secrets of their success, so the information gained from reference sites has to be treated with a degree of caution.

Pilot Implementations

Pilot implementations are becoming increasingly used to not only test the technology, but also to evaluate the benefits that can be achieved from new systems and ways of working. When there is no other feasible way of determining the degree of improvement that could result from the changes, a pilot implementation of the new process or practice is necessary if 'proof' of the benefit is needed. A pilot will normally test the new way of working on a small scale, so that the total benefit can be extrapolated. To provide the best evidence it is essential to identify, if possible, a comparable control group still working in the old way, as the current baseline. For example, when Thomson's holidays first introduced its online holiday booking system into travel agents, it was able to compare very accurately the sales of the selected pilot sites with a similarly representative sample of agents still making bookings over the phone. The pilot was undertaken in a sample of agencies selected to be representative of the range of different agencies that they operated. The pilot was also run for several months, to ensure that improvements were genuine and not just due to the initial enthusiasm of agencies selected to take part in the pilot. The 30% average increase in business handled by the pilot site agencies was sufficient evidence to justify the major investment required for all agents.

Box 5.1 describes how the use of modelling, benchmarking and a pilot implementation were used to develop the business case for a customer relationship management system in a major European paper manufacturer.

Box 5.1 Quantifying benefits in a European paper manufacturer

A major European manufacturer of fine and printing papers was considering the introduction of a customer relationship management system into its sales and marketing functions.

The company, which manufactures high quality papers and paper-based packaging materials, sold their products via distributors, to printers, large corporations and packaging manufacturers. While these organizations were their main customers, the decision about which paper to purchase was often influenced by graphic designers working for these customers. These designers therefore represented key influencers on sales and hence were also an important group for the manufacturer.

Sales were achieved by advertising and promoting (A&P) their products to both distributors and graphic designers, the latter generating pull through of product via the distributors. A key part of this A&P activity was a set of targeted marketing campaigns, in which marketing collateral about their products would be mailed out to the distributors and designers. This material was then followed up either by a visit from a member of sales staff or by a telephone call from the sales office. On average, the company carried out around 50 such A&P campaigns per year, costing a total of some 10 million euros. It employed 150 professional sales staff in the 15 countries and had over 6000 end customers.

While this promotional and sales activity was satisfactory, it was felt that the firm could achieve more sales from the significant amount it was spending. This caused the organization to consider trying to improve their knowledge of and hence relationship with their customers, and support this via the use of IS/IT.

Box 5.1 (Continued)

The specific drivers for the investment were identified as:

1 need for improved customer retention and increased market share in the high value market segments
2 maintenance of brand leadership despite increased marketing activity of competitors
3 desire to achieve more sales from significant amount being spent on A&P.

The two main objectives of the new system and associated business changes were agreed as:

1 to improve the effectiveness of A&P expenditure (defined as the ratio of sales revenue generated/advertising and promotion (A&P) cost)
2 to increase sales volume and value from new customers.

Benefits associated with these objectives included:

(a) reduced costs by avoiding wasted mailings and product samples to 'irrelevant' customers
(b) increased response rates from A&P campaigns
(c) increased rate of following up leads generated by campaigns – earlier and more customers
(d) increased conversion rate of leads to sales.

Developing a benefits dependency network, as described in Chapter 4, identified a number of significant business changes that were essential to delivering the benefits, including a complete restructuring of the customer database into new market segments to reflect customer lifetime value and purchasing patterns, rather than just industry sector; a new key account management process and sales commission system; a telesales centre for customers placing small orders and a new process for campaign planning, response tracking and sales targeting, based on the new customer and prospect database.

According to Figure 5.3, the main benefits of this investment would be measurable, that is, performance in that area was already being measured or a suitable measure could be defined and implemented. However, the company insisted that every IS/IT investment should deliver a financial return, which was difficult to prove unless a number of the benefits could be first quantified and then converted to financial values. The only two benefits that it was considered would lead to financial figures were (a) and (d) in the list, but value of benefit (d) was dependent on quantifying benefits (b) and (c).

Modelling

To calculate the direct A&P cost savings, a representative sample of campaigns from the previous year was analysed. This analysis sought to understand the types of leads generated and to identify patterns in responses and those customers who never responded to campaigns. As a result it was estimated that some 30% of the costs could be saved, without reducing the response rate.

Benchmarking

To quantify the expected improvement in responses from better campaign targeting, comparisons of the results from database marketing to industrial customers were obtained from a specialist consultancy. A modelling exercise on the new database within the paper manufacturer was then carried out, to show how targeting based on the timing in buying patterns would produce higher levels of response. This pattern was compared with the customer sales information held by a number of key distributors to confirm the likely improvements. This led to additional cost savings of some 10%.

To estimate the number of additional customers that could be visited by the salesforce or contacted by the telesales staff, depending on which was appropriate, all the sales staff logged their time and customer visits for two months. The mix of activity across different customer value profiles, leads generated from campaigns, regular customer meetings and time spent with different types of customer was analysed in relation to the sales that resulted over the next two months. Based on best practice benchmarks and information from similar organizations that had implemented the same key account management process, it was clear that by using the telesales approach to follow up many of the lower value enquiries, the sales staff could increase the time spent with potentially high value customers by some 20%.

Box 5.1 (Continued)

A Pilot Implementation

Having identified that changing how resources were used could enable customer contacts to be addressed more efficiently and effectively, thereby increasing the number of sales contacts made, the remaining issue was whether the more productive use of sales staff, combined with the improved targeting of campaigns would actually deliver more sales and specifically more sales caused by those campaigns.

No comparable information to help quantify the value of additional sales was available and although a few companies that had introduced similar changes were visited, none had the same combination of sales and distribution channels. The only remaining option was to pilot the new system and processes of managing the campaigns and sales follow-up. This was done based on a PC-based prototype of the system and paper-based 'workflow' control of activity on one typical campaign in one market. In order to provide a control for comparison purposes, existing processes were followed for the same campaign in another similar sized market. The pilot study lasted two months and sales from the two markets were monitored for a further two months, the normal 'depreciation' period for a campaign. Key distributors provided information about their sales to existing or new purchasers of the product set being promoted, such that the ability to find new customers and the underlying pattern of non-campaign derived sales could be understood.

At the end of the pilot, comparing the sales patterns in the two markets as accurately as possible, sales in the pilot market resulting from the new approach to the A&P campaign were clearly some 50% higher than in the control market, which was operating business as usual. If these figures were extrapolated across all campaigns and all markets the increased contribution from these sales would cover the investment costs in a few months. However the figure had to be moderated by the fact that the sales team involved in the pilot had, due to being under the spotlight, undoubtedly worked far harder to prove they could succeed than could be sustained over time by the whole sales force. It was agreed by the sales director that a 20% increase was achievable and sustainable across the whole business, and hence this more realistic figure was included in the business case (Figure 5.5).

Degree of explicitness	Do new things	Do things better	Stop doing things
Financial	d) Increased conversion rate to sales (p.a.) Additional conversions contribution Enquiries (+20%) £400K Mailings (+15%) £250K Samples (+20%) £350K Specifications (+40%) £200K Total £1200K (p.a.)		a) Reduced cost by avoiding waste on irrelevant customers 30% + 10% cost saving = £950K p.a.
Quantifiable	c) Increased rate of follow-up of leads by category (p.a.) New (Old) Enquiries 2000 (800) Mailings 15000 (<5000) Samples 5000 (2000) Specifications 600 (400)		
Measurable		b) Increased response rate from defined target group and earlier response from defined group Target group response rate increased from 5% to 10% 55% of responses received within 2 weeks of campaign (previously 45%)	
Observable			

Figure 5.5 The business case for the European paper manufacturer

The total financial benefits were sufficient to provide the necessary return from the combination of systems investment and business changes, and the proof that such improvements were achievable ensured all necessary resources were made available to complete the project as early as possible. The proof of the increased sales from the pilot also meant that the sales force provided all the help needed to implement the system and changes successfully, in order to increase their incentive payments at the earliest opportunity.

Financial Benefits

Definition: Financial benefit

By applying a cost/price or other valid financial formula to a quantifiable benefit a financial value can be calculated.

The aim of any business case should be to express as many of the benefits as possible in financial terms, so that the expected return on investment can be ascertained. Many organizations use primarily financial criteria to decide on IS/IT investments, although as discussed in Chapter 1, this can lead to a number of issues, for example:

- lack of innovative uses of IS/IT since the financial benefits are uncertain
- a focus on purely efficiency gains from IS/IT, which improve individual processes, but often at the expense of overall organizational effectiveness
- 'creative' calculations of financial benefits based on inadequate evidence
- making assumptions that enable sufficient financial benefits to be claimed to provide the necessary return in relation to the costs
- only declaring enough of the available financial benefits to offset the expected cost
- minimizing the costs of the system either by removing functionality, especially that which is not deemed immediately essential (e.g. integration of processes or information resources) or understating the organizational costs of implementation, such as training.

Overall, undue emphasis on purely financial returns will limit the range of investments in the applications portfolio, described in Chapter 2, to largely support or key operational applications, since it is only for these that sufficient knowledge normally exists to quantify the improvements and hence calculate a financial value.

The use of financial and economic appraisal techniques is discussed in overview later, with references to more detailed sources of information about the techniques. The emphasis in this section is on converting quantifiable benefits to financial ones as in the benefits analysis structure shown in Figure 5.3.

Due to the essential attributes of IT, its application to business processes frequently results in three types of benefit that can be quantified in advance. These benefits, which are discussed in Chapter 1 and shown in Figure 1.2, are related to increases in *efficiency* – that is using less resource to complete activities – increases in *accuracy* – greater precision and consistency or higher quality outputs from activities – and increases in *speed* – completing activities more quickly. Often these are combined under the heading of *greater productivity*, but productivity is not in itself a financial benefit, unless it results in an ability to either reduce costs by using fewer resources or reusing the resource or time savings to gain new revenue. How productivity gains are 'taken' as benefits varies considerably across organizations, especially those which save staff time. Box 5.2 describes three different ways in which a financial value was, or was not, derived from benefits which saved the time of staff within the organization.

Box 5.2 The productivity conundrum

Frito-Lay, the snack food manufacturer, decided to equip its sales/delivery force with handheld computers (Applegate, 1993). The pilot implementation showed that this saved three to four hours' administrative effort each week. The sales managers were asked to decide what that time saving could deliver as a benefit. It was agreed that each sales/delivery person should be able to increase their sales by between 3% and 10% per week, given the increased selling time available and allowing for their different customer mixes. This was measured shortly after implementation and an average of 6% over and above market growth was achieved.

A major motor manufacturer implemented an enterprise portal to enable all staff (over 100,000 people) to access all corporate information websites and carry out a wide range of 'self-service' activities such as maintaining their personal information, submitting expenses, making travel arrangements and making staff discount purchases. Based on a study, it was calculated that this would save an average of 8–10 minutes per person per day. Given the context of ongoing staff reduction targets in all areas, it was assumed that this would result, over time, in a possible reduction of 2% of staff. Obviously based on the large numbers of employees this provided a large cost saving, which was included in the business case, although it was known that it could never be explicitly proved after implementation that the savings were due to the portal.

A similar enterprise portal was implemented by a major healthcare company, employing approximately the same number of people as the motor manufacturer. Although they too calculated the daily time saving to be in the order of 6–10 minutes, this productivity gain was not converted into a financial benefit, since it would be possible neither to measure the saving after the event nor attribute it to the portal. The main objectives of the investment were to ensure all staff were better informed and to reduce

> **Box 5.2 (Continued)**
>
> staff frustration in finding information and carrying out administrative tasks, as well as save IT costs associated with supporting the proliferation of intranet sites built in non-standard ways.

In essence, financial benefits are only realizable from reductions in cost, including the avoidance of known future costs and the potential costs associated with unacceptable risks and from increases in revenue or avoidable revenue losses. Obviously cost reductions are easier to identify, quantify and 'prove' than additional revenues, but in both cases the final calculations are relatively easy provided the quantification, as described and exemplified in Box 5.1, has been based on legitimate assumptions and relevant evidence.

Not Targets

When producing a justification for an IS/IT investment it is often tempting to include target figures in the business case. Management may have stipulated a cost saving figure or an increase in revenues or some other quantified performance improvement they wish to realize from the investment and hence it appears necessary to include such figures if funding is to be obtained. However, we would caution against this. Rather we would suggest that the approaches described in earlier sections are followed, with the value of benefits being justified from evidence that is as objective and verifiable as possible, such as that from benchmarking and pilot studies. This approach will test how reasonable and hence achievable the targets that have been set are. Even if the target appears feasible, providing detailed evidence of how it will be achieved is not always straightforward, since it may depend on the cumulative effects of several smaller individual improvements. While management may be willing to fund achievement of an overall target, gaining involvement of other stakeholders often requires their understanding of how they can achieve the target that has been set. Deriving robust values for the individual benefits expected and how these contribute to the overall target can be an important part of that understanding.

Cost Reductions

To determine and verify cost reductions, it is necessary to consider how the combination of efficiency, accuracy and speed that creates the benefit can be converted to cost savings. This is a relatively simple calculation, based on the change in volume of activity and reduction in resources, people and other activity costs multiplied by an appropriate unit cost. It is important to maintain the 'audit trail' that led to the final financial figure, to be able to verify that the benefit is eventually realized or, if it is not, to explain the variances.

Cost avoidance benefits are essentially of three types:

1 Increases or changes in business activities or volumes, which can be accommodated without the need for commensurate increases in resources.
2 Certain future costs that will otherwise be incurred to improve efficiency, accuracy or speed merely to sustain the current level of business performance.
3 Uncertain future costs that may result from risks that have a significant probability of causing serious cost problems if changes associated with the investment are not made.

One issue with all types of cost reduction benefits is to determine whether the saving is of direct or variable costs only or if certain fixed costs will also be reduced. It is usually possible to calculate the variable element, such as direct labour, travel or materials and it is also possible to estimate the notional savings in fixed costs that could also occur, for example, savings in employment costs and accommodation. However, it is partly a matter of determining whether or not these savings will actually be realized and partly an issue of the organization's accounting policies as to whether and how they are included in the business case. Some organizations include a time element that allows for the direct cost saving immediately after implementation, but postpones the inclusion of indirect savings for a period, within which they can be realized.

For example, an engineering design company introduced a document management system, which would reduce the storage space required for documents and drawings in its London offices by several hundred square meters. By reorganizing and rationalizing the use of space, most of the 'floor space' saved could actually be released and sublet until the current lease expired, when the company could reduce its accommodation in the building. Given the cost of office space in London this produced a saving of over £100,000 p.a., which was included in the business case for year 2 onwards, to allow for the time taken after implementation to rationalize the space used.

Alternatively, some organizations take a longer term view and allow the savings to be included by transferring costs, normally from operational to overheads, in the understanding that other actions will be taken later to address those areas of cost. For example, the implementation of a new stock management and online purchasing system in a builders merchant operating over 100 branches, would reduce the yard area needed for 'heavy-side materials' by up to 40% in many of the larger branches. One performance measure for each branch site was 'profit per square metre', which would now provide misleading comparative performance information if it were not based on the area actually in use. The policy decision was to reduce the area to that actually in use in the branch profit and loss accounts, and include the area not in use in a head office business development account. Later, decisions would be made as to whether the space would be used to increase the branch product range and generate more revenue for the branch or, alternatively, sell the land and realize the value of the asset.

Whatever the policy or reason for a specific decision to include elements of fixed costs, it is important that the arguments and calculations are consistently applied across all investments, not just IS/IT projects.

Revenue Increases

Because there are always causes and reasons why costs are incurred, the effects of specific changes on existing costs can usually be estimated with some certainty, but the same is not true of many changes in revenue. Also the period over which any estimated revenue increases from the investment will be sustained is uncertain and in most cases probably shorter than for cost reductions, many of which are permanent. Therefore not only are revenue increases less easy to predict in terms of their likely value, how they are included in the overall calculation of the financial return will also differ.

Some revenue increases can be estimated reliably, especially those that involve improved financial systems to ensure revenue earned is actually received, for example, by more accurate invoicing and contracts or better bad debt control. If there are known causes of lost revenue, such as unavailability of product, unacceptable delivery or service response times or uncompetitive prices, it is possible to make an informed estimate of the sales that can be recovered by changes to correct the causes of poor performance. Of course other factors will simultaneously influence sales; for example supply problems of a competitor, a successful promotion campaign or, more negatively, a quality problem with a product or the launch of better service by a competitor. This makes it difficult to prove, following implementation, that the increase in sales was due to the changes made. And of course there may simply have been a change in customer demand between making the case and completing the project.

However, it should be feasible to construct a strong argument for recovering potential revenue that is being lost due to ineffective internal processes. For example, a professional services firm was unable to respond in time to a large proportion of the invitations to tender it received, which was a particular problem since future business was more dependent on winning tenders than on existing relationships with clients. Equally, it was losing a proportion of those bids it did make, which wasted the time of highly paid professional staff. It invested in a new 'shared knowledge base' that captured all the information from previous bids, successful and unsuccessful, such that proposals could be put together more quickly and comprehensively, by people with less experience. An evaluation analysis tool was also developed to enable experienced staff to pre-qualify whether, based on past success or attractiveness of the business, the preparation of a proposal was worthwhile. This increased both the number of responses it could make and the success rate.

In a similar way to considering how the efficiency, accuracy and speed attributes of IT can reduce specific costs, Parker and Benson (1988), in their approach to identifying increased revenue opportunities from information systems, describe three ways in which more value can be created. *Value linking* considers the impact of more effective integration of value-adding processes within the organization and externally to ensure that resources are coordinated to deliver better or more consistent levels of performance to meet customers' expectations. *Value acceleration* can identify where the system, in combination with business changes, can increase the speed at which the business performs, for example in developing new products or services, or by better synchronization of operational and decision-making processes. *Value restructuring* looks at ways of realigning job roles, management responsibilities and organizational structures to take advantage of the integrity and consistency of processes and synchronization of activities provided by the new information system. Empowerment of staff to make more decisions without the need to consult or involve their manager or another department is an example of value restructuring.

These concepts can also be used in organizations where revenue increases are not an option, but where more effective use of existing capabilities can be made through the introduction of the new system, resulting in a higher volume or quality of service delivery. For example, older people living in the community often require help both from medical services and social services, such as the delivery of pre-prepared meals. In the UK, as in other countries, these activities are currently carried out by two different agencies. The NHS is responsible for medical care and the local social services, which is part of local government, is responsible for social care. The UK central government is currently developing plans for such care, particularly the first assessment of an older person's needs to be carried out by just one of these agencies, rather than the two separate assessments that are currently undertaken. This new single assessment process will rely heavily on the use of information systems, with data being collected by the member of staff, on a laptop or other mobile device, while visiting the old person in their home. This information will then be shared with both the agencies responsible for ongoing care, ensuring not only that they both have complete and consistent information, but also that a higher number of such visits can be carried out by existing staff.

The ability to estimate the effects of any investment on sales revenue will depend on the organization's level of knowledge of its customers, their attitudes, behaviours, and resultant buying patterns for the products and services affected by the changes. This can be ascertained for existing customers by asking them or analysing customer sales data and then extrapolating the results to similar prospective customers in the same or similar segment.

Most of these examples are associated with increased revenue by improving current performance or eliminating causes of problems. Such benefits would be shown in the *better* or *stop* columns of the matrix shown in Figure 5.3. It is clearly more difficult to quantify and therefore put a reliable financial value on benefits resulting from doing new things, for example, opening up an online sales channel, or doing things in entirely new ways, such as applying workflow tools to new product development processes in order to bring new products to market faster.

Market research is needed when the revenue is expected from a new product, sales channel, type of customer, customer relationship process or geographic market. This is all rather obvious, but it is important that any claim of revenue increases is supported by reasoned argument about the causes of the increase, otherwise post-implementation review is impossible and, over time, scepticism about the benefits of even legitimate claims will increase. At best it may only be possible to provide a series of potential benefit levels, each based on a different combination of assumptions – *if the following assumptions are made then the increase will be between 5–10%, but if . . . then it could enable a 15% improvement . . . .* Different figures would then be input into the return on investment calculation to determine how sensitive or dependent the investment case is on the accuracy of the revenue estimates. 'What if' calculations can also be carried out to assess the effects of the sustainability of the increase over different time periods. If the business case is dependent on a particular revenue increase, then further work would be worthwhile, for instance, by testing the assumptions with customers to narrow the range of probable outcomes. However, it will always be a judgement rather than a clear-cut yes/no decision, implying that if any assumptions prove incorrect later in the project, the business case would be reassessed.

The preceding sections have described the ways that the value side of the business case can be developed into a comprehensive, substantive and robust argument for incurring the costs required to create the value. The full business case must obviously include these, as shown in Figure 5.6, but it is important that they are considered and evaluated in the context of the complete range of benefits that is expected to be achieved.

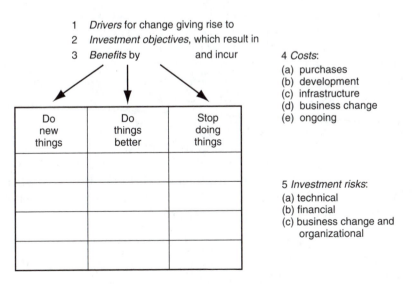

Figure 5.6 The full content of the business case

Project Cost Assessment

As has been discussed earlier in this chapter, estimating the benefits, both quantitative and financial, is complex and difficult. Equally, predicting the costs associated with an investment is often far from easy. Any financial assessment of the return or payback is sensitive to the potential inaccuracies in both. However it is relatively straightforward to measure the costs actually incurred, although often the non-IT-related costs, such as those associated with making business changes, are not recorded. The types of cost that should be included in the financial justification are shown in Box 5.3.

Box 5.3 Cost types in financial justification

Purchase costs of hardware and software, plus any external consultancy or specialist technical resources required.

Internal systems development costs, i.e. the costs of specialist internal resources for business analysis, designing the system, processes and procedures, developing or procuring the software, commissioning and implementing the technology and the system. How these are calculated varies across organizations depending on the accounting policies. In some cases they are considered a fixed cost and not allocated to individual projects, in others the direct salary costs are allocated and in many organizations the full costs of internal resources are recovered across the range of developments through an hourly or daily charge-out rate. The last of these provides the most realistic view of the full costs involved, which is necessary when comparing different options for resourcing the project, but implies the costs are discretionary, and will not be incurred if the project is not funded.

Charge-out or cost allocation policies have a significant influence on investment decision making, as discussed by a number of authors (see, for example, Earl (1989); Ward and Griffiths (1996)), and understanding the implications for different types of IS/IT investment decisions is essential in managing a comprehensive project portfolio.

Infrastructure costs that are incurred exclusively for the new system should be included, but again it will depend on accounting policies, including the policy for depreciating IT assets, as to whether the costs of shared infrastructure are allocated indirectly, for example, based on the number of workstations or recovered as a per unit cost based on the level of usage of the system. The options and issues associated with different ways of dealing with infrastructure costs are covered in the references mentioned above.

Costs of carrying out the business changes should also be included to provide a complete financial view of the investment, although apart from obvious costs associated with training, staff relocation or redundancy and refitting buildings (e.g. recabling or new office equipment) these are rarely included, being considered as 'business as usual'. This is realistic if there is no way of identifying the costs actually incurred by the project.

Ongoing costs associated not only with the operation of the new system, but also additional permanent costs involved in the new ways of working. For instance, many organizations are enabling staff to work remotely, which saves on travelling but increases telephone costs. These costs can either be included explicitly as additional costs or 'netted off' against the benefits from the changes to working practices.

Once a total financial value of the relevant benefits has been determined and the expected costs have been identified, a financial assessment can be made. It is not the purpose of this book to include a detailed description or critique of different financial appraisal techniques. The techniques applied to IS/IT investments are all derived from investment appraisal approaches for other forms of capital or revenue investment (Ballantine and Stray, 1998). Common approaches include calculation of a return on investment rate (ROI) or net present value (NPV), which can be compared with alternative uses of funds and the required return on assets (ROA) or return on capital employed (ROCE) for the organization's shareholders, or as needed to remain competitive in the industry.

While surveys such as that by Ballantine and Stray show that 90% of organizations – a proportion that has increased over the last 20 years – perform some form of financial assessment on all IS/IT investments, that does not imply that the decision to invest is based exclusively on the estimated economic return. The limitations of financial appraisal techniques are well known and, given the many uncertainties of IS/IT projects, even those organizations that apply them rigorously appreciate that basing decisions solely on estimated financial values will limit the types of business investment they make (Kohli and Devaraj, 2004). A comprehensive analysis of the types of accounting technique and their applicability to IS/IT investments is included in books by Hares and Royle (1994) and Renkema (2000).

Variations in Benefits and Changes across the Application Portfolio

The application portfolio was introduced in Chapter 2, as a strategic management tool to enable the contribution of different types of IS/IT investment to the activities of the organization to be understood. It has already been mentioned in this chapter that certain types of benefit and their required changes are associated with the different application types identified by the portfolio.

High potential investments are essentially research and development (R&D) activities to identify the benefits that could be achieved by innovative use of IS/IT. Benefits are therefore likely to be associated with changes that are new to the organization or associated with radically new ways of working. By definition, in such cases it is likely that little will be known about the benefits at the time of considering the investment. Hence the possible benefits associated with such investments can only be described in outline terms, based on external 'evidence' or from experience and judgement, and can at best be considered as observable or measurable, that is the activity can be measured now, but the potential improvement is not known. At this stage the nature of the changes required will not be known, except in the general sense of the potential differences from the current ways of working.

The purpose of most high potential evaluations is to provide sufficient evidence of the potential benefits and the costs and feasibility of the business changes required to achieve them, to justify initiating a major investment. The initial investment will not result in a working system at this stage, merely a 'proof of concept'. In many cases the work will demonstrate that further investment is not worthwhile.

Strategic investments are intended to achieve future advantages by creating new business and organizational capabilities which are superior to those of competitors. In non-profit-making organizations such investments aim to achieve transformations in the services provided to meet stakeholder needs. This usually implies significant change and innovation in the ways of conducting business or using resources, that is benefits will be associated mainly with doing new things, although some will result from performance improvements in existing activities. It is also possible that the new processes completely replace existing ones and elimination of those activities will save costs. Apart from the removal of old processes, the financial outcome cannot be predicted with much certainty. Benefits are therefore likely to be predominantly measurable, although some may be quantifiable or even financial, if the new processes have been successfully piloted to provide evidence to quantify them. If the investment is significant then it is often worthwhile undertaking a pilot or proof of concept first, so that more can be understood about the benefits, and the associated changes that will be required, before significant resources are deployed.

The changes will inevitably be extensive, possibly radical and can often involve restructuring roles, responsibilities and aspects of the organization. In many cases the changes will extend beyond the organization and involve customers, suppliers or trading partners.

Key operational investments are intended to ensure that the organization is not disadvantaged by the inadequacies of its essential processes and systems, leading to unacceptable levels of performance or significant business risks. Since these applications are aimed at improving existing activities, the majority of benefits will result from 'doing things better', although sometimes that is achieved by the elimination of unnecessary or duplicated tasks. The focus on existing activities also implies that there is sufficient knowledge of the consequences of the problems, that both the level of improvement required can be quantified and also how those targeted improvements could be achieved. It should be possible to estimate the financial value of many of the benefits, although some will be dependent on the severity, probability and timing of business inadequacies that the investment is intended to address. In the process of removing the causes of potential or actual disadvantages some new activities can be undertaken with the resources released. These benefits are less likely to be provable in terms of quantifiable or financial values.

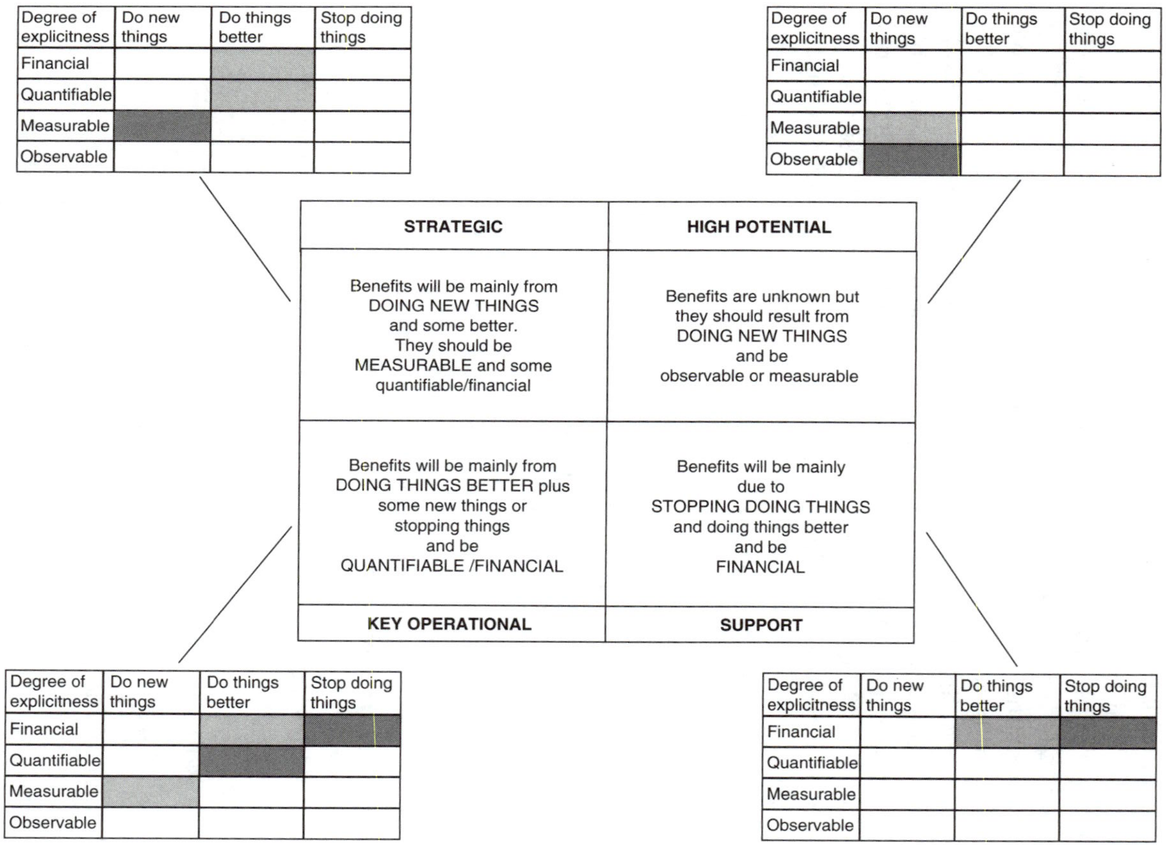

STRATEGIC

Degree of explicitness	Do new things	Do things better	Stop doing things
Financial			
Quantifiable		■	
Measurable	■	■	
Observable			

HIGH POTENTIAL

Degree of explicitness	Do new things	Do things better	Stop doing things
Financial			
Quantifiable			
Measurable	■		
Observable	■		

Central matrix:

STRATEGIC
Benefits will be mainly from DOING NEW THINGS and some better. They should be MEASURABLE and some quantifiable/financial

HIGH POTENTIAL
Benefits are unknown but they should result from DOING NEW THINGS and be observable or measurable

KEY OPERATIONAL
Benefits will be mainly from DOING THINGS BETTER plus some new things or stopping things and be QUANTIFIABLE /FINANCIAL

SUPPORT
Benefits will be mainly due to STOPPING DOING THINGS and doing things better and be FINANCIAL

KEY OPERATIONAL

Degree of explicitness	Do new things	Do things better	Stop doing things
Financial			■
Quantifiable		■	
Measurable	■		
Observable			

SUPPORT

Degree of explicitness	Do new things	Do things better	Stop doing things
Financial		■	■
Quantifiable			
Measurable			
Observable			

Figure 5.7 Variations of benefits across the applications portfolio

Changes associated with key operational applications can be extensive and complex, given the degree of integration and interdependence of such systems, but due to the role they play in making the core business processes operate, the changes would not normally be radical. However it is likely that many of the changes will be closely interlinked and may involve large numbers of staff.

Support investments are intended to improve organizational efficiency and eliminate unnecessary costs. They are therefore often related to stopping doing unnecessary tasks, automating clerical activities and reducing the costs of the resources required to perform the processes. This last case may involve outsourcing some activities. While cost savings are the primary aim, improvements in performing necessary processes and activities should also be achieved. It should be possible to predict the financial value of the majority of benefits in advance, since they are activities that the organization has been undertaking.

It might appear that because the changes largely involve automation, simplification and elimination they are easier to define and implement. However, they normally result in labour savings of some kind and this frequently creates resistance from those whose jobs are threatened or whose roles will be changed significantly. Critical to achieving benefits from support investments is the removal or decommissioning of old systems, many of which may be 'informal' systems that were developed by individuals or small groups to address local problems.

Figure 5.7 summarizes these differences across the portfolio.

The Importance of Recognizing the Variation in Benefits

It should be stressed that while different application types within the portfolio will give rise to the majority of benefits in different 'columns' in the business case, many investments do not fit neatly into one segment of the application portfolio and will give rise to a large number of benefits spread across the matrix.

A broad spread of benefits across the entire matrix, or clusters of benefits in more different rows or columns may be indicative of an investment that has a number of the different application characteristics within it. For example, the investment being considered may have elements of improving existing operations (key operational) and also new value-adding capabilities (strategic). In such cases, it is worth recognizing these are intrinsically different types of change and it may well be appropriate to phase the project to address them separately. Often the key operational part of the investment needs to be implemented first to remove constraints and problems in the current ways of working, before the innovations become achievable and the more strategic benefits can be realized. Also when the operational part of the project has been successfully achieved, it is likely that more will be known about the benefits that can actually be achieved from the strategic part of the investment.

Another implication of the variation in types of benefit that arise from different applications, and perhaps the most serious one, is that organizations should not expect all investments to produce similar business cases. In particular, high potential and strategic investments are unlikely to be able to yield a fully financially justified business case. Rather such business cases, if produced honestly, are likely to show mainly measurable benefits.

Risk Assessment

There are many well-established approaches to risk analysis, derived from case studies of IT failure or abandonment. Apart from the consistently obvious factors that increase risk, such as project scale, duration and technical or business complexity there are often organizational contextual issues that can create specific risks for certain projects at particular times. Comprehensive and practical sources of understanding the causes of risks, frameworks for assessing risks and approaches to managing them can be found in Cash et al. (1992), Ewusi-Mensah and Przasnyski (1994), Jordan and Silcock (2005), Renkema (2000), Sauer (1993), Ward and Elvin (1999), Willcocks and Margetts (1994) and the Office of Government Commerce (2002) publication *Management of Risk: Guidance for Practitioners*.

It is beyond the scope of this book to consider in detail all the types of risk associated with IS/IT investment. Apart from the risks associated with organizational and stakeholder factors, which have direct implications for the realization of available benefits, readers are advised to look at other texts, including those mentioned in the previous paragraph. Ways of identifying and taking action to address actual risks as they arise during the implementation of the business and enabling changes necessary for benefit delivery are considered in the following chapters.

At the time the investment decision is made the implications of the some of the risks can be allowed for by adding contingencies to the project costs or timescale. These contingencies would then be invoked as and when risks materialize, but the contingencies themselves need to be reviewed as the project proceeds to ensure that they are still appropriate to the remainder of the project.

Based on a synthesis of the literature just mentioned, for most IS/IT investments, three aspects of risk need to be assessed as early in the project as possible to enable a realistic appraisal of the probability of achieving the objectives and benefits. These risk types are described in Box 5.4.

Box 5.4 Risk types associated with IS/IT investments

Technical risks are those associated with the chosen technologies and suppliers and their ability to deliver the functionality, security and performance required. Whether the organization has the internal knowledge, skills and required infrastructure, and is using the most appropriate process to implement the technologies, must also be considered. Approaches to assessing and then managing technical risks, and risks associated with processes of development and implementation, are built in to most systems development and project management methodologies via risk registers.

Financial risks concern the predictability of the costs and confidence in the financial benefits. Such risks can be estimated by conducting sensitivity checks on the financial case assuming higher costs and reduced or delayed benefits. Other techniques including scenario planning and real options analysis can be used to compare the relative financial risks of alternative investments.

Business change and organizational risks include the capability of the organization, its management and staff and in some cases, external stakeholders to carry out the enabling and business changes that are essential to realize each of the benefits. A detailed analysis of stakeholder perspectives and concerns is the most effective way of taking action to reduce organizational risks, mitigate their effects or adjust the scope of the project to avoid them. This is described in detail in the next chapter.

Although the technical and financial risks of IS/IT investments can be significant and must be assessed and addressed, there is a increasing consensus that risks due to organizational issues are the most critical to the success of many projects, especially when the implementation affects large parts of an enterprise (Gibson, 2003).

A checklist of risk factors that need to be considered under each of these headings is shown in Table 5.3. The factors have been included in the category where they are likely to have the most impact, but clearly many will have secondary effects in the other categories. For example, the longer the duration of the project the more likely it is that key personnel will change, new requirements will emerge and resources will be required for other projects.

Table 5.3   *Checklist of investment risk factors*

Technical risk factors	Financial risk factors	Business change and organizational risk factors
Complexity of the system functionality	Size of the investment	Senior management commitment to the project
Technical novelty – to the organization and supplier	Project duration	User commitment of resources and knowledge
Number of system interfaces and systems being replaced	Degree of confidence in all the elements of project cost	Stability of organization and key staff
Certainty and stability of the business requirements	Confidence in the evidence for investment benefits	Extent of changes to business processes and practices
Technical skills of project team	Appropriateness of project cost control mechanisms	Number of departments, functions and business staff involved and affected
Business knowledge of the project team	Reliability of external suppliers estimates and enforceability of contract conditions	Degree to which organizational and role changes are needed to realize the benefits
Degree to which formal methodologies and standards are adopted	Rate of change of the external environment	Other change initiatives that will affect the same areas of business
Extent of the changes needed to IT infrastructure	Business criticality of the areas affected by the system	Existing change management capability and experience
Degree to which the system can be prototyped or piloted	Dependence of the benefits on other projects	Existing user IT and information skills and knowledge of 'how the business works'

Risk Variation across the Application Portfolio

It has been discussed earlier in this chapter how the benefits expected and the nature of the associated changes will vary across applications types. As shown in Figure 5.8, the type of risks that may be expected will also vary across the portfolio.

STRATEGIC	HIGH POTENTIAL
Risks are likely to be of all kinds TECHNICAL, FINANCIAL AND ORGANIZATIONAL	Risks are likely to be high and of all kinds TECHNICAL, FINANCIAL AND ORGANIZATIONAL Minimized by limited scale/scope
Major risks are likely to be ORGANIZATIONAL Financial and technical risks are addressed by strict application of methodologies	Major risks are likely to be ORGANIZATIONAL due to vested interests Low financial risks and technical risks minimized by use of proven technologies
KEY OPERATIONAL	SUPPORT

Figure 5.8   Variation of risks across the applications portfolio

High potential investments are, by definition, high risk and the risks are mitigated by controlling the time and costs allowed for the evaluation. This usually implies a limit on the scale or scope of the evaluation. It has to be accepted that in many cases the right outcome of the evaluation is not to proceed further, due to technical, financial or organizational risks being too great.

Strategic investments are intended to achieve future advantages by creating new business and organizational capabilities. This implies significant innovative change and the implementation of new ways of conducting business or using resources. Neither the costs nor the financial benefits can be predicted with certainty at the outset. The IS/IT requirements and business changes will evolve as it becomes clearer how the benefits can be best achieved and perhaps some potential benefits will prove impossible to deliver. If deploying new technology is integral to the project success, this, in turn, will introduce additional risks. Therefore the number of risk factors across all three categories is likely to be high and the approach to managing the project must allow for this.

Key operational investments are normally undertaken to improve existing essential processes and systems. Technical risks should be reduced by using established, proven technology, as far as possible. However, many key operational applications are complex and either have numerous interfaces or are required to be closely integrated. The strict application of systems development, quality assurance and project management methodologies, including risk registers, is needed to ensure that the system design and operational performance meet the business needs. Any financial risks should be relatively low, since the expected benefits should be financial or quantifiable and the costs associated with known technology should also be relatively easy to determine. However, such investments often require significant simplification, rationalization and integration of processes, resulting in widespread changes to organizational roles and responsibilities and the development of new skills or performance measures. Since these systems are at the core of the business, changes have to be carefully controlled to avoid deterioration in performance during the implementation.

Support investments are intended to improve organizational efficiency and eliminate unnecessary costs. Few, if any, of the changes will be innovative and given that the benefits should be achievable using proven technologies the investments should be relatively low risk. However, the achievement of many of the benefits will rely on changing and standardising organizational practices to make effective use of the technology available. Many of the efficiency savings will inevitably reduce the work required of some staff and often reduce the numbers of staff required, which will be seen as a significant 'disbenefit' of the changes by those affected. Consequently, the main risk factors are organizational, due to the unwillingness of some users to change their traditional ways of working, either individually or collectively.

A large financial services company applied this understanding of the different degrees of investment risk across the portfolio to include standard financial contingencies in the approval process. For example, overruns of up to 5% of costs were allowed for support investments, 10% for key operational and 20% for strategic, before further funding had to be fully justified through a revised business case.

Completing the Business Case

Organizations vary in the way they require proposed investments to be described, the criteria used to make funding decisions and the process by which those decisions are made. This chapter has described tools and techniques for converting the knowledge created by the development of a benefits dependency network into an argument for investment. Considerations of the costs and risks of the investment have been addressed but only in summary. The emphasis has been on creating a more realistic, comprehensive and substantive case for the benefits that should accrue and how those benefits can be realized. The business case should be supported by a detailed benefits plan, which can be based on the templates described in Chapter 4, and the benefits dependency network itself, to show the interrelationships of enabling and business changes and how in combination these can lead to the realization of each of the benefits. Details of responsibilities and how achievements will be measured should be clearly stated, to demonstrate the commitment of all the main stakeholders to carry out their agreed tasks. An example of a completed benefit template from the FoodCo case study is shown in Table 5.4, building on the earlier version shown in Chapter 4 (see Table 4.6). The corresponding change table is completed after undertaking a stakeholder analysis and is shown in Chapter 6 in Table 6.2.

For each of the benefits a more detailed description of both the benefit and the actions required to track its delivery would be included in the project manual, so that progress can be monitored during implementation

The business case itself should, if possible, be structured in a similar way to the process through which it was derived, to reflect the way the argument for investment was developed:

1 The business drivers that are causing the need to change.
2 The objectives of the investment and the contribution that their achievement will make to the relevant drivers.
3 The benefits that will be realized in meeting those objectives and whether they will occur due to new innovations or by improving the performance of essential processes or stopping unnecessary activities.
4 The quantified improvement expected and the financial value of those improvements where possible.

Table 5.4 Example of completed benefit template from FoodCo

Benefit number and type and related objectives	Benefit description	Benefit owner(s)	Dependent changes and responsibilities	Measures	Expected value (if applicable)	Due date
B2: Financial: O1	Eliminate invoice errors	Financial Controller	C1 – Production Manager	1 Number of customer invoice queries	Reduce by 90%	Oct 2004
				2 Admin time on corrections and reconciliations	Reduce by 15–20 hours per week (0.5 FTE) £30,000 p.a.	Sept 2004
B4: Financial: O2	Reduced costs of stock holding – including inventory reductions	Product Managers	C4 – Production Planners C5 – Purchasing Manager E3, E4 and E5 – Operations Director	1 Stock holding by product type for: (a) (RM) raw materials (b) packaging	Reduction of holding RM by 10% & packaging by 15%: one-off saving of £200,000	Oct 2004
				2 Number of stock write-offs	Annual saving of: RM (50%) £180,000 packaging (80%) £70,000	Nov 2004

5 The further measurable and observable benefits that will be delivered.

6 The expected costs involved in the project and a calculation of the overall financial implications of the investment, presented in whatever form the organization requires, including the different outcomes that could occur due to the uncertainties in some estimates.

7 An analysis of the potential risks involved and actions that can be put in place to address them.

Box 5.5 shows a part of business case for the FoodCo example developed in Chapter 4 and earlier in this chapter. Some of the benefits (for example, B2 and B3) have been split into components, depending on the parts of the benefit that could be quantified in advance. Some benefits could be quantified in the future if more work was undertaken, such as undertaking a pilot. However, they are left as measurable in the table until such further work has been undertaken or because the work involved would not be justified, given the expected value of the benefit.

Although most of the benefits arise from carrying out processes and activities more effectively (better) some have been entered into the 'stop' column, when problems will be eliminated (or almost eliminated) by the systems and process changes. Equally, some have been entered in the 'new' column because they occur due to the implementation of new processes and systems. This spreading out of benefits across all three columns and particularly having benefits in the stop and new columns, makes a more compelling case, demonstrating how the planned investment is going to stop wasteful activities and enable new ones.

The company was growing rapidly and needed to retain good staff to achieve the growth. Therefore, although efficiency gains through automation would release several operational staff, they would not leave the company, so no financial savings were claimed. Equally, the small savings of financial staff costs were 'notional', in that the staff would be offered alternative jobs in other areas, where vacancies existed.

The benefits dependency network shown in Figure 4.9 was appended to the business case, as were the full set of completed benefit and change templates. The latter is described in more detail in Chapter 6 once a stakeholder analysis has been completed for the investment.

Box 5.5 Summary business case for the FoodCo project

Business drivers

Forces acting on the organization that require the company to invest in new systems and change its processes in order to achieve its intended strategy of continuing profitable growth through product innovation and high levels of customer service are:

> *External* – price pressures due to the power of large customers, the need for traceability and for continuous product innovation.
> *Internal* – the need to improve grower relations, reduce the unacceptable levels of material wastage and reduce the cost and improve the effectiveness of internal processes.

Investment objectives

These primarily address the internal drivers but will also produce changes that will enable the company to improve its performance with respect to the external drivers. The investment objectives are:

1 to simplify and automate all business transactions
2 to integrate key processes and systems
3 to improve financial control of business assets and resources.

Benefits

The benefits that will be realized by achieving these objectives are shown in Table 5.5.

Project costs

Purchase of new hardware & software	£250,000
Cost of scanning equipment	£85,000
Cost of implementation technical consultants	£120,000
Internal systems development costs (for configuration)	£150,000
Infrastructure upgrade costs	£75,000
Business change costs	£170,000
Training costs	£80,000
Total	**£930,000**
Net increase in ongoing systems support & licence costs	£40,000 p.a.

Table 5.5 Benefits table for FoodCo

	Do new things	Do things better	Stop doing things
Financial		**B3a:** Improved production planning and control: release 4 FTE planning staff, cost saving £150,000 p.a. **B4:** Reduction in stock holding costs: one-off saving from reduction of stock holding of £200,000 and savings of £250,000 p.a. from reduced stock write-offs **B10:** Reduction in bad debts: Reduced payment write-offs: £35,000 p.a. **B9:** Improve cash flow: reduce debtor days by 15: £25,000 p.a. reduction in interest charges	**B2b:** Eliminating invoice errors: release 0.5 FTE staff in reconciliations, cost savings £30,000 p.a. **B5:** Stop unnecessary use of agency staff: £110,000 p.a.
Quantifiable	**B8b:** Improved speed and accuracy of grower returns: 90% reduction in queries		**B2a:** Eliminating invoice errors: reduce customer queries by 90%
Measurable	**B1:** Reduce number of dispatch errors due to scanning: number of dispatch errors	**B3b:** Improve business/production planning and control: number of breaks in production schedules/reduction in idle time **B6:** Reduced costs of customer service failures: number of returns	
Observable	**B8a:** Improved accuracy and speed of grower returns: improved grower relations	**B7:** Access to accurate and timely KPIs and management information: less time spent reconciling MI, more time spent on decision making and performance analysis **B11:** Better knowledge of customer and product profitability: credible and respected product and customer profitability information	

Box 5.5 (Continued)

Financial project return

A financial return for the project can be calculated by looking at the financial benefits shown in the top row of Table 5.5 and comparing these to the project costs.

One-off savings (B4) = £200,000, resulting in a one-off net investment of (£930,000 − £200,000) = £730,000

Recurring savings (B2b+B3a+B4+B5+B9+B10) = £600,000, resulting in a recurring net saving of (£600,000 − £40,000) = £560,000

Payback period=(£730,000/£560,000)=1.3 years (a NPV or IRR can also be calculated if required)

While many organizations will require a financial justification for projects, all of the benefits shown in Table 5.5 should be included in the business case. In some cases, these will help to show how the financial benefits will be realized.

Risk analysis

The following risks are identified that could prevent the realization of all or some of the benefits and need to be addressed in the approach to managing the project. Initial actions to address and mitigate the risks have been identified and a risk review agenda item established for each project management meeting.

Technical risks: complexity of the systems functionality; number of system interfaces and systems being replaced.
Financial risks: confidence in some elements of the project cost; confidence in the evidence for some of the benefits; business criticality of areas affected by the system.
Organizational risks: extent of changes to business processes and practices; number of departments/functions/staff involved; significant organizational changes needed to realize the benefits; limited existing change management capability.

Summary

The structure and logic for a business case presented in this chapter is intended to ensure the argument for investment is clearly understood by those who have to decide whether to proceed, but also by those who will be involved in managing the project to a successful completion. In many organizations the story is told largely in reverse – the costs are presented first and then the benefits are described. Hence the origin of the term 'cost benefit analysis'. This approach proposes a 'benefit cost analysis', which enables management to clearly understand the benefits that they can expect from an investment and hence decide how much they are willing to invest. Using the pro forma we have suggested in this chapter, the benefits that can be expected are clearly linked to the nature of business change required and hence management can also consider whether they are willing to make the complementary investments in change needed to realize the benefits.

The techniques have been described in terms of their ability to improve the quality of the business case. Later chapters explain how they can be adapted to ensure that the benefits management process is flexible enough to meet the needs of different situations and be integrated with the approaches to devising and implementing the technical solution or managing the project. The next chapter describes the finalization of the benefits plan, including a detailed assessment of stakeholder issues and considers the approaches needed to manage the changes that are essential to achieving the business case.

6
Stakeholder and Change Management

As has been emphasized throughout this book, IT, of itself, delivers few benefits. It is the complementary business and organizational changes that are made that produce the majority of benefits. Many studies have shown that it is organizational issues that either pre-date the project, or that arise during the project, which cause apparently available benefits not to be realized (see, for example, Doherty & King, 2001; Lederer and Nath, 1991). In the terms of the Soh and Markus (1995) model shown in Figure 1.5, it is having an *effective use process*, which ensures the changes needed to utilize the IT asset are carried out, that leads to improved business performance.

In the previous chapter the overall ability of the organization to manage the investment was considered an important component of risk analysis. However, it is the degree to which each of the specifically required changes can be accomplished that will determine the actual benefit set that is delivered. Not only is it necessary to understand the reasons why changes may be difficult to carry out, it is also important to adopt an approach to managing each change that deals effectively with the causes of problems as well as the effects. It is not the 'organization' that makes the changes. It is individuals and groups of people who have to change what they do or how they do it. These are normally known as 'stakeholders' in relation to a project or change programme and include the beneficiaries of the investment, those who have to make changes to bring about the benefits and, in some cases, other groups who are indirectly affected by the project, for example groups who may notice a reduced level of service or cooperation during the change period.

Some studies have suggested that IT-enabled change creates particular sets of issues as a result of the perceptions that are often held about the overall effects of IT or the implications of a specific change on individual roles or organizational relationships. These perceptions are likely to cause certain types of behaviour in relation to a new system or the introduction of a new technology. Not understanding these different views, and the reasons for the consequent behaviours, can create problems for the project team in its relationships with different stakeholder groups and may even result in conflicts among stakeholder groups. According to Swanson and Ramiller (1997) these *'problems are often the result of either a lack of common understanding of the purposes of change or different perspectives on how to achieve them'*. In their study, Kumar et al. (1998) identified three commonly held perceptions of IT-enabled change projects that can provoke quite different responses by stakeholders. The terms they use—system rationalism, trust-based rationalism and segmented institutionalism—are easier to understand (and remember!) as follows:

- *Rational* – which describes the behaviours of those stakeholders who subscribe to the economic goal of maximizing the organization's efficiency and effectiveness through technology.
- *Trust* – those stakeholders who trust others that they work with to only make changes that are mutually beneficial and are willing to collaborate with certain other stakeholder groups.
- *Self-interest* – those stakeholders who focus on satisfying their private interests and agendas, at the expense of others if necessary. This behaviour can, in the worst case, undermine the investment.

These are generic perceptions that will manifest themselves in a variety of ways depending on the effects of the particular project, especially the degree of change in relation to benefit, for each stakeholder. As will be discussed later in the chapter, these characteristics need to be addressed through different ways of managing the change components of the benefits plan. Otherwise the response of some of the stakeholders may be inappropriate, perverse or even destructive.

It is important to understand how the benefits are distributed across organizational processes, activities and stakeholder groups and whether the balance of 'pain' from change and 'gain' from the benefits is acceptable from each stakeholder's perspective and for the organization in total. The criticality of the influence of stakeholder perceptions on investment success has been argued by a number of writers. Jurison (1996) summarizes the issues well: *'An important challenge for management is to find a fair balance of benefits between the firm and its stakeholders. . . to implement the system successfully needs the cooperation of stakeholders . . . with no apparent benefits to them they are likely to resist the system.'*

It is not always the explicit changes that cause the resistance. It is often real or perceived secondary effects of the changes. For example, in many enterprise resource planning (ERP) implementations line managers are less than positive about changes that cause closer integration across processes and functions and the new interdependencies this creates. Typical concerns are:

- Increased accountability with less discretion and autonomy of decision making.
- The performance of their area of responsibility is more visible to others.
- They have to rely on others to achieve their performance targets.
- Recognition and reward structures reflect collective rather than individual performance.
- The significant learning curve required for them to manage in new ways and place greater reliance on the ERP system.

A further general concern of line managers, which is not exclusive to ERP projects, is that during implementation conflicts and issues will inevitably arise due to the difficulty in resolving priorities for resourcing the change programme and sustaining performance levels for 'business as usual'. Success of the project may depend on managers releasing the time of their most able and experienced staff – the same people they rely on to ensure existing operations run effectively.

This chapter first considers how stakeholder analysis can help understand the most appropriate way to deal with real and perceived issues. Then approaches to change management are discussed in relation to the types of issues that have to be addressed. Finally, the completion of the benefits plan is described.

Assessing the Feasibility of Achieving the Benefits: Stakeholder Analysis

Once a business case for investment has been developed and an overall risk analysis completed, a more detailed analysis is needed to determine how the organization can bring about each of the changes required for the benefits to be delivered. This can be considered as an aspect of risk analysis, based on an assessment of how willing or able the main stakeholders, or interest groups, involved in the project are to take the necessary actions and commit the time and resources required to achieve the benefits. In projects which require significant changes or involve a wide range of diverse stakeholders, it is advisable to do an initial analysis of stakeholder perceptions, prior to preparing the business case, to decide if any of the benefits are unlikely to be delivered, due to the difficulty of making the changes. The options and advantages of varying the sequence of use of the benefits management techniques, in different situations, are discussed in more detail in Chapter 8. It should also be remembered that during implementation many issues within or outside the project could arise that will affect stakeholder perceptions, interests and priorities, which in turn may change their commitment to the project. Stakeholder analysis may therefore need to be revisited a number of times during implementation.

In many cases a detailed stakeholder analysis will result in the identification of additional changes. These are most often in the form of additional enabling changes required to address stakeholder issues, either before implementation starts or at particular stages during implementation. Based on the issues that arise from the stakeholder analysis, different options for managing the changes can be identified, responsibilities finalized and the benefits plan completed.

There are many different techniques for stakeholder analysis, but here two of the most commonly used have been combined to provide an assessment of the real impact of the project on particular stakeholders and stakeholder groups but also allow for the importance of the stakeholder perceptions and the implications. Overall, the approaches assess the stakeholders' relationship to the project in terms of the balance of benefits they receive relative to the degrees of change they have to endure. This analysis also allows for the possibility that some stakeholders will receive '*disbenefits*' and actually be disadvantaged by the investment, an obvious example being the loss of jobs that may result. This assessment will also enable an overall judgement to be made of each stakeholder's (or stakeholder group's) attitude towards the project. The actions required to address any specific issues will depend on the influence that the stakeholder or group has in terms of affecting the achievement of the most important benefits.

In essence the purposes of stakeholder analysis are to:

- identify all the stakeholders whose knowledge, commitment or action is needed to realize each benefit

- determine the view held by each stakeholder (or stakeholder group) in terms of *'what's in it for me?'* and any disbenefits they perceive
- understand the change activities as they affect each stakeholder group and their motivation to achieve or resist the changes
- understand the actions needed to gain the required involvement and commitment of all the stakeholders
- develop action plans to enable or encourage the necessary involvement.

It also has to be recognized that there will be existing relationships or coalitions of interest among stakeholders and this will also influence their perceptions. These interrelationships can be either a major concern, if they cause empathy with groups that are against the project, or an asset if those who support the project can persuade others that, overall, the benefits justify the amount of change to be made, that is the organizational 'gain' is worth the individual 'pain'.

The enterprise-wide nature of many IS/IT investments means that the number of stakeholder groups affected by any one project can be very large and the feasibility of making changes is likely not only to be influenced by existing relationships, but also to cause working relationships among groups to change. It is also unlikely that all the stakeholders' issues can be addressed and neither is there always time in the project to reach agreement or a consensus with everyone concerned on every issue. Therefore it is important as a first step to assess which stakeholders' commitment of time and resources are critical to delivering the main benefits, either as benefit owners or change agents. Many new systems are aimed at improving or creating new ways of working with external stakeholders, such as customers, suppliers and other trading partners. An understanding of their perceptions of the benefits they will receive and willingness to make changes is necessary, but any actions to address external stakeholder issues will normally have to be undertaken by managers and staff with responsibility for those external relationships. It may well be the case that customers or suppliers may, if they will benefit without having to make significant changes, be very supportive and this can be a strong argument to persuade some reluctant internal stakeholders of the real need to change – external pressure can often create internal unity of purpose.

Identification of stakeholders will be based on the benefits dependency network in terms of benefit owners and those involved in making the business and enabling changes. These will include named individuals, people in defined managerial roles, specialists such as in human resources or regulatory functions, and often large groups of operational staff or external parties, such as customers. The latter may not be homogeneous groups in terms of their perceptions of the benefits or changes and it may be necessary to break them down into subgroups to reflect those different views and consequent issues. For example, in the health service, clinical staff will vary in their views of the role IT should play in their jobs and have widely different competences in using IT. Often some groups are strongly in favour of the changes, while for others the mere introduction of technology is threatening. Some customers may expect the organization to offer its products and services via electronic channels, whereas others will not want to change their traditional purchasing habits.

Often subdividing the group will be needed to allow for different levels of experience, time in the job, the age ranges of people or the location in which they work. For example, when introducing work-flow systems in a call centre in an insurance company, the operators split into two groups based on their attitudes to working overtime and shifts – the younger staff relied on overtime and shift payments to 'pay the mortgage' whereas those with families preferred to work fixed and certain, normal working hours. The project was expected to result in significant reductions in overtime required. Having identified the two views, action was taken to reorganize work groups to include people with both preferences and they were then allowed to agree the shift and overtime patterns among themselves.

Stakeholder Analysis Techniques

The first technique, which is frequently used by experienced project managers, implicitly if not explicitly, is shown in Figure 6.1. It enables an initial assessment of a large range of stakeholders and groups of stakeholders, and it is best to 'cast the net' widely at the start of any project to ensure no one who can affect the success of the project is ignored. Its main purpose is to provide guidance on the communication approaches that should be adopted by the project team in engaging with the different types of interest group. Stakeholders are first considered in terms of how important their involvement and commitment of resources is to achieving success with the project and then an assessment is made of their current attitude to the particular project.

Clearly, the main efforts of the project team should focus on gaining and retaining the commitment of those who have the greatest influence. However, the communications and engagement approaches will be different for those who are positive towards the project and can therefore be expected to actively support the project team and those who initially oppose the project. In the latter case much of the communication will involve negotiating or 'trading' with the stakeholder group, so that they do not have a negative effect on the project. At the same time the team needs to pay attention to some of the stakeholder groups, whose influence may be less critical at first but who could become more important as the project evolves.

This 'first-cut' analysis is particularly useful in large projects that involve many functions or business units that are starting from different levels of satisfaction with the current systems and ways of working and therefore have more or less to gain from organization-wide change. This situation is quite common in international organizations where units have different relationships with the centre and different cultures, both of which can introduce further divergence of interests and attitudes among similar stakeholder groups.

		Low	High
Attitude towards change project	*Supporting*	Keep informed, in order to retain their support but keep their involvement in the project limited	Keep well- informed, particularly if there is a problem with the project, to retain their confidence. Involve in aspects of project most directly affecting their interests
	Persuadable	Get them on board if only limited effort is required to persuade them. Pay more attention to them if their support will encourage other supporters and/or help to manage opposing groups	Engage in dialogue to develop more favourable attitude towards the project and to limit influence that groups opposing the project might have on them. Discuss how they might become involved
	Opposing	Usually require more effort to change their attitudes than is worthwhile. However, may be necessary to counter their negative influence on important groups	Require substantial time and effort to develop a positive attitude to the project and to manage their demands. Effort may also be needed to counter their impacts on other groups
		Low	High
		Importance to project success	

Figure 6.1   *Prioritizing the attitudes of stakeholder groups (after OGC, 2003)*

This classification of stakeholders is largely subjective and identifies the 'communication strategies' required by the project manager and team to deal with the different types of relationship, but does not take an overall organizational perspective of how best to address the specific concerns about the project or other factors that may be causing reluctance to become involved. However, such analysis does identify the stakeholders who have considerable influence on whether or not the project will succeed and therefore whose interests must be aligned with the way the business case is presented and the change plan is managed.

The second technique is based on the work of Benjamin and Levinson (1993), which was developed to address the particular organizational issues of IT-enabled change. It considers each stakeholder perspective on the project from the balance of change and benefit affecting them. The first step is to identify from the benefits dependency network, normally by asking the stakeholders themselves, how many and how significant are the benefits that they will receive or recognize as benefits for the organization, and also the number and scale or complexity of the changes they are involved in. An initial analysis can be made on a matrix as shown in Figure 6.2, which plots the relative positions of stakeholders on two axes, those of benefits received and changes required.

High	NET BENEFITS Should champion the project – but must be aware of implications for others and use their influence *Collaborators*	BENEFITS BUT... Will be positive about benefits but concerned over changes needed – ensure sufficient enabling changes are identified to offset any resistance *Compromisors*
Benefits received	FEW BENEFITS BUT... Must be kept supportive by removing any inertia/apathy that may influence others *Accommodators*	NET DISBENEFIT Likely to resist changes – must ensure all aspects of resistance dealt with by enabling projects *Resistors*
Low	Low	High
	Changes required	

Figure 6.2 Summary stakeholder assessment

While the relative positions on each of the axes are important to show the gradations of views held, this analysis identifies four basic groups of stakeholders:

1 *Collaborators (net benefits)* – those who should champion the project because they will receive benefits with little change and therefore should be able to influence others, provided they are sensitive to the need for others to make or undergo changes for their benefit. They should be kept actively involved in the project planning and their opinions sought when any issues or uncertainties arise.

2 *Compromisors (benefits but. . .)* – those who will obtain worthwhile benefits, but have to make considerable changes to obtain them. Inevitably, the changes come first and if the benefits are not certain or the project begins to have problems, their commitment may waver as the benefits seem either a long way off or look unlikely ever to be achieved. If the project can deliver some early visible benefits or 'quick wins', it will increase confidence that the more difficult changes are worthwhile and will, in due course, result in the delivery of the other more significant benefits. It is likely that throughout the project this group will change their views and some renegotiation of the change programme or further actions to address emergent issues will be needed, hence they will have to make some compromises at times. This will be particularly the case if they are making the changes at the same time as existing workloads involved in 'keeping the shop open' increase. If the interests of these groups are not continually and explicitly addressed, they may gradually become less committed and even resist some of the change aspects of the project.

3 *Resistors (net disbenefit)* – those stakeholders who have to make changes largely for the benefit of others, while they have little or nothing to gain. In the worst case they may feel that the project will only result in disbenefits for them. These groups are the most likely to resist the changes and it will normally require specific actions to be taken, early in the project, to address their concerns or make changes to the benefits plan, especially if they are very influential stakeholders and action to change their perceptions is unlikely to succeed. It is important not just to identify and take action but to make it clear that their concerns are being considered seriously and addressed as far as is possible. These groups are always likely to give priority to maintaining performance levels in existing business as usual activities rather than devote time and resources to the change programme.

4 *Accommodators (few benefits but. . .)* – those who are involved in or affected by the investment but more marginally, in the sense that they will see few benefits and have little if any change to make. Provided that they are kept informed of how the project is proceeding and specifically when and how their time or involvement is needed they will normally accommodate the project activities

within business as usual. This may change if they perceive that other stakeholders, with whom they work, are negatively affected by, or are struggling to cope with the changes.

An initial assessment of the stakeholder positioning in the FoodCo example discussed in previous chapters is shown in Figure 6.3. The pattern is a positive one in the sense that there are clearly a number of stakeholders, including the managing director, who will gain significant benefits with little effort. However, some of these are external and will need to be informed about the investment and the benefits that they can expect. It may not be practical for them to directly influence the other stakeholder groups, but in the case of the customers the customer services manager and marketing director should represent their interests in discussions with other stakeholders. However, there are three groups of internal stakeholders who have to make significant changes for little if any 'personal' benefit: the purchasing manager and buyers; the production manager and his staff; the production planners. These groups could form a powerful alliance to reduce the impact of the changes, given the critical parts of the operations they control. Four other groups or individuals are in the 'benefits but. . .' category and will have to be convinced that the changes required justify the expected benefits if they are to use their influence to persuade others to make the relevant changes. This example will be considered in more detail later in the chapter.

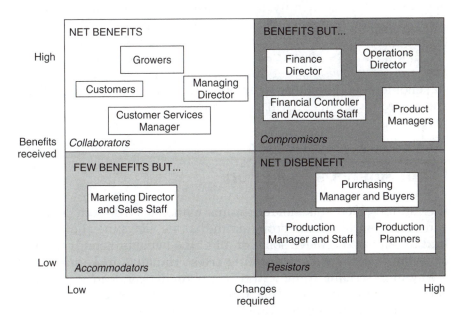

Figure 6.3 *Stakeholder assessment from FoodCo*

The results of this form of stakeholder assessment should be considered in three ways. First, the positioning of the stakeholders on the matrix relative to their ability to influence the project as defined in the analysis shown in Figure 6.1 should be considered. This suggests the type of 'engagement strategy' the project team needs to adopt with each stakeholder (or stakeholder group) and whether there is a need to involve more senior management in addressing some of the issues.

Second, the pattern of the stakeholders across the matrix will give an initial indication of the viability of the project. If the majority of influential stakeholders are in the 'benefits but' and 'net dis-benefits' groups, then it is likely that, overall, it will be very difficult to obtain the required commitment to achieve the business changes. The project scope may have to be revised either to find more benefits or to reduce the extent of the changes required, or be restructured into stages that deliver some early benefits from limited changes. It also enables interrelationships among stakeholders to be depicted in order to consider how one group could exert a positive influence on others, or to identify where negative views might be reinforced.

Third, the assessment helps to identify those whose position must be considered in depth using the more detailed analysis described later, to identify specific actions required and who, in the context of the potential impact on the project will have to be responsible for taking this action. This more detailed analysis should always be carried out for all those classified as *resistors* and *compromisors*, but may also include selected influential stakeholders in the other segments, to ensure their perceptions and hence involvement will be sustained over the duration of the project.

From Analysis to Action

Having identified stakeholder groups with concerns, both practical and perceived, about the project such that the views they hold could lead to failure to achieve some or all of the benefits, actions need to be defined to reduce the resulting risks. The table in Figure 6.4 is a way of describing those issues in a way that can lead to relevant and practical action plans. Each individual stakeholder or group of stakeholders identified as a resistor or compromisor, as well as other key stakeholders should be listed. For each stakeholder the benefits they receive directly and their view of the other organizational benefits are summarized in the second column. It may be that a benefit to the organization overall is a disbenefit to a particular stakeholder group, such as the need to relocate or a threat to their long-term job security and this should be expressly shown in the analysis. The changes that they either have to make or which will affect them are also summarized.

Stakeholder group	Benefits perceived (disbenefits)	Changes needed	Perceived resistance	Commitment (Current & Required)				
				Anti	None	Allow it to happen	Help it happen	Make it happen
List of stakeholders and stakeholder groups – especially resistors and compromisors	Individual and organizational benefits for each stakeholder and group	Changes to be made by or which affect each stakeholder or group	Resistance of each stakeholder or group and reason for this	Are against the project and will attempt to stop it or hinder progress	Are either unaware the project is going on or do not think it affects them	Will comply, when requested to do tasks required by the project, e.g. attend training	Will provide know ledge, time and resource to ensure the project meets object-ives and time scales	Will instigate, oversee or carry out changes and ensure that all relevant changes are completed success fully
					C ——▶ R			
						C ———————▶ R		
				C ——————————————▶ R				

Figure 6.4   *Stakeholder analysis and actions required*

Finally, preferably in discussion with the stakeholders or their representatives and based on the balance of the benefits and changes, any resistance should be identified and understood. Reasons for resistance may be due to the particulars of the changes affecting them or more general issues, such as 'change fatigue', 'technofear', the need to learn new skills or apparent deskilling of their role, new systems being too prescriptive or the introduction of detailed measurements of individual performance, leaving little or no discretion in the job. Often the concerns are about the ability to introduce the changes and simultaneously maintain current levels of performance, without any additional resources during the transition. Alternatively, they may just be due to scepticism that the new system will actually work, based on experience of other investments in the past. In the worst cases, it can be due to cynicism that there is a hidden agenda and that these particular changes are only the start of more serious reductions in staffing or deskilling of their jobs through technology. There may be other reasons due to the current context of the business and other changes taking place.

The current view or position of each stakeholder is then indicated (C) in one of the five columns using the definitions:

anti – will overtly resist the changes due to the overall negative effects on them

none – no commitment to what is needed to be done or perhaps are unaware of the need for change

allow – will do the minimum needed, by compliance rather than cooperation

help – will cooperate and actively support actions as requested

make – will instigate the necessary actions and ensure they are completed successfully.

Based on the role the particular stakeholders need to play in achieving the changes, the required level of commitment can also be agreed and indicated (R). It is the extent of the gap between the current and required levels, that will determine the nature of the action and who is best able to achieve it. If the current and required positions are identical then clearly no action is needed. If they are in adjacent columns, no additional action is required since good project management practices, plus attentive and consistent communication, should be sufficient to address the concerns.

When the gap is over two columns, for example from *none* to *help it happen*, then a specific action is required, which becomes another enabling change on the benefits network, linked to the relevant changes affecting that stakeholder. As with all changes, responsibility and evidence of achievement need to be explicitly identified. For many of these further enabling changes responsibility will lie with line managers, or specialists in other business areas, rather than within the project team itself. Where the gap extends over more than two columns, especially in the case of *anti* to *make*, either the feasibility of achieving the dependent benefits has to be reconsidered or a series of actions is needed, to first reduce the antipathy towards the project, as soon as possible, and later to achieve the level of positive commitment required. Again the need for action and the nature of that action will depend on the degree of influence the stakeholder has, as described in Figure 6.1.

One interesting variant that can appear in this analysis is the need to reduce the enthusiasm of some stakeholders, often including the project champion, to personally *make* everything happen as quickly as possible, without being willing to allow others time to understand and buy into the changes.

Figure 6.5 shows an example of a detailed analysis of some of the stakeholder groups in FoodCo – those who were in the high change segments of the earlier assessment (see Figure 6.3). It can be seen from this that in five cases further actions were needed to address the genuine stakeholder concerns that might prevent their giving the project the necessary level of commitment. In the case of the production planners, action would be needed in two stages. First, to overcome existing resistance, due to the fear that jobs would be lost, before further action could be expected to obtain the cooperation required to implement the new system successfully.

Stakeholder group	Perceived benefits or disbenefits	Changes needed	Perceived resistance	Commitment (Current & Required)				
				Anti	None	Allow it to happen	Help it happen	Make it happen
Finance director	Improved cash control and info	New KPIs and Controls	None					C ——→ R
Finance controller and accounts staff	Fewer errors, better control	New systems and procedures	*Extensive retraining*			C	Action	→ R
Operations director	Reduced stock costs	New planning processes	None					C ——→ R
Production manager and staff	Fewer production problems	New systems and technology	*Fear of new technology and lack of skills*			C	Action	→ R
Purchasing manager and buyers	None	Inventory-driven procurement system	*Reduced discretion and tougher KPIs*		C	———	Action → R	
Product managers	Better cost info and accurate grower payments	New grower system and inventory KPIs	*Risk that grower needs will not be met*			C	Action	→ R
Production planners	None – *fewer planners needed*	More automated scheduling	*Fear of job losses*	C	Actions	———		→ R

Figure 6.5   Stakeholder analysis from FoodCo

Many stakeholder or interest group views can be changed by appropriate actions to address their concerns, but their perceptions are also likely to change over time as the project evolves, especially if problems arise, and due to factors outside the project. In projects that last more than a few months the stakeholders themselves are also likely to change and reorganizations may change the roles of stake-holders in the project as well as the individuals involved. Therefore it is important to revisit the stakeholder analysis whenever any of the more influential stakeholders change.

Completing the Benefits Plan

Having carried out a comprehensive stakeholder analysis, the final details can be completed on the benefits plan, which is the set of 'tables' that define all the activities, interdependencies, timing and responsibilities involved in managing the changes and realizing the benefits. The stakeholder analysis may have added additional enabling changes to the benefits dependency network, clarified or redefined some of the business changes and may even have amended some of the benefits, based on the practicalities of achieving them.

In Chapter 4, templates for describing the benefits (see Table 4.6) and changes (see Table 4.7) were introduced and, at that stage, initial information derived from the benefits dependency network could be entered into the tables. In Chapter 5 as the business case was developed the benefits information could be completed as described and exemplified in Table 5.4.

The final stage in completing the information regarding the change elements of the plan involves ensuring that all the stakeholders who have to contribute to effecting the changes understand the roles they are expected to play and the resource commitment they will need to make during the project. From the change dependencies and the project plan the timing of when each change activity needs to be completed can be estimated and the earliest start date identified. By estimating the resource commitment from each stakeholder for the change activity, standard PERT networking techniques can be used to schedule the change activities within the overall project plan. This will almost certainly result in some compromises from the ideal sequence of activities, due to resource constraints. If such constraints impact the tasks on the critical path, the overall timescale of the project will need to be revised to accommodate them. This is not a simple task but is a normal aspect of any project planning and control methodology.

The information from this planning process can then be used to complete the details required for the benefits plan, as shown in the example template in Table 6.1, which is based on the sample of

Table 6.1 *Completed change template example from FoodCo*

Change or enabler number and dependent benefits	Description	Responsibility (and involvement)	Prerequisite or consequent changes	Evidence of completion	Due date	Resources required
E8 B7, B9 and B10	Develop new KPIs based on Balanced Score Card	Executive Directors	P: None C: C6 Implement performance management process	Balanced Score Card and KPIs agreed by board and published	April 2004	2/3 executive meetings + 1 day per departmental manager
C2 B3, B4	Implement new raw material stock replenishment algorithms	Purchasing Manager and Product Managers	P: E1 Restructure stock coding C: None	Tested and agreed algorithms for all A and B class materials	June 2004	20 days of inventory controllers, 10 days of product/purchasing managers + 4 days of accounts staff

the business and enabling changes in the FoodCo project, initially described in Chapter 4 (see Table 4.7). As for the benefits, the activities required would be described in more detail in the project manual and be updated as implementation proceeds. For complex or extensive changes it is probably necessary to develop a more detailed 'sub-project' plan and to manage and track the progress of all the activities required to complete the change.

Approaches to Managing Change

In principle, there are a number of ways that actions can be implemented to address stakeholder change management issues in the project environment. Ury et al. (1993) suggest three different types of management approach, which can be used to bring about change successfully, although each can also cause both helpful and adverse stakeholder behaviours:

1 *Top down* – imposition of the changes by senior management. This can be quick and effective but, although it usually obtains compliance in the short term, it can breed a feeling of resentment and reduce future cooperation, especially when there are genuine causes for the concerns that appear to have been ignored.
2 *Coalition* – working together to understand and resolve the concerns and, if possible, the causes of those concerns, at least for the duration of the project. Concessions will probably have to be made in terms of the change plan or by finding additional benefits to encourage the required commitment.
3 *Negotiation* – involves making very specific trade-offs between the organization's need for the benefits and the means by which the stakeholder group will help those benefits occur. This may involve agreeing to terms and conditions to protect the jobs of staff or the introduction of new incentive or reward schemes to 'buy in' the new ways of working. The danger here is that special treatment for those taking a negative stance may reduce the commitment of others who initially were in favour of the project.

The style of action best suits the situation and people involved and would have least undue side-effects on others must be decided. The alternative is, even at this early stage, to reduce the scope and ambition for the investment to that which can be accommodated without making unduly risky changes. Which of these approaches can be adopted is also dependent on the nature of the organization, the culture and existing management style. For example, in an organization with a strong command and control structure, change can be implemented from the top down more frequently and with less risk than in an organization with devolved professional responsibilities and a more social culture that relies on interest group collaboration to achieve improvements and change. An alternative approach described by Markus and Benjamin (1997) is to recognize that 'change is a contact sport' and establish specific types of change management roles and allocate responsibilities for change 'advocacy' and 'facilitation'. These roles should, preferably, be filled by experienced line managers and organizational development specialists, who are not part of the project team and therefore wedded to the particular IT solution, and who will be open to different options for achieving the changes.

Matching the Management Approach and Stakeholder Behaviours

As described earlier, stakeholder behaviours in relation to IT-enabled change can be categorized in three ways – rational, trust and self-interest – based on their views of the changes and benefits of the project. At the same time, the approach adopted for managing the project can be essentially one of three types – top down, coalitions or negotiation. These are inevitably simplifications of all the possible alternatives available, but they are helpful when combined, to understand how the interplay between the approaches adopted by the project team and the different stakeholder perceptions and consequent behaviours, can influence the outcome of the investment. In a study of international enterprise systems implementations, Ward et al. (2005) used these classifications to analyse the stakeholder and project team interactions over the course of the projects to understand how effectively the management approaches addressed different stakeholder behaviours, in terms of the effects on time, cost and benefits delivered. The study revealed that the different management approaches provoked responsive behaviours from certain stakeholder groups that influenced the outcome. Table 6.2 summarizes the main effects of the different combinations of management approach and stakeholder behaviour on the projects. A more detailed discussion is given in Box 6.1.

Table 6.2 *Interplay of stakeholder behaviours and management approaches*

		Management approach		
		Top down	Coalitions	Negotiation
Stakeholder mode of behaviour	Rational	1 Clear vision of potential benefits – business case and overall plan	2 Mutual benefits from changes and shared learning – but tends to reduce scope to changes that can be agreed by all	3 Agreement on timescales, resources and local benefits, but tends to reduce scope and lose some major benefits
	Trust	4 Shared vision of potential benefits and acceptance of the need to change to overcome problems	5 Cooperative change management to achieve mutual benefits	6 Trade-offs in resources, benefits and changes can be agreed across interest groups
	Self-interest	7 Localized view of benefits only – resistance to change if no local benefit, leading to software customization	8 Trade-offs between coalitions to minimize negative effects of changes (and probably reduce benefits)	9 Detailed 'contracts' on all aspects of implementation – benefits, resources, changes, etc. with each interest group

Box 6.1 Implications of interactions of management approaches and stakeholder behaviours

Top down/rational

As discussed previously in Chapter 4, at the start of a project it is essential to ensure the project is consistent with the stated vision or strategy of the senior management. The best way of gaining consensus at this level is via rational discussion of the drivers for change, the investment objectives and business benefits expected and present these in a business case. Senior executives are more likely to agree to and support a well-argued business case, linking the investment benefits to the business strategy, than for any other reason. Equally, it is their confidence in the business case that enables senior managers, individually and collectively to persuade others of the need or change. However, it is possible that senior management will be unaware of some serious issues that may prevent delivery of all the benefits and they will want the benefits delivered by minimum resources and change effort. The business case also provides a 'mandate' for the project manager and team.

Coalitions/rational

From the mandate for change, the project team supported by senior management needs to establish the appropriate relationships with 'coalitions' of key stakeholders to develop the change plan that will deliver the business case. If the project requires significant innovation in processes and ways of working, then organizational learning will be required to create and achieve the changes. This can take some time and require more effort than expected to achieve agreement among the affected stakeholders. The rational view will tend to balance the change effort with the importance of the benefits, which may result in a reduction in scope, in order to deliver what these coalitions perceive as the major benefits, within an acceptable timescale and manageable change plan. Given that these coalitions need to see the mutual benefit from their agreements, their existence may not be sustained if the situation changes.

Negotiation/rational

The project team's relationship with the business managers will tend to focus on rational negotiation about the facts, that is, timescales, schedules, resources and the most obvious benefits. The more complex issues such as change implementation and new working relationships require more subtle types of negotiation to resolve. Again the project team can use the business case to argue the need for other changes to deliver the benefits, but the line managers will argue it is 'their job to deliver the benefits' and the project team's job to deliver the necessary technology at the right time and cost. This leads to a focus on the project costs and the technology rather than the business changes. The result is that the relatively easy local benefits will be delivered but the efforts needed to obtain the more difficult benefits are likely to be reduced.

Box 6.1 (Continued)

Top down/trust

When senior management attempt to impose 'their' plan without allowing time and effort for understanding how the changes will be made, existing relationships among stakeholders based on 'who trusts whom' will often be reinforced. They may well agree with the benefits, but the attitude to change will be acceptance rather than commitment to make it happen. The project team will be faced with stakeholder groups who represent the current organization structure, and senior management's inability to delegate to or empower the groups can inhibit achievement of consensus about the change plan.

Coalitions/trust

This is the best combination for moving from 'intent' through planning and into implementation when major business and organizational changes are needed. It requires the same actions by senior management and the project team as in 'coalitions/rational', but recognizes the existence of current relationships and the need for a facilitated process to enable those stakeholders to determine the changes in working relationships required. Line managers are allowed discretion to define new working arrangements or perhaps conclude that not all the changes are worthwhile in relation to the benefits. This should mean that the investment objectives can be converted into a viable plan, so that the majority of benefits can be achieved because the changes will actually be made.

Negotiation/trust

This combination enables the more complex organizational issues to be addressed, since the existing trust among stakeholders will enable a degree of trading off between both benefits obtained and changes needed, as well as the resources and timescales required to achieve implementation. Again, the effect may be to reduce the overall benefits delivered to those where well balanced, 'fair', trade-offs can be agreed. However, the trading process is likely to delay the project since the trade-off arrangements may well produce a non-ideal implementation schedule in terms of the use of the project team's resources.

Top down/self-interest

When senior management attempt to impose a 'solution' without reference to existing stakeholder issues and constraints or trust their line managers to achieve the plan using their knowledge and resources, the riskiest combination can occur. It is often compounded when the project team has only focused on its relationship with senior management and paid little or no attention to line managers' change and resource issues. In effect the line managers will only accept the need for change in line with the specific benefits they will obtain and will not cooperate in changes that result in benefits to others or the organization overall. This more often happens in multiunit, multinational implementations where a corporate solution is imposed without consultation and involvement in the initial planning. When the project team consists primarily of 'head office' staff, the problems are compounded!

Coalitions/self-interest

This combination can be a problem when the coalitions required to work together to define the changes and the project team, usually implicitly supported by senior management, have little confidence and trust in each other's motives. Behaviour closer to self-protection can occur, especially if those outside the coalitions have more to lose than gain. Trade-offs with the project team and among the groups are likely to result in minimal negative impact but this will reduce the benefits to those achievable by minimal change. It is this combination that often turns the implementation into a 'software project' to avoid contention between groups and the project team, who achieve what they can with the resources they actually control.

Negotiation/self-interest

At the point of implementation and change over to the new system and associated ways of working, each individual line manager needs to be clear about the 'contract' they, and their staff, have to achieve the new performance levels implied by the

Box 6.1 (Continued)

benefits. The project team also needs clear criteria as to priority areas of business concern and to have clear contingency plans for any actual deterioration of business performance following implementation. It is more likely that the conditions for constructive negotiations will exist close to implementation, if the self-interest behaviours, that are now acceptable, have not prevailed earlier in the project.

In large projects with multiple stakeholders all three management approaches are likely to be required over the duration of the project, and also possibly need to be used simultaneously, to deal with concurrent stakeholder behaviours. It should be remembered that the project team can choose its management approach but the stakeholder behaviours are not under its control. Therefore the project team has to be sensitive to the stakeholders' views in selecting their approach, but also aware of the possible adverse or even disruptive behaviours a particular approach may cause.

In Box 6.2 the implications of the routes that projects take through the matrix are also considered in relation to the intentions of the investment and the extent to which innovative changes as opposed to changes to resolve or overcome problems, are essential to delivering the benefits. The routes discussed are not intended to be prescriptive, but do reflect experience of analysing different types of project using the framework.

Box 6.2 Alternative routes through the matrix

Figure 6.6 suggests three main routes through the matrix leading to varying degrees of probable success. All avoid the top-down/self-interest box, a combination that can cause major setbacks and delays, increase risk and may even derail the whole project. Each route is workable and will produce success to a degree, but the top and bottom routes (dots and dashes, respectively) are likely to deliver fewer benefits.

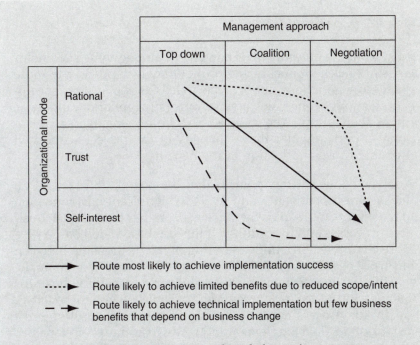

Figure 6.6 *Routes through the matrix*

The 'best' route is shown by the full line, since the management approach adapts to match the organizational behaviours as they will probably evolve during the project. The top-down/rational combination in the planning phase is effective in establishing the investment intent, expected benefits, business case and project structure. But following that, a change to coalitions/trust is best for developing and agreeing an achievable plan – one which will deliver the majority of the benefits via a manageable change programme. This needs to continue through the early stages of implementation, but move to negotiation/self-interest close to final implementation in order to enable the effective control needed to commission and operate the new system and processes.

If, following the project set-up the purely rational view prevails, it is likely to move the project to the coalitions/rational box (dotted route). In which case, the project may be redefined to some extent to reduce the scope and, consequently, some of the benefits, to enable changes to be managed with fewer problems. The focus will be on the stakeholders who will gain

Box 6.2 (Continued)

most from the investment. If agreement among these stakeholders is not reached quickly, the project may well proceed to more detailed negotiations about 'facts', such as the system specification, project timescales and resources (negotiation/rational), rather than resolve the more subjective or sensitive organizational aspects. Again, these changes to the project scope will probably cause a reduction in the benefits.

Another danger at this point is that the negotiation focuses on the system functionality and leads to significant customization to meet users more idiosyncratic needs, rather than change business processes and procedures. If this can be avoided based on a more comprehensive understanding of the relationship between business change and benefit, it should be possible to make sensible trade-offs to undertake the most beneficial business changes, provided resources are available (negotiation/trust). Again, the process needs to change to negotiation/self-interest just prior to final implementation. Because the project passes through more combinations of approach and mode in this route, there are likely to be delays due to the 'trading' to reach agreement plus potentially additional costs due to iterations in design and planning. However, this route is likely to lead to the achievement of a significant proportion of the benefits, but probably those that are more local than corporate.

The third (dashed) route is likely to produce a successful IT project in terms of moving the organization onto a new suite of software and associated technologies but due to the potentially destructive aspects of the top-down/trust combination and the protectionism which often follows (coalitions/self-interest) few of the benefits apart from the 'low hanging fruit' will be delivered, probably after considerable delay and at higher than expected cost. In this route, all the project team can do is deal with aspects under their direct control and accommodate the diverse stakeholder interests by meeting the basic requirements only or customizing the software, which usually implies replicating much of the functionality in the existing systems. In essence the organization essentially rejects the investment as a business initiative and it becomes primarily an IT project.

The model does not imply that once a route is being followed the outcome is inevitable, but it is likely that either benefits achieved will be reduced and project timescales extended or costs increased when the project becomes 'stuck' in an element of the matrix where the management approach and mode of behaviour are conflicting rather than reinforcing.

The Nature of IT-Enabled Change Management: Is it Different?

Markus (2004) coined the term 'technochange management' to differentiate the issues associated with managing IS/IT implementations from other types of change projects. Like Ward and Elvin (1999), she describes this type of change as 'a complete intervention' in which the interdependency of technology implementation, business changes and the benefits to be realized has to be recognized in the way the investment is managed. This is in part due to the uncertainty of the outcome of the combination of changes, but also due to the limitations of traditional IS/IT project management and organizational change management approaches. The former focuses on delivering a working solution and the latter on the ability of people to adapt to new organizational processes, roles and structures.

The organizational change literature rarely considers the role of technology in creating change, yet in many cases the changes are dependent on the capabilities of IT or require major changes to the organization's IS (and possibly IT) to make them work. For example, the OGC (2003) guidelines, *Managing Successful Programmes*, differentiate between IT, and other low ambiguity, 'facilities' programmes, where the emphasis is on construction and delivery, and programmes that 'change the way the organization works' where organizational change management is the focus. The issues associated with programmes in which IT enables the beneficial changes in how the organization works, are consequently not specifically addressed. As argued throughout this book it is the complementary organizational changes that deliver the benefits of most technology investments. Markus lists a wide range of these types of change, which are very similar to those described as typical business and enabling changes in Chapter 4. The critical difference between the 'technochange' perspective and more traditional approaches is that the benefits realized depend on the design of new technology-enabled ways of working and the synchronized implementation of technology and organizational change.

While many IS/IT implementations can be planned in detail based on prior experience and by adopting best practice methodologies in design and project management, many more require significant new knowledge to be created during the project. This implies an iterative development approach, frequently involving prototyping or piloting key IS/IT solution components *and* the new ways of working, to understand both the potential benefits and whether they can be actually realized. This, according to Markus is important not only when new technology is involved, but also when the organization is resistant to change and prototyping is used to create the ability to change ways of working incrementally, rather than risk major business and IT changes at the same time.

Interestingly the UK National Health Service's 'Connecting for Health' programme, (discussed in Chapters 1 and 4), which has many aspects that have the characteristics of 'technochange', was initially set up to be managed with separately defined roles, responsibilities and even structures addressing technology delivery, change management and benefits realization. While this may have been appropriate for some of the more traditional task automation components of the deployment of IT, it was unlikely to be successful in the more complex and innovative uses of IT to change the way that many healthcare and other professionals work together to achieve the major social and economic benefits intended from the programme. The need to integrate and synchronize these streams of activity soon became increasingly apparent to the clinical and managerial staff, who were expected to use the new technology and systems to deliver those benefits.

The discussion thus far implies that different change management strategies are required for different types of IS/IT investment, to deal with the inherently different interactions between the IS/IT and organizational changes needed to use them effectively and the benefits that will result.

Alternative Change Management Strategies

Research by Simon (1995) proposes four types of change control or management, to be used in different circumstances, depending on whether senior management wish to encourage *contribution, performance, innovation* or *initiative*. Achieving these different intentions requires senior management and the project team to apply varying degrees of control to the change activities, based on the need for senior management to contribute their knowledge and influence and the extent to which decision making can be safely delegated. This will of course vary across organizations and depends on both the nature of the application, the business and the organizational culture. For example, in retail organizations with many branches or stores, there is usually little discretion allowed in new systems implementations in the branches and local stores, whereas the organization's market researchers would be expected to demonstrate their initiative to extract and analyse customer information from point-of-sale stored in a data warehouse. Equally, in the R&D functions in pharmaceutical companies, different communities of scientists will be given much local discretion in how they make best use of knowledge-sharing applications.

These different forms of management control are closely related to the different benefits, changes and risks to be managed across the four segments of the application portfolio presented in Chapter 2. They also recognize the need to address many of the change management and learning issues that are characteristic of 'technochange' described earlier. Achieving each of the four types of outcome requires different types of change control.

Boundary Control

This is most appropriate when the intended *contribution*, that is, the investment benefits, can be stated clearly, but senior management are indifferent as to the means by which they are achieved within some stated parameters, such as the cost they are willing to incur or the timescale that can be allowed. Within these constraints, people are empowered to achieve the stated benefits in the way they think most appropriate, given the resources available. This is most effective when the benefits can be expressed in financial or quantifiable terms and the changes needed to achieve them can be explicitly defined in terms of cause and effect. It also requires a clear statement of the extent to which software will be customized or whether a 'vanilla' IS/IT solution will be accompanied by changes to procedures and practices, in order to achieve the benefits. This normally implies that the stakeholder implications can be identified early in the project and action taken to mitigate any adverse issues. Discretion is then allowed for the project team and the line managers involved, to negotiate with each other, to agree the detail of when and how the required changes can be made.

All these attributes imply that this approach is most feasible when the changes are mainly to stop inefficient existing practices or make efficiency improvements. Therefore boundary control is likely to be most suitable for support application investments that are not critical to the organization's strategy or do not have any significant interdependencies with other investments.

Diagnostic Control

If the required benefits can be specified in detail, but their delivery is dependent on a complex and perhaps interrelated set of changes, then the progress of the change management components of the implementation needs to be carefully monitored to ensure that all the benefits remain realizable. This can be especially difficult if decisions have to be made during implementation, regarding whether to make changes to the IS/IT or to business practices. Best practices in project management force each of the stakeholders to plan thoroughly, to monitor progress against key milestones and deliverables and to use this feedback to take any necessary corrective action. There may be a clearly stated rationale for the changes in terms of how performance improvements can be achieved, but key stakeholders may have different views about the best way of achieving them. In such projects it is likely that new stakeholder issues will arise as the project progresses, due to problems of detail in the changes or alternative options for achieving the benefits. As we saw in Box 6.1, these emergent issues often result in 'trade-offs' being required between different stakeholders and also between benefits and the costs or risks of some changes. These trade-offs are most easily understood and negotiated when the target benefits are explicitly quantifiable or financial.

This form of control is used when achieving *performance* improvements are the main objectives but it relies heavily on the stakeholders' ability to prescribe in detail at each stage, what has to be delivered and how it will be done. It is most appropriate for key operational or large organization-wide support investments, that involve many, often interrelated, but not radical changes to business processes or structures.

Interactive Control

The previous two management control approaches are appropriate when the benefits or value side of the business case for investment can be explicitly stated, even if the change plan may have to be modified during implementation. This, in turn, may result in changes to the business case, and in some cases this may cause the project to be abandoned, if the realizable benefits become insufficient to justify further expenditure. In some investments senior management are not able to state in detail what they expect beyond an outline vision or concept, with perhaps some explicit objectives, and iterations are required to assess, in detail, the benefits that can be delivered from different change options. These uncertainties mean that it is difficult to identify or address all the stakeholder issues at the start of the project. In this case, senior management need to develop and share their knowledge by facilitating and supporting an organizational learning process to identify more precisely what the benefits could be, and the risks, if any, the organization is willing to take to achieve them. In these circumstances, senior management need to monitor the evolution of the project and the business case and be able to intervene to make critical decisions, when appropriate, while encouraging *innovation* and creative thinking.

Senior management need to maintain a top-down and rational view of all the likely consequences of the investment, but also allow stakeholder groups to define the optimum achievable combination of technology, change and benefit relationships. This is a delicate balancing act, which relies on establishing effective, trusting working relationships between stakeholders as well as adhering to good project management practices. It requires senior management to be kept informed of both project progress and of potential problems only they can resolve, especially stakeholder conflicts or issues that require changes to organizational roles and responsibilities. They may also be required to make decisions to change the scope of the project due to the organization's inability to carry out the changes successfully or if business circumstances change and the potential benefits become less important. Clearly, these situations are more likely to arise in large, cross-functional projects where significant, even radical, business changes are involved or where there are a range of possible trade-offs between technology investment and business changes. *Innovation* through 'technochange', or radical business change based on proven technologies, is most frequent in strategic applications, to create advantages through new business processes or models, or for key operational investments intended to carry out existing processes in significantly different ways.

Belief System

If senior management wish to encourage *initiative* and empower people to create something radically different then they must establish a belief system, or set of values, that enables people to explore options that align with the strategic intentions of the organization and have an impact on the business drivers. The belief system also gives guidance regarding the types of change the organization is willing to undertake and the rationale or justification needed to initiate different types of change programme. In many organizations the argument for 'technochange' programmes has to be particularly compelling, given senior management scepticism about the business benefits. Hence the early stages of new technology projects often need this form of control. Management do not have the knowledge to understand the potential benefits of the technology and the project team cannot prove a simple cause and effect link between technology change and improved results of the organization. In this case the only means of control is through actively facilitating behaviours in line with the organizational values they have established.

This form of management control is most commonly used in conjunction with a variant of boundary control, such as a strict limit on authorized expenditure for each project stage, to reduce the potential business and financial risks associated with the degrees of freedom being allowed. High potential evaluations exploring new business opportunities or the potential benefits of new technologies, including prototypes or pilots to test the concepts, would fall into this category. If the evaluation is successful, then the form of control should change to one more appropriate to the nature and purpose of the resulting major investment.

STRATEGIC	HIGH POTENTIAL
Benefits: from innovation Characteristics: organizational learning Stakeholder issues: uncertain, evolving and complex Risks: technical, financial and organizational Change control: INTERACTIVE	Benefits: to be determined Characteristics: create knowledge Stakeholder issues: unknown Risks: all types but minimized by limited scale/scope Change control: BELIEF SYSTEM + BOUNDARY CONTROL
Benefits: by performance improvements Characteristics: knowledge application Stakeholder issues: predictable but complex and inter-related Risks: mainly organizational – financial and technical reduced by application of methodologies Change control: DIAGNOSTIC	Benefits: from financial savings Characteristics: automation with empowerment to deliver savings Stakeholder issues: predictable but often negative due to cost savings Risks: mainly organizational, due to vested interests Change control: BOUNDARY
KEY OPERATIONAL	SUPPORT

Figure 6.7   Change management approaches and the applications portfolio

Building on Figures 5.7 and 5.8 in the previous chapter, Figure 6.7 summarizes the relationship between these four change management approaches and the nature of the benefits, changes, risks and stakeholder issues that are commonly associated with each of the application types in the applications portfolio.

Summary

It has been recognized for some time that IS/IT development and implementation is a socio-technical rather than technical process but, although many methodologies allow for this, there is still a strong tendency for technical considerations to dominate the implementation process. The iSociety report in 2003, *Getting By, Not Getting On*, mentioned earlier in the book, provided many examples of failure to achieve performance improvements from IS/IT, due to a lack of attention to the critical role that understanding and managing individual stakeholder expectations and concerns plays in IT-enabled change projects.

While stakeholder analysis can be considered as a component of risk assessment in developing the business case, its real value is in anticipating and determining the actions needed to address stakeholder issues as early as possible in the project. This enables the planning and management of the organizational and business changes to accommodate and deal with the genuine, legitimate concerns of individuals or groups of stakeholders. Defined by Soh and Markus (1995) as the *effective use process*, which converts the IS/IT asset into performance improvements through a combination of successful IS/IT adoption and organizational change management, the ability of the organization to create benefits from new or changed ways of working is the key to realizing the value of most IS/IT investments.

Many organizations now understand that *benefits realization* is both an organizational competence and a major component of IS/IT implementation (see, for example, the OGC (2003) guidelines, *Managing Successful Programmes*). However, it is often considered an activity separate from change management. In many organizations the responsibilities for change management and benefits realization are assigned to different people. Again this tends to reinforce the belief that the benefits largely result from the implementation of technology and that people must change the way they work in order to achieve those benefits. This can often be the cause of resistance to change, since the reasons for the changes seem, to many people, to be merely due to the implementation of the technology. Coupled with the scepticism, resulting from many IS/IT disappointments (or inflated promises), this can cause many stakeholders to avoid becoming actively involved in contributing their knowledge or resources to the change programme, resulting in the perception that 'IT is being done to them'.

Recognizing the importance of managing stakeholder interests and adopting a change management strategy appropriate both to those interests and what the organization is trying to achieve, increases the organization's ability to realize the investment benefits. Change management and benefits realization should be closely integrated and the approaches to stakeholder and change management discussed in this chapter explicitly recognize this interdependence. There is considerable literature that offers valuable guidance on how to manage organizational change, but very little of that literature makes specific reference to the issues arising from technology enabled change. Hence this chapter has concentrated on the particular aspects of IT-enabled change projects.

The next two chapters consider how the benefits management process can be aligned and integrated with other established best practices and methods of IS/IT implementation management and governance, and how it can be adapted to be used effectively in different organizational contexts and for different types of IS/IT investment.

7
Implementing a Benefits Management Approach

Business managers and professionals in most organizations realize that benefits from IS/IT investments do not just happen, but there is less appreciation of the fact that to achieve greater success, an organization must change the way it thinks about, commissions and manages those investments. As stated in Chapter 3, merely improving existing processes and methodologies is insufficient, because that does not address the central issues involved in managing the benefits. However, having new processes, tools and techniques is only the first step. In the terminology used earlier in the book these are just the *means*, and it is how they are used that will determine whether the *ends*, of improving the value from investments are realized. Therefore the 'mode of engagement', that is the *ways* that IT specialists, business managers, users and executives are involved and contribute to the project, the roles each plays and how decisions are taken, also has to change if these new tools are to be used effectively.

The previous three chapters described a suite of tools and techniques that enable organizations to change the way they identify business benefits, build business cases and manage the changes needed. Through consistent application of these concepts, techniques and frameworks an organization can develop the competences needed to manage the variety of investments it undertakes more successfully. This chapter describes how these changes, in the ways of managing IS/IT investments, can be introduced and made effective in the day-to-day conduct of project activities.

First, the reasons that organizations introduce a benefits management approach, and the implications of those different rationales for how the process and tools are implemented, are considered. Then we return to the process outlined in Chapter 3, to describe how the approach and process can be operationalized, in practice. This includes how benefits management can be integrated with existing methodologies for planning and managing IS/IT projects. Throughout the chapter, the discussion reflects the experiences of a wide range of organizations that have adopted this new way of managing their IS/IT investments.

Rationales for Introducing Benefits Management

Having been involved in the introduction and observed the adoption of the benefits management techniques described in this book in many organizations over the last 10 years, there are a number of reasons that commonly lead to the recognition that a new approach is needed. The different reasons often influence the resulting extent of the implementation, ranging from the implementation of new organizational processes and governance to simply the addition of new tools and techniques to existing methods.

Perhaps the four most common causes of adoption are:

1 *A crisis*: a major investment is out of control, costs are escalating and it appears that few if any of the benefits will be delivered. The benefits management toolkit is then used to reappraise the project business case and develop a benefits plan to redefine the overall scope or revise the implementation plan. This would include in some cases cancelling the project. Use of the tools and techniques is then usually extended to other projects to prevent them from suffering the same fate.

2 *An intervention*: business managers are reluctant to engage in the development of business cases for IS/IT projects or to play an active role in delivering the changes and benefits. Instead they prefer to leave it to the 'project team'. This often occurs when the project team insists on following rigorous systems development and project management methods that are not 'user-friendly' ways of working. This can result in managers feeling that, rather than being involved in the process it is being 'done to them'. The introduction of the tools and techniques plus the new process can enable business managers to apply their knowledge in a simple and effective way. If, however, the focus remains exclusively on short-term financial payback, there is a danger that the tools are used merely to provide better argued financial figures, rather than follow through the change management and benefits realization.

3 *A new initiative*: either as result of an IS/IT strategic planning process or due to the initiation of a number of strategic change initiatives that include significant IS/IT investment, the organization realizes that its current methods are insufficient to deliver the investment objectives. This perhaps coincides with an understanding of the demanding challenges of 'technochange' projects and the need to integrate and synchronize IS/IT implementation with business changes in order to achieve the benefits. Normally this produces the recognition that the organization needs new ways of working over the whole investment cycle, which ensure that IS/IT professionals and business managers work together more effectively and combine their knowledge and skills. The complexity of implementation also indicates the need to take into account a wider range of stakeholder interests and how the balance of benefits and changes will affect their commitment to the programme or project. The introduction of a benefits management process in this context is seen as a means of improving collaboration between project teams and line managers over an extended period. As such it tends to lead to the adoption of the approach as a central component of the ways all major IS/IT investments, as well as many other change programmes, are conceived, assessed and managed.

4 *Improved governance*: as organizations become aware that the range of IS/IT investments it makes has a significant effect on current performance and its future ability to succeed in its industry, the need for more effective and adept governance processes becomes paramount. The intention is not only to manage its IS/IT investments and change initiatives more effectively, but also to improve the decision making that instigates those investments, in order to ensure they are either driven by the strategy or are instrumental in creating new strategic options. This view also requires the 'loop to be closed', by using formal post-implementation reviews to understand how well investments that have been made have achieved their objectives. This 'top-down' governance usually recognizes that there is a gap in current methods that is preventing the organization from exploiting the IS/IT capabilities it has or can acquire. The introduction of a comprehensive benefits management approach is a business-based way of ensuring the interdependency of IS/IT implementation and business change is understood and dealt with effectively leading to the delivery of measurable business improvements.

The first two causes are perhaps characteristic of organizations that do not have comprehensive IS strategies aligned with their business strategy, but tend to be problem driven and opportunistic in terms of IS/IT investments. This 'point solution' approach tends to foster a similar attitude to the disciplines required to carry out the projects consistently well, resulting in new tools and techniques being implemented reactively to overcome problems, rather than improve organizational competences and capabilities in managing IS/IT. These new ways of working are normally introduced to the organization by the IS/IT function, which can be interpreted by business managers as the IS/IT function alone needing to improve its competences and processes. Having said that, in some instances these modes of introduction have led, over time, to the approach becoming the basis for all IS/IT investment planning and management as well as other organizational change initiatives.

These four different starting points described are depicted in Figure 7.1. It is when a benefits management approach is implemented due to reasons 3 and 4 that it is able to make a significant improvement in not only benefits realized, but also to the ability of the organization to identify the most advantageous investments to make.

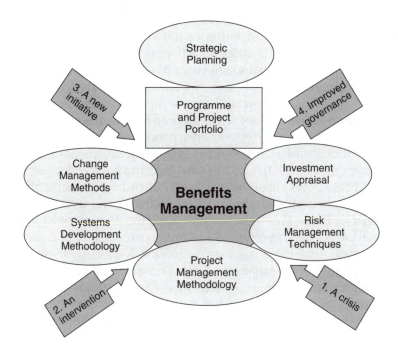

Figure 7.1   Different rationales for implementation of a benefits management approach

Box 7.1 describes in more detail how a major UK retailer introduced the approach, not only as an initiative to improve the value delivered from each of its major IS/IT investments, but also to improve the governance of the whole IT-enabled transformation programme.

Box 7.1 Adoption of benefits management within a major retailer

A major supermarket in the UK had embarked on a multimillion programme to replace many of its core information systems and redesign its operational processes. In order to ensure the programme did not simply become a technology replacement initiative, but would deliver benefits that addressed the strategic drivers on the organization, it decided to adopt the benefits management approach throughout the programme. However, introducing the process was also seen to require significant changes to how the organization initiated, justified, managed and evaluated the success of its IS/IT and change projects. Therefore, a benefits management approach was used to plan the new process introduction, both to demonstrate the improvements it should produce and to ensure that the key stakeholders, the business managers, would become more appropriately involved in the projects. The benefits dependency network that was developed to identify the benefits from adopting this approach across the programme, and the changes to working practices needed, is shown in Figure 7.2.

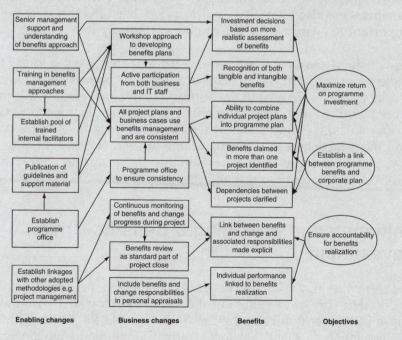

Figure 7.2 *Benefits dependency network for benefits management adoption*

It can be seen that the investment objectives for the adoption were agreed as: to maximize the return on the programme investment; to ensure the programme addressed the issues identified as important in the corporate plan; and to identify accountability for the realization of business benefits from a programme, that to date had been driven by the desire to replace technology.

The benefits management approach can improve the outcomes of single projects. However, as exemplified in this case, the approach also provides additional value when applied to the multiple projects within a programme. (This is discussed in detail in Chapter 9.) Use of the benefits management process allowed the organization to combine the individual project benefits plans into a coherent programme plan that recognized dependencies between the individual projects, and importantly, recognized when multiple projects were claiming the same benefits. Basing the programme benefits plan on the detailed individual project plans ensured a more realistic assessment of the benefits expected from the programme, allowing expectations to be set particularly among the shareholders of the organization who were watching the significant investment with extreme interest. While such shareholders were keen to see a financial return on the investment, adoption of the benefits approach ensured that attention was not solely focused on financial benefits, but more qualitative benefits were also identified, which, as has been discussed, are often important to ensuring the use of new systems by individuals.

Use of the dependency network meant that the changes to existing project management and systems development methods and ways of working needed to enable the approach to be successfully adopted, were identified and made. Key changes identified included the need to involve both IT and business staff in developing the benefits plans and the establishment of a programme office that could monitor the consistency of plans and issue guidance on using the approach on projects of different types within the programme.

Initiating and Managing a Benefits-Driven Investment

As shown in Figure 7.3, the benefits management approach involves a different way of carrying out the activities associated with initiating a project and developing the business case for the investment. It also involves a specific focus during implementation on tracking progress towards the achievement of each of the benefits. The ability to achieve the maximum benefits from the investment will depend on the degree of certainty of the benefits plan and, during its execution, identifying if and when it needs to be amended and adjusting it appropriately. Therefore it is important that all the necessary knowledge is included during the planning stage and that everyone understands the implications of the plan and their role in its execution.

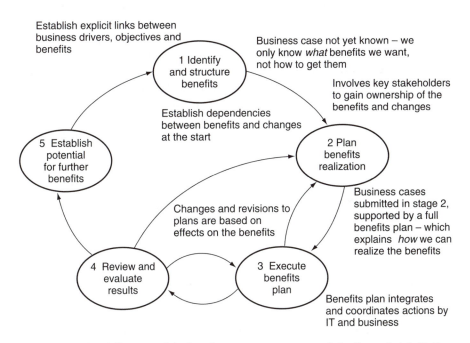

Figure 7.3 *Key differences of the benefits management approach in the project initiation and implementation stages*

As described in earlier chapters, success in the first two stages of the benefits management process depends on the effective sharing of knowledge between business managers and IS/IT specialists, an exchange which is facilitated by conducting workshops rather than holding meetings or one to one discussions. Overall the workshops should ensure that all the necessary links with the business drivers are made and can be sustained and that the relationship between benefits and changes is made explicit. The ability of all stakeholders to commit the time and resources required by the project should also be ensured. The outputs from the workshops will form the basis of the business case and benefits plan and should become integral components of the overall project plan. The number of workshops needed to develop the benefits plan will vary depending on the scale and complexity of the project, but normally at least two will be necessary. Each workshop should involve the key stakeholders in order to agree the investment objectives, elicit the benefits, define the scope of the change programme and understand the potential risks.

Between the workshops a considerable amount of work will have to be done by both the project team members and other key stakeholders to obtain the required information and document and review information from the first workshop. While it is impossible to prescribe a guaranteed way of achieving the best benefits plan and business case, there are a number of areas where good practices can improve the process – both in the content and management of the workshops and their conduct. Figure 7.4 suggests the main activities that are involved in the establishment of a benefits-driven approach.

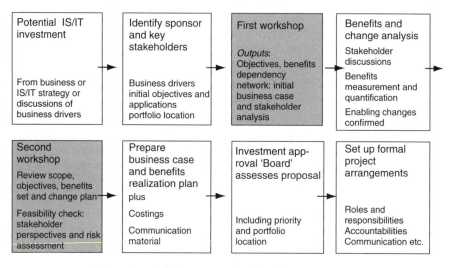

Figure 7.4 *Initial activities in a benefits-driven project*

It is assumed that prior to the first workshop a potential investment need or opportunity has been identified either through a formal strategic assessment or planning process or it has emerged from the current operational or application issues. Or it may have arisen as a new business idea or due to the availability of new technology. If so it should be considered as a high potential opportunity to be evaluated, rather than require the development of a rigorous business case and benefits plan, to justify significant investment. How the benefits management approach and techniques can be adapted for high potential evaluations are considered later in this chapter.

Before considering the details of the project set up activities, it is helpful to define and describe two roles that are critical to making the benefits-driven approach effective: the project sponsor and business project manager.

The Project Sponsor

At the start of the project a business project sponsor or champion should be appointed – a senior business manager who will take over-all responsibility for ensuring the investment produces the maximum value for the organization. The need for this senior business management leadership and involvement has been identified in many surveys as a factor that can significantly affect the outcome of IT investments, as well as other types of business change initiative. This is recognized in most organizations and project sponsors are often appointed, although how the role is executed varies across organizations and individuals. Depending on the nature and scope of the investment, the seniority level of the sponsor will vary from, probably, executive level for a strategic or large key operational project to departmental or functional manager for support or smaller key operational projects. For large projects, especially those that are strategic or span a number of business functions, a project steering group of senior managers from all the functions involved is often established, to assist the project sponsor and business project manager.

According to most best practice guidance (Kerzner, 2004; Morris and Pinto, 2004) the role of the sponsor includes:

1 Involvement from the start of the project to set or endorse the investment objectives.
2 Having the power, authority or influence to get things done by other managers, especially ensuring resources are made available and that organizational issues that may affect the project are addressed.
3 Understanding and articulating the vision of the project in terms of how the new ways of working and other business changes will result in the benefits.
4 Being the managerial link between the project and the wider organizational and other business initiatives.
5 Chairing the project steering group or review meetings, when decisions regarding any changes to the investment plan are made.

These imply that the sponsor should give the project strong, public support, actively monitor the progress from the business improvement perspective and be available, at any time, to the project manager and team to help resolve issues that arise. The sponsor should see the success of the investment as a significant personal objective and should demonstrate some personal contribution to the project.

The attendance of the sponsor at the benefit workshops is essential and preferably the sponsor should convene them to ensure that other senior managers attend. At the first workshop he or she will articulate and confirm the business drivers and ensure that appropriate investment objectives are defined and agreed, thereby setting the aims, scope and high level success measures for the project. The scope is particularly important since the temptation for extra functionality to be added needs to be challenged, as does overengineering and unnecessary integration.

The Business Project Manager

Also, preferably before the project starts, a business project manager should be appointed, although in some cases it may not be clear who the best person would be until after the first workshop when the scope is better understood. As mentioned in Chapter 3, many organizations now appoint business managers to project manage IS projects. However, the role is not always clearly defined, and can often be summed up as 'to ensure the project proceeds in the best interests of the business'. This is too vague and can lead to misunderstandings and uncertainties of how the role relates to the IT project manager or leader who has responsibility for the 'technical' aspects of the project.

As has been often repeated in this book and elsewhere, it is the organizational issues associated with IS/IT projects that most frequently lead to failure to deliver the benefits. The appointment of a business project manager is intended to deal with these aspects of the project and the investment. The term *business* project manager is used to distinguish the role from that of the IT project manager or leader and to ensure the management of the investment is seen as an investment in IT-enabled business change. He or she must ensure that the non-IT activities and responsibilities are defined, understood and executed. This includes many of the enabling changes and all the business change management and benefits realization tasks. But it is not the responsibility of the business project manager, who is part of the project team, to personally carry out the tasks. Benefit and change owners have to fulfil their responsibilities and be held accountable for activities assigned to them in the benefits plan. The role of the business project manager is to coordinate all the non-IT activities, ensuring that they are planned and controlled as integral components of the project.

The primary roles the business project manager fulfils are:

1 The coordination and monitoring of the change and benefits management activities on the benefits dependency network.
2 The development of the benefits plan and preparation of the business case and that the benefits measurement and tracking mechanisms are in place at the appropriate points in the project.
3 The custodianship of the benefits plan on behalf of the senior management.
4 The project management of the non-technical elements of the plan.
5 Responsibility for the communication strategy that keeps all stakeholders and other business managers informed about the investment and progress towards the objectives.
6 Maintaining a continuous dialogue with the key stakeholders to maintain their commitment and participation and to help them address issues as they arise.
7 Ensuring that the education and training programmes are developed and delivered at the required times so that everyone is able to fulfil their responsibilities.

These are extensive responsibilities and require expertise and knowledge of project management techniques and methods. In many cases we have observed, people who are appointed to such positions have little experience of managing projects. Even if they are excellent operational managers they find that the skills required to manage large projects are quite different. Therefore it is important to select a business project manager who has both a good knowledge of the business area being addressed and practical experience of project management.

For small projects, the business project manager is likely to be a part-time role, but for large or strategic investments full-time dedication will be necessary. In very large investments the business project manager may need specialist support to assist in coordinating, and perhaps facilitation of, the change management activities and also to develop and monitor the measurement processes that ensure the benefits are delivered.

The project sponsor and business project manager roles are essential to the orchestration of the benefits planning activities at the workshops and the further tasks that need to be performed between workshops and throughout implementation.

The First Workshop

The purpose of the first workshop is to establish whether the investment looks viable in terms of the potential benefits and whether those benefits are relevant to the organization's strategy. This assessment requires the input from the key stakeholders who are likely to be involved in the project, to not only ensure their knowledge is included, but also to get their collective agreement to the investment objectives and commitment to the further work needed to produce an achievable business case and benefits plan. The project sponsor should identify who those key stakeholders are and personally invite them to the workshop, and brief them on what is expected to be accomplished.

At the workshop the main tasks are to:

1 Review the business drivers to ensure there is clarity about why changes are needed. The organizational context within which the project has to be undertaken should also be assessed to identify any factors that will influence the feasibility of the project, such as other strategic change initiatives or impending reorganization. The overall contribution the investment is expected to make should be clarified in terms of its positioning in the applications portfolio, to enable the appropriate management processes to be established.
2 Discuss and agree the objectives and overall scope of the investment and develop an initial benefits dependency network that identifies the benefits expected and the main business and enabling changes needed to achieve them.
3 Carry out a preliminary structuring and assessment of the benefits, including whether or how they can be measured and determine whether the investment looks viable. If it is, then the further work required to develop the benefits parts of the business case needs to be defined.
4 Agree ownership of all the benefits and changes to ensure that both the necessary work to refine the details will be carried out and also that there is longer term commitment to the investment plan.
5 Conduct an initial stakeholder analysis to identify any additional stakeholders who will be affected by the project, whether any stakeholders will suffer 'disbenefits' and make an assessment of any potential organizational issues that will affect the success of the project.

The outputs from the workshop are agreed investment objectives, an initial benefits dependency network with identified owners and measures, an outline business case and an understanding of the organizational and stakeholder issues that will need to be accommodated or addressed. An action plan to refine each of these should be established to obtain further essential information required for the second workshop.

Activities between Workshops

The key activities that need to be undertaken before holding the second workshop involve ensuring that all stakeholder implications of the project, their perceptions about how it will affect them and their consequent ability and willingness to fulfil their expected responsibilities have been understood. This includes their view of any 'disbenefits' that may result from the investment, so that any potential resistance has been identified and can be considered at the next workshop.

Additionally, each of the proposed benefits needs to be examined in more detail, to define measurements and, if possible, quantify the benefit, if it is material to the business case. For those benefits which will need considerable effort to quantify, for example a pilot study, the work required should be specified and the implications for the timing of the business case submission considered. Between workshops, those involved may also need to investigate and understand in more detail the implications of the changes and their interrelationships, so that the benefits plan will reflect the timing and resources required to carry out the changes.

The technical feasibility of the project should also be evaluated during this period and an initial estimate of the likely IT costs made.

The Second Workshop

The main purpose of the second workshop is to decide whether it is worth proceeding with the investment. This will be based on the best estimate of the business case and the feasibility of providing the required IS/IT components and carrying out the business changes. Although the objective is to find the best way to proceed, it is also the best time to stop investments that do not appear to have a viable business case, before large amounts of resource begin to be consumed. Alternatively, only parts of the project may provide significant benefits, some of the changes may be deemed too risky or elements of the technology solution may be too expensive or not sufficiently proven, such that the project scope has to be revised.

Clearly, it may not be possible to have all the required information available for this second workshop, unless there is a lengthy gap between workshops. Even if this is the case, a second workshop should be held when the 'value side' of the business case is reasonably clear and then either a third workshop planned to produce the final business case, or actions put in place for the project team and stakeholders to complete the plan. In any project it is important to maintain the momentum and keep the key stakeholders involved and interested in the investment planning. Therefore it is better to hold more workshops at reasonable intervals (probably one to two months apart), than to wait until the business case is perfected and then 'present' it back to those whose commitment is critical to the project.

The main tasks to be completed at the workshop include:

1 To review and refine the investment objectives and scope in terms of which changes can be successfully achieved and deliver the most benefits, without undue risks. This will inevitably be iterative and depend on the other tasks described here. At this stage a risk analysis, as described in Chapter 5, should also be formally undertaken.
2 Each of the benefits and changes on the network should be revisited and the interrelationships among them confirmed or adjusted, such that the logic inherent in the network is fully understood and agreed by all the main stakeholders. In particular, the enabling changes need to be reviewed to ensure that the organization will be capable of adopting the new technologies and any new capabilities, competences and processes will be in place to achieve the business changes once the technologies are implemented.
3 For each of the benefits, either the current performance or the timing of when such baseline measures will be taken should be confirmed.
4 The need for all the proposed IS/IT functionality should also be reconsidered, to determine whether all of it is essential to the realization of the benefits or if some of the benefits could be obtained by changing working practices, processes or roles and responsibilities, without introducing new technology. Equally if the IS/IT comes as a 'package' the possibility of achieving further benefits from the deployment of functionality that will effectively be obtained 'free' should be explored. However, as discussed in earlier chapters, if such functionality offers little or no benefit or will require significant additional business changes, the temptation to implement it, simply because it was free, should be resisted.
5 All stakeholder responsibilities should be confirmed, or amended if necessary, and actions put in place to address all the organizational issues that have been identified from the stakeholder analysis, as described in Chapter 6.

6 The overall structure of the dependency network should be reviewed to identify potential benefit 'streams', that is, sets of changes and benefits that are capable of being delivered more or less independently of the rest of the network. In that case, it may be better to phase the project implementation to deliver each benefit stream independently, to enable some benefits to be achieved early and reduce the overall project risks. Although from a technology perspective it may appear more economic to install all the technology as one implementation, from a stakeholder perspective it may be preferable to realize some of the 'easier' benefits earlier, especially those that require less extensive or sensitive changes. This is a matter of judgement, but it is based on the general experience that large projects have the most risks and hence breaking a project down into more manageable phases can reduce risk. Also the realization of some early benefits can increase the commitment of some stakeholders to the rest of the project, as discussed in Chapter 6.

The main outputs from this second workshop are the business case and benefits plan with completed benefits and change 'templates' for all the activities, as described in previous chapters. This documentation should be completed as soon as possible after the workshop, although as stated earlier, it may, for large or risky investments be necessary to convene a further workshop or meeting to confirm some elements of the business case.

Although workshops are commonly used in organizations to bring people with different knowledge sets together to agree what needs to be done, experience of conducting many benefits management workshops has identified some useful 'tips' or guidance on how to make them work successfully. These are listed in Box 7.2.

Box 7.2 Guidance for conducting benefits management workshops

First and foremost it is important to ensure that the right stakeholders can attend the workshops. That is those who have the knowledge required, are of appropriate seniority and also have the ability to commit time and resources to the project. It is always preferable to delay the workshop to enable those key people to attend rather than go ahead without them, even if there is pressure to 'get on with it'.

Box 7.2 (Continued)

It must be remembered that it is a workshop and not a meeting, to encourage everyone to participate fully without concern for the organizational hierarchy or roles. It is often the more junior staff who have the detailed knowledge required to identify potential benefits, be specific about the changes and understand how others affected by the investment might respond.

The quality of the facilities in which the workshop is held is important. Workshops require more space than meetings so that people can stand up, move about and have small group discussions as well as plenary sessions. This emphasizes the relative informality of the working relationships and also increases the energy people put into the work. It can be a long and demanding process and it is important that energy levels are sustained over several hours. The 'mental energy' that will be applied is higher when people spend time standing rather than sitting. It is tempting to suggest removing chairs altogether, but people need a rest from time to time! However, the 'furniture' should be pushed to the side to avoid people sitting round a table, as in a meeting.

The room should have large areas of whiteboards or wall space, which can be used to 'pin' large sheets of paper on which to record and structure the work produced, such as the benefits dependency network and stakeholder analysis. These working sheets will become the output from the workshop, so it is best to record them on paper or an electronic whiteboard to avoid transcribing time and potential errors. It is important that everyone can see the wallcharts and work on them, which again requires a good working space.

The best way of initially constructing the networks and other outputs is to use Post-its™, due to their innate flexibility in terms of changing the content and moving them around to visually represent the dependencies and relationships. The process involves both creative or brainstorming tasks and, later, analytical assessment of the options identified. During the process, many Post-its™ are created, changed, discarded or moved about to develop the agreed output. Following the initial workshop the outputs should be converted to an electronic form, using a suitable drawing package and at subsequent workshops this can be displayed on a whiteboard or wall and changes made either via more Post-its™ or directly. An interactive whiteboard is ideal for this.

It is important that everyone contributes their knowledge and therefore it is better not to channel all the ideas, suggestions and comments through one person who 'has the pen'. It is preferable that each individual writes down his or her own knowledge and then once it is displayed, he or she can explain their reasoning and others can question, comment or add to it and then the group can reconcile different views where required and agree the final version. It may be appropriate to subdivide a large group into smaller teams, partly because of the practical problems of large group discussions being dominated by some individuals and partly to ensure the knowledge in the room is applied most effectively. These subgroups should consist of people who do not normally work together to facilitate the knowledge sharing. The output from each group should be displayed and explained to enable others to express their views.

Even at the earliest stages people should be encouraged to be as explicit as possible when writing on the Post-its™, to avoid uncertainty later about what was meant. For instance 'reduce costs' will frequently be a benefit, but which specific costs are meant should be stated. 'Change the culture' is often identified as a necessary business change. However, a change in organizational culture results in the changes in behaviours and working practices of groups and individual staff. So, who should make such changes and what changes are required should be specified.

Finally, all this implies that the workshops have to be well planned and organized, with an emphasis on producing comprehensive high quality outputs that will be able to be refined, developed further and eventually finalized. This normally requires someone to facilitate the process and ensure that all that could be done by those present, in the time available, is achieved. The facilitator should be someone not directly involved in the project, but who is familiar with the business areas being discussed. He or she needs to have expert knowledge of the tools and techniques of the benefits management approach plus skills

Box 7.2 (Continued)

and experience in facilitation. In part the role is to ensure that the process works and that everyone is appropriately involved, but also to challenge the outputs, normally by asking simple, even naïve, questions to help clarify what is meant and the assumptions on which it is based.

Equally the facilitator should identify when conflicting views need to be reconciled and whether or not consensus or agreement needs to be reached on a particular point. It is the facilitator's role to help prevent or resolve differences of opinion that will significantly reduce the quality and usefulness of the outputs from the workshop.

As has been stated earlier, documentation arising from the benefits management process should be kept up to date as the project proceeds, so that at any time it reflects what has been agreed and achieved so far. Any changes will need to be recorded, so that after implementation the review of the success or otherwise of the investment can take due account of anything that influenced the eventual realization of each benefit.

At this stage it is also valuable to define a communication strategy for the project, to ensure that everyone in the organization (and perhaps external parties such as customers, suppliers and regulatory bodies) is informed at the earliest possible time of the intentions and implications of the project. This is normally the responsibility of the project sponsor and business project manager. When there are significant organizational change implications, it is important that everyone is told what is actually planned, as openly and honestly as possible, rather than allow rumour and speculation to create a different and almost inevitably less favourable impression of what is going to happen. It is also important to tailor the communication content to particular stakeholder groups, based on the implications for them and their role in the business. Poor communication at this stage can introduce unnecessary additional risks. For example in the 'Connecting for Health' programme in the UK NHS, failure to communicate with general practitioners and other clinicians, in a language that encouraged their involvement in the programme, caused delays to the programme and created initial resistance to some of its key components.

Inclusion of the Benefits Plan in the Management of the Project

From this stage onwards the activities identified in the benefits plan should become integral components of the project plan and be monitored accordingly at all progress review meetings. Often such meetings focus mainly on the IT delivery plan and issues resulting from any problems with functionality, cost or timeliness. These are, of course, important but the same discussions should also include updates on progress towards implementing the business changes and delivering the benefits and the resolution of any issues affecting these aspects of the project. The overall success of the investment relies on the accurate alignment and synchronization of the IT and business activities, and that is less likely to happen if they are reviewed separately or at different times.

It is important that the project sponsor is involved in the review process on a regular basis, to ensure that the project team and other stakeholders are aware of any changes in the organization or business context that could affect the project. Any changes that have occurred in the business drivers or the strategy of the organization will require a reappraisal of the whole investment to decide whether it is worth continuing with the project as it is, or whether it should be changed significantly. Equally other events or external changes that have made some of the benefits more or less important may require the business case to be revisited or revised. Should the expected costs or timescale for the project increase significantly, again, achieving the investment objectives or realizing net benefits may have become problematic. If the investment is dependent on deliverables from other projects or business changes in those projects, the sponsor and business project manager should consider the implications of delays or changes in these to the viability of the project.

In most cases, changes affecting the project identified at review meetings will result in revisions to the implementation plans, but in some cases they may cause the project to be abandoned. This is clearly a difficult decision, especially when implementation is well under way or close to completion. However, many failed projects could and should have been stopped before all the expenditure was incurred, because they were no longer going to deliver any benefits to the organization. There are always other investments competing for the funds and resources available and it is better to free up those that are being wasted than to continue to deploy them when failure is seen to be inevitable. Equally, people working on a project that is clearly of little or no organizational value will become demoralized and this is likely to decrease the chances of 'salvaging anything of value from the wreckage' even further. In spite of this, in too many cases a 'we've started, so we'll finish' rationale causes projects to carry on, as if they had developed a life of their own.

Evaluating the Results and Establishing Potential for Further Benefits

As described in Chapter 3, following the full implementation of the new IS/IT and business changes, the achievement of the business case and benefits plan should be formally reviewed, as indicated in stage four of Figure 7.5. The purposes of the review include a detailed assessment of whether each of the benefits intended have been achieved or not. If they have not been achieved, the reasons for this should be established and any remedial action that could cause them to be realized should be identified. It is also important to ascertain any unexpected positive or negative consequences of the new ways of working enabled by the project.

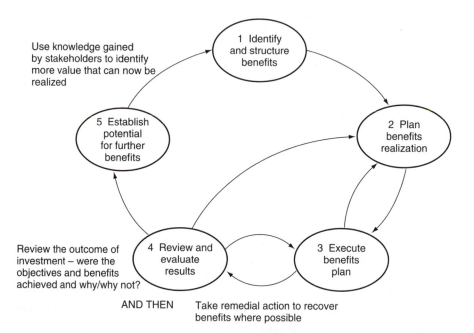

Figure 7.5 *The key activities in the review process*

At the same time as reviewing the delivery of the intended benefits from the project, the review meeting should also consider the opportunity for further benefits, as shown in stage 5 of Figure 7.5. Using the knowledge that has been gained from the project, new benefits that are now available from further business changes or IS/IT developments should be considered.

While these are the purposes of any particular benefit review, the reason for carrying them out systematically for all major projects is to learn how to improve the overall value that the organization derives from all its IS/IT investments, by learning from success and failure. Those generic lessons should be communicated to the managers of other projects.

Because there are a number of reviews or audits that can occur at the end of a project, it is probably worth stating what a benefit review is *not*. It is *not* a project management review, which focuses on variances in time and cost from the project plan. It is *not* a system quality or performance review, which assesses the conformance of systems functionality and performance with the requirements specification. It is *not* a financial audit, although in public sector organizations an audit is an official requirement to ensure funds have been spent appropriately. Neither, as emphasized in Chapter 3, is it a 'witchhunt' to allocate blame!

In order to gain the most from a benefit review, and avoid the potential downsides, the process has to be managed effectively. It is also important to be as consistent as possible in how the reviews are conducted across projects, to ensure that the outputs provide fair comparisons and enable lessons to be transferred to future projects. Visible consistency and objectivity will also encourage people to engage in the process openly and honestly, rather than attempt to ensure that any blame belongs elsewhere. Figure 7.6 shows the main inputs and expected outputs of the review process.

The review should be planned in advance, in order to gain maximum value from the process. Ideally it should be clearly identified as a key date or milestone in the project plan, probably about two to three months after implementation is complete and when it should be possible to determine whether the benefits have occurred or are beginning to be realized. It should follow any project or systems quality reviews, since they may provide some relevant explanations concerning the lack of achievement of some of the benefits.

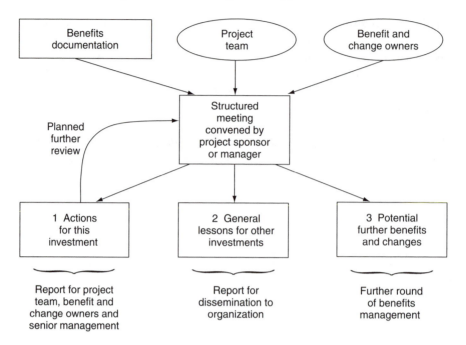

Figure 7.6   Main elements of the benefits review process

Preparation will be required in advance of the review, in order to revisit and update the business case and benefits plan documentation and enable the participants to provide the necessary evidence for the review meeting. The meeting should be convened by the project sponsor. The business project manager, IT project leader, and all the main stakeholders should be invited to attend. In respect of the benefits, each of the benefit owners should prepare a statement, with the appropriate evidence, as to what extent the benefit has been realized and, if it has not be achieved, any reasons that might explain this. Other documentation that will probably be essential to the discussions includes: the business case and benefits plan (both the original and the latest versions); any project or system quality review reports and a summary of key decisions that were taken to alter the scope or other aspects of the project during implementation.

The review meeting itself should be run as a structured discussion based on what has happened as a result of the investment, with emphasis on the final outcome rather than what happened during the project. In order to gain the most from the meeting time, the order of discussion should match the objectives of the review. That is: it should commence with the benefits intended that have been achieved and any unexpected consequences, both positive and negative. It should then consider benefits that have not, as yet, been achieved, the reasons and any actions that can be taken to retrieve them. Finally, any benefits that have to be 'written off' should be identified including the reasons for this. Actions and responsibilities should be agreed for any benefit that could still be retrieved and to deal with the effects of unexpected 'disbenefits'. Finally, the meeting should identify any further benefits that can now be realized and instigate actions to investigate the feasibility of actually realizing them.

The meeting should conclude by identifying the main lessons learned from the project, in terms of how the use of the benefits management process within the organization could be improved and advice for other projects that could improve the way they are managed, or implemented, in order to increase the value delivered. For example, it is worth revisiting the initial risk analysis and identifying which risks actually materialized, how they were dealt with and the overall effect on the project outcome. As shown in Figure 7.6, the outputs from the review meeting should be three 'reports':

1 A full review of the investment in terms of benefits realized and any actions still outstanding to achieve the business case, which should be confidential to the meeting attendees and the appropriate senior managers, such as the 'investment board' that sanctioned the funding. They should agree the extent to which the review report can be made 'public'. If there are significant actions still to be taken, this report would probably be the basis of a further review meeting to be held when the actions have been carried out.
2 A summary of the lessons learned that may benefit future investments, which should be communicated as soon as possible to all other current project sponsors and managers, and made available through updates to 'best practice guidelines' for future projects.
3 A report describing the further potential benefits now available and actions that have been put in place to examine them. These potential benefits effectively form new projects and should be added to the list of future projects within the organization. For instance, an engineering organization installed imaging technology as a more efficient way of archiving diagrams and documents. Once the new technology was working well, it became clear that improving the whole document management process was now possible, leading to an ability to provide more effective exchanges with clients during design and to shorten the time taken to respond to invitations to tender for new contracts. If, as in this case, the further opportunities require significant resources, they will need

to be evaluated against alternative future investments, but often they can be achieved through low cost small projects that are part of the organization's continuous improvement 'programme'. For example, if a new stock control system improves the accuracy of stock figures, it might lead to revisions of replenishment policies in planning systems through the sharing information with suppliers. Alternatively some may be innovative or speculative ideas that should be progressed as high potential projects.

It should be stressed that these reports do not need to be long documents. Indeed, it is better, particularly in the case of the general lessons to be shared with other projects, that such reports are brief and to the point. In the case of the general lessons learned, it may well be worth sending this summary directly to the business project managers of other current projects to ensure that it is seen. Many organizations have found that posting such documents on intranets or in electronic knowledge bases ensures that they never see the light of day again!

The overall contribution that benefits reviews make to an organization's ability to increase the benefits derived from its IS/IT cannot be overstated. It is at this stage in the process that knowledge about the investment is greatest and when the organization can learn how to improve its ability to utilize IS/IT successfully. However, ensuring that the review process makes such a contribution relies on three critical factors: that the review is rigorous in understanding cause and effect relationships regarding changes and benefits; that the meeting concentrates on what can be done now and in the future, rather than dwell on the past (or even try to re-manage it!); and that no blame is allocated or seen to be, however difficult this may be. If the last of these cannot be achieved, it is likely that many people will be suspicious of the process and not be open and honest when taking part.

Monitoring the Benefits after Implementation

The benefits review should normally be held as soon after implementation as it is possible to assess, with sufficient evidence, whether the intended benefits have been achieved. This would normally be some two to three months after the system and associated business changes have been made, although some benefits may materialize immediately. However, it may be necessary to wait longer to evaluate some benefits adequately, especially those that were dependent on using new capabilities created by the investment. In many cases it is wise to implement new systems when business activity or volumes are at their lowest, to reduce the risk of the changes causing performance to deteriorate. The benefits may involve the ability to deal with 'peak loads' and it will only be when volumes are high that the benefits can accurately be measured. Benefits associated with more accurate and timely information leading to more effective decision making are notoriously difficult to prove after the event, because there is likely to be a time lag between the information being available and its use in decisions.

Another concern is that, although benefits do occur soon after implementation, they can 'decay' once the changes have become the normal practices and people's enthusiasm for the improvements has waned. It therefore may be worth having a second review some months after the first to determine whether certain, vulnerable benefits have been sustained. Some organizations also want to be able to prove that their IT investments have delivered the expected value over an extended period, even several years. This cannot really be done project by project since, after a year or more has elapsed, other changes have been made that will obscure the benefits realized from any particular investment. Any such assessment therefore is probably best done through an annual review of investments completed during the previous year and the cumulative benefits delivered, verified by the reviews of the individual projects. As discussed later, this can be considered an aspect of 'governance' and relates to managing the overall investment portfolio.

For very large or complex projects, especially where the benefit streams are delivered at different times, it is best to treat the investment as a 'change programme' of related projects as discussed in the next section.

Fit with other Methodologies

As was described in Chapter 3, the benefits management process complements other methodologies. Proven systems development best practice and methodologies, such as structured systems analysis and design methodology (SSADM) or dynamic systems development methodology (DSDM) should be used, as appropriate, to develop the IS enablers identified for the project in order to ensure conformance to requirements, performance and resilience. While it is not possible to be prescriptive, the highly structured methodologies (such as SSADM) are usually more appropriate for key operational and support application investment, whereas the more iterative methodologies (such as DSDM) are needed for strategic and high potential applications.

A range of change management methods can be employed to achieve the changes identified in the benefits dependency network. The nature, scale or impact of a change may require or suggest the use of a particular approach to effecting the specific change, and other changes that depend on it, successfully. If it involves redeploying, or even no longer employing significant numbers of staff, the organization's employment policies and practices would influence or determine the approach to be taken. Equally, corporate communications policies would influence the way in which the implications of the project are communicated to internal or external stakeholders and may require different groups to be informed at different times in different ways.

The benefits management process also complements the most commonly used project management methodologies. Most such methodologies tend to focus on conformance to cost, time and quality issues, rather than explicitly identifying the benefits the organization is seeking to achieve from the project. The benefits management process can be used in conjunction with any of these methodologies in order to ensure that the organization is explicit about the benefits it is seeking and that it remains focused on these throughout the project. Most methodologies also require that the project is broken into a number of discrete steps or work packages, to define the deliverables and time and resources required and then focus on identifying the optimum order in which to carry these out, often by using a Gantt chart or some form of critical path analysis. Use of the benefits management approach can identify the work packages that the project can be most effectively broken into and also, suggest a sequence for these. How the benefits management process can be used in conjunction with the well-known project management methodology PRINCE2 is described in Box 7.3.

Box 7.3 Benefits management and PRINCE2

PRINCE2 is an example of a structured project management approach that is used widely in both the private and public sectors. It was developed by the Office of Government Commerce (OGC) and is the recommended approach for UK government projects.

PRINCE2, a refinement of an earlier approach PRINCE (Projects IN Controlled Environments), was based on existing best practice in project management and other methodologies. The OGC was involved in the early stages of the research that led to the development of the benefits management process described in this book. There is a high degree of consistency between the two approaches allowing them to be used together in a way that draws on the specific strengths of each approach.

PRINCE2 defines eight processes for the effective management and governance of a project. Each process is described briefly here and then how benefits management and PRINCE2 can be combined to complement each other is discussed.

1 *Directing a project* – this is a process for senior management responsible for the project to direct its activities and resources. The process lasts for the full duration of the project and has five major strands within it: authorizing the development of a business case and project plan; approval of the business case; review of the project at stage boundaries and ensuring the project comes to a controlled close and that lessons are shared with other projects.
2 *Starting up a project* – this tends to be a short process in which the project management team is appointed and the aims of the project are communicated.
3 *Initiating a project* – this process seeks to develop a business case for the project, which is contained in a project initiation document (PID). It is suggested that a PID contains much information about a project including:

- objectives
- critical success factors and key performance indicators
- impacts and assumptions
- constraints and option evaluations
- benefits analysis
- project costs
- cost/benefit analysis
- risks
- delivery plan – including stages or milestones.

Box 7.3 (Continued)

4 *Controlling a stage* – a key principle in PRINCE2 of controlling projects is to break them into manageable stages. This process describes the monitoring and control activities required to keep a stage on track.

5 *Managing product delivery* – specifies the contract between the project and suppliers. PRINCE2 calls the work agreed in this process a 'work package' and seeks to ensure agreement on issues such as timing, quality and cost.

6 *Managing stage boundaries* – this process includes reporting on the performance of the previous stage, approval from senior management to move to the next stage, updating the project plan and detailed planning of the next stage.

7 *Planning* – the planning process continues throughout the project. A key recommendation of PRINCE2 is that detailed planning is only undertaken for the next stage of the project to be undertaken.

8 *Closing a project* – this process seeks to understand the extent to which the objectives of the project have been met, ensure follow-up actions are undertaken and to share lessons learned with other projects.

While PRINCE2 is very comprehensive, provides very detailed guidance to improve project management practices and is widely used, its treatment of benefits tends to be cursory. In particular, while it is suggested that the PID in the project initiation stage includes a full benefits analysis, including linking benefits to the changes required to deliver them, appointing benefit owners and setting measures for each benefit, little detailed guidance is given on how to identify these. The benefits are the most important outcome from a project, since that is presumably why the project is being undertaken. This limited treatment of benefits is therefore a noticeable area of weakness. We would suggest that the tools and techniques relating to the first two stages of our five-stage process are used to develop a full benefits plan as has been described in earlier chapters. If the organization has mandated the use of PRINCE2, then this benefits plan can be incorporated into the PID in an appropriate form.

The simplicity of the benefits management approach is also important in this early stage of a project. The strength of PRINCE2 lies in its comprehensiveness, formality, attention to detail and its robustness. However, it is inevitably complex and most business managers do not want, or have the time, to learn the methodology, or even be subjected to it. The simple frameworks of the benefits management approach, coupled with the participative workshops, ensure that individuals, both from the business and specialist areas can input and combine their knowledge in a way that they find intuitive – and occasionally even fun! This willingness to participate early ensures agreement for the project is gained from those who will be impacted and, importantly, knowledge within the business is captured in the benefits plan.

We would therefore suggest that the PRINCE2 processes of controlling stages, managing stage boundaries and managing product delivery are used if required to undertake the third stage of our benefits management process: the execution of the benefits plan. A key part of the PRINCE2 approach is the breaking of projects into phases. The benefits plan, particularly the benefits dependency network, can prove a means of identifying and comparing possible phases. The identified dependencies between changes and benefits, allow an understanding of which benefits can be expected from undertaking a certain set of changes. An identification of such linkages can enable the delivery of benefits early in a project, which may be important if the project is a long one or if there is particular stakeholder resistance.

Finally, while the closing of a project process in PRINCE2 suggests a review of the success of the project and a sharing of best practice, these are not focused explicitly on benefits. Also it does not expressly include the important stage included in the benefits management process of identifying the potential for further benefits. Given the centrality of benefits delivery to the success of the project, we would suggest that the benefits management process is adopted for these activities. For organizations that have mandated the use of PRINCE2, the evaluation of benefits realized from the project and the identification of further benefits should be included in the project closing process.

Figure 7.7 illustrates how the benefits management process and PRINCE2 are related and which approach we suggest should lead at each stage.

Box 7.3 (Continued)

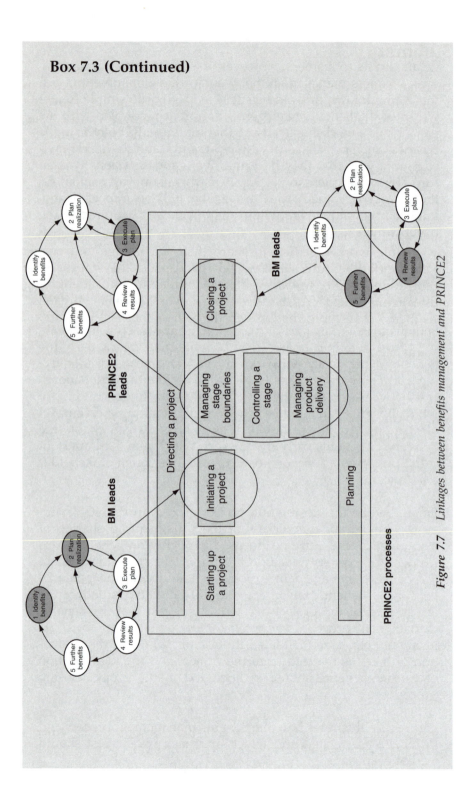

Figure 7.7   Linkages between benefits management and PRINCE2

Summary

This chapter has described how the benefits management process can be introduced and implemented in organizations and has provided practical guidance on how the tools and techniques can be used effectively to address issues that can arise over the investment life-cycle. This guidance is based on the experiences of a large number of organizations that have adopted the approach. Whatever causes the need to adopt a benefits management approach, those organizations' experiences also prove that it is not sufficient merely to introduce a new process and to train staff in the use of new set of tools. It is the way in which the process and tools are then used to change how people work together, to share their knowledge and enable the appropriate resources and skills to be applied, that improves an organization's ability to carry out the complex tasks of identifying and realizing benefits. As discussed in Chapter 2, for many organizations their weakest information systems competence is 'exploitation'. Building that competence requires both IS/IT specialists and business managers to contribute their expertise and experience and to adopt a disciplined and rigorous approach to managing all IS/IT investments.

Much of the emphasis of this chapter has been on the first two stages of the benefits management process. This was quite deliberate, even though the investment objectives are only achieved by sustained attention to all the activities that influence benefit delivery throughout the duration of the investment. As has been said earlier in the book, developing a business case and benefits plan is more than a means of obtaining funds. The process by which it is done will not only effect the integrity of the investment case, but also the viability of achieving each of the benefits, through the willingness and ability of all the stakeholders to fulfil their commitments. The level of commitment is often dependent on the benefits they perceive and the extent to which they understand, and are involved in defining, the scope and nature of the business changes required.

Without stakeholder commitment at the outset of a project, the issues that inevitably arise during implementation can prove difficult to resolve, leading to increases in cost and time as well as failure to realize some or all of the benefits. With a comprehensive and detailed benefits plan it is easier to assess the implications of events that occur during implementation and then adjust the appropriate elements of the plan. The evidence from both project failures and successes strongly supports the argument that careful planning at the start, combined with identifying and resolving contentious issues early in the project, leads to higher levels of success. The more complex and extensive the programme of change, the more important it is to plan and replan for the benefits as the project proceeds. The formats of the outputs from the benefits framework are relatively easy to maintain and update and the techniques can, and should, be reapplied throughout the project when either uncertainties arise or more becomes known.

This chapter has discussed the general aspects of introducing and adopting the benefits management approach, but has not considered factors that influence the use of the process and techniques in different situations and organizational contexts such as the inherent nature of an organization, whether it is a corporation or public body, its size and the types of IS/IT applications or infrastructure being implemented. Chapter 8 considers the implications of these context specific issues and how the approach can be adapted to address them is exemplified.

In Chapter 9, the use of the approach to improve the management of major change programmes and how organizational governance mechanisms can be established to manage whole portfolios of IS/IT investments and change programmes are discussed.

8
The Importance of Context

In previous chapters, we have sought to emphasize the linkage between the realization of benefits from IS/IT investments and the need to make organizational changes. This is highlighted in the benefits dependency network introduced in Chapter 4. The other tools and frameworks introduced, such as the stakeholder analysis discussed in Chapter 6, also link benefits realization with the need for change within, and perhaps even outside, the organization.

The particular changes that an organization needs to make will depend on its current status. Even if implementing similar applications, some organizations may be starting from 'further behind' than others and hence will need to make more changes in order to achieve the same benefits. Alternatively, an organization may not be able or willing to make certain changes, due to resource or capability constraints or the risks involved, and hence may only realize a limited set of the available benefits. For example, smaller businesses, on average, have fewer financial and human resources at their disposal (Ballantine et al., 1998; Pollard and Hayne, 1998). They are often unable to accomplish large change programmes and might therefore expect a more modest set of benefits. However, those benefits they can realize may improve their performance in a greater proportion than larger organizations, which can fund significant change programmes.

Context is also important when considering benefits. What is considered a benefit will depend on the current performance level of the organization, relative to its competitors or business targets. For organizations that are investing to overcome business disadvantages, the benefits expected will be of different types from those intending to create advantage from innovative uses of IT. What is viewed as a benefit will also depend on the strategy of the organization and its external and internal drivers, as discussed in Chapter 2.

Although some drivers may be common to many organizations, such as improvements to customer or client service, others, particularly internal drivers are likely to vary across organizations, giving rise to differences in what are perceived to be benefits.

Factors to Take into Account

Generic Benefits

The importance of specific organizational context on the realization of benefits means that it is not possible to develop a generic set of benefits and associated changes for given application types, or for types of organization, or for IS/IT supply arrangements such as outsourcing. The fallacy of the 'silver bullet' approach to IS/IT investment (Markus and Benjamin, 1997), when vendors describe product features or functionality as a list of standard benefits, has already been discussed in earlier chapters. Then it was noted that the lack of consideration of organizational change was a significant problem in this view of technology. However, it is also flawed in that it disregards the context of individual organizations and suggests the improvements listed can be achieved by all organizations and are beneficial to all of them.

This leads to a warning. Given the inability to produce generic lists of benefits and associated organizational changes for a particular application or type of organization, then it is equally not possible to produce generic versions of the tools and frameworks that we have presented here. Although we have shown a number of completed frameworks in this book, these are simply to illustrate their use and they should not be applied wholesale to other projects, however similar these may appear.

In projects where the implementation of the same system, or components of a system are being replicated across different business units within an organization, or in large public programmes where the same system is to be deployed in multiple settings, it is very tempting to generate a 'standard' version of the frameworks, such as the benefits dependency network. While this might save time in the first stages of the benefits management process, as explained later in this chapter, the temptation to do so should be resisted. It makes an assumption that the benefits are the same or similar for each unit and can be achieved through a prescribed set of changes. Not only is this rarely the case, it can significantly reduce the commitment of the unit's management and staff to the project implementation.

Different Types of Organization

A key element of context is the nature or type of organization. Organizations can be classified in many different ways. The factors that are most likely to have a bearing on the benefits realization process described in this book and are most frequently encountered are:

- Whether the organization is in the private sector, when a significant driver is always to maximize returns to shareholders, members or partners, or in the public sector, where its drivers are more likely to be related to service provision and providing value for money.
- Size of the organization, that is if it is large or if it is what is termed a small and medium sized enterprise (SME), which is usually taken to mean an organization with 250 employees or fewer.
- If the organization is a single business unit or is comprised of multiple distinct units, for example different lines of business or different geographic territories, in which IS deployments are replicated.

We have already presented a number of examples that relate to investments by large organizations in the private sector in single business units and so in this chapter we consider investments by other types of organization, that is: the public sector, small businesses and multiunit businesses that require replicated deployments.

The Public Sector

A number of examples of public sector investments in IS/IT has been included in previous chapters. One component of the National Health Service programme 'Connecting for Health' is a system to allow patients to book hospital appointments at a time convenient to themselves. This was introduced in Chapter 1 and discussed further in Chapter 4, where a benefits dependency network was shown, and it is considered in more detail later. The use of single assessment of the needs of older people by social workers and healthcare professionals was included in the discussion of business cases in Chapter 5. These examples show that the benefits management process can be successfully applied to such contexts. While use of the process is similar to that described for other types of organization, there are a number of issues that are frequently encountered in public sector organizations.

Imposed Drivers

The drivers acting on public sector organizations, which cause them to consider investment in IS/IT and undertaking the associated changes, are often the result of government policies. While private sector organizations will have significant external pressures, for example from their customers or competitors, they can, in many cases, choose whether to respond or not, and also how and when. However, in the case of the public sector, the drivers are often in the form of a requirement to meet a specific target and by a given deadline, whether or not this is feasible or appropriate for that organization.

Such imposed drivers can often make it appear that benefits identification and management is unnecessary, since there is a feeling of 'we have to do it anyway'. We would argue that, while the identification of benefits to prove a business case may not be relevant, the other frameworks and ways of working presented are highly beneficial. Agreement of the objectives of the investment will begin to ensure that all those involved have a common and shared view of what the organization is seeking to achieve. Most investments yield a range of benefits and by identifying these, a focus can be placed on those that are of most importance to the organization, given its current position, and will demonstrate to stakeholders what they might expect to gain from the investment. While not undertaking the project may not be a option, identification of the business changes needed may well show ways of making changes that are more acceptable or effective than others, and also determine those that are critical to realizing the benefits that are of most value to the organization itself. Indeed, identification and successful achievement of the business and enabling changes can ensure that an imposed investment does actually yield benefits to the organization, rather than just becoming a bureaucratic requirement that absorbs resources, or worse, an expensive and time-consuming failure. An example of the benefits approach used to ensure benefits from a mandated project is described in Box 8.1.

Box 8.1 Choice-based lettings of public housing

In the UK, the government is pursuing a far reaching programme of innovation and change in the public sector. In many cases a central element of these improvement programmes is the modernization of services through process redevelopment and the adoption of new information technologies and systems. A major element of the vision for the future is that all public services, both centrally and locally provided, should be accessible electronically by 2005. The definition of electronically accessible includes both telephone and online access, ensuring the ability to meet the needs of the widest range of citizens.

Like all other public services, the housing department within a local authority was therefore considering how it might meet this government requirement. A key area of responsibility for the department is the provision of council or social housing to families and individuals. Rather than simply develop a telephone and website facility that would provide an additional channel for their usual enquiries from residents and families seeking a home, members of the housing team wished to take the opportunity to improve the service they offered. Traditionally, those seeking social housing were held on a waiting list and, from time to time, were sent details of properties the housing team thought were appropriate. Considerable time was wasted as the properties were often not suitable and, while details were sent back and forth, the properties stood empty. Occupancy rate was a key performance indicator for the housing team, since it had a number of consequences, including increased rental income and reduced vandalism, to which empty properties were highly vulnerable.

It was recognized that the new electronic channel could be used to provide access to all the available properties held by the local authority. Residents could then select the property that they were interested in and communicate this to the authority without delay, a service they termed *choice-based lettings*.

Through the use of the benefits management process the team were able to identify the benefits that could be expected from

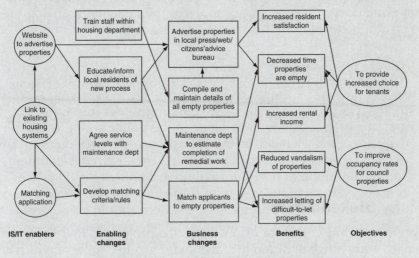

Figure 8.1   Benefits dependency network for a social housing department

Box 8.1 (Continued)

such a choice-based approach. A simplified version of the benefits dependency network they developed is shown in Figure 8.1. Benefits included increased rental income and a reduced number of properties standing empty, something the housing team were sensitive to being criticized about. However, when exploring the necessary changes it became apparent that, in order to ensure there were sufficient properties to provide choice, the maintenance team had to refurbish previously let properties more quickly and be prepared to estimate the time work will take and adhere to agreed service levels. In this particular case, the maintenance team was part of a separate department and heavily unionized.

It was recognized that achievement of the changes required by the maintenance team would require an influential change owner. A well-respected senior manager in the maintenance department was asked to join the project team. He broke the necessary changes down into a set of smaller changes that could be implemented sequentially. He also linked each of these changes to the performance targets for his own teams and ensured that they understood the rationale for the changes they were being asked to make. Although there was some initial resistance from the maintenance staff, their understanding of the reason for the changes and the stepwise approach meant that they were achieved successfully. Concern about the possible transfer of this activity to the private sector also helped to ensure the changes were made.

The system went live on time allowing the authority to meet the imposed deadline from central government. However, more importantly the authority has realized significant benefits in terms of both client satisfaction and occupancy rates, leading to increased revenues.

Many Stakeholders

Another common feature of public sector projects is that they often have a wide range of different stakeholder groups, some of which are very large in terms of the number of people involved. Many public sector organizations have strong social and consultative cultures, due to the nature of services they provide and the mix of professionals employed. The staff expect to be able to express their views on how the investment will affect their work and roles, and importantly, to have these views taken into account in the development and implementation of the project.

Many projects also often include stakeholders outside the organization itself, including the general public. The realization of benefits from investments may be reliant on changes to ways in which external stakeholders access or make use of the services or how they contribute to them. In addition, there is a need for most public sector projects to be inclusive. Unlike private companies, they can rarely decide to serve only some of their clients or users. Instead, they must ensure that all parts of their community are properly served. For example, the NHS 'Choose and Book' system, which seeks to allow patients to book hospital appointments at a time convenient to themselves is referred to again in Box 8.2. For significant benefits to flow from this project, the majority of patients must be encouraged to either book an appointment online or via the telephone while with their GP or once they have returned home. However, it may be that patients do not understand what is required of them or are reluctant to take responsibility for a task that was previously carried out for them by the doctor and the hospital. Indeed, it may be those patients who are most in need of medical attention, such as the elderly or those with complex needs, who are the least able to book their own appointments. Actions must be identified to support these vulnerable groups and included as enabling or ongoing business changes in the benefits plan.

The changes that will be required from different stakeholder groups should be shown on the benefits dependency network, even if these groups are outside the organization. Where possible, enabling changes or even ongoing business changes should be identified to address any difficulties that can be foreseen. So, for example in the project discussed in Box 8.2, it is recognized that patient education programmes will be required, but also a process that identifies those patients who fail to make appointments for necessary consultations and tests. In such projects, having completed a dependency network, it is important to also undertake a careful stakeholder analysis, as discussed in Chapter 6. While a consideration of the views of stakeholders is important for all investments, stakeholder analysis is often the most crucial part of public sector projects.

Box 8.2 'Choose and Book' in public healthcare: multiple stakeholders

As introduced in Chapters 1 and 4, the National Health Service in the UK is currently undertaking what has been estimated to be the largest civilian investment in IT (NHS, 2005). 'Connecting for Health', as it is called, has a number of strands of activity: a centrally managed email and directory service for all organizations in the NHS; the provision of an electronic health record for all citizens; the use of IT to improve prescribing; systems to capture and distribute medical images; and the ability of patients to choose a date and time for appointments.

This last strand of the programme, which has been termed 'Choose and Book' was discussed in Chapter 1. The intention is that patients whose doctor has referred them to their local hospital for a consultation, a therapy or a diagnostic test such as an X-ray examination, should be able to choose a date and time for that appointment that are convenient to them.

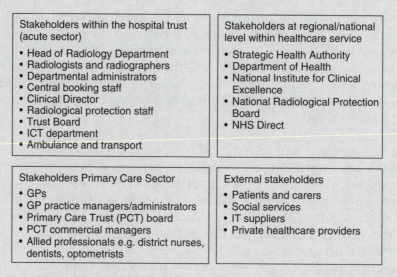

Stakeholders within the hospital trust (acute sector)	Stakeholders at regional/national level within healthcare service
• Head of Radiology Department • Radiologists and radiographers • Departmental administrators • Central booking staff • Clinical Director • Radiological protection staff • Trust Board • ICT department • Ambulance and transport	• Strategic Health Authority • Department of Health • National Institute for Clinical Excellence • National Radiological Protection Board • NHS Direct

Stakeholders Primary Care Sector	External stakeholders
• GPs • GP practice managers/administrators • Primary Care Trust (PCT) board • PCT commercial managers • Allied professionals e.g. district nurses, dentists, optometrists	• Patients and carers • Social services • IT suppliers • Private healthcare providers

Figure 8.2   *Stakeholder groups for the 'Choose and Book' project*

Figure 8.2 shows the stakeholder groups associated with appointments for X-rays in the 'Choose and Book' project. It can be seen that while there are a significant number of stakeholders within the hospital trust, such a project must be viewed as a

Stakeholder group	Perceived benefits (disbenefits)	Changes needed	Perceived resistance	Commitment (Current and Required)				
				Anti	None	Allow it to happen	Help it happen	Make it happen
GP	Fewer enquiries Tracking of patients	Training – use new system only	Rejection of referral Extra work and costs		C	*Action required?* →		R
Head of radiology	Better use of clinic staff Reduced cost per X-ray	New appointment process in radiology dept Support needed to establish new ways of working	Difficulty in making changes due to staff shortages			C	*Action required?* →	R
Clinical director	Better clinical care	Adherence to defined protocols	Need to be involved – just a scheduling issue?		C	*Action required?* →	R	
Patients	Choice of appointment Better information Reduced waiting time	Need to have info about the service/process to enable them to use it	Unknown (needs to be investigated)			C	R	
ICT department	Awareness of future need for databases/networks	More resources (staff time) needed for IT developments	None			C →	R	
PCT chief executives	Better use of funds and resources	Raise priority/ownership	Overstretched			C →	R	

Figure 8.3   Partial stakeholder analysis for the 'Choose and Book' project

Box 8.2 (Continued)

partnership with the primary care sector, since there are also a significant number of important stakeholders in this sector, such as the GPs who must encourage their patients and their practice managers to adopt this new way of booking appointments. Figure 8.2 highlights that public sector projects often have a number of regional or national bodies as stakeholders, since they have set the initial intention or targets that are driving deployment and will wish to monitor progress or they issue overall guidelines and monitor activity in the sector. Finally, the figure highlights that such projects are likely to have a number of groups of external stakeholders, including here the patients who it is intended will be the beneficiaries of the improved service.

Figure 8.3 shows a stakeholder analysis as described in Chapter 6 for some of the key stakeholders involved in the 'Choose and Book' project. It can be seen that, for a number of the stakeholders whose involvement is required to either make the changes happen or to help them happen, actions must be identified to address their perceived resistance. The activities identified to address such resistance should be included in the benefits dependency network for the project, and hence the final benefits plan. The roles of these stakeholders mean that without undertaking the identified changes, the benefits expected from the project will not be realized.

Small Businesses

As stated in the introduction to this chapter, it is likely that smaller firms will have more limited human and financial resources than large organizations. Additionally they are less likely to possess, or will have less access to, technical resources and capabilities when compared to their larger counterparts (Keeling et al., 2000). However, smaller firms do have the advantage of flexibility and receptivity to try new approaches because their processes, structures and systems are normally simpler than in larger firms (Chang and Powell, 1998). Such observations imply that while smaller firms can adapt to new ways of working, their limited resources mean that they must select these new ways very carefully. Hence, rather than being less relevant to smaller organizations, it could be argued that the process and tools presented in this book are more pertinent. They can help to ensure that benefits are realized from those projects that are undertaken and, just as importantly, they can also be used to avoid projects that are unlikely to deliver benefits or waste the limited funds and resources available.

The tools and frameworks that comprise the benefits management approach can be applied in a small business in a similar manner to that described for larger organizations. However, there are a few particular issues that arise in the use of the approach in SMEs. In very small businesses, it is likely that most of the staff would be involved in the benefits planning process described in Chapter 7. Some of them may not benefit from the investment directly, but it is very likely that they will be involved in or affected by the changes that are needed. Another important consideration that arises from the development of a benefits dependency network is whether the organization has the capacity or capabilities to carry out the changes that have been identified. As is shown in the case study described in Box 8.3, thought should not only be given to the organization's ability to undertake the necessary changes, but also to who should be responsible for ensuring they occur.

Box 8.3 B2B e-commerce in a gift manufacturer

A small, UK-based gift manufacturer wished to explore the benefits and implications of implementing an internet distribution channel for use by retailers who stocked and sold their gifts. These retailers ranged between small single-site newsagents and gift shops to large, national chains. The sale of gifts by supermarkets in the UK was also beginning to grow and the manufacturer hoped that this internet offering might help them win business from these important and powerful players.

The planned internet offering would allow retailers to enter their orders for gifts online at any time of day. The manufacturer would then receive orders immediately, cutting out the errors and delays that were being experienced with the telephone and fax-based ordering system that was in place. It was expected that the online ordering facility, if implemented well, could provide a point of differentiation from other gift manufacturers.

Box 8.3 (Continued)

A simplified version of the benefits dependency network developed by the management team is shown in Figure 8.4. A number of significant benefits were identified. By speeding up and improving the accuracy of order fulfilment to retailers, the number of 'turns', that is, the rate at which the gifts in a display stand are sold could be increased, as the right stock would be in place without any stockouts. This would lead to improved sales, both for the retailer and the manufacturer. The order information could also be used, both by the retailer and manufacturer, to understand those gifts that had been selling well and, conversely, those that had not. Unprofitable lines could therefore be removed and the number of gifts that were returned from retailers as unsold could be reduced. Overall, it was expected that the service to retailers would be improved, but at a lower overall cost.

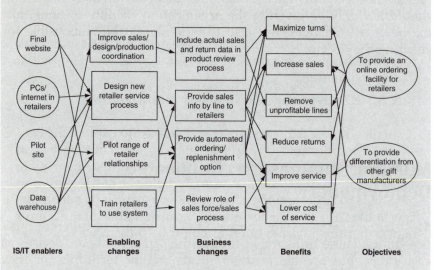

Figure 8.4   Benefits dependency network for a gift manufacturer

A number of business and enabling changes and supporting IS/IT requirements were identified. These included the important tasks of ensuring that the system met the needs of the retailers, that a large number of them could be trained to use it and that new service processes were designed and implemented to support their use. If both the retailers and the manufacturer were to benefit from the additional information the system could provide about sales, then both parties would need to learn how to interpret this information and in the case of the manufacturer, consideration of this information would need to be included in the product review and new design process. An important change that was identified was in the role of the current sales staff. If the system was successful, it was hoped that such staff could move from being effectively 'order takers', to providing real customer service, such as helping retailers select the best product range and improving the displays to increase sales.

While some of the changes identified would be challenging, none was felt to be impossible. However, when identifying owners for each of these changes, the chief executive's name kept recurring. Given his other responsibilities, it would be unlikely that he would have enough time to manage all the necessary changes and ensure they were successfully achieved. However, without this attention to the changes, the network clearly demonstrated that the expected benefits would not be realized. A new senior member of staff was therefore appointed into a sales director role. In addition to taking on other duties, she took responsibility for a number of the most significant changes that had been identified.

Multiunit Businesses: Replicated Deployments

Most large businesses are composed of a number of different business units. These units may produce the same goods or services as each other, but operate in different geographic territories, or they may be organized according to product and service lines. In order to implement organization-wide strategies, realize operating synergies, provide a consolidated picture of performance across the different units and also achieve IT procurement economies, many organizations seek to deploy the same IS/IT applications across all their units. Many public sector initiatives also require the same or similar systems to be deployed in a large number of locations and separate organizations, such as local authorities or in all state schools or in all publicly funded hospitals.

As discussed earlier in this chapter, while it may be tempting to assume that the benefits and necessary changes for such similar implementations will be the same and hence save the time and cost of developing individual benefits plans, this temptation should be avoided. Each unit, even when part of the same organization, is likely to be starting implementation from a unique position in terms of its current performance and capabilities. For example, they will have differing resources and staff skills or be using a particular set of existing systems and they will be operating in different local business or social situations. A benefits plan that identifies the specific and significant benefits and associated changes that can be achieved by the unit in question, given its current position, should therefore be developed. Participation in the development of the plans, or explicit recognition that the plans reflect the local context, will encourage stakeholder participation in the change activities identified and increase willingness to use the new system.

Variations across the Applications Portfolio

The applications portfolio was introduced in Chapter 2. This framework allows investments in applications to be considered according to the contribution that they are expected to make to the organization's strategy or operations. Key operational applications improve the effectiveness of the current business operations while the main contribution of support applications is to reduce costs by eliminating or reducing organizational inefficiencies. As shown in Figure 8.5, investments in these two application types are aimed primarily at overcoming existing business problems and constraints in order to avoid current or future disadvantages.

In contrast, investments in strategic applications are intended to provide advantage by differentiating the organization from its competitors or improving its operational performance, so that it sets new standards of excellence in its industry. Such improvements usually require the organization to do new things or to create new ways of conducting aspects of its business. High potential investments are R&D activities that seek to create future opportunities by exploring and evaluating new business ideas or new technologies. Once such ideas are proven, they can become the basis for full-scale strategic investments. Hence, as shown in Figure 8.5, these latter two application types are associated with gaining advantage through innovation.

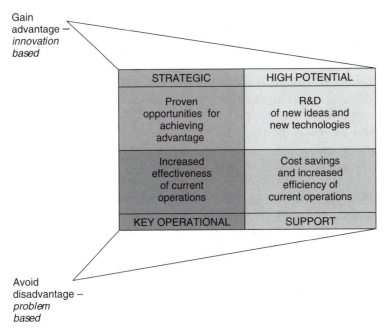

Gain
advantage −
innovation
based

Avoid
disadvantage −
problem
based

STRATEGIC	HIGH POTENTIAL
Proven opportunities for achieving advantage	R&D of new ideas and new technologies
Increased effectiveness of current operations	Cost savings and increased efficiency of current operations
KEY OPERATIONAL	SUPPORT

Figure 8.5   *Different contributions of applications in the portfolio*

As discussed in Chapter 4, the degree of knowledge and understanding of the 'why, what and how' – *why* is the investment being made, *what* has to be done to realize all the potential benefits and *how* this can best be achieved – will also vary across the portfolio. The reasons for investment in both key operational and support applications are likely to be clear and well understood, since they are related to current operations. In the case of support applications both the 'what' is expected from the investment and 'how' this will be realized from a combination of organizational changes and IS/IT is likely to be fairly easily ascertained. This may require more detailed analysis and consideration of the feasibility of various options in the case of key operational investments, due to risks that might be incurred if the benefits are not realized. Strategic applications, in contrast, are related to new opportunities for the organization and the rationale for an investment may be difficult to state explicitly, at least initially. Again, since strategic applications relate to new activities or new ways of working, the 'what' and 'how' will be less well understood and hence less certain.

In essence, these differences across the applications in the portfolio can be expressed in terms of the 'ends, ways and means' view of strategy development and implementation introduced in Chapter 2.

For support applications the 'ends', that is the investment objectives and benefits expected from the investment are likely to be relatively easy to express and agree at the start. Similarly, the 'ways' that business changes can be made to achieve the stated objectives, are likely to be known or can be fairly easily ascertained. The most appropriate set of 'means', that is the combination of enabling changes and the IS/IT required to effect the business changes, is also relatively easy to determine, once the necessary business changes have been agreed.

In contrast, due to their innovative nature, for strategic applications the 'ends' may be difficult to state with certainty at the start. Therefore, although it is suggested that the development of a benefits dependency network should start by establishing and agreeing the investment objectives and identifying the expected benefits, this will probably prove difficult when new strategic investments are initiated. Consideration of the 'ways', that is the organizational changes that can be made and whether the 'means' exist to achieve those changes must be made before the 'ends', that is the benefits and the investment objectives, can be predicted with certainty and finally agreed. Those final objectives may, in some cases, be dependent on the ability of the organization to develop new information systems or other organizational capabilities, in order to bring about the changes needed to realize the potential benefits.

These variations in the extent of existing knowledge and degrees of certainty about the expected benefits and the associated business changes across the portfolio, suggest the need for different emphases and approaches when using the tools and frameworks. In particular the way the benefits dependency network is developed will differ, depending on whether the main intention is to remove or reduce business or organizational problems or to achieve a successful innovation. These variations, which depend on whether the investment is essentially 'ends', 'ways' or 'means' driven, are considered in more detail in the following sections.

Problem Based: Key Operational and Support Applications

Problem-based investments arise when an organization is primarily considering the use of IS/IT to improve performance in order to:

- avoid an existing disadvantage compared with competitors
- prevent performance deteriorating in the future to a level that would be a disadvantage

- achieve stated business targets
- remove constraints that are preventing known opportunities being taken.

Examples of such investments might include: integrating customer data to provide a single point of contact for customer enquiries; implementing an ERP system to remove reconciliation problems between production and finance; providing employee self-service applications via a portal to reduce administration and purchasing costs, or providing laptops to sales people to ensure the accuracy of customer quotations.

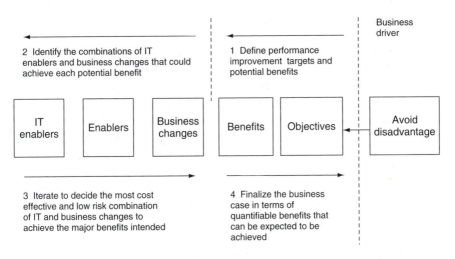

Figure 8.6   Developing an 'ends'-driven, problem-based network

The main purpose in constructing a benefits dependency network for problem-based investments is to identify the most cost-effective and lowest risk combination of IT and business changes that will achieve the required improvements, most of which can be expressed as explicit, quantified benefits. Those benefits will largely be the result of changes that enable the organization to stop doing unnecessary activities or make it able to carry out essential tasks better, either more efficiently or effectively.

As shown in Figure 8.6, development of the network commences as described in Chapter 4. It is important first to define and agree the investment objectives, expressed as the level of performance improvement required to overcome the problems or constraints being faced. The particular benefits that can be expected by achieving the objectives should also be identified. Ownership of the benefits and how they can be measured should then be determined before considering the changes, since this will help to ensure that the required ends have been accurately defined.

The possible combinations of business and enabling changes and IT functionality can then be considered together. The analysis should emphasize the use of existing or off-the-shelf software and minimize the need for new IS/IT development, as far as possible. The preference should be to change business processes and procedures wherever feasible, either to make better use of existing systems or to minimize the costs of customizing software. These approaches will both reduce initial investment costs and risks and reduce ongoing systems maintenance and support costs.

The alternative IS/IT and change combinations should then be prioritized based on overall cost effectiveness and least risk, in relation to achieving the highest value set of benefits. It is then advisable to carry out a stakeholder analysis on the preferred option to identify any reasons why implementation could be problematic and, if necessary, revise the business case accordingly. Alternatively, if the stakeholder issues suggest that implementation may fail, the 'next best' option should be considered. This approach sometimes results in a new 'hybrid' option that is achievable. The objectives and benefits can then be finalized for the preferred option and a full business case and benefits plan developed.

Overall, the process is relatively linear. Consideration of benefit commences with an identification of the improvements required. Different combinations of business and enabling changes and IT are then considered in order to determine the best way of achieving as many of the required performance improvements as possible.

Innovation Based: Strategic and High Potential Applications

Innovation-based investments occur when an organization is deploying IS/IT to exploit a business opportunity, to create potential business opportunities or to create new organizational capabilities:

- by doing something new involving the use of IT
- by doing something in a new way using IT
- by using new IT to do something it could not do before.

This is the area of 'technochange' described in Chapter 6, where innovation is dependent on a combination of the technology, the organization's technical expertise and the ability of the organization to change in order to make effective use of the new technical capabilities. Examples could include creating an online sales channel to reach new customers; introducing vendor managed inventory by key suppliers; allowing customers to do self-billing or deploying a data warehouse and analytics to support operational decision making.

A key reason for constructing a benefits dependency network for innovation-based investments is to understand whether a combination of business changes and technology deployment can create a worthwhile advantage and how that can best be achieved. Such investments will often require extensive customization of available software or the bespoke development of software to meet the new and possibly unique requirements. Advantage gained from such investments normally results from a combination of doing things better, that is, to a performance level that competitors cannot match or doing new things that others cannot easily copy.

These investments are of two types, both of which are aimed at creating advantage for the organization. The first is essentially 'ways' driven and the second is 'means' driven.

'Ways'-driven investments are more appropriate for strategic applications, where an opportunity exists and the purpose is to identify whether and how the organization can make the necessary business changes and IS/IT investment to gain advantage from the opportunity. As shown in Figure 8.7, this involves a number of stages.

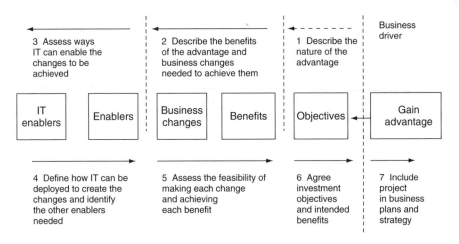

Figure 8.7 Developing a 'ways'-driven, innovation-based network

The first step is the creation of a vision statement that describes the nature of the advantage. This is a set of initial objectives that 'paint a picture' of what the situation would be if the advantage were gained. Within that overall picture all the possible business benefits should be brainstormed, but for each, the likely business changes that would be essential to achieving it should also be identified, on the assumption that IS and IT can be implemented to support these new ways of working. The feasibility of making the business changes and risks involved should then be assessed to determine those benefits that are most likely to be achievable and the benefits revised as necessary. It would be appropriate at this stage to do an initial stakeholder analysis as part of the assessment to ensure that all the key stakeholders are appropriately involved.

Then the extent to which technology could be used to enable each of the business changes is assessed and the overall likely cost of the technology needed is compared with the estimate of the benefits to determine whether, overall, the investment will be beneficial. Given this is an innovation, it is likely that a range of enabling changes will also be required to develop new processes, and even new competences, and redefine responsibilities. Finally, a full assessment of the organization's ability to deliver the combinations of IT and business changes is needed, to establish the achievable benefits of the investment before developing the final business case, based on the refined and agreed objectives.

Compared with the problem-based network development, the process is more iterative, since the benefits are difficult to define initially. They are also dependent on the nature of the changes the organization is willing and able to make plus its ability to develop and deploy new technology. It is likely that the potential benefits originally identified will change considerably during these iterations.

'Means'-driven investments are appropriate for high potential projects when a business idea for using IS/IT or other new technology appears to offer an opportunity to create advantage for the organization. As high potential projects, many of these evaluations will lead to a decision not to proceed further because it is shown not to work or is financially unfeasible.

As shown in Figure 8.8, although high potential projects should be considered as R&D activities, it is still important to define the business context and drivers, in order to spell out why the creation and evaluation of new business options is important to the organization. This will also provide the rationale for deciding how these R&D projects are prioritized. For such projects, the main purpose in creating a benefits dependency network is to identify if there are sufficient potential benefits to justify the use of resources to obtain the necessary information to build a business case for further, more significant investment.

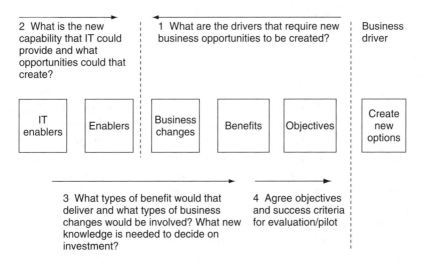

Figure 8.8 *Developing a 'means'-driven, innovation-based network*

In the case of new technology, the capabilities of the technology need to be understood in order to establish a proof of concept, not just of the technology, but of the enabling changes needed to use it effectively. It is then possible to make an initial estimate of the potential business benefits and describe the nature of business changes that will be needed. If the initial estimates of the benefits and scale of changes needed suggest that the project could be worthwhile, success criteria for a more detailed evaluation or a pilot implementation should be defined and the level of funding needed to complete the evaluation agreed.

This use of the benefits dependency network is less a formal process than a way of ensuring that all the necessary aspects of the potential innovation are considered and interrelated. It does not include the development of a full business case or benefits plan, but it requires a more structured analysis of the nature of the investment than the benefits management 'lite' initial assessment described in Chapter 9. Like the 'ways'-driven innovation investments, the use of the benefits dependency network is iterative. The initial network is certain to be amended significantly during the process of evaluation and revising the network is a useful way to record new knowledge about the benefits or changes, as and when it is acquired.

Different Application Types

Many organizations are implementing similar information systems, often using the same software package, for example systems for customer relationship management or enterprise resource planning. However, as described at the start of this chapter, the particular context of individual organizations will have a significant influence on the nature of the benefits achievable and the changes required when considering the implementation of similar systems in different organizations or business units. Although generic benefits and changes should not be assumed for any given application, some recurring patterns in benefits and changes and interrelationships between these can be observed. We cannot cover all types of application, but we include here some of those that are currently being deployed by a wide range of organizations. They include those applications that have the most significant impact on organizational performance and development and present the greatest challenges in terms of identifying and managing the expected benefits. The different applications considered illustrate the majority of issues encountered in using the benefits management approach and that need to be addressed if organizations are to increase the benefits realized from their IS/IT investments.

E-Commerce and E-Business

Since the demise of the dot.com boom, most e-business and e-commerce developments are now expected to be managed like more traditional IS/IT projects, in terms of the identification and realization of benefits. However, there are some particular issues associated with e-commerce investments and e-business applications that involve extensive interaction with outside parties.

The two terms electronic commerce (e-commerce) and electronic business (e-business) are often used interchangeably. However, as discussed in Chapter 1 more precisely, e-commerce describes the use of IS/IT to perform business transactions and other trading activities with third parties, for example with customers and suppliers, while e-business describes the use of IS/IT to improve information communication and use, both within the organization and with external parties. By definition, a characteristic of e-commerce investments is the requirement to involve external stakeholders, typically either customers or suppliers and hence it is critically important to understand 'what is in it for them'. All external stakeholders will not perceive the same benefits, indeed some may not perceive the new system as beneficial at all, yet they may be required to make significant changes in the way they conduct business with the organization. Implementation of an e-commerce system cannot be made 'mandatory' for external organizations, except by threatening to reduce the level of business with them, that is, by emphasizing the 'disbenefits' of not cooperating. Understanding the potential reactions, both positive and negative, to an e-commerce investment requires a thorough stakeholder analysis as early as possible in the project, in order to elicit genuine concerns, but also to appreciate the range of contexts within which the application has to be successfully used. Ideally, representatives from the range of external parties who will be affected should be consulted directly in this analysis. Additional actions that must be undertaken to encourage or facilitate their participation should be identified from the stakeholder analysis. These are likely to include communications plans that inform each of the different external parties about the benefits they can expect from using the new system and the changes they need to make to achieve those benefits. They may also include other actions such as incentive payments or discounts to encourage usage, the provision of necessary technology and assurance mechanisms.

In addition to the involvement of external stakeholders, e-commerce and e-business investments are often innovative in nature, allowing the organization to do something new or to do something in a distinctly different way. They are therefore likely to have the characteristics of the 'innovation-based' investments described earlier. Hence, in developing a benefits dependency network, it may be difficult to define clearly the objectives and benefits until the nature of the changes required by both the organization and the trading partners affected are known. The ability of the organization to develop the new system and work effectively with those external parties, which will have varying levels of IS/IT capabilities, to deploy the new technology also need to be considered. It will therefore be necessary to iterate between the 'ends' and the 'ways and means' until an acceptable and feasible solution is identified. One constraint that is frequently identified is the extent of integration needed with existing systems, for the organization itself and its business partners. In order to yield benefits, e-commerce investments frequently require integration with a wide range of existing systems and that data are shared in real time or near real time with those systems. Limitations in terms of the quality or performance of existing systems or the ability to exchange data and documents of different formats may require modification to the scope of the system or require implementation to be phased over time.

E-commerce developments have to date also been characterized by several, overlapping cycles of application identification and implementation. Rapid changes in many industries and markets, often brought about by e-commerce itself, have necessitated organizations in those industries to respond almost immediately to innovations by others. Although much of this haste originated in the dot.com boom, these shorter development times seem to have remained a consistent feature of e-commerce. While the benefits management process described in this book could be seen to add additional time to the consideration of investments, careful planning will tend to reduce the actual time taken and cost to implement the new processes and systems, because what actions are required and the expected benefits are more clearly understood. Using the process can also prevent an organization from embarking on ill-conceived investments that may become very expensive or in the worst case cause some trading partners to prefer to do business elsewhere.

Information Management

While knowledge management has generated much heat, and arguably less light, over the last decade, effective information management continues to be an enduring requirement for the majority of organizations. Information management may be defined as: *'The treatment of information as an asset to enhance an organization's competitiveness and responsiveness. It results from effectively identifying, collecting, and analyzing information – and then directing it to the points of decision-making and customer service'* (Impact21 Group, 2005). This definition stresses that information is an organizational asset, and like other assets it should be actively managed and supported by appropriate cross-organization policies, guidelines and roles, rather than being left to the idiosyncrasies of individuals or different teams. It is also intended to support decision making at all levels of the organization. Information gathering is often seen as a means by which senior managers can monitor and control what is going on within the organization, rather than to enable a wide range of staff to improve local decision making.

While organizations' information management activities pre-date the use of IT, the sheer volume of information within organizations and the need to share this in a timely way with a large number of staff, result in IS/IT investments being at the heart of information management. Since the majority of information systems capture, organize, store and disseminate information they are all, to some extent, information management investments. However, the term is usually confined to systems whose primary aim is to provide the information required to improve decision making. An example of a relatively simple IT-based information management investment is described in Box 8.4.

Box 8.4 Information management in clinical trials

A driver for all pharmaceutical companies is the ability to develop new drugs and to bring them to market as quickly as possible. Undertaking clinical trials is a critical stage in new drug development. Clinicians, often dispersed around the world, will be approached by the pharmaceutical company to participate in trials of new drugs. The trials can last for a number of years in order to prove the efficacy of the drug and that it has no adverse side-effects. A major challenge in such trials is the recruitment of suitable patients. For rare medical conditions, or trials that require very large numbers of patients, recruitment may take a considerable time and hence lead to a delay in bringing the final product to market.

A pharmaceutical company decided to develop a web-based system that would encourage the timely recruitment of patients, by allowing the dispersed clinicians involved in trials to share their progress with the others involved in the trial, including scientists and medical staff within the pharmaceutical company. Figure 8.9 shows a simplified version of the benefit network that was developed for the system.

Rather than rely on a technical solution alone to encourage information sharing between those involved in the trial, the company

Box 8.4 (Continued)

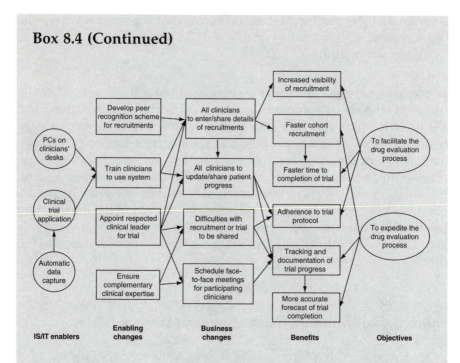

Figure 8.9 *Benefits dependency for a clinical trial application*

recognized that they must also make changes to the way the team worked. It was important to make the participants in the trial feel as if they belonged to a team. A respected clinical leader was appointed to form links among the individual clinicians and also finance and time were set aside to enable the participants to meet each other face to face. Participating clinicians were encouraged to share difficulties in patient recruitment, or issues that they encountered in treating the patients with the new drug with others in the trial. This provided the pharmaceutical company with valuable insights into the progress of the trial and its likely successful completion date.

Commonly encountered IS- and IT-based investments in the information management domain include data warehouses and data marts, analytics or data mining tools and corporate portals and intranets. Figure 8.10 shows a schematic diagram of a number of such IS and IT elements that can be used to form an integrated approach to the storage of data and the use of analytical tools to provide comprehensive information to monitor organizational performance. In this particular case the set of information analysis tools and the underlying data are accessed via a portal which provides a single point of entry, navigation and searching tools to help find the appropriate information resources. Enterprise portals are discussed in more detail later in the chapter.

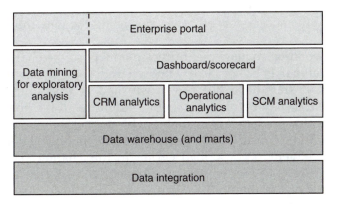

Figure 8.10   Integrated performance analysis system (after Hemingway, 2005)

Information management investments tend to present a number of particular issues in relation to the identification and realization of benefits.

Given that information management investments seek to improve decision making, it is important to commence the consideration of the objectives and benefits by understanding and defining those decisions that need to be improved and why. Who currently makes such decisions, the process by which the decisions are made and the results monitored, the information required to make the decisions and how this could best be presented or made available to them, should also be defined and agreed. This applies to both regular provision of management information, such as monthly financial reports and ad hoc analyses. Also, the improvements in business performance or development the organization is expecting to realize as a consequence of better decision making should be clearly articulated. 'Better decision making' should not be viewed as an end in itself and should never be considered as a sufficient description of a benefit. The benefits will depend on the nature of the decisions, the impact on the business of getting the decisions 'right' and to what extent having more accurate, more timely or more comprehensive information can influence the success rate.

For example, analysing customer buying patterns could provide information about the launch of a new product. Take-up could be enhanced by targeting the most appropriate customers and identifying the optimum timing for the launch. To determine whether the use of the improved information had been successful in terms of target customer selection and the timing of launch, it would be necessary to compare the launch with previous equivalent ones. This implies also being able to provide information on earlier launches in order to measure the success or, otherwise, of using the new information.

Many information management investments pose the challenge that their full value may not be clearly known until some time after implementation. If staff have not previously had access to appropriate information, it may be hard for them to identify all the benefits that could be realized when it is available. This suggests that such investments should be considered in two phases, the first being a 'problem-based' investment, as described earlier in this chapter. That is, the investment seeks to remove the problems or constraints causing the current lack of the required information. This phase could include accessing additional information sources, improving the integrity of the information by implementing new data and content management processes or consolidating data from several sources into one integrated database or data warehouse. The second phase then is essentially an 'innovation-based' investment, or series of developments, when the new opportunities open to individuals and the organization due to the information they now have available are identified and evaluated. It may be appropriate to formally divide the project into these two phases, a 'production phase' and a 'utilization phase' and produce a distinct benefits plan and case for funding for each. The benefits of the first phase could include significant efficiency improvements, whereas the second would require the level of understanding of the decision-making processes described earlier. In general terms, obtaining evidence to prove the benefits of the second phase would tend to be by reviewing a representative sample of decisions, rather than by more systematic measurement.

While Figure 8.10 may suggest that information management investments are primarily about system and technology deployment, identification of the changes to ways of working is as critical to the delivery of benefits, if not more so, than other types of application. Careful use of the tools and frameworks presented in this book often highlights a number of important areas that organizations need to consider. One of these is the availability of analytical skills within the organization. While current analytical and business intelligence software is very powerful, it must be used by individuals who understand the analysis being undertaken. If decisions will be made based on the results, it is particularly important to understand the limitations of the analytical techniques or reliability of the underlying information being used. Such skills tend to be highly specialized and in short supply in most organizations, as witnessed by the reports of many organizations that have invested in large data warehouses and associated analytical software, but have derived little or no value from them. Indeed, as they fill with vast amounts of data, such data warehouses can often simply add to the costs of information management without providing any significant benefit.

Another important area that may require changes, if benefits are to be delivered, is the ways the organization makes decisions, both the formal processes and the less formal customs and practices, including the timings of decisions and who is involved in making them. For example, if information management investments can allow greater information access throughout the organization, it may be appropriate to devolve decision making, so that decisions can be taken closer to the point of need. Instead of simply being able to make decisions more quickly, it may be possible to move to more 'just-in-time' decision making. This contrasts with having to make decisions rapidly, often under pressure, based on incomplete information. It may also be possible to allocate responsibility for more decisions to individuals, rather than require agreement of a group of people, because the individual now has all the necessary information available. If investments seek only to support existing decision-making practices, then the benefits may be limited as much by those practices as by the available information.

Customer Relationship Management Systems

Many organizations in both business-to-consumer markets and in business-to-business markets have invested and continue to invest considerable sums in customer relationship management (CRM) systems. While the details of the rationale for these investments will vary from organization to organization, the general intention is to enable organizations to understand their customers or clients and hence build enduring relationships with them (Knox et al., 2003). Such relationships are in turn expected to increase the revenue that the organization can earn and reduce the costs associated with customer attrition and acquisition. CRM systems have also been deployed by not-for-profit organizations, including local authorities, seeking to improve the service they provide to their users and the value for money provided to the source of their funding.

As with the other types of application considered here, CRM systems have a number of particular characteristics that influence the nature of the benefits to be realised and how the investment is managed.

An important characteristic of the benefits arising from CRM systems is the considerable time taken for many of the significant benefits to be realized. Many CRM systems have been sold with vendors' promises of rapid improvements to organizational performance. However, an increasing number of studies are beginning to show that it may take up to five years or more after the initial implementation for many of the major benefits to be realized (Peppard and Ward, 2005). For example, in 2002, the Britannia Building Society in the UK won an award for the best CRM implementation in the financial services sector, but had begun its CRM initiative in 1995. Similarly, one particular life assurance company was recently voted by a countrywide survey of brokers, who are their main channel to market, as the 'best company to deal with'. However, this accolade was three years after the implementation of their CRM system. The long-term nature of the benefits calls into question figures quoted for the failure of such initiatives. For example, Gartner Group (2002) found that 65% of CRM deployments failed. However, given a much longer timeframe for measurement, it may be found that the failure rate is much less.

The nature of the benefits from CRM is shown schematically in the return on investment (ROI) curve shown in Figure 8.11. It can be seen that operational benefits, such as process efficiencies and cost savings, can be expected to emerge relatively quickly after implementation. However, the benefits that result from improved customer relationships require those relationships to be built and will therefore take years, rather than months, to realize. The organization's customers also have to appreciate the value of the new type of relationship. Groups of customers will expect different benefits from a closer association, implying that the organization will need to tailor the way it works to satisfy a variety of customer requirements.

The long-term nature of many of the benefits from CRM systems has implications for the use of the benefits management process, in particular in setting the measures for benefits and how their achievement will be assessed. Since it is not feasible to delay the review of a project for several years, in order to establish if long-term benefits have been realized, the review stage of the process must recognize that all the benefits expected will not have yet been achieved. Instead, it should focus on the shorter term operational benefits. If there have been difficulties in realizing these, it suggests that action may be required to ensure the longer term benefits will still be achieved. In addition, it may be possible to design measures for the longer term benefits that, while not confirming their full realization, indicate that the organization is on track to obtain them in the future. To demonstrate that the changes are causing the improvements expected, it may be appropriate to pilot the new ways of working with a particular group of customers and compare them, over time, with a 'control group' of other similar customers. A complex set of measures, in addition to traditional sales analyses, may be required to show that both the organization and its customers are benefiting from the new arrangements. Such measures may relate to the amount and quality of the information being collected from customers or a reduction in the number of queries about routine transactions, but they would normally also include careful assessment of customer satisfaction. While this will not guarantee improved service and increased purchases in the future, it may be expected to contribute to these.

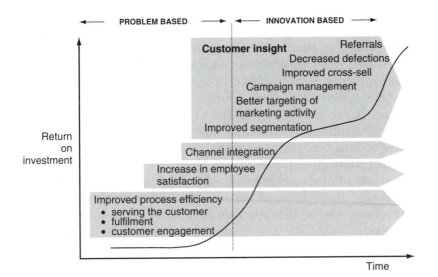

Figure 8.11   Return on investment curve for CRM systems (after Peppard and Ward, 2005)

When building the business case it may be worthwhile to do an initial stakeholder analysis to identify not only the range of perceptions customers may have of the changes, but also to define the benefits different types of customer could expect to see. This may produce a number of benefit streams, requiring different changes to be made to address the needs of different customer segments. In turn, this may help phase the implementation to gain some quick wins by delivering some benefits to large numbers of customers without major changes.

Other issues that are particularly pertinent in CRM deployments are related to the critical role of frontline staff, both to the collection of customer information, but also to the effective use of the system and the information it contains. In many organizations staff are accustomed to focusing on the products sold or the performance of the team or unit in which they work. They are less familiar with focusing on the customer, whose needs may not precisely match the organization's ways of doing business or cut across product or unit boundaries. The areas where staff are able to use their discretion or must follow the prescribed processes need to be clearly defined. In seeking to realize the benefits from CRM systems, it is therefore important to understand the views these frontline staff have of the system and ways of working, and particularly to understand 'what is in it for them'. Due to the central role these staff will play in making many of the changes happen, the stakeholder analysis must identify actions that will address their issues and concerns.

Another issue that frequently occurs in the consideration of the views of individuals regarding the use of CRM systems is the perceived link between information and power in organizations. Individuals often believe that if they share their information with others, their personal value and hence power within the organization will diminish. The development of new performance measurement or incentive schemes may be one means of addressing such views. For example, rather than rewarding individual performance alone, providing some financial bonus for team or organizational achievement may be required.

Finally, many of the benefits expected from CRM systems depend on successfully dealing with many of the information management issues discussed earlier. In particular, if an organization intends to derive insights about customer behaviour from the information they have collected, they will require access to sophisticated analytical skills. Given the fundamental changes implicit in implementing a CRM system, that is moving from an organizational-centric to a customer-centric view of the business, it will probably also be necessary to reconsider the decision-making roles and processes within the organization.

Enterprise Resource Planning Systems

Enterprise resource planning (ERP) suites are configurable, off-the-shelf software packages that provide an integrated suite of systems and information resources that coordinate operational and management processes across a broad range of internal business activities, including procurement, accounting, finance and human resources (Davenport, 1998). As with CRM systems, many organizations have invested in or are currently considering ERP suites. While the focus of CRM developments is improving relationships with external parties, ERP deployments tend to focus primarily on improving the performance of internal processes and operations, often by rationalizing and integrating not only the systems and processes, but also the data and information sources used in operational and managerial decision making. As a consequence, the quality and reliability of the data in the ERP system is critical to achieving the majority of the benefits.

A number of the issues that characterize the realization of benefits from ERP systems have already been discussed in Chapter 1 and are summarized in Figure 1.8. One issue identified is that many ERP investments can be viewed, by both the business managers and IS staff as primarily software replacement projects. This may lead to reluctance from business staff to fully participate, leaving the IS staff to lead the project. Although the IS staff may believe they know how the business operates, it often transpires that what they do know is how the systems in the business operate, rather than how business is actually done. The lack of involvement of business staff means that business changes to utilize the new systems effectively are overlooked. Even when business managers and staff are involved, they often ask for the system to be configured or amended to reflect current business practices. If such requests are met, this can result in both increased initial investment and ongoing support and maintenance costs. This approach is also likely to reduce the benefits realized since it reduces consideration of new ways of working. As is shown by the case study presented in Box 8.5, this can result in keeping the old ways of working after having incurred the significant cost and disruption associated with introducing new technology.

Box 8.5 Implementing an ERP at PharmaCo

A major global pharmaceutical company, termed here PharmaCo, recently invested £11 million in a SAP-based ERP

Box 8.5 (Continued)

and supply chain management system to replace 17 separate legacy systems in different business units and functions within the organization. Due to this heavy emphasis on systems replacement, the project was viewed almost solely as *'a technology replacement project, with little change to the underlying business'*. This resulted in the planning stage of the project being characterized by a clear belief that the project and its implications on the organization were well understood.

Problems began to emerge when it became apparent that successful implementation and operation would require greater changes to the way units and functions within the business operated and interrelated than had first been anticipated. These groups were traditionally highly autonomous and were not willing to have changes to the way they worked mandated by the project team. In particular it became clear:

> *We needed to work according to processes – however, the organization is predominantly organized along unit and functional lines. Process ownership and governance were problems that surfaced that needed to be resolved.*

Concerned about the challenge to their traditional functional control, many of the managers began to look after their own and their function's interests.

At the end of the implementation stage, although the system was operational, significant problems remained and few benefits had been delivered. The organization therefore set about an active shakedown phase, which it referred to as *'commissioning'*, in an attempt to achieve the benefits that had justified the investment. This phase sought to identify explicit benefits for each of the different functions involved and to improve the relationships between these groups. For example:

> *A process based knowledge-sharing intranet site has been established to help staff share experiences and learning with the new system across functions. This has hints, tips and how-tos on it – and it is generally seen as a success.*

The implications of these common characteristics of ERP deployments for effective benefits realization emphasize the importance of the choice of business project sponsor and business project manager for such projects. These roles are discussed in Chapter 7, where it is argued that, for projects with significant degrees of business change, the individuals who fulfil them should be experienced senior managers drawn from the business. Given that most ERP deployments will affect a large number of groups or functions within the organization, it is important that the two individuals can garner respect and cooperation right across the organization and are not seen to represent certain interest groups alone.

The project manager in particular should ensure that all functions that will be significantly affected by the ERP deployment are involved in the development of a benefits plan. This includes identifying those benefits that they might expect to receive and those changes they will be involved in, either by having to make the identified changes or by being affected by them. Such involvement of different groups will often show that some groups or functions may already have well-functioning processes and access to appropriate information, while others do not. Therefore some groups will be less willing to change, because they are satisfied with their existing systems, while others will see it as an opportunity to upgrade to better systems and technology. The benefits plan and business case should therefore be sensitive to and reflect the varying degrees of change that may be required by different functions and units in relation to the level of benefits that each may realize. A comprehensive stakeholder analysis should be undertaken as early as possible in the project, to ensure that actions are put in place to address the range of different starting points and perceptions of those groups.

A study exploring the organizational issues of enterprise system (ES) deployments, including ERP systems, identified a number of issues that often occur during the implementation. Based on the varying degrees of success observed in the cases studied, some conclusions can be drawn that help organizations address these issues to ensure more successful deployment (Ward et al., 2005). Among other findings, the project proposed the model for typical enterprise system implementation described in Box 8.6.

312 *The Importance of Context*

Box 8.6 Model of enterprise systems deployments

In an ideal enterprise systems (ES) development and implementation, the organization has an overall business strategy that will lead to achievement of its medium and long-term business vision. The implementation of an enterprise system is seen as essential to that business strategy. Either the ES implementation is intended to operationalize the strategy or provide the basis for the new business model that underpins the vision. In the latter case the business and organizational changes required are likely to be very extensive, but are difficult to identify in detail at the start of the project.

If, however, there is a lack of clarity about how the enterprise system will contribute to the business strategy, the business case tends to be based on the functionality offered by the system. Due to the lack of focus on required business changes, during implementation unexpected organizational issues and constraints emerge, usually related to making changes to working practices and processes, rather than the implementation of the technology.

While most IS deployments can encounter such problems, the sheer scale of most enterprise systems, both in terms of complexity and the number of functions and individuals that are impacted, means they are particularly susceptible to organizational issues. In such cases, it was found that organizations sought to reduce the scope of the project to something that is achievable. The benefits realized from the systems were significantly reduced and the original vision was also scaled back. In the worst case, the result was an expensive deployment of new technology that offered little in addition to the original systems that were in place.

The two-stage model shown in Figure 8.12 is based on how those organizations in the study that had implemented an ES successfully had addressed the complex set of issues they encountered. The model draws upon the work of Markus and Tannis (2000), but many others have also proposed or observed a staged approach, albeit with a varying number of stages.

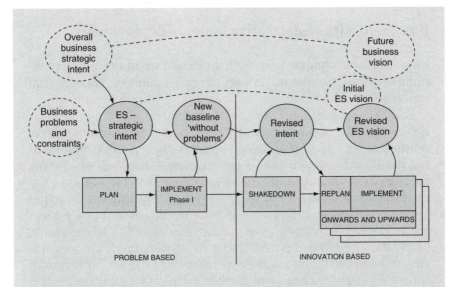

Figure 8.12   *The two-stage model of ES implementation*

This approach commences with the identification of how the enterprise system can contribute to the overall strategic intent of the organization. However, a large part of the planning is driven by the wish to overcome existing constraints and problems within the business. Implementation is effectively broken into two phases. The first phase is consistent with the problem-based investments discussed earlier in this chapter. This phase of the implementation seeks to overcome known problems in the organization, producing 'a new baseline', where the existing problems and inhibitors to more innovative change have been removed. This accepts the logic of others that it is difficult to operationalize a new vision when surrounded by current problems. Equally, it allows for the fact that different stakeholder groups will be at different stages of development in terms of the capabilities of existing systems. Those with excellent existing systems will have a different perspective on the need for and nature of the changes required compared with those with poor systems who have much to gain simply by replacement to remove problems. The compromise usually errs on the side of bringing the weaker areas up to the new baseline and deferring the riskier and more innovative changes. Another key issue is clarity of the need for and benefits of systems integration, where again different stakeholders have more to gain or

Box 8.6 (Continued)

lose from the change and the compromises made often post-
pone changes to take advantage of integration of systems and
processes.

Following any ES implementation there is some form of shakedown phase, which may involve resolving serious problems if
business performance has been adversely affected, or merely
tuning the system and business processes to achieve the
expected performance levels. Any implementation should anticipate and plan for this stage, ensuring resources and procedures
are in place to deal with the consequences of implementation.
Once the 'baseline' benefits have been delivered, the organization needs to define a revised intent for the ES, in terms of
future business change (and further ES investment if necessary)
to deliver new business options that will be available following systems and process integration or having common systems
across the business units.

Having established a new or revised intent in relation once
more to the business vision, which may have changed during
the period of implementation, a new stage of planning and
implementation, often in smaller steps, focused on specific business processes can be carried out. This onwards and upwards
stage, which is consistent with the innovation-based networks
described earlier in this chapter, is more innovative and requires
more business change. It is often therefore only really feasible
in discrete steps if business risks are to be avoided. It is important that organizational knowledge gained during the first, often
large-scale implementation is retained and transferred to this
second phase.

Enterprise Portals

Enterprise portals have been described as *'the most important business information project of the next decade'* (Collins, 1999) and are
perhaps the most recent embodiment of enterprise systems. These
systems seek to provide a single electronic location where staff can go
to do their job, which they seek to do by integrating all the disparate

information sources and applications within organizations. The information and applications presented to staff can be customized to reflect their role in the organization or their location, and can be further personalized by each member of staff to reflect their own preferred ways of working. Enterprise portals can therefore help individuals seeking information and can also be used to provide information to staff while mitigating the effects of 'information overload'. Portals can further enhance effectiveness by supporting communication between individuals and work groups, allowing increased collaboration. In addition to these improvements in internal operations, portals can also improve collaboration with external business partners such as customers and suppliers.

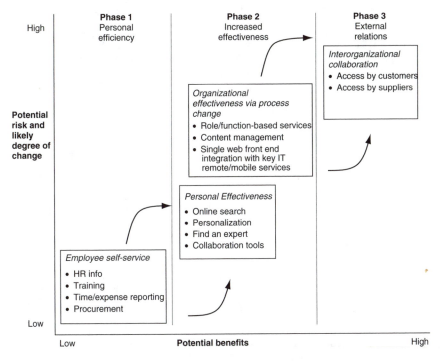

Figure 8.13 *Phases of enterprise portal deployment*

Enterprise portals are effectively a collection of separate services and functionality within a single framework. Organizations can therefore choose the order and sequence of how they deploy these. Research on the patterns of deployment of portal services (Daniel and Ward, 2005) has shown a common pattern of phased service and functionality deployment, as shown in Figure 8.13. These phases echo those shown in Figure 8.12, first removing the inefficiencies

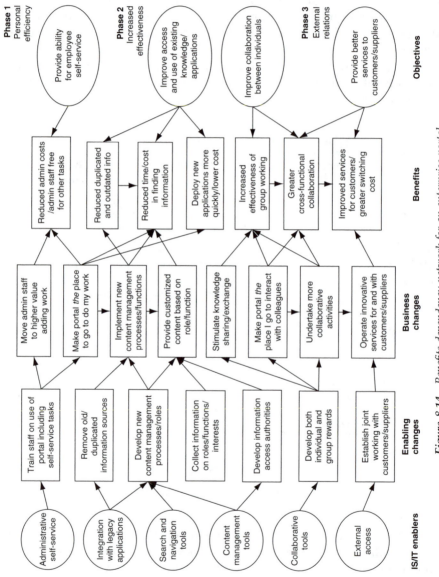

Figure 8.14 Benefits dependency network for an enterprise portal

associated with staff undertaking simple administrative tasks, often termed employee self-service. The next two phases allow increased effectiveness, first at the individual and then at the organizational level. The latter, in particular, will require changes to processes and associated roles and responsibilities. Only when organizations are confident with the operation within their organization are they prepared to move 'onwards and upwards' and make the portal available to customers and suppliers in order to develop closer working.

A benefits dependency network describing the phased implementation of an enterprise portal, which has once again been simplified, is shown in Figure 8.14. If the entire network is considered, reflecting a big bang approach to portal deployment, then it can be seen that there are interdependencies between benefits, with the realization of some benefits being reliant on the achievement of earlier ones and similarly for a number of the business changes. In addition, the later benefits and changes, including those associated with more collaborative working and developing new services for or with external parties are not well specified, since experience of using the system is required to understand the changes needed to realize benefits in these areas. Alternatively, it can be seen that the network suggests implementation can be divided into a number of separate benefit and change streams that reflect the stages or phases shown in Figure 8.13. Each of these phases can be addressed sequentially, allowing the learning and experience from previous phases to be fed into the later stages.

Infrastructure Investments

Infrastructure, such as new network capacity, processing capability, data storage or operating and general utility software, can often be one of the most difficult areas of IT investment to justify in terms of business benefits. In many cases it is equally difficult to measure the actual benefits realized after implementation. It can be argued that some aspects of IT infrastructure are required just to be in business and should be justified in the same way as other essentials, such as office space. This would normally mean on a cost per employee basis. However, this is not appropriate when major new infrastructure investments or upgrades are being considered. New infrastructure may be required for one or more application being planned by the organization, but frequently the benefits arising from these are insufficient to justify the significant investment involved. It is also often the case that many other existing or future applications will use the same infrastructure. Hence the argument for infrastructure investments often needs to be based on unknown benefits from, as yet unspecified future use, making it difficult to justify the costs involved.

A suggested approach to justification is to consider the various ways in which a particular type of infrastructure can contribute to improvements in organizational and individual performance or create new business options. Figure 8.15 suggests five different ways in which this contribution can occur. Any specific investment is likely to produce benefits in a number of these dimensions, each of which should be examined in order to build a combined business case.

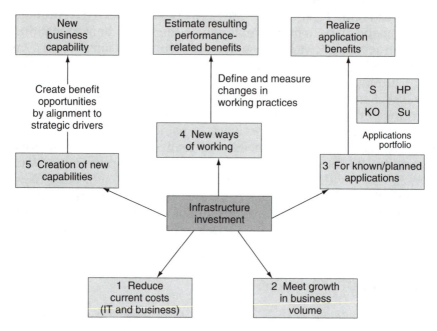

Figure 8.15   *Infrastructure investment justification*

The five ways in which infrastructure investments can contribute to organizational performance, and which, if appropriate, should be included in a business case, are:

1 *Reduce current costs*: Modern technologies often incur lower costs in terms of support and maintenance than older versions, hence new infrastructure can often be, at least partly, justified by a reduction in IT operating costs. Such savings are most likely to arise in relation to the running costs of extensively used support or key operational applications and personal productivity and communications tools. There may also be business cost savings, especially by providing

easier to use desktop tools or lower cost means of communication or information access.

Included in this category is also the 'forced' need to replace a technology that is or is becoming obsolete, i.e. it will no longer be supported or further developed by the vendor. As with any technology investments that involve supporting existing applications, it is prudent to question whether all those applications are still essential to the business. If they cannot be discontinued, alternatives which will result in different benefits and costs should be considered, for example:

- transferring the applications to another existing technology already in use in the business or a new technology consistent with the IT strategy and policies relating to nominated platforms and standardization across the business
- modifying, replacing or redeveloping the applications to take advantage of new, lower cost technology platforms
- reducing the functionality of the applications to the essentials before transferring them to another technology.

2 *Meet growth in business volume*: Infrastructure investments may be required to meet the growth in the volume of business transactions both internally and externally. However, it needs to be clear whether the increased volume is related to real business growth that leads to increased revenue or higher service levels, rather than merely increased internal activity. Much of the increased network and storage capacity required by organizations is simply due to poor practice in the management of emails, intranet content and documents, rather than growth in volume or value of business being conducted.

Additional infrastructure may also be required to accommodate a changing mix of transactions, for example, customers switching to the internet ordering from the call centre, or to meet changing business practices, customer or employee expectations. In some markets, customers now expect just-in-time deliveries from suppliers in order to avoid their holding stocks. They are therefore undertaking more single line ordering, rather than consolidating purchases, leading to an increased volume of transactions for the supplier, but no additional revenue.

3 *For known or planned applications*: As already discussed, infrastructure costs can be justified, in part, based on the benefits delivered by known future applications that will use the infrastructure, and the relevant proportion of the costs should be included in the business justification for those application investments. Normally,

more than one application will make use of any significant infrastructure investment, therefore explicit links should be identified between the planned infrastructure and each of the applications in the portfolio, both being developed and currently in operation, that will use the new infrastructure. This is also important to ensure that as new applications are planned and implemented they use the existing infrastructure as far as possible, or take advantage of the new infrastructure investments and avoid further, unnecessary, costs being incurred.

4 *Emergent and planned new ways of working*: Although many changes to business processes and working practices are associated with specific applications, increasingly, improvements in the ways of working can result from people using the tools and facilities provided by the infrastructure, without major application investment. For example, a bank having set up its 'product catalogue' on an internal website, stopped sending product update information on paper to its several hundred branches. Two benefits resulted: a large paper cost saving and faster, consistent, up-to-date information could be provided to customers in the branches. Filing the mass of paper received in the branches was also a problem, often leading to delays in staff receiving the latest information at the counter.

Some of changes can be identified by analysing working practices while others evolve over time as individuals and groups find new or better ways of carrying out their tasks and roles. These emergent new ways of working should be considered as pilots, which will be reviewed after a certain time to determine whether they could be beneficially adopted elsewhere. When a new type of infrastructure is introduced it may be possible to identify potential benefits by seeing what has happened in other organizations that have already adopted the technology. This may also yield insights into the types of change that are needed to take full advantage of the capabilities provided as well as enable the organization to avoid believing the technology will provide certain benefits, when others have failed to realize them.

5 *Creation of new capabilities*: In some cases, IT infrastructure investment is essential for building a new capability required for the future business strategy to be achieved or for a particular strategic initiative. For example, a multinational energy company stated that one of its strategic intentions was 'to become location independent', thereby enabling its technical and professional staff to perform their jobs wherever in the world they happened to be. This was subsequently used as the main justification for a major

investment in network capacity, mobile devices and high function-ality portable workstations. In the UK, a requirement to move to electronic access and delivery of services to citizens, has led many local authorities to justify major infrastructure investments as an integral part of delivering e-government services. It has also been recognized by a number of such authorities that the deployment of improved IT infrastructure will, over the long term, reduce the need for more traditional types of infrastructure, such as offices and depots. As the infrastructure to enable online access and mobile working by staff is implemented, savings in the capital and oper-ating cost of existing physical sites are being used to balance the IT costs incurred.

Non-IT Projects

While the emphasis of this book is on realizing benefits from IS/IT enabled investments, the process described has also been successfully applied to change projects that have little or no IT element to them. Each of the stages of the process, outlined in Chapter 3, and the more detailed tools described in later chapters, can be applied as described. The one exception will be that the final column in the benefits dependency network that identifies the required IS/IT may be empty or sparsely populated.

Non-IT projects that the process has been applied to include:

- corporate restructuring and reorganization
- diversification into new markets (geographic or product)
- changing staff pay and reward schemes
- office relocation
- creating the conditions within an organization necessary for sus-tained innovation
- adopting a key account management approach to marketing/sales
- adoption of the benefits management approach throughout an organization.

The last of these projects is described in more detail in Chapter 7, which considers implementation of the benefits management process.

The disciplines encouraged by the benefits management process, such as the linking of investment objectives to the drivers acting on the organization, the identification and measurement of benefits and the importance of changing working practices to realizing benefits all resulted in improved implementation and benefits of these change projects.

As noted in Chapter 4, while a project may have commenced as an IS/IT enabled project, in developing a benefits dependency network, it may become apparent that the organization does not need to invest in new IS/IT. Rather, if the necessary changes identified are undertaken, many of the benefits could be realized with current systems.

Different IS/IT Supply Arrangements

In addition to the type of organization and the nature of the application being considered, how an organization provisions its IS/IT will have an impact on the way it plans for and manages the realization of benefits. An organization has two basic options when considering the provision of IS/IT: to provide systems and technology using in-house staff or buy products and services in from external suppliers. The increasing number and range of the uses of IS/IT by organizations require increased expertise to implement and support. This has led to many organizations either outsourcing some of their existing IS/IT resources or increasing their reliance on external suppliers for the skills and services needed to support the use of new technologies. However, effective IS/IT exploitation is dependent on the way an organization integrates the use of the technology with its other capabilities and this requires knowledge and skills within the organization, either in a dedicated IS/IT group or within other business functions.

The discussion of the use of the benefits management approach so far has assumed that the majority of the expertise and resources needed to implement the systems and changes is available in-house or can be obtained as and when required from external sources. If an organization relies on outside parties to provide much of its IS/IT capability, there are particular implications for the management of IS/IT investments and hence the use of the benefits management approach.

External Supply: Outsourcing and Offshoring

Driven by a desire to reduce costs, share risks, increase flexibility and also often by a shortage of relevant skills, many organizations have outsourced the provision and ongoing operation of their IS/IT activities. To date, outsourcing has tended to be applied to specific activities, such as programming, IT support or the operation of computer networks. However, as the number of organizations undertaking outsourcing has increased, this has also been accompanied by an increase in the number of activities outsourced, to the extent that whole business processes, such as human resources, accounting and supply chain management can now be outsourced. The term *business process outsourcing* is used to describe the provision of such services by a third party. Interest in and the uptake of such arrangements has been further fuelled by the recent dramatic growth in low cost providers in countries such as India and China, a phenomenon that has been termed *offshoring*.

Bendor-Samuel (2000) describes a popular view of outsourcing when he describes it as an exchange between buyer and provider, in which the buyer exchanges control of a process or activity in return for the ability to define the results. Keen to ensure the performance of their outsourcing providers, many organizations have sought to clearly define the results that they expect, putting in place highly specified service-level agreements. In some cases, buyers have sought to make the outsourcing provider responsible for business benefits. However, as has been emphasized throughout this book, the realization of business benefits is seldom dependent on the deployment and operation of IS or IT alone, but requires changes to working practices within the organization buying in the services. It is not possible for an outside provider to take responsibility for these changes and hence they cannot be responsible for the delivery of business benefits. As shown in Figure 8.16, although an outsource provider can be made responsible for the operation of the IS and IT enablers and some of the related enabling changes, responsibility for the majority of the enabling changes and the business changes remains firmly with the business managers and staff within the purchasing organization.

As also shown in Figure 8.16, use of an outsource supplier will create the need for additional business changes, for example, the need to manage the relationship with the provider, monitoring of their level of service and the inclusion of the services provided into the ongoing operations of the organization. The management of the relationship with the outsource provider should include a two-way sharing of information, covering both their level of service, issues and future development plans and also the issues and business plans of the purchasing organization. Mechanisms and responsibilities for the management of the relationship should be expressly identified. While it may be tempting to view the management of the contract with the service provider as the responsibility of the IS/IT group, the criticality of their service to the operations of the business suggests that one or more business managers should have a significant input to that relationship management process.

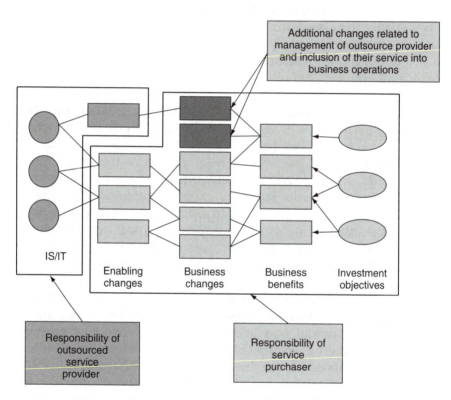

Figure 8.16   *Responsibilities in outsourced IS/IT arrangements*

In the case of the outsourcing of entire processes, it may be that the number of business changes to be undertaken by the organization is reduced, since whole groups of activities will be undertaken by the third-party provider. However, once again business changes related to the management of those services will be needed. In particular, it must be ensured that the operation of the outsourced process is aligned with the other internal operations of the organization, if the improvements in the particular process are to produce overall net benefits to the organization. As an increased number or range of activities is outsourced, it may become difficult to clearly differentiate areas of responsibility of the supplier and the service purchaser. While attempts should be made to clarify responsibilities from the start in a contract of engagement, it will not be possible to cover every eventuality, particularly in long-term relationships. Blurred boundaries should therefore be recognized and means for dealing with issues arising from them must be developed and included in the necessary changes or enablers.

The experience of the UK government in outsourcing the supply of IT is discussed in Box 8.7.

Box 8.7 Outsourcing in the public sector: UK public finance initiative

In order to improve the delivery of public services in the UK and in particular to address the reduction in spending on such services that has been witnessed since the 1970s, the UK government has sought to develop partnerships with the private sector in what are termed public private partnerships (PPPs). One particular form of PPP is the private finance initiative (PFI) in which private sector organizations take on the responsibility for constructing and operating a public service, which the government undertakes to purchase on a long-term basis. While many of the over 600 initiatives to date have been for the construction and operation of civil engineering projects, such as the building or refurbishment of schools and hospitals, a number of them are to provide IT projects.

The key objectives in undertaking PFI projects in the IT sector have been described as to *'effect risk transfer and impose commercial discipline'*. However, despite the definition by the public sector client of what is required from the private sector partners in such initiatives, a recent study by the Treasury itself (HM Treasury, 2003) found that such projects had *'not delivered the step-change in performance the Government originally intended and still requires'*. As shown in Figure 8.17, the PFI IT projects were no more successful than traditional IT projects, with over 70% realizing under 80% of the expected benefits, consistent with the success rates discussed in Chapter 1.

Box 8.7 (Continued)

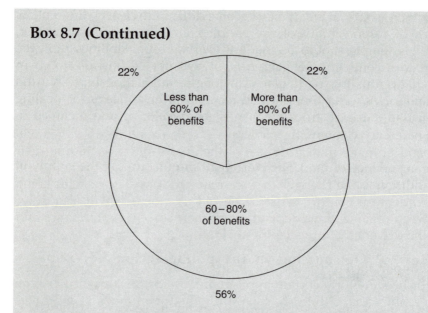

22%   Less than 60% of benefits

22%   More than 80% of benefits

60–80% of benefits

56%

Figure 8.17   Percentage of benefits delivered from IT PFI (after HM Treasury, 2003)

Factors identified as giving rise to this poor performance include:

- The fast pace of change in the IT sector makes it difficult for the public sector to effectively define the outputs it requires from a long-term contract.
- The high level of integration of IT into other business systems of the client make it difficult to clearly delineate areas of responsibility of the client and the provider.
- In addition to up-front investments, IT projects have a high proportion of ongoing running costs.
- IT projects have a much shorter life than other types of project and often require significant asset refresh, making it difficult to define and enforce long-term service needs.

These challenges are not unique to the public sector. They are commonly encountered in all IT outsourcing and underline the fact that the realization of benefits from IT cannot be passed to a third party. The client organization must retain or develop skills and working practices within its own staff to manage the relationship with the outsourcer and this occurs in such a way that the services provided continue to be aligned if the strategic drivers acting on the organization change.

Summary

This chapter has explored the implications of context on the realization of benefits from IS/IT investments. The recurring theme of this book is that the realization of benefits will in most cases require changes to the roles, responsibilities and processes and working practices within the organization. The changes required to make effective use of a new system will vary between organizations, since they will depend on particular attributes of the organization, including their current operations and on the skills and motivations of their staff. In addition to the changes that are required to realize benefits being dependent on context, what is viewed as a benefit will also differ between organizations depending on their current performance and on the drivers that are shaping their strategy.

The importance of context precludes the ability to specify a generic set of benefits for a certain application type or for a particular type of organization. While we have presented a number of examples of the tools and frameworks in this chapter, it should be stressed that these are to illustrate their use and they cannot be taken as templates for actual projects. Not only would such use ignore the particular situation of an organization, it would also prevent the sense of shared ownership among the project team and benefit and change owners that results from generating their own benefits plan together. The importance of context also warns against the 'silver bullet' approach to system deployment, in which generic lists of functionality or features promised by vendors are assumed to be benefits that will be realized by an organization. If such features and functionality do not address the particular drivers acting on the organization, they are unlikely to translate into benefits. Even if they do address those drivers, the organization must ensure that it understands what business changes will be needed to translate that functionality into a business benefit and be willing and able to make such changes.

The next chapter goes beyond single projects and considers how the use of the benefits management process can provide additional value when applied to multiple projects, within a programme and for the whole investment portfolio. Use of the process enables organizations to combine individual project benefits into a coherent programme benefits plan that recognizes the dependencies between the individual projects and, as importantly, identifies when several projects are claiming the same benefits.

9
From Projects to Programmes to Portfolios

So far we have discussed IS and IT investments as discrete projects, which has been the traditional way of considering and managing such activities. However, as more and more organizations have embarked on much larger scale change initiatives, often impacting the entire organization, the term 'programme' has become more widely used. Many of these change programmes are to a large extent either enabled by new IS/IT options or required significant investments in IS/IT to make them successful. Examples include the investments in enterprise-wide suites of applications, such as enterprise resource planning (ERP) and customer relationship management (CRM), and inter-organizational e-commerce, which were discussed in the previous chapter. In many cases it is not possible to foresee all the potential benefits or define all the changes needed at the start and the programme investment objectives and benefits will evolve as the organization learns what can, and cannot, be achieved. Also business circumstances may change during the extended time involved in completing the full implementation of the systems and business changes, requiring a reappraisal of the benefits that can be realized. The nature of large-scale IT enabled change programmes and the applicability of the benefits management approach in that context is considered in this chapter.

Governance in respect of IS/IT covers a broad spectrum of general management responsibilities for the deployment of information systems and technology and the use of information in an organization (see Ward and Peppard, 2002). It includes defining roles, accountabilities, decision rights and mechanisms for ensuring that IS/IT is utilized effectively and successfully by the organization. A key aspect of IS/IT governance involves ensuring that investments made realize the maximum possible business benefits. Just as a large organization is likely to find itself planning and implementing a number of projects at any one time, it is equally likely that it will be undertaking more than one major change programme. This extent of activity will put pressure on resources within the organization and will hence require a means of prioritizing and balancing competing demands. The use of portfolio approaches, particularly the applications portfolio introduced in Chapter 2, is an effective means of achieving a complete picture of current and planned activity and ensuring this is appropriate for the organization. The latter part of the chapter considers how using the benefits management approach can be accommodated in governance processes and thereby increase the value derived from an entire portfolio of IS/IT investments.

Defining Programmes

There are many definitions of the term 'programme', most of which are intended to differentiate a programme from a 'very big project'. It may sound trivial, but in many cases the word 'programme' is used to ensure that appropriate senior management attention is paid to the investment, attention they would fail to give to a 'mere' project. The OGC guidelines *Managing Successful Programmes* defines the differences as follows:

> *A project is a particular way of managing activities to deliver specific outputs over a specified period and within cost, quality and resource constraints.*
>
> *A programme is a portfolio of projects that are co-ordinated and managed as a unit such that they achieve outcomes and realise benefits.*

Other definitions are largely as imprecise, although Williams and Parr (2004) suggest that there are two essential differences – that programmes create new organizational capabilities and change the existing organizational capabilities in order to complete the programme successfully. That implies that not only are some of the final benefits difficult to forecast, but also that some of the changes will not, directly, produce performance improvements, merely the capability to achieve them through further changes. Projects, by way of contrast, normally deploy existing capabilities to achieve definable benefits.

There is considerable evidence that many project risks are directly related to the scale and duration of a project and so breaking them into smaller, more manageable tasks – effectively a programme of interrelated projects – can help reduce risk. It can also enable some benefits to be realized earlier, an increasingly important factor in today's uncertain and changeable business environment, when investment priorities have to be reassessed frequently. In concept, programmes allow an organization to adjust its use of resources to match changing priorities and emergent opportunities. This implies that programmes are used to bring about major changes over extended periods, whereas projects focus on achieving specific deliverables, in as short a timescale as possible. The emphasis in projects is to define and agree the project content, scope, costs and benefits as early as possible to enable the business case to be made and the schedule and necessary resources for implementation to be planned in detail. One reason for a programme-based approach is the recognition that, although this is possible for areas of definable change, in others the situation is unstable and it would be better to leave the finalization of content until as close as possible to the target date for implementation.

An example of a significant change programme enabled by IS/IT is described in Box 9.1.

Box 9.1 'Connecting for Health'

'Connecting for Health', the £6.5-billion programme being undertaken by the UK NHS, which has been discussed in earlier chapters, consists of a number of major projects in their own right. As introduced in Chapter 4, these include a centrally managed email and directory service for all organizations in the NHS, the provision of an electronic health record for all citizens, the use of IT to improve prescribing, systems to capture and distribute medical images and the ability of patients to choose a date and time for appointments.

Each stream requires considerable investment in IT and changes to working practices to transform the delivery of primary and secondary healthcare. The overall aim is that patients will obtain care appropriate to their needs, wherever they enter the system, based on the clinical staff having a full patient history available to them, an approach that is being described as 'patient-centred care'. In order to achieve this, a new communications capability is needed to transmit the health record information, both text and images to all the points in the community and acute care sectors where a patient may attend, such as GP surgeries and out-patient clinics. This would also enable groups of separately located clinicians to provide second opinions, more quickly and easily, and generally to apply collective rather than individual knowledge to patient diagnoses and care plans.

The creation of the underlying network and associated infrastructure is almost exclusively an IT project, which has been outsourced to a consortium of suppliers. This infrastructure, although complex and expensive delivers few immediate benefits itself. The significant benefits from the programme will arise from the suite of new applications that can operate on this infrastructure and more importantly, the changes to healthcare processes and practices that are agreed with the key stakeholders.

Types of Programme: Planned and Emergent

A programme consists of a portfolio of projects that have to be managed as an interrelated set, if all the available benefits are to be realized over time. If the benefits management process and tools are used consistently across the projects within a programme, it is relatively straightforward to bring those outputs together to manage the benefits of the entire programme. However, there are a few aspects that need further consideration.

There are two distinct types of programme. The first is those that are defined as a programme at the outset: as a set of related projects that all need to be undertaken to achieve a required change. This also includes programmes resulting from an appreciation that a large project needs to be broken down into smaller components, due to changes that have emerged since it was initiated. The second type of programme is those that result from the realization that existing or planned projects are interdependent and need to be managed as a coherent set to avoid the failure of one of them putting the others at risk. The latter may also be an appropriate approach when a number of projects require changes in the same area of the business at the same time or over a short period of time. The focus of the programme is then on scheduling the related projects, particularly in coordinating the business changes needed so that organizational risk and stress is minimized.

It is also appropriate to adopt a programme management approach to large IS/IT investments, when they consist of a number of applications that are in three or more segments of the application portfolio, in order to accommodate the inherently different types of change to be managed during implementation and the varying degrees of certainty of realizing the benefits. For example, a project may involve significant automation of clerical activities to release 'back office' resources and reduce systems and information duplication (support) and, at the same, implement a data warehouse to replace its existing legacy reporting systems (key operational) *and* support the introduction of a new balanced scorecard approach to performance management (strategic or high potential). While the overall benefits to be realized depend on all three being successful, each could be managed separately, in parallel, in terms of the business changes that need to be made.

Programme Dependency Networks

The interrelationships between the elements of a programme should be explicitly defined in terms of a programme dependency network that shows the interdependencies among the underlying projects. The development of a programme network will be slightly different for the two types of programme discussed earlier; those that are defined as a programme from the outset and those that result from the realization that certain projects are interdependent.

The development of a programme network for the first of these types of programme is depicted in Figure 9.1. This shows the simplified case of a programme that has been broken into three component projects A, B and C. The drivers acting on the organization will form the basis for the definition and agreement of a set of investment objectives for the programme. These will form the objectives for the component projects. As shown in the case of projects A and B, it may be helpful to agree additional investment objectives at the project level, in order to ensure that the project has sufficient definition and focus. These will typically relate to the higher level programme objectives, providing greater detail about these, but they could also be additional objectives, if the organization wished to use the underlying projects to tackle issues outside the remit of the programme. The benefits that could be expected if each of the programme objectives is met might then be agreed. The agreed set of objectives and benefits can then be used to divide the necessary activities into a set of projects. For each of these, a full benefits dependency network

Programme

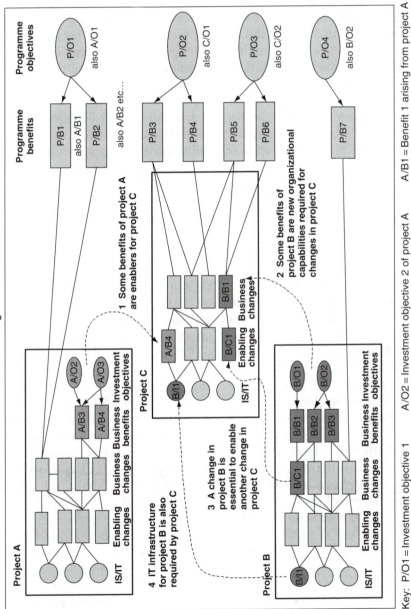

Key: P/O1 = Investment objective 1 of overall programme
A/O1 = Investment objective 1 of project A
A/O2 = Investment objective 2 of project A
A/B1 = Benefit 1 arising from project A

Figure 9.1 Programme dependency network for a planned programme

should be developed and interdependencies between the component projects highlighted by means of linkages between the individual project networks.

Typically, there are four distinct ways in which individual projects can be interdependent. These are exemplified with regard to a programme to improve both the efficiency and quality of service provided by the field service engineers of a major utility company. This major programme was divided into a number of component projects that addressed all parts of the service cycle:

1 *Benefits of earlier projects can be enablers of later projects.* For example, in the utility company, efficiency improvements in the administrative operation of the field service division allowed a reduction in the staff needed in the back office. This was expressed as a benefit in the 'back office administration project'. Rather than being released, these staff were transferred to the customer service division where they were retrained in order to provide improved customer service. The requirement for additional customer service staff had been recognized as a necessary enabling change in the 'customer service transformation project'.

2 *Some benefits of earlier projects are new or improved organizational capabilities required for later projects.* In the case of the utility company, they wished to offer a premium service to customers. However, it was not possible to offer this until the organization could provide faster response times to service requests. The ability to improve response times relied on improved service engineer productivity, which was a benefit expected from the 'field engineer mobile working' project.

3 *A change in one project is required to enable a change in a later project.* For example, at the utility company, in order to reduce the time taken for field engineers to service equipment, it was necessary for them to have complete and up-to-date information about the equipment, such as components and circuit diagrams. Rapid access to this information was seen to rely on the changes in an early project that sought to identify, compile and index the most up-to-date versions of such information.

4 *IS/IT developed in an earlier project is a prerequisite for later projects.* For example, for the utility company, a new broadband mobile working infrastructure was required as part of the 'field engineer mobile working' project that sought to improve service engineer productivity. This network was also a key part of reducing customer complaints since it allowed information generated in the field to be passed back to the service centre immediately. Most complaints experienced by the utility were due to work being carried out in the

field. The ability to provide accurate and timely information about such work, such as duration and likely interruptions to supply, allowed customer concerns to be dealt with effectively.

Having developed benefits dependency networks for the individual projects, it may be necessary to iterate back to the programme objectives and benefits, and the division between individual projects, to ensure that, in combination, these address the drivers acting on the organization and appear achievable. A business case should be developed for each of the projects within the programme, since this will clarify the nature of the benefits expected and the costs associated with these, as well as for the entire programme. It may be that some of the projects cannot be justified as standalone investments. However, their criticality to the realization of the programme should be recognized.

For programmes that were not planned from the outset, but have arisen from the recognition that projects being planned or undertaken are interdependent, a programme-level dependency network should also be developed. This will look similar to that shown in Figure 9.1, although development of the network will commence with the individual project-level networks. Again, the interdependencies between these should be clearly shown and will typically be those described in Figure 9.1. In addition to identifying the project interdependencies, the programme network should be used to bring together all of the benefits expected from the individual projects and their investment objectives. Such a consolidated view is useful in identifying benefits that are expected, or claimed, by more than one project. If this is the case it should be investigated whether the expected benefits can be cumulative. The transformation programme of a large retailer in the UK, discussed in Chapter 7, provides a good example of benefits identified in separate projects that can be cumulative in nature. The regular customer satisfaction surveys undertaken by the retailer are a key performance indicator and any project that could claim improvements in this was likely to be well received. Many projects within the programme had potential to improve customer satisfaction, such as reducing queuing times at tills and improving the on-shelf availability of stock, and hence identified an increase in customer satisfaction ratings as a benefit. Such improvements are likely to be cumulative and hence the benefit can be counted in more than one project. However, care should be taken that the overall cumulative benefit claimed by the programme does not suggest a satisfaction rating of over 100% or any other such unfeasible outcome.

In other cases, benefits cannot be cumulative. For example, a benefit of the introduction of EDI or e-commerce for procurement may be the elimination of errors in orders caused by re-keying of information. Clearly, the elimination of errors cannot be claimed by more than one project. In the case where benefits are being claimed by more than one project and these are not cumulative or would result in an unfeasible outcome, such as more than 100% satisfaction or less than zero stock holding, the project that can most easily give rise to the benefit should be identified. The benefit, and any associated changes, should then be removed from both the benefits dependency networks and the business cases of the other projects in the programme. If the benefit that has been claimed more than once is significant, it may be necessary to reappraise the business cases of those projects from which it has been removed.

Bringing together the benefits and investment objectives of individual projects can also highlight when there are contradictions. For example, in the case of a major organization that was undertaking an improvement programme within its customer call centre, on examining the benefits from individual projects, it was found that one project claimed the benefit of 'shortening call durations', while another claimed, 'lengthen call durations to allow greater cross-selling'. In cases such as this, the organization must reappraise what it is trying to achieve. Once it has done this it should remove the benefits that are no longer relevant from the individual projects, together with their associated changes. As before, if such benefits were significant, this may require reappraisal of the business cases of the individual projects affected. Finally, a consolidated programme network will also show when the realization of a benefit is reliant on the successful completion of more than one project. Such instances can result in 'double-counting' of the benefit or alternatively not including the benefit in any of the project networks or business cases.

An approach to address the issues relating to consolidating benefits across individual projects is to establish a 'register' of all the intended programme benefits. As the benefits of each project are identified, the register should be updated to specify which project will deliver 'how much' of each benefit, based on the changes that each project will bring about. The register would also be updated with the benefits realized as the projects are completed.

The Management of Programmes

In addition to developing a programme level network, it is important to explicitly define the management structure and responsibilities for the programme. Such a structure is shown schematically in Figure 9.2.

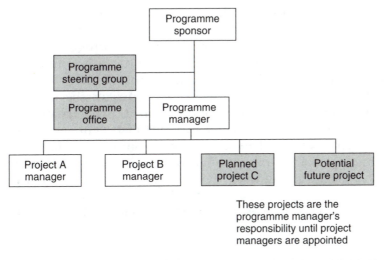

Figure 9.2 *Outline structure for programme management (after OGC, 2003)*

The roles as shown are variants on the roles of project sponsor and business project manager described in Chapter 7, however, given the greater scope and uncertainties inherent in programmes, there are some essential differences. First, executive sponsorship relates to the overall programme and a programme manager, or director, should be appointed, as well as business project managers for each of the projects. It needs to be recognized that the skills and abilities required to be a programme manager include, but go beyond, those of a good project manager. He or she will require what Partington et al. (2005) describe as higher order conceptions and competences, which enable a programme manager to cope with the ambiguities and conflicts that inevitably arise in large programmes and know when it is necessary to be directive, achieve consensus or effectively reconcile conflict among stakeholders. While project managers can usually rely on adherence to a project management methodology to judge how well the project is progressing, a programme manager has to be aware of the broader organizational context within which all of the projects have to be accomplished. It is also likely that the programme manager will need to be very senior, in order to have sufficient credibility and authority to have the respect of the project managers.

Second, since almost all programmes will involve changes in many parts of the organization, many of which cannot be defined at the outset, the sponsor and programme manager will need to consult and be advised by a range of other senior managers from the areas involved. This is described here as a 'programme steering group', which should be involved in all the key investment and priority-setting decisions that have to be made as the programme evolves. As stated earlier, some of the projects will not be justified as stand-alone investments, and the steering group will need to assess the combined business cases and how they deliver the objectives of the programme. As the programme evolves, the later projects will be able to be defined explicitly in terms of benefits and costs and the steering group will have to reassess the scope and viability of the remainder of the programme as more becomes known, in rela-tion to other organizational developments or changes in its strat-egy. This implies that the membership of the steering group will also need to evolve over time as the emphasis of the programme changes.

In most cases the programme manager, sponsor and steering group will also need the support of a 'programme office', that is, collating all the relevant information across the projects. It would normally be the job of the programme office to maintain the benefit register discussed earlier and also to ensure that all the benefits are accounted for once, and once only, in all project business cases.

Governance of the Investment Portfolio

As explained in the introduction to this chapter, IS/IT governance covers a broad spectrum of responsibilities, only one of which, man-aging the portfolio of investments, is discussed here. Obviously it is an integral component of governance, since making the wrong investments or not realizing the business value from the investments made can seriously impact both organizational performance and the achievement of future strategy. Effective governance is required to ensure that the organization does not waste its funds and resources on investments that do not adequately contribute to the business. It also has to ensure that, in the worst case, the organization does not incur disadvantages or become uncompetitive, due to lack of investment in key operational and support systems and essential infrastructure. Therefore it must not only be reactive, vetting and approving investments as they arise, but be proactive in ensuring that the overall portfolio of current and planned investments supports the strategic priorities of the business.

Most organizations realize that making the right decisions is complex, requiring both accurate and reliable information about each of the investments and also collective agreement at a senior management level that the mix of investments is using organizational resources in the most appropriate ways. This complexity means that rarely, if ever, can the decisions involved be delegated to one individual and normally some form of 'investment board' or 'steering committee' is set up to ensure that the specific investments made, in combination, contribute effectively to achieving the organization's strategy. The term *investment board* is used throughout the rest of this discussion, meaning a group of senior managers charged with deciding on the contents of the IS/IT investment portfolio and therefore by implication, responsible for priority setting and defining the appropriate level of overall IS/IT spend on new investments.

The basic terms of reference for the group can be considered as ensuring that:

- There is an information systems strategy that expresses the areas where investment will have the most beneficial contribution to business strategy, as discussed in Chapter 2.
- The organization has, or can acquire or develop, the required IS/IT resources and capabilities to deliver the critical components of the IS strategy in the timescale needed. Also the group needs to be assured that future capabilities will be in place to meet known future investment plans.
- All investments that require significant resources or funds are approved based on comprehensive and rigorous business cases supported by adequate evidence that the benefits plans inherent in those cases are deliverable.
- When contention for resources occurs, as it inevitably will, that decisions to allocate or reallocate funds and resources are based on achieving the highest level of overall business benefit possible from the resources available. This may, from time to time, mean removing resources from existing projects or even cancelling some, because their contribution is insufficient compared with new opportunities available.

- All investments are reviewed after implementation, so that the benefits achieved from the overall investment plan can be assessed and that lessons learned are taken up by other projects in order to improve the quality of benefits plans and, as a consequence, the overall value realized.

The threshold level for requiring the investment board to approve expenditure will vary from organization to organization and setting it at a low level will not only increase the work of the board, but also involve it in considering projects that demean its role. It should also be recognized that whatever level is set will encourage large numbers of investments to be estimated to cost just below the threshold! Therefore the board should also review the overall IS/IT budgets from time to time.

Where projects are a part of a major programme, some of the responsibilities of the investment board can be delegated to the programme board, providing it is adopting the same rigorous approach to investment management. However, it needs to retain its role in overseeing the priorities for deploying the organization's limited resources to overall maximum benefit, since new or emergent opportunities may provide a better return than existing programmes. Equally, the governance of many smaller investments, especially support applications, can be delegated to line managers who have to justify them financially within an allocated budget and the approval of high potential funds can be made within a budget reserved for R&D activities. All the investment board needs to know is whether the resources absorbed by these investments are preventing more significant investments from proceeding.

Setting Priorities

The discussion thus far shows the complexity of the task. Not only do all investments have to be assessed on their individual merits, they need to be assessed in the context of alternative investments available, including existing ongoing projects and emergent opportunities that could, in the near future, deliver more benefits from the resources available. To do this the board must establish rules by which it will determine the priorities and also make those rules and the reasons for its decisions known to avoid unnecessary conflict and even 'game playing'. It will also need to have a full set of information available when making approvals otherwise each investment will be considered in isolation. This is normally provided by a central support 'project office', which both vets the proposals to check their validity before submission to the board and also provides the additional information required to ensure any issues of relevance to a decision are not overlooked. This role is very similar to the 'programme office' described earlier, but the focus is on all the IS/IT projects that are components of those programmes or independent of them. The development of such an investment board by a major telecommunications company is described in Box 9.2.

Box 9.2 Priority setting at a major telco

A major telecommunications company established an investment board to oversee its IS/IT investments, which ran to over £250m per annum, the majority of which were components of strategic change programmes. In this case the programme directors were required to submit regular reviews of the overall business cases for their programmes in order to obtain continuing funding. In addition, each business case and benefits plan had to be peer reviewed by another senior manager, not associated with the project, who advised the board on the rigour used to build the business case and change plan. This was in addition to the work of the project office, whose remit was to vet the evidence supporting the claimed benefits. As a result the board received high quality input to its decision making and the whole organization had increased confidence in the decisions it made.

The board was equally demanding regarding the submission of post-implementation benefits review reports. Imposing such stringent disciplines and cross-checks meant that very few 'weak' cases were ever put forward to the board.

This example implies that the very existence of a governing process that insists on the rigorous use of a benefits management approach makes the task of managing the investment portfolio somewhat easier, since the projects that cannot provide adequate evidence of benefits do not get 'off the drawing board'. However, there are some additional techniques that can assist this process further.

The Applications Portfolio for Priority Setting

The applications portfolio, for classifying IS/IT investments according to their expected contribution to the organization, was introduced in Chapter 2 and has been used to explain the implications of different types of application investment throughout the book. It is also a valuable technique for informing the investment board of the implications of choices between alternative investments. In terms of current projects and programmes being put forward for approval, all should be presented to the board with a full business case and benefits plan as described in earlier chapters. Other more emergent ideas for investment, that are likely to be in the high potential quadrant of the applications portfolio, cannot be the subject of such detailed assessment, but still require a reasoned argument explaining why they should be considered.

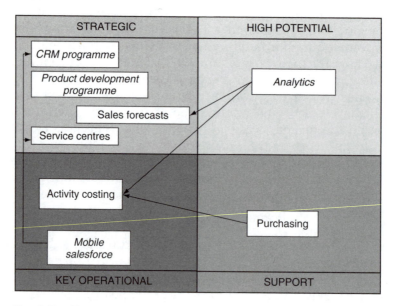

Key: *Italics*= Projects and programmes underway   Non-italics = Planned projects

Figure 9.3   *Example applications investment portfolio*

A simplified example of an applications portfolio is shown in Figure 9.3. It includes both individual projects, some of which are interdependent, and programmes that contain a number of projects. The two programmes, customer relationship management and new product development, were instigated at executive level to directly address a number of strategic drivers, while the projects were initiated through the IS planning process. Projects and programmes that are underway are shown in italics. These require an update of the business cases at regular intervals when the investment board reviews the overall plan or if priorities need to be reassessed. The other projects shown require decisions on whether to approve funding for the project to proceed or defer a decision until a later date, due to the need to reserve funds for other projects.

It may be in some organizations that funds are not the constraining factor, but the availability of critical resources, people or skills. Scarcity in any of these may affect the timing of investments. Some projects will be in competition for the same resources whereas others will not be, and therefore could go ahead sooner even if they promised less net benefit. The portfolio view does not provide 'rules' for such decisions, but allows the context within which a particular decision is made, to be understood, such that funds and resources are not committed prematurely to low value projects.

Another variant on the approach, which can help resolve the possible contention for funds within the overall portfolio, includes the consideration of the relative value of the investments and the level of risk involved, due to the extent and complexity of the changes (Jeffrey and Leliveld, 2004). This approach is shown in Figure 9.4, together with the most likely locations for the different application types identified by the applications portfolio. Strategic applications are likely to yield high potential value to the organization. The decision to be made is effectively between 'priority investment' and the commissioning of an evaluation to find out more about the investment. Most key operational applications are also likely to yield high value, but some may be able to be deferred in order to use funds on more urgent or higher return options. While some support investments are likely to provide a significant financial return at low risk, many will be able to be postponed, if strategic or key operational investments require resources or funding first, since efficiency benefits will always be available at a future date. High potential applications are those that the organization needs to learn more about before committing significant investment. Having undertaken an R&D or pilot project, it should become clear if the organization could expect significant value or if they should not invest.

Managing the investment portfolio is not merely about the approval of funding and setting priorities, it includes ensuring that the range and pattern of investments reflects the business priorities. It also involves assessing whether the overall plan is the best way of using the resources, over time, to achieve the maximum set of intended benefits. This requires an understanding of the dependencies between projects and the relative risks involved. To increase the overall level of benefits realized the portfolio of investments should be balanced carefully between high value, but high risk, and lower value projects, where the certainty of benefit delivery is higher. It would of course be ideal for all investments to be high value, low risk, but this is rarely, if ever, the case.

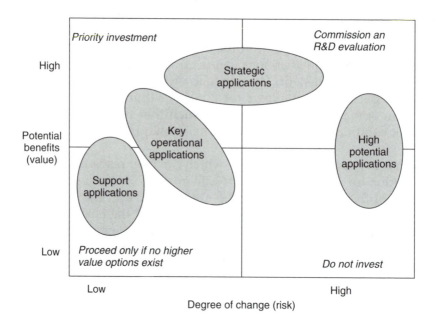

Figure 9.4   *A portfolio approach to funding decisions (after Jeffrey and Leliveld, 2004)*

Links to Drivers

More detailed information about the investments and their relevance to particular business drivers is also required in order to assess the relative priorities of applications in the same segment of the matrix. The relationship between the investments and the drivers should be clearly understood, in case the drivers change and the project plan has to be revised to realign the IS/IT contribution to the changing business priorities.

Table 9.1 shows such information for the example portfolio shown in Figure 9.3. (As in Figure 9.3 the projects and programmes in italics

Table 9.1 Linking projects and programmes with business drivers

Drivers/investment options	Cost reduction	Customer service	Safety legislation	Sales growth	Staff retention	New product development	Costs, dependency and comments
CRM programme							Cost £1.2m
Project A	High			*Low*			90% done
Project B	Medium	High					50% done
Project C	*Low*	Medium		High			Project A
Project D		High		Medium			Projects B, C and 3
Product development programme							Cost £800k
Project A			High	Medium		*Low*	80% done
Project B				High		High	Project A
Project C			Medium	*Low*		High	Projects A and B

Table 9.1 (Continued)

Drivers/investment options	Cost reduction	Customer service	Safety legislation	Sales growth	Staff retention	New product development	Costs, dependency and comments
Project 1: sales forecasts (strategic)				High		Medium	Cost £600k Project 6
Project 2: service centres (strategic)	High	High		Medium			Cost £750k Project 3
Project 3: mobile sales force (key operational)	Medium	Medium	Medium	High		Medium	Cost £400k 70% done
Project 4: activity costing (key operational)	High			Medium		Medium	Cost £250k Project 5 Project 6
Project 5: purchasing (support)	Medium		Low				Cost £150k
Project 6: analytics (high potential)	?			?		?	Cost £25k Pilot for projects 1 and 4

are already underway, whereas the others have yet to start.) This table includes the strategic drivers, the contribution of the projects to each driver (high, medium or low), progress to date and the estimated overall costs of the investment. Additional information such as project start and expected end dates could also be shown. For the two major programmes, the contribution of each of the projects is shown, since although it may be a high priority now, some of the later elements or phases of the programme may become less important if the business imperatives change.

The links between investments and drivers can also be presented in the form of a high level network as shown in Figure 9.5.

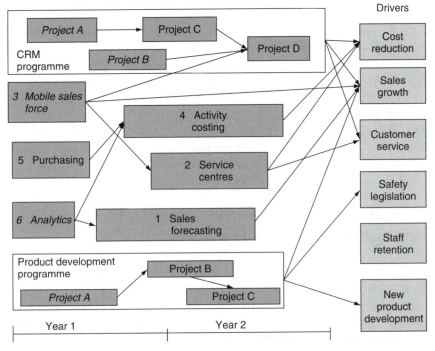

Note: Projects in *italics* are already in progress.

Figure 9.5   The investment plan dependencies

Presenting the portfolio of investments in such a table or high level network highlights critical dependencies and the degree to which the drivers acting on the organization are being addressed. For example, as shown in Table 9.1 and Figure 9.5, although the purchasing project does not contribute major benefits, it is an enabler of the activity costing project. Before deciding on funding it, the degree to which the benefits of the activity costing project would be reduced, if the purchasing project is deferred or cancelled, should be considered.

Second, the mobile salesforce project, in addition to providing significant direct benefits is an enabler of two others, including a future project in the CRM programme. Ensuring that it is adequately resourced to enable its timely and successful completion should be a high priority, even if other projects have to be deferred. Project B in the CRM programme and project A in the product development programme should be given priority for resources to ensure that the downstream projects in those programmes can go ahead as planned.

Third, the investment board should be concerned that although a number of investments address five of the drivers, no investments are underway or planned to address the remaining driver: *staff retention*. The board should consider or even commission work to identify whether any change programmes or IS/IT investments could be made to improve the organization's performance in respect of this driver. Any stated business driver implies 'that change must occur' and therefore an initiative or project to bring about change should be included in the strategic plans, certainly within a two-year horizon. Alternatively, the organization's executive should revisit the rationale they used to determine that staff retention was actually a particular issue to the business.

Including Emergent Investments in the Management of the Portfolio

As argued earlier, the investment board should only assess an investment when the full business case has been developed and it is supported by a complete benefits plan. However, not all decisions can be made on that basis because the timings of business problems or issues and opportunities that require investment are unpredictable. Organizations must be able to respond quickly and coherently to new choices as they arise. The danger is that these new options are not considered in an equivalent way to the existing or planned investments that have been put through a comprehensive benefits planning process. In many organizations it is these emergent opportunities that cause repeated disruption to existing plans, resulting in funding and resourcing uncertainties and frequently changing priorities.

To be fully effective, the portfolio management approach should also allow for 'emergent' opportunities to be assessed in relation to those that have been through the rigour of the benefits management approach. It is possible that new options that emerge will be better potential investments than those already in progress, however there is a danger that a 'planning blight' will occur if the board requires all projects to be dealt with on the same basis.

Benefits Management 'Lite'

To overcome this problem a number of organizations have introduced a simpler, cut down, variant on the first stages of the benefits management process, which allows a rapid appraisal of new options. This we describe as benefits management *lite* – a simplified approach that enables the essentials of an investment to be described. It could be argued that all new options and ideas could be considered as 'high potential' investments and be tested and evaluated through an R&D approach. However, many will not be particularly innovative and justify in-depth exploration. Those that genuinely have the potential to deliver strategic advantage need to be identified as early as possible and an R&D phase commissioned as a priority. If there is contention for particular resources or a need for extra R&D funding, this new opportunity should be compared with other current high potential projects to determine whether it should take priority.

The remaining emergent investments need a quick, but incisive, evaluation to determine whether the benefits available are likely to be worth the costs of the technology and risks associated with business change, particularly when compared to existing investments. The purpose is not to make a decision about the new investment, but to decide whether to delay decisions about better formulated investments, until a comparable business case can be developed. It would not be appropriate, based on this simplified evaluation, to stop already approved projects from proceeding.

Figure 9.6 describes the essentials of this light-touch approach, for both technology-based opportunities (in italics) and business-based opportunities. It contains all the components of the benefits dependency network, but only requires a summary of the main benefits and changes, sufficient to determine its portfolio positioning. This allows it to be compared with other alternative investments of the same type. If it is a new technology opportunity, the first stage is to identify the potential benefits it offers in relation to the drivers acting on the organization. If they are significant, the second step is to assess the organization's capability to deploy the technology in the short term and the extent of the business changes needed to achieve the potential benefits. If it is a business-based idea, it should have been derived from the drivers and the purpose of the assessment is to define the main benefits that could be realized, the extent of the changes and if the necessary technology is already available or can easily be acquired and deployed.

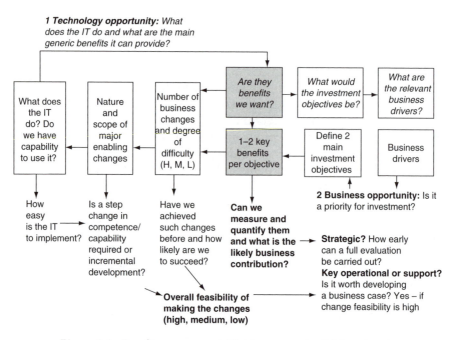

Figure 9.6   Benefits management 'lite' to assess potential investments

In both cases the resulting argument for considering the investment further is based on the contribution and relevance of the potential benefits to the business drivers and the estimated feasibility of achieving them (high, medium or low). The assessment of the ability to accomplish the changes should be based on the organization's previous experience of achieving similar changes successfully in the recent past. This appraisal will only be rigorous enough to commission the work needed to produce a full business case or decide not to pursue the investment further.

Summary

Organizations of all types are increasingly finding themselves confronted with interrelated projects and large-scale programmes of change. Expecting projects to be well defined and being able to establish a controlled environment for all projects, as required by leading project management techniques, is often no longer possible. As has been described in this chapter, the benefits management tools and frameworks allow organizations to explore the interdependencies between multiple projects or, in the case of planned programmes, how to break these into sub-projects. In both cases, the monitoring of benefits throughout the process allows those managing the projects or programmes, to assess the progress made towards the desired objectives. While such monitoring is important for standalone projects, it is often even more important in multi-project and programme environments, since there is opportunity for important benefits to fall between projects or to be duplicated by different projects. In large programmes it can be difficult to specify all the final benefits expected with much certainty and the benefits plan will need to be revised, as more becomes known about the achievable benefits.

Given the significant number of projects, and in some cases, the multiple programmes, being planned and undertaken within organizations, governance structures must be ever more robust. As well as regularly monitoring the progress of ongoing projects and programmes, a key element of governance is making appropriate investment decisions. Statistics continue to show that the majority of IS/IT investments fail to deliver the expected benefits. While much of this is due to poor implementation, poor investment selection also plays a part. The benefits management approach provides better information for making a decision to fund, or not fund, a particular investment. However, such decisions have to be made with the best available knowledge about alternative uses of resources and funds. It is therefore important that management are presented with adequate information about the choices in a consistent way so that such comparisons can be made. Benefits management, coupled with the use of a portfolio management approach, can allow such consistency to be achieved across projects and programmes.

It is suggested that an investment board, or similar executive group, should be established to manage the investment portfolio. The role of the investment board is to ensure that the best possible decisions are made, across the range of potential investments and then put the necessary disciplines in place so that the benefits expected from each investment are actively managed during the project and accounted for on completion. If the board's remit is extended to include all projects and change programmes, it can also ensure that other, non-IT-based investment options are similarly assessed.

The final chapter broadens the application of benefits management and considers the process of strategy development and implementation as essentially a process of identification and delivery of benefits to the organization and its stakeholders. How the use of the benefits management frameworks and tools can help is therefore introduced and exemplified and the insights such an approach can offer are discussed.

The chapter then considers the further development and use of IS and IT within industries and organizations and by individuals in terms of the implications and future challenges likely to be involved in identifying and realizing benefits from new applications of IT. Many current IS/IT investments seek to create new business capabilities. For example, the mobile devices currently being deployed by many organizations, to extend access to organizational systems, reflects a wish to provide the capability for staff to be able to work where it best suits them and for them to be connected to the organization and their colleagues wherever they choose to work. The realization of benefits will then depend on how both individuals and the organization make use of these new capabilities. This implies that it may be necessary to develop new ways of identifying and assessing how different types of IS/IT investment create value for organizations.

10
Creating a Better Future

In this chapter the key characteristics of the benefits management approach are summarized and further evidence of the improved outcomes resulting from the use of the approach is described, including a comparison of two projects in one organization. The first project did not take a benefits management approach and produced very few benefits for the organization. The second project, that did use the benefits management process, not only delivered the technology on time, on budget and all the expected business benefits, but also involved the business managers in the IS/IT development in a way that changed the relationship between those managers and the IT function, to the benefit of all future projects. From being thought of previously as a high cost/low value unit, the IT function became viewed as a strategic capability that could significantly enhance the company's competitive position.

Investments in IS/IT projects and other change programmes are the means of improving organizational performance and creating new strategic options and capabilities. If an organization adopts a benefits management approach to managing its complete investment portfolio, it is effectively using it to manage the implementation of significant components of its business strategy. As a result, some organizations have seen the value of using the same frameworks, tools and techniques as a way of helping the formulation and improving the implementation of organizational strategies. Strategy formulation can be viewed as a process in which objectives are identified, the achievement of which gives rise to sets of benefits, both to the organization and its stakeholders. Extending the use of the benefits management approach to strategy formulation and implementation is discussed in this chapter.

To conclude the book, we turn our attention to the future. We consider the future of IS and IT within organizations, with particular regard to envisaged developments, the nature of the potential benefits and the implications for their realization. Speculating on the future is always likely to be a hazardous business, so to reduce the inherent risks we have based the discussions on the views of many researchers and experts in the field.

The Continuing Challenge of IS/IT Investments

As was discussed at length in Chapter 1, investment in IS and IT continues to be challenging to managers within all types of organization. Recent studies show that somewhere between 70–80% of all IS/IT projects are considered as failure (for example, Lambert and Edwards, 2003), a figure that does not seem to have improved over the last 30 years. While we cannot argue with the many studies that show the continued high rate of disappointment, we would argue that the bald statistics hide a number of more subtle issues. The first and most simple is that organizations, and the individuals within them, do transfer some of the lessons learned from previous investments to future projects and thereby improve the results. However, as has been discussed throughout this book there are a variety of reasons why, in spite of organizations learning from their past successes and failures, this pattern of perceived failure continues. The following list identifies the problems common to many organizations:

- Expectations created by the IT industry are not realistic in terms of proven value or the time it takes to realize them.
- Organizations are implementing more complex and sophisticated applications, which require increasing levels of managerial and employee skills to use them effectively.
- The applications are often enterprise wide and impact more people inside the organization and also relationships with external trading partners and customers. One organization cannot prescribe how others will conduct their business, and achieving benefits relies on the active cooperation of a wide range of stakeholders.
- The types of benefit that IS/IT can deliver are increasingly diverse and less easy to identify, describe, measure and quantify.
- In many cases, it is difficult to relate business performance improvements to specific IS/IT investments, as they usually result from a combination of improved technology and other changes in the ways of working.

- The prevailing focus of many organizations on achieving a short-term financial return from its investments, prevents many of the longer term benefits of a coherent and sustained IS/IT investment strategy from being achieved.

While these are challenges that largely result from the rapidly evolving use of technology and the complex problems associated with the scale and scope of deployment, there are a number of management issues that are critical to successful investment. These can perhaps be best summarized by drawing on studies of other authors of IS/IT implementations:

- Business benefits realized, depend on achieving a 'fair balance of benefits between the organisation and its stakeholders. The issue of gain sharing is of critical importance... with no apparent benefits to them, stakeholders are likely to resist the system' (Jurison, 1996).
- 'There may be a major disconnect between the strategic intent of a decision to implement a system and the resulting actions that must be completed' (Bancroft et al., 1998).
- 'Benefits are typically delivered through extensive changes to business practices and decision making. There is a growing consensus that organisational factors are far more critical to successful IS implementation than technical considerations' (Markus et al., 2000).
- 'Problems are often the result of either a lack of common understanding of the purposes of change or different perspectives on how to achieve them successfully' (Swanson and Ramiller, 1997).

Traditionally, attempts to increase the value derived from IS/IT investments have focused on improving the management of supplying and implementing the technology and the projects within which this occurs. Existing methodologies reflect the best practices learned over many years and enable activities such as systems development and project management to be managed effectively. However, they do not directly address many of the organizational or socio-technical issues noted earlier.

In order for an organization to address these challenges it needs to develop a set of competences that enable it to identify how and when to use IS/IT to improve its performance and then manage each investment successfully. The nature of those competences was described by Mata et al. (1995), who found that many issues related to IT, such as technology, access to capital and technical IT skills could not provide sustained competitive advantage. However, they did find that the capability of managers to conceive of, develop and exploit IT applications in a way that supported or enhanced the activities of their business was a skill that took time to develop and could provide a source of sustained competitive advantage. A key part of developing these skills was the ability of IT managers and other functional managers to work together to understand the particular context of the organization and each other's needs and use this combined knowledge to develop appropriate new systems. Having a coherent and effective approach to managing the benefits of its investments can be considered as a critical competence for an organization.

Characteristics of the Benefits Management Approach

The characteristics of the benefits management approach, which are incorporated in the process and the tools presented in this book, are summarized below. These characteristics, which can be considered as the key success factors for benefits management, are:

- Ensuring that the links between IS/IT investments and business strategic priorities are explicitly stated and understood.
- A clear understanding that benefits only occur from active involvement of business managers in defining and owning those benefits and carrying out the changes that deliver them.
- Business cases have to be realistic, reflecting the ability of the organization to realize as well as identify the benefits.
- Not all investments will be able to be justified financially. However, the ability to explicitly measure the benefits is essential to their delivery.
- The business case should be based on evidence that shows how the value of each benefit was derived.
- When the investment involves significant innovation it may be necessary to pilot the new ways of working, as well as prove the technology, in order to be confident that the benefits can actually be achieved.
- Achieving benefits requires the sustained commitment of business resources and extends beyond the delivery of the new systems and technology.
- Reviewing the benefits that are, and are not, realized from each investment, is essential, if an organization is to increase the value it obtains from all its IS/IT investments.

- The 'softer' benefits that accrue to individual stakeholders are often important prerequisites for the achievement of the 'harder' organizational or business benefits. Understanding, attending to and overtly addressing the interests and perceptions of stakeholders are essential aspects of the change management and benefits realization activities.
- Implementations should be phased, if possible, to deliver some benefits as early as possible – the 'quick wins'– and sometimes these are benefits that require business changes rather than major technology implementation.

We know, from our work with organizations in all sectors, as well as from other research (Wentworth Research, 1998), that the majority of organizations appreciate the relevance of these points. Many have subsequently changed how they plan, justify and manage investments in IS/IT based on the benefits management approach.

The Value of the Process

Our own experience, corroborated by independent research, has shown that the adoption of a benefits management approach results in projects that are more successful than those carried out without such an approach. In making this assessment, our measure of success is that used by the researchers DeLone and McLean (2003) discussed in Chapter 1, that is, the net benefits realized. Figure 10.1 was derived from actual investments undertaken in a major pharmaceutical company. They analysed a number of IS/IT investments to which the benefits management approach had been applied and compared these to earlier investments to which it had not.

The numbers have been removed from this comparison, due to the sensitivity around the large sums that are often involved in investments in this sector. However, the comparison clearly shows that the benefits management approach resulted in greater benefits. The comparison only included the benefits to which a financial value could be attributed. There was also a concomitant increase in the non-financial benefits realized.

It can be seen that use of the benefits management process can increase the costs of some investments. The additional cost involved is that of management time. This is the time spent by business managers and IS/IT colleagues working together to develop a coherent and agreed benefits plan, monitoring progress against that plan and finally reviewing the outcomes of the project. However, this additional management time produces a proportionally greater increase in the net benefits actually realized.

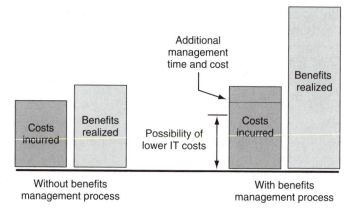

Figure 10.1   *The value of benefits management*

Although an additional management cost may be incurred, this can often result in the reduction of other costs; particularly IT costs, as shown in Figure 10.1. This can arise for three reasons. First, the development of a robust benefits plan early in the investment cycle identifies projects that do not yield sufficient benefits and these can be stopped before significant sums are spent. The second reason is related to the right-to-left working of the benefits dependency network. The logic of the network is to ensure that all activities in the project are driven by business need. As introduced in Chapter 1 and discussed more fully in Chapter 4, this results in an identification of the IT 'sufficient to do the job'. This can avoid the commonly encountered problem of organizations developing or buying additional IS/IT functionality that does not deliver any real business value. This not only increases the cost but also often slows down implementation, thereby deferring the realization of some or all of the benefits. Although there is no rigorous research to support the statistic, many observers have suggested that organizations often use less than 20% of the features or functions of software they purchase. The third reason is an extreme version of the second. In some cases, adopting this approach enables organizations to appreciate they can realize the benefits that they are seeking simply by making changes to working practices, often in order to use existing IS or IT better and hence do not need to invest in additional hardware or software.

A brief case history of the implementation of an enterprise-wide system within one organization is given in Box 10.1. The implementation occurred in two phases, the first did not make use of the benefits management approach, while the second phase did.

Box 10.1 Implementing enterprise systems in Ctel

Ctel provides systems and hardware for broadband IP networks for voice and data communications. Sales to large organizations are made directly to customers, while sales to smaller companies are made through resellers. The company also provides equipment and software to original equipment manufacturers (OEMs) for inclusion into their own networking solutions. Ctel has operations in over 70 countries, divided into two regions: North America and Europe, the Middle East and Africa (EMEA). Ctel's corporate headquarters is located in North America and the EMEA headquarters is in the UK.

Ctel's implementation of an enterprise system (ES) occurred in two phases, the first of which did not adopt a benefits management approach and the second of which did. By the time of completion, the first phase of the project was four times over budget and had taken twice as long as expected. It was also recognized that the project resulted predominantly in the delivery of a technical solution, with little benefit to the business. In contrast, the second phase of the investment realized the expected benefits and, importantly, involved business staff in a positive way that left them well disposed to use of the system and participation in future IS and IT projects.

Phase 1: project genesis: a global ERP implementation

In late 1998, the executive management of the EMEA region tasked a project team with evaluating options for implementing an ERP system. This team recommended the adoption of SAP, since it was being successfully used within a recently acquired semiconductor business. When staff in Ctel's headquarters in North America learned of this project, several senior managers argued that the benefits of improved business integration through ERP would be even greater if Ctel deployed SAP organization-wide. Accepting this argument without a careful consideration of the expected benefits, the board approved a single, global implementation.

Box 10.1 (Continued)

A complex project management structure, reflecting the regional and business unit structure, was created with the project management role being distributed across four separate project managers. Each project manager was given responsibility for implementation in specific business units, with a requirement to cooperate on technical matters. This was described by the EMEA project manager as encouraging a *'premature focus on technical issues'*, rather than clearly evaluating the business benefits that might be expected and the changes to organizational processes and working practices that would be needed to realize them. Without a clear understanding of the benefits that they might expect, the business managers were reluctant to commit the resources that were needed for implementation. Instead the managers preferred to protect their own interests, which concerned maintaining the smooth running of their respective units.

Cooperation was eventually gained from the managers and their staff, however the limited consultation was regarded as a sign of a technology-centred approach to implementation that neglected SAP's impact on core business processes and working practices: *'to many of those in the business, it felt like SAP was being done to them, rather than they were involved or part of it'*. After much delay and considerable overspend, the SAP software was implemented and went live without significant problems. Few stakeholder groups believed that they had benefited from the ERP implementation, as was observed: *'it's our old business on a new system'*.

Phase 2: service management implementation in EMEA

Phase 2 involved the deployment of SAP modules in the EMEA after-sales service division. The approach witnessed during this phase was significantly different from that of phase 1. While the geographic scope and the number of business activities involved were less than in phase 1, the modules implemented affected the most complex parts of the business and the version of the software installed had not, at that time, been installed in Europe by any other organization.

Unlike the first phase, phase 2 commenced with the EMEA senior management establishing a vision of why and how the service organization had to change, and how this could be achieved by implementing the new SAP modules. There was an explicit statement of the intended benefits and an understanding that these would result from a combination of organizational, process and system changes.

As the project moved to the implementation stage, the project team presented the business case at workshops where stakeholder groups were extensively involved in discussing how the changes would be implemented and benefits realized. This stage, which lasted for over half the duration of phase 2, included developing a system prototype for demonstration to key business users and gaining their feedback about how implementation could be refined. Once technical and business changes were agreed, responsibility for achieving them was explicitly assigned to cross-functional teams, involving both field engineers and central service management staff, who committed to cooperate with each other to deliver them.

Also in contrast to phase 1, phase 2 was managed by a single senior business manager who had access to sufficient financial and other resources. As the changeover to the new system approached, key stakeholders were becoming concerned about the details of implementation and changes within their own areas. The project manager was able to discuss the implications with each stakeholder group and provide extra resources, where needed, to affect the necessary changes, thus avoiding any deterioration in services to customers.

A formal post-implementation review of the project gave a detailed account of the benefits achieved, both from a financial perspective and according to the views of key stakeholders. The project had been delivered on time and on budget, but more importantly, almost all the intended benefits were achieved.

Going Further: Using Benefits Management to Formulate and Implement Strategy

As discussed in Chapter 2, an enduring challenge for any organization is to ensure the investments it makes in IS/IT are aligned to its business strategy and where possible, allow it to create new strategic opportunities. The rate of change of the business environment and technology development make this a very demanding task. The evidence quoted earlier in the chapter proves how difficult it is to successfully identify and implement investments that will make the best possible contribution to the organization. In Chapter 2, approaches and tools to develop an IS/IT strategy that defines the investment portfolio required to achieve the organization's strategy were discussed. However, as considered in Chapter 3, if an organization is unable to realize the benefits of its investments, not only does it waste funds, it is less able to select the appropriate investments to make. Improving the management of the implementation of new systems and technology, so that more of the available improvements are delivered, will enable the organization to manage its whole portfolio of investments more successfully and thereby achieve its strategy.

While there has been greater publicity about the failure of IS/IT investments to deliver the expected performance improvements, there is a body of evidence that suggests other major change initiatives are, on average, no more successful. Increasingly, many major change initiatives and programmes depend on IS/IT enablers or require significant changes in how IS/IT is used, which would suggest that IT-enabled change programmes are doubly difficult! Managing such IS/IT-enabled change programmes is exacerbated by the problems many organizations face in understanding how IS/IT can be used to improve business performance. There is a need therefore to consider investments in IS/IT as two different types. Some are needed to continuously and incrementally improve the performance of current, 'business as usual' activities through increased efficiency, accuracy and effectiveness in those core processes. In these investments the effects on performance should be directly identifiable.

Other investments are the enablers of strategic change, when the performance improvements will be less directly related to the IS/IT components but be dependent on a number of factors, not least the identification and successful implementation of the other types of change needed. The reasons why organizations initiate change programmes are either to respond to drivers that are causing them to have to do things differently to remain successful or to create and exploit new opportunities. Therefore the programmes are effectively the means by which strategic change is accomplished. Few organizations can succeed, in a rapidly evolving environment, by just continuing 'business as usual', which implies that the main issues in strategic management are identifying when and why changes are necessary, knowing what benefits the changes should produce and how they can be successfully realized.

The Purpose of Strategies: To Deliver Benefits to Stakeholders

It would therefore appear that, if an organization's aims and objectives could be expressed as the benefits that will be delivered by achieving them, it should be possible to use the overall logic of the benefits management approach to improve at least the implementation of business strategies and possibly help formulate new strategies. This makes sense if the definition of strategy is looked at carefully. Probably the simplest of the many definitions, in the context of business is that of Porter (1980): *'An integrated set of actions aimed at increasing the long-term well-being and strength of the enterprise'*. In order to achieve this, the enterprise must satisfy the requirements of a wide range of stakeholder groups, including those who fund the enterprise and those who work in it. Therefore a possible equivalent definition could be: *'An integrated set of actions aimed at providing benefits over the long term to enterprise stakeholders'*. This perspective is particularly relevant for public sector, mutually owned and not-for-profit organizations, but can also be appropriate for commercial corporations.

If this view is taken, then each of the organization's objectives should result in the provision of benefits to one or more groups of stakeholders, such as its shareholders or its customers. In many ways this is similar to the concept of the balanced scorecard (BSC), which shows how a combination of objectives that meet the expectations of a number of stakeholders, if achieved, results in improved financial performance (Kaplan and Norton, 2001). In essence, the BSC suggests that investment in innovation leads to better products and services, which, in turn, capture more customer value and better processes, which results in lower unit costs. In combination these produce more revenues at less cost and therefore greater profits. However, there are more stakeholders than just customers and investors, who can influence the outcome of the strategy and they will be more willing to support the organization's actions if they too are beneficiaries of the strategy. Most notable are the employees, but modern organizations are also dependent on how well they satisfy the expectations of other interested parties. Typically, enterprise stakeholders include:

- Shareholders and other investors, such as partners or members in the case of mutual societies.
- Customers and consumers who benefit from the use of the products and services.

- Suppliers, distributors and other trading partners, who benefit from the income they receive by doing business with the organization.
- Employees who benefit not only financially but also from the skills they acquire, career development, job satisfaction and an enjoyable working environment.
- Government, which benefits directly from the tax revenues raised, but also from the overall improvements in economic and social welfare created by the organization.
- Regulators who ensure industry standards are complied with, to the benefit of society.
- The communities in which the organization operates benefit from the economic activity it generates and also from, in many cases, the provision of local amenities and sponsorship of social developments.
- Even competitors benefit, albeit indirectly, from the success of one another, due to the continuing improvements in standards of product and service quality. Having a competitor with a poor reputation or, worse, one that breaches the law, is detrimental to others, since it can tarnish the industry image and create fears and uncertainties in customers.

This is not meant to be a comprehensive list, but is intended to show that there is a wide range of potential beneficiaries from an organization's activities. Also few of these categories of stakeholders can be treated as a homogeneous group and most will have to be divided into segments or subgroups that reflect their different relationships with the enterprise and the benefits they are seeking from that relationship. Segmentation is commonly applied by marketers to customers, but can also be applied with useful effect to other stakeholder groups such as suppliers and employees.

Incorporating Benefits Management into Strategic Thinking

Figure 10.2 depicts how the benefits management approach described throughout this book can be applied to business strategy. Following an analysis of the business drivers, using a combination of techniques such as PEST, competitive forces and competence analysis, the organization establishes objectives for the future, but then expresses these as the benefits that particular stakeholders will receive if and when the objectives are achieved. These benefits will be produced by both incremental improvements resulting from specific projects and/or step changes resulting from major programmes. The IS/IT projects may be either standalone, in the sense that they deliver a specific set of benefits to certain stakeholders, or be components of larger change programmes, as shown in the figure.

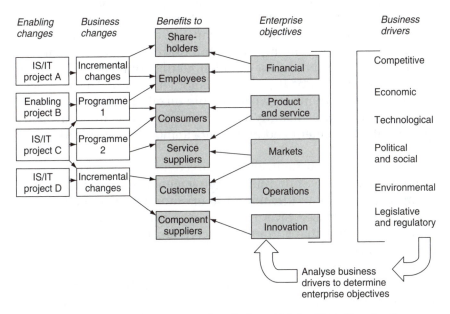

Figure 10.2 *Business strategy described as a high level benefits network*

Once the strategy has been expressed as benefits to groups of stakeholders, the organization can define the types of changes needed to achieve sets of those benefits, assess the feasibility and cost of achieving them, devise the programmes and projects required to make them happen and then develop plans for the achievement of the benefit streams, within and across the projects and programmes. This is, of course, a very complex task, but it does maintain a focus on benefits from the formulation of the strategy through to the scoping of projects, such that all project and programme activities will all be related back through the network to intended benefits and hence the business objectives. This in turn means that projects should not have to search for benefits to justify themselves; instead they will be commissioned to realize subsets of the range of benefits that the organization wants to deliver. The feasibility and costs must still be determined, in order to decide whether the benefits can be justified or to decide between investment options. Of course, once this is done the decision may be not to proceed, in which case the enterprise objectives will have to be revised.

This approach should also enable a more coordinated and structured approach to the ownership of benefits from the senior executives, who own the overall benefits that derive from the business objectives, and the managers, who are responsible for realizing subsets of those benefits from the programmes and projects. Equally, all staff involved in managing change and benefits realization will understand the contribution they are making to the organization's strategy. It also enables a problem described in Chapter 9 to be addressed more easily. In a complex multi-project, multi-programme environment, benefits can either be double-counted or not counted at all, that is they are assumed to be the result of another project. This emphasis on strategic benefits management should enable a structured cascade from the top down, making it easier to align benefits to the most appropriate investment and avoid benefits 'falling down the cracks' between them.

As strategies evolve or drivers change it should be possible through the master network to identify those existing investments that have increased or decreased priority or are even no longer required. Also additional projects that address emergent needs not already covered can be defined. This does not imply that all strategies and the resulting activities should only be devised and managed top down since that has been shown to be inadequate for modern organizations. Inevitably, many investments will be initiated in response to operational issues. Having a network of all the strategic initiatives and other projects will enable an organization to reconcile and coordinate changes resulting from both top-down and bottom-up initiatives.

How the benefits management tools and techniques can be included in the strategic planning process can be summarized as:

- The organization should carry out a regular strategic analysis to understand and interpret its business drivers and establish or revise its medium and longer term objectives.
- Each objective should be interpreted in terms of the benefits that it could produce for different organizational stakeholders and how these benefits can be measured through key performance indicators (KPIs).
- By assessing the nature and mix of those objectives across the stakeholder groups the range of changes required to deliver them can be identified and described.
- These changes can be analysed, synthesized and structured to enable programmes and projects to be designed and configured to achieve particular subsets of the benefits. It may be that some

benefits are not feasible and the strategy as originally intended cannot be realized and a revision should be undertaken.

- A high level map of the projects and initiatives can show the dependencies among projects. Detailed benefits dependency networks and plans for each component should be developed.
- Business cases should be developed for each project and programme. A consolidation of these individual cases will therefore represent the business case for the implementation of the overall organizational strategy. The investment board, as described in Chapter 9, would then be able to assess more comprehensively the overall contribution of each case submitted for funding, based on its role in achieving the organization's strategy rather than only on the financial implications.
- The benefits management process should be used to guide implementation and review in each individual project and programme in order to ensure that the benefits of each are delivered.

Examples of Benefits-Driven Strategies

This approach to strategy formulation and implementation has been adopted, at least in part, by a number of organizations that were already using the benefits management process for all major projects. Two examples are considered in Box 10.2. In the first example, the organization had developed a new business strategy and it then used the benefits management approach to determine how to implement the strategy successfully. In the second, the organization was faced with significant changes in its industry and used the benefits management techniques to help in developing a business strategy to address the new situation. In both cases using this approach made it possible to develop a long-term plan for the major IT infrastructure changes needed to support the new strategy. This benefits view of strategy can therefore help in the difficult task of justifying infrastructure investments discussed in Chapter 8.

Box 10.2 Benefits management use in business strategy formulation and implementation

A medium sized bank – implementing a new strategy for personal banking

At the height of the dot.com boom a medium sized bank (MSB) developed a new strategy for its personal customers to provide

Box 10.2 (Continued)

online banking services. At the time many of its competitors and some new entrants to the banking sector had developed online 'e-banks' as separate organizations. MSB however had decided that over the long term electronic banking would become just one of a number of ways customers would expect to use banking services. Therefore its strategy should be to integrate its e-banking services with all the other forms of personal banking offered through its branches and telephone banking centre. The main objectives of the strategy were, first, to retain existing customers who might be attracted to the new e-banks by attractive initial offers and, second, to attract new customers, particularly younger people, by its 'one-stop-shop' services. It also realized that although the integrated approach would be more complex to establish, it would over the long term be a more cost-effective way of using its existing resources and assets.

Having established these objectives and an understanding of the scale of changes needed to achieve them, the bank embarked on a benefits management-based assessment of how best to achieve those objectives within the resources at its disposal.

It first identified, based on extensive market research, the benefits it could expect to deliver to its different types of customer, based on the products and services they used and the extent of their current financial commitment to the bank. These were then assessed in terms of the benefits the bank would expect to realize if it provided a comprehensive and integrated service. In particular there would be considerable cost savings if many customers switched to online transactions, many processes could be automated and there would be increased cross-selling opportunities to encourage customers to take up new products.

The changes needed to achieve each of these customer and organizational benefits were then defined. These were considerable and ranged from new marketing strategies, consolidation of all customer accounts around a unique customer identifier, redesigning the back office processes to provide consistent levels of service to each of the customer channels, integration of all front office systems in the branches and service centre with the new online service, providing a common 'look and feel' to those systems and retraining staff to provide a full service to the customer across the whole product range. This led to the need for other previously unidentified changes in the processes for new product development and a need for a rationalization of the products currently offered in order to avoid the cost of supporting old products across multiple channels.

Finally, the changes required to the existing IT applications and infrastructure, including the replacement of some and the implementation of new ones were identified. In addition to the e-banking suite, the need for additional systems such as a customer relationship management suite was highlighted.

Before finalizing the implementation plan, all the existing change initiatives and IS/IT projects were reviewed to determine those that were still valid in the context of the new strategy, those that needed to be revised and those that could be cancelled. Those that were still relevant were then integrated into the 'master network', which became the basis of the implementation plan. From this new change programmes and workstreams and associated responsibilities were defined, so that the maximum number of activities could be pursued in parallel, in order to bring the new personal banking services into operation as soon as possible.

The new services were successfully launched within six months and not only were the objectives achieved in the following year, but the share price increased at a higher rate than its main competitors'.

Ctel – formulation of a benefits-driven strategy

The use of the benefits management approach at the project level in Ctel was discussed earlier in this chapter. Following its successful introduction on the project described in Box 10.1, it was used on all subsequent IS/IT projects and a number of change programmes.

Due to major changes in the industry and also a restructuring of the company in order to concentrate on its core products and services, which included selling its semiconductor business, the executive recognized the need to overhaul the business strategy. In particular, the company's R&D group had developed a new product range that would open up new markets, but would

Box 10.2 (Continued)

require the development of new ways of selling to customers and providing after-sales support. The new products would also cannibalize existing products and the organization realized it would have to manage the transition away from the old product set effectively.

Once again, based on thorough market research and industry forecasts the executive established a clear understanding of the drivers and agreed an initial set of objectives, to be achieved in phases over two to three years. The benefits that could be expected to be achieved, by all the relevant stakeholders, over that period were identified and where possible ratified by discussions with key stakeholders. An initial priority was set to introduce the new products and services to existing customers first in order to prevent losing them to competitors.

This framed the main objectives of the first change programme and five other programmes were also defined. Each programme was broken into projects, many of which were to create the new competences and capabilities to enable the new services, including a number of IS/IT application and infrastructure projects. Once all the projects and programmes had been defined in terms of the changes they would produce and measurable benefits they should deliver, the whole strategy was reappraised to determine whether there were alternative ways that could either realize the benefits earlier or achieve more ambitious targets overall. This reappraisal resulted in reducing the programmes to five and consolidating a number of the change activities and IT projects. It was agreed that to increase the flexibility of bringing about the changes, it would be advisable to implement all the major changes to the IT infrastructure as early as possible, so that it did not become a constraint to amending the priorities or sequence of the change programmes and associated projects.

Early development of the IT infrastructure proved to be a wise move because it soon became apparent that the initial plans for the programmes were constrained by the skills and resources available. The plans had to be revised to avoid some parts slipping back unacceptably. The strategy itself had to be revised as economic conditions deteriorated and fewer customers than expected were willing to invest in new systems. As a result the company was forced to focus on the cost reduction components of the strategy, including the programme to rationalize its after-sales service by using more outside contractors. Fortunately, the benefits already realized from the field service system, described earlier, meant that the transition to external service provision was achieved without any customer service problems.

Future Trends in IS/IT and their Implications for Benefits Management

In this final section of the book, we consider some of the expected future trends in IS and IT. Many developments and changes in IS/IT functionality, capability and use are being forecast. It is therefore not possible for us to be exhaustive and we have concentrated our attention on those issues that appear to be most significant and that have particular implications for the realization of benefits from investments. Rather than turn to a single source for our view of the future, we have blended together the views of other academics and commentators. Our consideration of the future is consistent with the concerns of most managers and their organizations, that is the short to medium term, which we have taken to mean the next one to five years.

Mobile Working

The last few years have seen a rapid growth in the use of mobile devices such as laptop PCs, mobile phones and PDAs in all developed countries. This growth has been fuelled by the falling prices of the devices and their increasing functionality and also by improved data transmission rates, particularly through access to broadband fixed networks and the availability of 3G mobile networks. The functionality available and greater connectivity means that people can now access the applications and information that they need to do their job almost wherever they choose or are required to work. While many types of staff, such as sales representatives and field engineers, have always worked away from a fixed location, many organizations are now considering this approach for a much wider range of their employees. Some organizations may adopt mobile working in order to allow their staff to work from home, with the aim of providing a better 'work–life balance'. Others, with multiple locations, may use mobile working as a way of improving collaboration among their staff by allowing individuals to work at different sites as the need arises.

Mobile working appears to offer many advantages to both organizations and the individuals within them. Productivity can be increased by reducing the time taken commuting or travelling between sites. If staff can be encouraged to enter data or update records while in the field, then a more accurate and even a real-time picture of organizational performance can be achieved. Access to complete and up-to-date information means it is more likely that mobile staff will be able to meet the needs of customers or clients, thus increasing satisfaction. However, organizations and individuals adopting this way of working are also beginning to identify challenges. Individuals find that once provided with the ability to be connected to the organization *at any time*, the organization expects them to be connected *all of the time*. Work and home life can begin to blur. Many individuals enjoy coming to work in order to interact with others. Without such contact, they can begin to feel alienated, which may in turn reduce their loyalty to the organization.

One of the biggest challenges organizations currently face when considering mobile working is being able to demonstrate an acceptable return on the investment, since it is difficult to identify the achievable benefits and ascribe a realistic financial value to them. An implication of using the benefits management approach in relation to mobile working is, as discussed in Chapter 8, the importance of understanding the organizational context in which it is being introduced. The general advantages forecast for the uses of mobile technologies cannot simply be adopted by an organization as benefits, since generic benefits do not exist. Rather, those general points should be carefully considered in the particular case of the organization, their staff and their current ways of working. Reduced commuting is likely to be a benefit, but how this benefit is realized and by whom will vary. If the individual works for longer, then the organization benefits from the additional output. However, if the individual does not use the time saved for work, the organization may still benefit by having a less tired and more effective member of staff, but it is unlikely to be able to place a direct financial value on this.

The difficulty many organizations are currently experiencing in developing a robust business case for mobile working can be understood by considering the applications portfolio first presented in Chapter 2. Mobile working should be considered as a high potential application in most organizations, that is it may provide considerable advantage in the future, but as yet not enough is known. As discussed earlier in the book, high potential projects are unlikely to produce any financial benefits until more work is undertaken, to provide sufficient evidence of the achievable benefits, the costs and the feasibility of the required business changes, to justify initiating a major investment. The initial investment will not result in a working system, merely a pilot implementation or a 'proof of concept'. Indeed, the high potential project may well demonstrate that mobile working is not appropriate for the organization or not at that time.

Greater Support for Collaboration

The activities being carried out by organizations are becoming ever more complex. This increase in complexity and scale usually requires the organization to draw on a greater range of skills and involve more staff. As teams become bigger and more diverse, it is less likely that they will be able to be colocated or meet face to face regularly. Mobile working will further exacerbate this, with individuals preferring to work where it suits them, rather than be tied to a team location. Organizations are therefore seeking to use IS and IT to support collaborative working between dispersed teams.

As was discussed in Chapter 1, Griffith et al. (2003) considered the use of IS to support virtual teams. They found that while it could offer support for this way of working, it could also act as a *jealous mistress*, capturing the tacit expertise of individuals without offering them the opportunity to replace this. We would suggest that for IS and IT to successfully support collaborative working, it should offer benefits at three distinct levels: to the individual, to teams and to the organization. When developing a benefits plan, changes to working practices may need to be designed to ensure benefits at all three levels are realized and balanced. For instance, although mobile technologies can allow all team working to be carried out remotely, saving the organization travelling expenses, it may be necessary to fund staff to have face-to-face meetings with colleagues and even longer periods of working together. This may be essential to developing the personal trust, which is often required to gain the individual- and team-level benefits that depend on sharing knowledge and ensuring that tasks are allocated appropriately and equitably.

Degree of Embeddedness: Pervasive and Nomadic Computing

Developments in a number of areas of IT and communication technologies are creating the possibility to move beyond the ideas incorporated in mobile working, to the concept of *ubiquitous computing*. Such developments include: the integration of wireless communication technologies and computing; the increased power and reduced cost of processors; continued miniaturization and improvements in battery power and life.

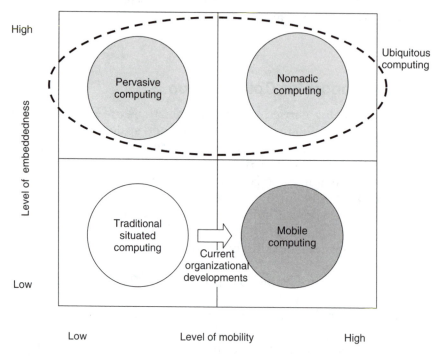

Figure 10.3   Embedded computing (after Lyytinen, 2005)

As illustrated in Figure 10.3, a key part of the vision of ubiquitous computing is the degree of 'embeddedness' – the degree to which various computing and communication devices can be included in a wider range of locations or types of equipment. Nomadic computing offers an increasingly convergent view of the future, in which a single device, which can be used in many locations, can be used to carry out a wide range of functions (a 'one-does-all' view). In contrast, the pervasive view offers a world in which processing and communication capabilities are included in everyday objects and can increasingly communicate with each other (a 'many-do-all' view). Examples of the nomadic approach include the increasing range of portable technologies that can carry out multiple functions, such as camera phones and Blackberry devices. The current significant interest and growing use of smart radio frequency identification (RFID) is an example of the growth of pervasive computing. In addition to the use of RFID in the supply chain to improve the flow of goods, stock control and the speed of checkout in stores, considerable development activity is being directed to a wider range of applications that could benefit from intelligent device to device communication. Developments include transportation ticketing, blood and organ identification, access control and border security.

The recent emergence and rapid development of the technologies and applications associated with both nomadic and pervasive computing suggests that investments in these areas should be recognized today as high potential opportunities in most organizations. Hence a relatively limited amount of funding should be sought to learn more about the potential benefits that can be achieved in the particular organizational context. Given the very early adoption stage of these technologies, organizations that do not feel comfortable being at the 'bleeding edge' of technology, should adopt a fast follower approach. This could involve joining cross-industry groups to stay aware of technology developments and their implications and only invest when there is a clearer understanding of best practices in adoption and use.

While new technologies can provide an opportunity to revise or develop new business strategy, organizations should be careful that they are not seduced by the hype often surrounding such technology. As discussed in the next section, they should ensure that they do not become a victim of technology push, but always clearly identify the business benefits that will arise from the use of the technology and ensure that these are relevant and important to their future strategy.

Continued Technology Push

It could be argued that both mobile and ubiquitous computing are examples of technologies that are seeking a problem and hence examples of technology push. Technology and system vendors will continue to develop new products and enhance existing ones and then seek to convince organizations that they must invest in these new products either to keep up with competitors or to gain advantage. While some increases in product functionality or new products are of real benefit, others are of only marginal value and will only add to the considerable amount of functionality that is already not used in most applications. However, even if organizations are aware that they will get little benefit from upgraded functionality, they are often required to migrate to such versions as vendors limit or even stop their support for earlier versions.

Many organizations seeking to stop the control of powerful software vendors have opted for open source solutions. Interestingly, their study of the use of open source software (OSS) in a large-scale deployment in a hospital in the Republic of Ireland, Fitzgerald and Kenny (2003) found that users became more interested and involved in the deployment when they learnt that it was OSS and were also more accepting of the limitations of the system than they were for systems from large vendors.

In applying the ideas within the benefits management process to the issue of technology push, it is useful to remember how the benefits dependency network was constructed starting with the investment objectives, that is the business need or demand. The network is developed from this, ending with an identification of 'the technology that is sufficient to do the job'. This approach will help prevent the investment in new systems and technology simply because they are available or because other organizations are investing in them. Rather, it will ensure that an organization understands how it can expect to realize benefits from the IS and IT it has identified as useful.

Cost Containment and Demonstration of Value Added

A perennial concern for senior managers in all types of organization is the continued increase in the sums spent on IS and IT. Despite the falling cost of processing power, data transmission and data storage, organizations are spending ever greater sums on IS/IT and this trend is expected to continue in the future. The growth in expenditure is in part due to the fact that organizations are using IT to carry out a greater range of activities. It is also fuelled by particular events such as Y2K and the dot.com boom and also in part due to the continued push of technology from vendors, as discussed previously.

This concern for value realized becomes particularly intense in difficult economic times or after a period of significant investment in IS/IT, when senior managers are likely to seek to leverage more value from the investments they have already made. As the costs of IS and IT, as a proportion of total business costs, continue to climb in the future, the focus on extracting more benefits from existing investments will increase. This focus increases the importance of the last two stages of the benefits management process, that is the review of the benefits realized from an investment and the identification of further benefits. As described in Chapter 7, one objective of the review is to establish those expected benefits that have not been realized, so that actions can then be put in place to recover them, where it is feasible. The identification of further benefits should also be given greater emphasis, particularly since it is often possible to identify new benefits that do not require additional investment in IS/IT but can be realized from changes in working practices or processes.

Continued Growth in Outsourcing and Offshoring

Many organizations are turning to outsourcing and offshoring as a route to reduce costs and increase flexibility. It is expected that this trend will continue in the medium term, for example, in the case of offshoring to India, revenues are expected to grow from $7.7 billion in 2001, to over $57 billion in 2008 and account for 7% of India's GDP (McKinsey Global Institute, 2003).

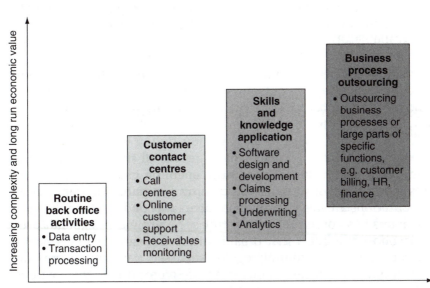

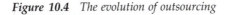

Figure 10.4 *The evolution of outsourcing*

The increased value of outsourcing and offshoring is expected to reflect not only increased volumes of work transferred to third parties, but also an increase in the complexity of the work. Figure 10.4

depicts an evolution of outsourced activities. Outsourcing typically commences with the transfer of routine activities, such as data entry and the operation of call centres. As organizations become more familiar with this way of operating, they are increasingly prepared to transfer more highly skilled and value-adding work. A question remains as to the impact of the transfer of increasingly skilled and knowledge-based activities on the future innovative potential of the sending organizations.

While outsourcing and offshoring have many parallels, outsourcing refers to the transfer of activities to a third-party organization. In contrast, in addition to describing the transfer of work to third parties overseas, offshoring can also be used to describe the transfer of work to the overseas operations *within* an organization. In these cases the organization may be willing to transfer activities beyond those shown in Figure 10.4, including the transfer of research and new product development. An example is provided by GE. At their John F. Welch Technology Centre in a suburb of Bangalore there are 1800 scientists and engineers undertaking research and development activities for all divisions of the organization. They are developing new products for GE and have helped to contribute to the 1000 patents filed by the Indian units of such firms at the US Patent Office over the last few years (Rai, 2003).

Chapter 8 considered a number of issues relating to the realization of benefits when adopting outsourcing of either IS/IT or entire business processes. The most fundamental and important of these is that the provider or supplier cannot be made responsible for the delivery of business benefits. Their traditional contribution is to provide IT and IS enablers or other enablers that function to the specified service level. They may also provide other enabling changes, such as the provision of a help desk or of training for staff. As organizations outsource increasingly complex and open-ended activities, such as entire business processes, these will become business as usual and hence should be represented as business changes on a dependency network. However, contracting for such services will not be sufficient to ensure business benefits are delivered to the organization. Competences in the management of such external services, such as monitoring of performance and the management of exceptions must be developed and become ongoing operational activities. Additional challenges of working across considerable distances, timezones and cultures may also have to be addressed. Specific enabling changes or ongoing business changes should be identified to address these and other issues that may arise and included in the benefits plan. Hence outsourcing may not reduce the competences required by an organization, rather shift their nature from the traditional operations of the organization to the management of distributed and remote activities.

In their book *Gurus, Hired Guns and Warm Bodies*, Kunda and Barley (2005) note a tension that results from the use of hired staff to undertake increasingly complex work. They observe that the outsourcing and contracting market seeks to turn staff, even those with particular experience and expertise, into commodities that can be hired as and when required. Furthermore, the organization's employees often wish to see clear demarcations between such temporary staff and themselves, such as in the provision of office space or the latest equipment. However, to address the business issue being tackled, it is usually necessary for the hired staff to become highly involved and operate as part of the team. Enabling changes or ongoing business changes should be identified to address these competing forces, if such 'hired guns' are to contribute effectively without disaffecting existing employees.

Having it All: Productivity and Agility Benefits from IS/IT

Traditionally IS/IT has been used mainly to improve organizational performance through its ability to increase the productivity of existing processes or create new, more effective and efficient processes. Hence the focus has been largely on increasing organizational productivity. Improved productivity, as typified by just-in-time manufacturing practices, suggests highly standardized approaches with the minimum of redundancy. However, in increasingly changeable and unpredictable business environments, organizations need to continually improve performance and also be able to adapt quickly and effectively to changing business conditions. This ability to adapt to dynamic market conditions is being termed organizational agility. Agility can apply at two levels: the ability to respond accurately and quickly to changes in levels of activity, such as changes in demand, and the ability to use the resources it has available to create new business options, in anticipation of changes in the business environment. In contrast to high productivity, high levels of agility imply the need for flexible approaches, and also spare capacity, to be able to respond rapidly to changing demands. It also suggests the empowerment of staff, to be able to both recognize and respond to changing conditions.

This raises a number of issues and challenges for IS/IT investment decision making and management in the future, if they are to provide benefits across the spectrum of organizational productivity as well as organizational agility. To address these challenges, it has already been suggested earlier in the chapter that the benefits realized by individuals and teams are important in making staff accept and use new systems and undertake the required changes. Such individual- and team-level benefits are therefore equally important to or even more important than organizational level benefits. Identifying, measuring and realizing these benefits will require a different focus of attention, moving away from processes to the way people work individually and collectively. Organizational performance improvements will derive from both productivity gains and the flexibility of individuals to carry out a wider range of tasks. It would seem that, in the future, more attention should be paid to the overall mix of work an individual does, in order to understand how he or she can be more effective in performing all those activities.

Many organizations continue to pursue organizational performance improvements that require people to adapt continually to new systems, which are designed to improve specific business processes, but take little account of how people actually use technology. Usually staff will have to use a number of different systems in the course of the working day, each of which was designed differently and often requiring considerable knowledge to use all of them effectively. This causes individuals to either use only limited parts of the functionality available or avoid using some systems or procedures whenever possible. This can result in disappointing levels of benefit from existing investments, but also may be inhibiting the organization from understanding and identifying the benefits that could result from *all* its staff using IS/IT more effectively. It is worth noting that the quality of the IS/IT facilities provided by an organization is now one of the reasons why some applicants accept or decline job offers.

Central to achieving increased and more effective use of IS and IT by staff will be the levels of IS/IT and information skills of individuals, the quality of the information resources available and the ease of use of the applications they are expected to use. As described in Chapter 8, enterprise portals are being implemented in many organizations to begin to address some of these issues, by providing a customized and, in some cases, even a personalized workspace which becomes 'the place all staff go to do their jobs'. That includes the processes they contribute to, the tasks they perform, the information they need and the connectivity that is essential to enabling them to work with colleagues, both within and outside the organization. The complex set of relationships that enterprise portals are attempting to facilitate is depicted in Figure 10.5.

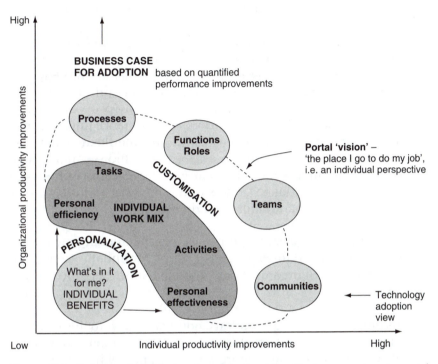

Figure 10.5 *Balancing individual and organizational benefits from an enterprise portal*

In Chapter 1, the use of an enterprise portal to increase both staff productivity and flexibility following the merger of the Woolwich with Barclays Bank was described (see Box 1.3). It was also critical to rapidly exploiting the new internal capabilities that were one of the main aims of the merger. Without having to change the main business applications in the two organizations, the combined product suite of the merged company was made available, almost immediately, to all customers.

In addition to allowing staff to work in ways that suit them, two other aspects of IS/IT investment become more significant when considering agility. The first is that resource flexibility, at both the individual and organizational level requires an extensive and standard infrastructure, so that people can carry out all the tasks required, without constraints or a long learning curve whenever they change roles or move jobs. This implies that an increasing proportion of IT investments will be infrastructural, either to create new capabilities or sustain performance. As previously discussed, the justification of infrastructure investments is an enduring problem, which requires some new ways of thinking now that it is integral to how almost every organization conducts its business.

The second challenge that is implied is that their move towards more dynamic capabilities requires extensive knowledge sharing and reuse across the organization. This includes the knowledge that has been captured in the form of proprietary information and also ensuring individuals can and do collaborate to share their personal knowledge. As with infrastructure investments, it is difficult to identify and then put in place specific actions to realize the benefits that result from investments in information resources and related retrieval and analysis tools. Again, unless there is greater understanding of how staff use information and make decisions, individually and collectively, it will be increasingly difficult for organizations to make information management investments that actually support the creation of new capabilities. Worse still, as suggested by the research by Griffith et al. (2003) inappropriate deployments of IS/IT with the intention of improving the use of organizational knowledge can actually produce the opposite effect.

All this implies that organizations not only have to improve the way they decide on and implement new systems and technology, they also have to introduce more coherent approaches to monitoring the ongoing and emergent benefits that result from the total set of IS/IT investments made. This will not only provide the learning needed to improve the value derived from future investments, but also help prevent the organization from making expensive, and perhaps disastrous, mistakes in its use of IS/IT. This, in turn, suggests that organizations need to adopt a range of different approaches to assessing IS/IT investments, due to the inherently different roles that the use of technology plays. In some cases, it is clearly now a cost of doing business, in effect a utility, without which the organization cannot function. In that sense, it is an essential organizational hygiene factor and should be justified as part of the cost of employing staff or occupying premises. In others, it is clearly a means of improving aspects of business performance to produce specific benefits. However, in more and more cases, technology investment is an essential enabler of new organizational capabilities, but the benefits only materialize when those capabilities are deployed successfully to create new opportunities, or enable the organization to adapt effectively to changing circumstances. In these cases, the benefits realized are dependent not only on how well the technology is used, but also on how well the organization identifies, defines and implements its business strategies.

A Final Word or Two

The benefits management approach was developed to enable organizations to improve the value realized from specific investments. However it can be, and is being, used to assess how well organizations are employing their IS/IT assets and to increase the benefits they can leverage from them, as well as to formulate, manage and implement strategic change programmes. It can even help formulate and implement business strategies themselves. Overall this enables organizations to stop focusing on the *cost of ownership* of IT and start to understand the *value of ownership*, by first considering the potential benefits it can obtain from investments, rather than search for sufficient benefits to justify the costs involved. Having a coherent and comprehensive approach to identifying and realizing the benefits of each of the IS/IT investments it makes is essential to understanding the value that IS/IT contributes to the organization.

However, this cannot happen unless that approach enables business managers and IT specialists to work together in new ways, to share their knowledge in order to identify the best ways to combine IS/IT implementation with business changes. This will ensure the maximum benefits are delivered and, importantly, it will allow the organization to learn from what it has and has not achieved.

The benefits management process, tools and techniques, described in this book have been adopted by many organizations, because they provide a comprehensive, yet commonsense approach that business managers and IT specialists can easily understand, learn and use together.

It has also been said many times, by both groups, that working in this way, when compared with more traditional approaches to managing IS/IT investments, is also more *enjoyable*!

Glossary

Benefits Management The process of organizing and managing such that the potential benefits arising from the use of IS/IT are actually realized.

Benefit owner An individual or group who will gain advantage from a business benefit and who will work with the project team to ensure that benefit is realized.

Benefit streams A set of related benefits and their associated business and enabling changes and enabling IS/IT.

Business benefit An advantage on behalf of a particular stakeholder or group of stakeholders.

Business changes The new ways of working that are required to ensure that the desired benefits are realized.

Business and organizational drivers Views held by senior managers as to what is important to the business – in a given timescale – such that they feel changes must occur.

Change owner An individual or group who will ensure that a business or enabling change identified is successfully achieved.

Enabling changes Changes that are prerequisites for achieving the business changes or that are essential to bring the system into effective operation within the organization.

Financial benefit By applying a cost/price or other valid financial formula to a quantifiable benefit a financial value can be calculated.

Investment objectives Organizational targets for achievement agreed for the investment in relation to the drivers. As a set they are essentially a description of what the situation should be on completion of the investment.

IS/IT enablers The information systems and technology required to support the realization of the identified benefits and to allow the necessary changes to be undertaken.

Measurable benefit This aspect of performance is currently being measured or an appropriate measure could be implemented. But it is currently not possible to estimate by how much performance will improve when the changes are completed.

Observable benefit By use of agreed criteria, specific individuals/groups will decide, based on their experience or judgement, to what extent the benefit has been realized.

Quantifiable benefit Sufficient evidence exists to forecast how much improvement/benefit should result from the changes.

Stakeholder(s) An individual or group of people who will benefit from the investment or are either directly involved in making or are affected by the changes needed to realize the benefits.

Why, what and how of a potential investment *Why* is the investment being made – why does the organization need to change and how critical to its future is the successful management of the changes? *What* types of benefit is the organization expecting to achieve by making the changes – to reduce costs, improve operational performance, gain new customers, create a new capability etc.? *How* can a combination of IT and business changes deliver those benefits at an acceptable level of risk?

References

Alshawi, S., Irani, Z. and Baldwin, L. (2003) 'Benchmarking information technology investment and benefits extraction', *Benchmarking: An International Journal*, 10(4): 414–23.

Amit, R. and Zott, C. (2001) 'Value creation in e-business', *Strategic Management Journal*, 22(6): 493–520.

Applegate, L. M. (1993) 'Frito-Lay Inc. Strategic transition (A)', *Harvard Business School Case Study*, Boston, MA.

Avison, D. and Fitzgerald, G. (2002) *Information Systems Development: Methodologies, Techniques and Tools*, 3rd edition, London: Pearson Education.

Ballantine, J. and Stray, S. (1998) 'Financial appraisal and the IS/IT investment decision making process', *Journal of Information Technology*, 13(1): 3–14.

Ballantine, J., Levy, M. and Powell, P. (1998) 'Evaluating information systems in small and medium-sized enterprises: Issues and evidence', *European Journal of Information Systems*, 7(4): 241–51.

Balogun, J. and Hope Hailey, V. (2004) *Exploring Strategic Change*, 2nd edition, Harlow: Pearson Education.

Bancroft, N. H., Seip, H. and Sprengel, A. (1998) *Implementing SAP R/3 – How to Introduce a Large System into a Large Organisation*, 2nd edition, Greenwich, CT: Manning Publications.

Barney, J. B. (1991) 'Firm resources and sustained competitive advantage', *Journal of Management*, 17(1): 99–120.

Bell, S. and Wood-Harper, T. (1998) *Rapid Information Systems Development: Systems Analysis and Systems Design in an Imperfect World*, Maidenhead: McGraw-Hill Education.

Bendor-Samuel, P. (2000) *Turning Lead into Gold: The Demystification of Outsourcing*, Provo, UT: Executive Excellence Publishing.

Benjamin, R. I. and Levinson, E. (1993) 'A framework for managing IT-enabled change', *Sloan Management Review*, 34(4): 23–33.

Breu, K. and Hemingway, C. J. (2001) *Creating the Agile Workforce*, Cranfield School of Management and Microsoft.

Breu, K., Hemingway, C. J., Strathern, M. and Bridger, D. (2002) 'Workforce agility: The new employee strategy for the knowledge economy', *Journal of Information Technology*, 17(1): 21–31.

Broadbent, M., Weill, P. and Neo, B. S. (1999) 'Strategic context and patterns of IT infrastructure capability', *Journal of Strategic Information Systems*, 8(2): 157–87.

Brynjolfsson, E. and Hitt, L. M. (2000) 'Beyond computation: Information technology, organisational transformation and business performance', *Journal of Economic Perspectives*, 14(2): 33–48.

BT (2004) 'Egomaniac execs and shoddy tech hampering UK business', *CNET News.com*, 5 February.

Carr, N. (2003) 'IT doesn't matter', *Harvard Business Review*, 81(5): 41–9.

Cash, J., McFarlan, W. and McKenney, J. (1992) *Corporate Information Systems Management*, Boston, MA: Irwin.

Chan, Y. E. (2002) 'Why haven't we mastered alignment? The importance of the informal organisational structure', *MIS Quarterly Executive*, 1(2): 97–112.

Chang, L. and Powell, P. (1998) 'Towards a framework for business process re-engineering in small and medium-sized enterprises', *Information Systems Journal*, 8(3): 199–215.

Checkland, P. and Holwell, S. (1998) *Information, Systems and Information Systems: Making Sense of the Field*, Chichester: John Wiley & Sons.

Checkland, P. and Scholes, J. (1999) *Soft Systems Methodology in Action*, Chichester: John Wiley & Sons.

Collins, D. (1999) 'Data warehouses, enterprise information portals and the Smart-Mart Meta Directory', *Information Builders Systems Journal*, 12(2): 53–61.

Daniel, E. M. and Storey, C. (1997) 'On-line banking: Strategic and management challenges', *Long Range Planning*, 30(6): 890–98.

Daniel, E. M. and Ward, J. M. (2005) 'Enterprise portals: Balancing the organisational and individual perspectives of information systems', *European Conference of Information Systems (ECIS)*, Regensburg, Germany, May.

Davenport, T. H. (1998) 'Putting the enterprise into the enterprise system', *Harvard Business Review*, 76(4): 121–31.

Davenport, T. H. (2000) *Mission Critical: Realizing the Promise of Enterprise Systems*, Boston, MA: Harvard Business School Press.

DeLone, W. H. and McLean, E. R. (1992) 'Information systems success: The quest for the dependent variable', *Information Systems Research*, 3(1): 60–95.

DeLone, W. H. and McLean, E. R. (2003) 'The DeLone and McLean model of information systems success: A ten year update', *Journal of Management Information Systems*, 19(4): 9–30.

Dobson, M. S. (2003), *Streetwise Project Management*, Avon, MA: Adams Media Corporation.

Doherty, N. F. and King, M. (2001) 'An investigation of the factors affecting the successful treatment of organisational issues in systems development projects', *European Journal of Information Systems*, 10(3): 147–60.

Doran, G. T. (1981) 'There is a S.M.A.R.T way to write management goals and objectives', *Management Review*, November.

Earl, M. J. (1989) *Management Strategies for Information Technology*, Englewood Cliffs, NJ: Prentice Hall.

Earl, M. J. (1992) 'Putting IT in its place: A polemic for the nineties', *Journal of Information Technology*, 7(1): 100–108.

Eisenhardt, K. M. and Martin, J. A. (2000) 'Dynamic capabilities: What are they?', *Strategic Management Journal*, 21(10–11): 1105–121.

Ewusi-Mensah, K. and Przasnyski, Z. H. (1994) 'Factors contributing to the abandonment of information systems development projects', *Journal of Information Technology*, 9(3): 185–201.

Farbey, B., Land, F. and Targett, D. (1993) *IT Investment: A Study of Methods and Practice*, Oxford: Butterworth-Heinemann.

Farrell, D. (2003) 'The real new economy', *Harvard Business Review*, 81(9): 105–12.

Fitzgerald, B. and Kenny, T. (2003) 'Open source software in the trenches: Lessons from a large scale implementation', *Proceedings of 24th International Conference on Information Systems (ICIS)*, Seattle, December.

Galliers, R. D. and Leidner, D. E. (2003) *Strategic Information Management: Challenges and Strategies in Managing Information Systems*, Oxford: Butterworth-Heinemann.

Gartner Group (2002) 'Moving from disillusionment to real value: An introduction to the eight building blocks of CRM', *CRM Conference*, Paris, May.

Gates, W. (1999) *Business @the Speed of Thought*, Harmondsworth: Penguin.

Gibson, C. F. (2003) 'IT-enabled business change: An approach to understanding and managing risk', *MIS Quarterly Executive*, 2(2): 104–15.

Grant, R. M. (1996) 'Toward a knowledge-based theory of the firm', *Strategic Management Journal*, 17(2): 109–22.

Griffith, T. L., Sawyer, J. E. and Neale, M. A. (2003) 'Virtualness and knowledge in teams: Managing the love triangle of organisations, individuals and information technology', *MIS Quarterly*, 27(2): 265–87.

Harding, D. (2003) 'Can't grasp IT? Don't ask the techies', *Metro*, 5 September.

Hares, J. and Royle, D. (1994) *Measuring the Value of Information Technology*, Chichester: John Wiley & Sons.

Hemingway, C. (2005) *Information Management*, Information Systems Research Centre, Cranfield School of Management.

Hill, C. and Jones, G. (1998) *Strategic Management. An Integrated Approach*, Boston, MA: Houghton Mifflin.

HM Treasury (2001) *Choosing the Right Fabric: A Framework for Performance Information*, London: The Stationery Office.

HM Treasury (2003) *PFI: Meeting the Investment Challenge*, London: HMSO.

The IMPACT Programme (1998) *Achieving the Benefits from Software Package-Enabled Business Improvement Programmes: Best Practice Guidelines*, London: Impact.

Impact21 Group (2005) 'Definition of information management', www.impact21group.com/glossary.html.

iSociety (2003) *Getting By, Not Getting On*, London: Work Foundation.

Jeffrey, M. and Leliveld, I. (2004) 'Best practices in IT portfolio management', *Sloan Management Review*, 45(3): 40–50.

Johnson, G. and Scholes, K. (1999) *Exploring Corporate Strategy*, 5th edition, London: Prentice Hall.

Johnson, K. and Misic, M. (1999) 'Benchmarking: A tool for web site evaluation and improvement', *Internet Research*, 9(5): 383.

Jordan, E. and Silcock, L. (2005) *Beating IT Risks*, Chichester: John Wiley & Sons.

Jurison, J. (1996) 'Toward more effective management of information technology benefits', *Journal of Strategic Information Systems*, 5(4): 263–74.

Kalakota, R. and Whinston, A. (1997) *Electronic Commerce; A Manager's Guide*, Reading, MA: Addison Wesley.

Kaplan, R. S. and Norton, D. P. (2001) *The Strategy-Focused Organisation: How Balanced-Scorecard Companies Thrive in the New Business Environment*, Boston, MA: Harvard Business School Press.

Keeling, K., Vassilopoulou, K., McGoldrick, P. and Macaulay, L. (2000) 'Market realities and innovation in small to medium enterprises: Facilitators and barriers to the use of electronic commerce', *New Product Development and Innovation Management*, 2(1): 57–70.

Kerzner, H. (2004) *Advanced Project Management: Best Practices on Implementation*, Hoboken, NJ: John Wiley & Sons Inc.

Knox, S., Maklan, S., Payne, A., Peppard, J. and Ryals, L. (2003) *Customer Relationship Management: Marketplace Perspectives*, Oxford: Butterworth-Heinemann.

Kohli, R. and Devaraj, S. (2004) 'Realizing the business value of information technology investments: An organisational process', *MIS Quarterly Executive*, 3(1): 53–68.

Kumar, K., Van Dissel, H. G. and Bielli, P. (1998) 'The merchant of Prato – revisited: Toward a third rationality of information systems', *MIS Quarterly*, 22(2): 199–226.

Kunda, G. and Barley, S. (2005) *Gurus, Hired Guns and Warm Bodies: Itinerant Experts in a Knowledge Economy*, Princeton, NJ: Princeton University Press.

Lambert, R. and Edwards, C. (2003) 'A survey of IS/IT project appraisal', IS Group, Cranfield School of Management.

Lederer, A. L. and Nath, R. (1991) 'Managing organisational issues in systems development', *Journal of Systems Management*, 24(11): 23–7.

Lyytinen, K. (2005) 'The move to mobile', *Mobile Interaction Workshop*, London School of Economics, April.

Markus, M. L. (2004) 'Technochange management: Using IT to drive organisational change', *Journal of Information Technology*, 19(1): 4–20.

Markus, M. L. and Benjamin, R. I. (1997) 'The magic bullet theory of IT-enabled transformation', *Sloan Management Review*, 38(2): 55–68.

Markus, M. L. and Tanis, C. (2000) 'The enterprise system experience – from adoption to success', in R.W. Zmud (ed.), *Framing the Domains of IT Research: Glimpsing the Future through the Past*, Cincinnati, OH: Pinnaflex Educational Resources.

Markus, M. L., Axline, S., Petrie, D. and Tanis, C. (2000) 'Learning from adopters' experiences with ERP: Problems encountered and success achieved', *Journal of Information Technology*, 14(4): 245–65.

Mata, F. J., Fuerst, W. L. and Barney, J. B. (1995) 'Information technology and sustained competitive advantage: A resource based analysis', *MIS Quarterly*, 19(4): 487–505.

McGolpin, P. and Ward, J. M. (1997) 'Factors affecting the success of strategic information systems', in J. Mingers and F. Stowell (eds), *Information Systems: An Emerging Discipline*, London: McGraw-Hill.

McKinsey Global Institute (2003) *Offshoring: Is It a Win–Win Game?*, Washington, DC: McKinsey & Co.

McManus, J. and Wood-Harper, T. (2002) *Information Systems Project Management: Methods, Tools and Techniques*, London: Prentice Hall.

Melville, N., Kraemer, K. and Gurbaxani,V. (2004) 'Information technology and organizational performance: An integrative model of business value', *MIS Quarterly*, 28(4): 283–322.

Mintzberg, H. (1983) *Structure in Fives: Designing Effective Organisations*, Englewood Cliffs, NJ: Prentice Hall.

Morris, P. W. G. and Pinto, J. K. (2004) *The Wiley Guide to Managing Projects*, Hoboken, NJ: John Wiley & Sons Inc.

Mumford, E. (2003) *Redesigning Human Systems*, Hershey, PA: Idea Group Inc.

Neely, A. (2003) *Measuring Business Performance: Why, What, How*, London: Economist Books.

Neely, A., Adams, C. and Kennerley, M. (2002) *The Performance Prism: The Scorecard for Measuring and Managing Business Success*, London: Financial Times Prentice Hall.

NHS (2005) www.npfit.nhs.uk/introduction/ataglance/#cost.

OGC, Office of Government Commerce (2002) *Management of Risk: Guidance for Practitioners*, London: The Stationery Office.

OGC, Office of Government Commerce (2003) *Managing Successful Programmes*, London: The Stationery Office.

OGC, Office of Government Commerce (2004) *Project Initiation Guidelines*, www.ocg.gov.uk.

Parker, M. M. and Benson, R. J. (1988) *Information Economics*, Englewood Cliffs, NJ: Prentice Hall.

Partington, D., Pellegrinelli, S. and Young, M. (2005) 'Attributes of programme management competence: An interpretive study', *International Journal of Project Management*, 23(2): 87–95.

Peppard, J. and Ward, J. M. (2005, forthcoming) 'Unlocking sustained business value from IT investments: Balancing problem-based and innovation-based implementations', *California Management Review*.

Peters, T. and Waterman, R. (1980) *In Search of Excellence*, New York: HarperCollins.

Pettigrew, A. and Whipp, R. (1991) *Managing Change for Corporate Success*, Oxford: Blackwell.

Pollard, C. E. and Hayne, S. C. (1998) 'The changing face of information systems issues in small firms', *International Small Business Journal*, 16(3): 70–87.

Porter, M. (1980) *Competitive Strategy: Techniques for Analysing Industries and Competitors*, New York: Free Press.

Porter, M. (1985) *Competitive Advantage: Creating and Sustaining Superior Performance*, New York: Free Press.

Rai, S. (2003) 'From India, genius on the cheap', *International Herald Tribune*, 15 December: 12.

Remenyi, D., Sherwood-Smith, M. and White, T. (1997) *Achieving Maximum Value from Information Systems*, Chichester: John Wiley & Sons.

Renkema, T. (2000) *The IT Value Quest: How to Capture the Business Value of IT-Based Infrastructure*, Chichester: John Wiley & Sons.

Rose, M. (2002) 'IT professionals and organisational ascendancy: Theory and empirical critique', *New Technology, Work and Employment*, 17(3): 154–69.

Ross, J. W. and Beath, C. M. (2002) 'Beyond the business case: New approaches to IT investment', *MIT Sloan Management Review*, 43(2): 51–9.

Royal Statistical Society (2004) *Performance Indicator POST Presentation*, London: Royal Statistical Society.

Sauer, C. (1993) *Why Information Systems Fail*, Henley: Alfred Waller.

Simon, R. (1995) 'Control in an age of empowerment', *Harvard Business Review*, 73(2): 80–88.

Soh, C. and Markus, M. L. (1995) 'How IT creates value: A process theory synthesis', *Proceedings of the 16th Annual Conference on Information Systems*, Amsterdam, The Netherlands: 29–41.

Stabell, C. B. and Fjeldstad, O. D. (1998) 'Configuring value for competitive advantage: On chains, shops and networks', *Strategic Management Journal*, 19(5): 413–37.

Strassmann, P. A. (1999) 'The search for productivity', *Computerworld*, 33(32): 52–3.

Swanson, E. B. and Ramiller, N. C. (1997) 'The organising vision in information systems innovation', *Organisation Science*, (8): 458–74.

Teece, D. J., Pisano, G. and Shuen, A. (1997) 'Dynamic capabilities and strategic management', *Strategic Management Journal*, 18(7): 509–33.

Thorp, J. (2003) *The Information Paradox*, Whitby, Ontario: McGraw-Hill Ryerson.

Treacy, M. and Wiersma, F. (1993) 'Customer intimacy and other value disciplines', *Harvard Business Review*, 71(1): 84–93.

Ury, W. L., Brett J. M. and Goldberg, S. B. (1993) *Getting Disputes Resolved*, San Francisco: Jossey-Bass.

Venkatesh, V., Morris, M., Davis, G. and Davis, F. (2003) 'User acceptance of information technology: Toward a unified view', *MIS Quarterly*, 27(3): 425–78.

Venkatraman, N., Henderson, J. C. and Oldach, S. (1993) 'Continuous strategic alignment: Exploiting information technology capabilities for competitive success', *European Management Journal*, 11(2): 139–49.

Walsham, G. (1993) *Interpreting Information Systems in Organisations*, Chichester: John Wiley & Sons.

Ward, J. M. and Elvin, R. (1999) 'A new framework for managing IT-enabled business change', *Information Systems Journal*, 9(2): 197–221.

Ward, J. M. and Griffiths, P. (1996) *Strategic Planning for Information Systems*, 2nd edition, Chichester: John Wiley & Sons.

Ward, J. M., Taylor, P. and Bond, P. (1996) 'Evaluation and realisation of IS/IT benefits: An empirical study of current practice', *European Journal of Information Systems*, 4: 214–25.

Ward, J. M. and Peppard, J. (2002) *Strategic Planning for Information Systems*, 3rd edition, Chichester: John Wiley & Sons.

Ward, J. M., Hemingway, C. J. and Daniel, E. M. (2005) 'A framework for addressing the organisational issues of enterprise systems implementation', *Journal of Strategic Information Systems*, 14(2): 97–119.

Wentworth Research (1998) *Many Happy Returns*, London: Wentworth Research.

Wernerfelt, B. (1984) 'A resource based view of the firm', *Strategic Management Journal*, 5(2): 171–80.

Willcocks, L. and Margetts, H. (1994) 'Risk and information systems, developing the analysis' in L. Willcocks (ed.), *Information Management: The Evaluation of Information Systems Investments*, London: Chapman & Hall.

Williams, D. and Parr, T. (2004) *Enterprise Programme Management*, Basingstoke: Palgrave Macmillan.

Index